Kant after Duchamp

OCTOBER Books

Annette Michelson, Rosalind Krauss, Yve-Alain Bois, Benjamin Buchloh, Hal Foster, Denis Hollier, and John Rajchman, editors

Broodthaers, edited by Benjamin H. D. Buchloh

AIDS: Cultural Analysis/Cultural Activism, edited by Douglas Crimp

Aberrations, by Jurgis Baltrušaitis

Against Architecture: The Writings of Georges Bataille, by Denis Hollier

Painting as Model, by Yve-Alain Bois

The Destruction of Tilted Arc: *Documents,* edited by Clara Weyergraf-Serra and Martha Buskirk

The Woman in Question, edited by Parveen Adams and Elizabeth Cowie

Techniques of the Observer: On Vision and Modernity in the Nineteenth Century, by Jonathan Crary

The Subjectivity Effect in Western Literary Tradition: Essays toward the Release of Shakespeare's Will, by Joel Fineman

Looking Awry: An Introduction to Jacques Lacan through Popular Culture, by Slavoj Žižek

Cinema, Censorship, and the State: The Writings of Nagisa Oshima, by Nagisa Oshima

The Optical Unconscious, by Rosalind E. Krauss

Gesture and Speech, by André Leroi-Gourhan

Compulsive Beauty, by Hal Foster

Continuous Project Altered Daily: The Writings of Robert Morris, by Robert Morris

Read My Desire: Lacan against the Historicists, by Joan Copjec

Fast Cars, Clean Bodies: Decolonization and the Reordering of French Culture, by Kristin Ross

Kant after Duchamp, by Thierry de Duve

Kant after Duchamp

Thierry de Duve

an OCTOBER book

The MIT Press
Cambridge, Massachusetts
London, England

This book was set in Bembo by Graphic Composition, Inc.

Library of Congress Cataloging-in-Publication Data

Duve, Thierry de.
Kant after Duchamp / Thierry de Duve.
p. cm.
"An October book."
Includes index.
ISBN 0-262-04151-0 (hc : alk. paper)
1. Aesthetics. 2. Aesthetics, Modern—19th century. 3. Aesthetics, Modern—20th century. 4. Duchamp, Marcel, 1887–1968. 5. Modernism (Art)—France. I. Title.
BH39.D85 1996
111′.85—dc20 95-38235
CIP

In memoriam Michel Foucault,
who wrote:

Do not ask who I am and do not ask me to remain the same:
leave it to our bureaucrats and our police to see that our papers are in order.
At least spare us their morality when we write.

Contents

Acknowledgments

I met Michel Foucault only once—it must have been in 1980 or 1981. He was then a guest of honor at the University of Louvain, where his thinking had been anathema when I had been a student there, some fifteen years earlier. He was giving a series of lectures on the topic of "avowal." I didn't miss a single class, and when I learned that he had office hours of which very few students took advantage—out of shyness, probably—I went to visit him. I told him how much his work meant to me, and then how the idea had insinuated itself into my mind that the time had come for artistic modernity to be looked at archaeologically, the way he had looked at the global *episteme* of the classical age. "Do you think this is feasible?" I asked. "Why?" he said, "What bothers you?" I said I was convinced that the fish doesn't know the tank water—that's what bothered me, and not just methodologically. He seemed puzzled. "Your work on the classical age benefits from a historical distance of more than two centuries," I said. "Modernity is too near. And I feel caught up in this dilemma: either an archaeology of modernity is feasible, but then this would mean that we are no longer modern; or we are still modern, and so the archaeology of modernity is not feasible." Foucault laughed—he had this incredibly charming and conquering laughter, very healthy. "Don't worry. It's not up to you to decide whether you are modern or postmodern. Do what you think you have to do, and let your readers decide. Perhaps your work will make the transition." I thanked him and left, in a rare state of elation. I knew he had been preposterously generous, as if such a transition could rest on a single person's work. But his encouragement did the trick: I was liberated.

When I first met Clement Greenberg—it must have been in 1985 or 1986—it was at his place, on Central Park West. I had sent him an article, and he had expressed his interest and his disagreement. It was the disagreement I wished to discuss with him. He wasn't interested in talking theory; he offered me a drink and set about to check out my taste instead. When, after a while, I told him I was convinced that Andy Warhol was one of the greatest living artists (he was still alive then), Greenberg jumped to his feet and said—not angrily but both mockingly and sententiously—"You just disqualified yourself as a judge of art." It was I who laughed, this time, and proceeded rather cruelly to discuss some of the paintings he had on his walls. Eventually we had another drink, and a few years later we had our theoretical discussion—in public—but that's another story. We never settled our disagreements of taste, however; that wasn't necessary. It remains that in matters of art criticism and aesthetic judgment, there is no one from whom I learned more.

I am sad that Michel Foucault and Clement Greenberg are no longer here to receive the expression of my gratitude, for they are the two people to whom this book owes the most, as I hope the book will show. The two of them together—to many a reader an uncanny pairing, I guess—have allowed me to practice a perhaps unusual switching of "hats": the modern when the issue at stake (in both theory and practice) is the appreciation of art; the postmodern when it is a matter of looking back, "archaeologically," on modernity, on its achievements and its disillusionments.

There are many too many people to whom I would like to express my deepest thanks: artists, critics, colleagues who offered criticism and fueled my thinking; my students at the University of Ottawa, who had to bear with me as many of the ideas expressed here were tested with them, and perhaps on them, in helter-skelter order; the people who attended my seminar at the Collège International de Philosophie in Paris in 1989 and who submitted those ideas, by then slightly better arranged, to fierce but friendly criticism. Though thoroughly reworked, the material in this book has appeared elsewhere, either in French or in English or both. Chapters 1 (written in 1985), 5 (1982–1988, in a very different version), and 6 (1983) compose *Au nom de l'art* (Paris: Minuit, 1989); chapters 2 (1987), 3 (1985), and 4 (1986) were originally written and published in English; together with chapter 7 (1979–1989), their French versions compose *Résonances du readymade* (Nîmes: Jacqueline Chambon, 1989); the (shorter) French version of chapter 8 (1989) was published separately. The writing of each chapter has received incentive—and sometimes the bite of a deadline—from magazine editors and conference organizers, who are heartily thanked here for the opportunities they gave me: Wladimir Krysinski for chapter 1, Dennis Young for chapter 2, Ingrid Sischy for chapter 3, Serge Guilbaut for chapter 4, Pierre-Jean Labarrière for chapter 5, Pierre Gravel for chapter 6, Rosalind Krauss for chapter 7, Emilie Daniel and Patrick de Haas for chapter 8. My very special thanks go to Rosalind Krauss, who supported me throughout the years this book took in making, and who magnificently translated chapters 1, 6, and 7. I am also deeply grateful to Judith Gintz-Aminoff, who translated chapter 8 and went over the whole manuscript several times to make it look as if I had written it in my native tongue.

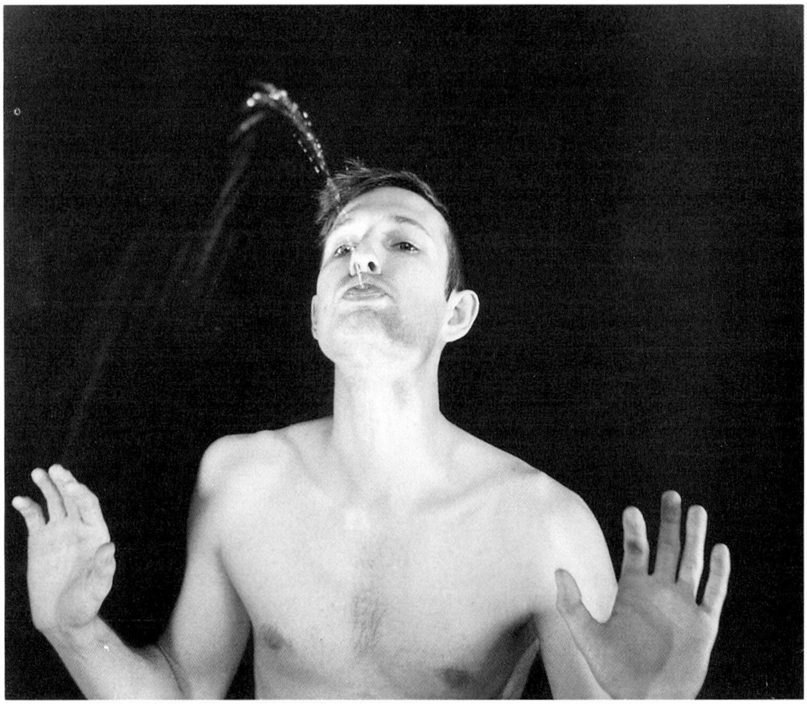

Bruce Nauman, *Self-Portrait as a Fountain*, 1966, color photograph. Collection of Whitney Museum of American Art, New York. © 1995 Bruce Nauman/ARS, New York.

Part I:

The Universal and the Singular

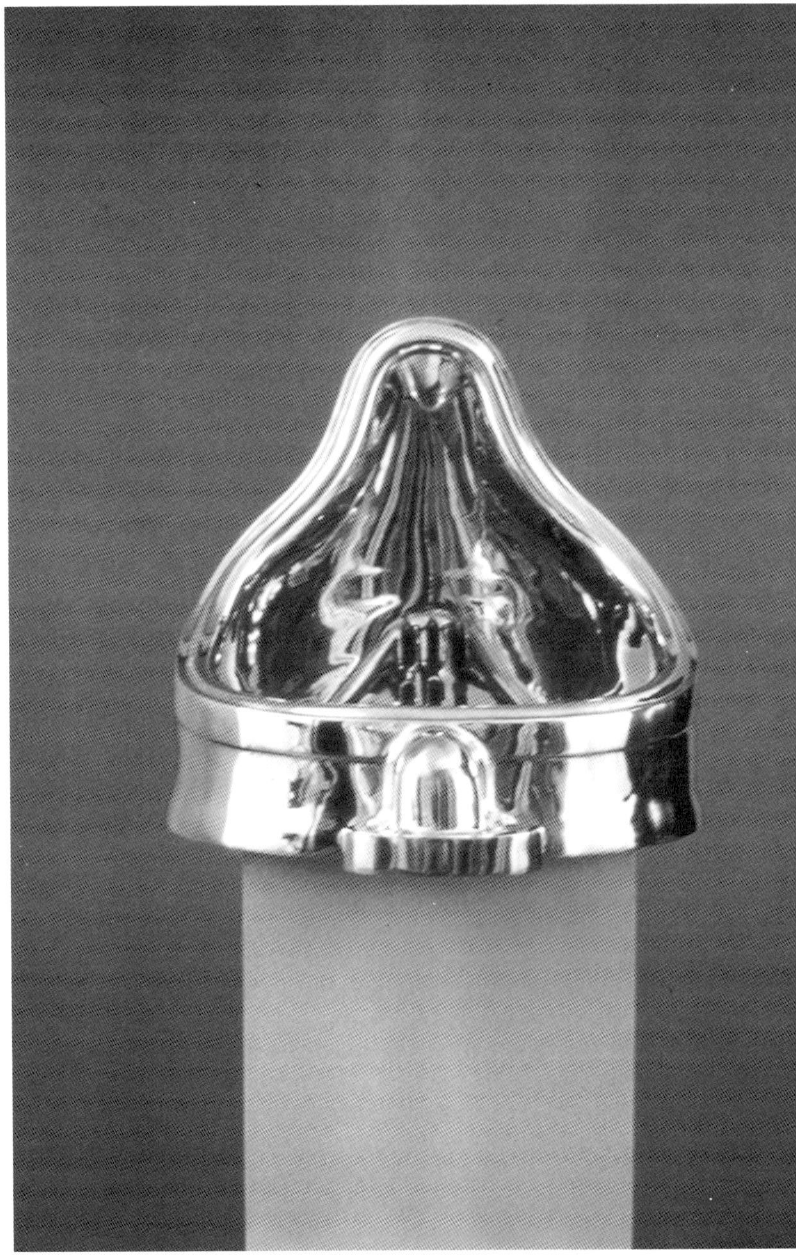

Sherrie Levine, *Fountain (After Marcel Duchamp),* 1991, edition of six, cast bronze, 15 × 25 × 15″. Courtesy Marian Goodman Gallery, New York.

1

Art Was a Proper Name

> For us, art is that which we find under this name: something which simply is, and which doesn't need to conform to laws in order to exist; a complicated social product.
>
> —*Robert Musil*

Act One: In Which You Are Coming from Outer Space and Ask Yourself "What Is Art?"

1.1.

Imagine yourself an ethnologist—or an anthropologist—from outer space. You descend to Earth. Knowing nothing about it, you are unprejudiced—except perhaps that you see everything through E.T.'s eyes. You start observing humans—their customs, their rituals, and above all, their myths—in the hope of deriving a pattern that will make Earth-thought and its underlying social order intelligible. You quickly notice, among other things, that in most human tongues there is a word whose meaning escapes you and whose usage varies considerably among humans, but which, in all their societies, seems to refer to an activity that is either integrative or compensatory, lying midway between their myths and their sciences. This word is *art*. Having noticed that it designates things, and goaded by your empirical curiosity as a researcher, you set out to inventory these things.

With the help of your informants, chosen to be as numerous and diverse as possible, at some point you will have collected a corpus, as exhaustive as possible, empirically defined by the rubric: all that is called art by humans.[1] So gathered, the corpus seems incredibly heterogeneous to you. It includes images, but not all images; sounds, but only some; written or printed texts, but only certain ones; two- and three-dimensional objects, some made in the image of humans, but also others that are unrecognizable; gestures, cries, and speeches, but performed or uttered only under certain, extremely variable, conditions; and so on. You sort. You compare. You scan your corpus in all directions, counting on discovering those features, which through their recurrence and their opposition to other neighboring features, will little by little establish the field of pertinence of the human word "art."

The job seems endless to you. You can tenaciously undertake it only because you are relying on a postulate that at times seems to you an intuitive certainty, but at other times only a methodological hypothesis: the comparative procedure is worth the expenditure; the taxonomic enterprise looks promising. Perhaps, being a follower of the functionalist school of some Martian Malinowski, you postulate that art has a social function proper to itself, independent of the diversity of its manifestations, or that it fulfills a fundamental need of humanity in general, or further, that it corresponds to a shared instinct of the species constituting one trait of any human's "basic personality." As such, the classification of the various domains of their activities that humans spontaneously construct when they distinguish between art, religion, ethics, and science,

1. "An art object, by definition, is an object recognized as such by a group." "The study of aesthetics consists mainly of the simple collection of objects. Everything will be collected, including what is easy to collect." Marcel Mauss, *Manuel d'ethnographie* (Paris: Payot, 1971), p. 89. (My translation.)

seems well founded to you. Or perhaps you have been nurtured by the structuralist school of a Martian Lévi-Strauss (more prestigious on your planet), in which case the spontaneous taxonomy of humans seems to you no less well founded, although for other reasons. You take it to be an empirical fact, whereas they refer to it, perhaps unwittingly, as to a set of transcendental conditions. Thus, it is with good reason that humans give art an autonomous place, with magic and religion on one side, and science on the other. With the certainty that "in anthropology as in linguistics, it is not comparison that supports generalization, but the other way around,"[2] you postulate the existence of a universal unconscious structure that underlies the disparate corpus constituted by everything humans call art. A set of regular transformations, tedious to inventory but limited a priori by the combinatory system, will perhaps one day explain the profound isomorphism which you suppose underlies the variety of practices, but which, for the time being, seems to be lacking in content the more universal it is in form. At the intersection of magical *action* and scientific *knowledge,* artistic *making* attributes a symbolic power to the things it names, at times gathering together, at times dispersing, human communities.

And you conclude that these symbols that humans exchange in the name of art must have—for them, who are perhaps unaware of this, it is a minimum; for you, who know nothing but this, it is a maximum—the undeniable function of marking one of the thresholds where humans withdraw from their natural condition and where their universe sets itself to signifying. Likewise, you conclude that the name "art," whose immanent meaning still escapes you—indeterminate because overdetermined—perhaps has no other generality than to

2. Claude Lévi-Strauss, *Structural Anthropology,* trans. Claire Jacobson and Brooke Grundfest Schoepf (New York: Basic Books, 1963), p. 21. Where the word "art" is lacking and does not, therefore, allow the empirical census and the structural postulate of invariance to refer to it, another postulate of universality takes over. Thus Boas: "In one way or another, esthetic pleasure is felt by all members of mankind." Franz Boas, *Primitive Art* (New York: Dover, 1955), p. 9.

signify that meaning is possible. In this game of symbolic exchanges, the word "art" would be nothing but the empty square that sets them in motion.[3]

1.2.

As an extraterrestrial ethnologist, this is probably all you could say about art viewed from the perspective of its humanness. Beyond this symbolic function, what humans call art loses its unity and thus fractures into arts, in the plural—into countless styles and motifs. But you will probably have noticed that these things humans name art have different ages; that some are being preserved with great care; that they are transmitted from generation to generation even while new things are continuously produced, and while from time to time some things are discarded and forgotten. Therefore, it might occur to you to consider your corpus as a synchronic section resulting from a long diachronical sedimentation, one whose history you undertake to write. Without really leaving your watchtower, you now give your attitude as an anthropologist a twist of humanism, and so, you become an art historian.[4]

3. In so few lines, one cannot do more than indicate the starting point of Lévi-Strauss's aesthetic thinking, the theory of the *floating signifier* (developed in his *Introduction à l'oeuvre de Marcel Mauss*), where he explains the emergence of the symbolic in general as the condition of art as well as of myth and science. Without this condition and its structuralist explanation, the comparisons Lévi-Strauss introduces (as in the chapter "Art" of *Structural Anthropology*) between artistic productions that are similar but that come from peoples completely separated in time and space would not even be plausible, except through a diffusionist explanation. One could thus imagine that an anthropologist landing from outer space and, inversely to Lévi-Strauss, looking for the unity of very heterogeneous artistic productions which, however, arise globally from one and the same society, one from which he himself is separated in time and space, would stumble on the same hypothesis, but in reverse order, so to speak. The reflexive singularity of art—that it is symbolic about the symbolic—would only strike him all the more forcibly.

4. The writing of art history always presupposes an anthropology, albeit a deceivingly simple one, as is shown by H. W. Janson, who chooses this starting point to his *History of Art:* "We

With one foot inside and one foot outside of time, you see the nature/culture threshold repeating and renewing itself in each of the mementos humans leave on the earth, sometimes as documents, sometimes as monuments. With the help of the necessary documentation, you climb back up the trail and try to bring to life the monumental corpus of what humans have called art in the course of their history and which they still preserve under this name. Your corpus is given from the moment your point of view is established, your point of view established from the moment your corpus is set. Art is your domain, your speciality, your chapter in universal history. Whether or not you argue your point of view, for you art is the autonomous *raison d'être* of your corpus, something like a substance or an essence, a noumenal invariant, the evolution or decline of which you describe as fluctuations or variations that are only phenomenal. Perhaps you reflect on the noumenon that makes art art, hoping that historical inquiry will clarify it for you; but first you have postulated its identity, there where history, lost in the search for its origins, confesses its own impotence in linking the evolution of art to the major discontinuity that must have presided over its birth, there also where *Kunstwissenschaft* takes over from *Kunstgeschichte*. Perhaps you dream to find this identity, essence, or origin of art in the ideal of Greek antiquity, and your discipline only engages in time the better to restore atemporality. Perhaps, on the contrary, you project it into the future and the facts gathered by your discipline arrange themselves accordingly as an eschatology. Or else, it is the organic cycle of generations or the mechanical swing of the pendulum that spells history for you. In any event, you hypothesize about the shape of time even if you haven't done so about the being of art. In both cases the hypothesis is unverifiable, either lost in its origins or permanently out of sight, beyond the horizon line where history ends.

Having the taste neither for metaphysics nor for speculation, perhaps you prefer monographic studies: the concrete history of objects rather than the abstract history of being. Your work is scientific, like that of the natural scientist.

---

might say that a work of art must be a tangible thing shaped by human hands" (New York: Abrams, 1966, p. 9).

But you are a historian of art and not of things. You can't help but recognize an intention in each "art-thing," nor fail to see that the intentions form certain groupings, following lines of force that are geographical and chronological. And if you recall having been a functionalist, you will be tempted to say that these lines of force draw a common design, a *Kunstwollen,* everywhere and always different in its manifestations, but everywhere and always constant in its aim. According to whether your inclination pushes you toward difference or constancy, you write *The Life of Forms* or *The Voices of Silence,* biomorphism in movement or psychology as metamorphosis. But you never write the history of *art,* since art as such is without history. Of course, you are aware that the conceptions humans have of art history have changed in concert with the things and the forms called art, but if in their succession you are above all tracking the evolution of the idea, you will see your discipline melting into *Geistesgeschichte* and art, having become one of the historical figures of Spirit, losing its concrete specificity. If, on the contrary, buttressed by the concrete, you allow yourself to see nothing but form and its variation, and if you suppress all speculative temptations, you will have reduced your discipline to *Stilgeschichte,* but not without making the concept of art reappear under the name of style. It, too, maintains itself in the singular throughout all pluralities. For if history periodizes styles, style periodizes history. And if you recall having been a structuralist, you will be tempted to order the temporal evolution of styles with the help of a few paired, formal criteria—the opposition of painterly and linear, of open and closed, and so on, those truly distinctive features of style in general.

Whatever the history of art—most often indeed the history of styles—does, it postulates (when it doesn't simply prejudge) the continuity of its substance, the invariance of its concept, the permanence of its foundations, and the unity of its limits. You are a historian of art and this is why, even though (all things considered) you don't know what art is, as far as you are concerned its history must be cumulative. Despite changes, even despite revolutions, the history of styles, accumulated in the mass of things that humans have called art over the course of time, appears to you as a cultural heritage. It belongs, you say, to humanity, and this is why your discipline is humanist. It is made up of objects but also of relations between these objects, ties of filiation, hinges of influence through which history obeys its own causality, broken influences and new departures through which art renews itself, naked as on the first day. As an extraterrestrial anthropologist visiting Earth, you had defined art empirically as being constituted by everything humans call art. As a humanist historian, you redefine this corpus historically: it is a patrimony. Its manifest heterogeneity gives way to its cumulative continuity, which is grounded in the fact that an essence called art maintains itself unchanged throughout its succession of avatars.[5]

---

5. This rather cavalier summary of the biases of (mainly German) art history relies on a few landmarks that are well known for having indeed oriented the profession and which it will be enough to mention here: Winckelmann for founding art history on the Greek ideal; Riegl for the notion of *Kunstwollen;* Wölfflin for the distinguishing features of style; Riegl and Max Dvorák, respectively, for the history of art as *Stilgeschichte* and *Geistesgeschichte;* Panofsky for the distinction between document and monument and for "the history of art as a humanist discipline." Art historians are not unaware of the implicit postulates of their discipline. On the contrary, there is no great historian of art who has not treated this problem theoretically. But neither is there one who has "resolved" it, for that would imply going beyond the limits that the discipline has drawn round itself. Certain ones, like Germain Bazin and Lionello Venturi, gave the problem a historical and reflexive twist or, in the instance of George Kubler, a more radically epistemological one. But that is to grasp the problem on the bias, as it were, either redoubling art history as the "history of art history," or posing the problem of the shape—itself ahistorical—of the history of art itself. It is rarer to see the problem approached frontally by embarking on a theoretical and methodological work. Yet this is exactly what, for example, Hans Sedlmayr does, as he ranks the tasks of art history along a series that begins in the *being of the work of art,* postulated but unknowable, and ends, after a long detour in historical science, in the *factors* or *forces* that must ground this being in its universality. (*Kunst und Wahrheit, Zur Theorie und Methode der Kunstgeschichte* [Mittenwald: Mäander, 1978], p.11.) If this is rare—and risky—for a theoretical work, it is, on the contrary, almost the rule in popularizing works which, before offering the reader a grand historical panorama guided by the red thread of an atemporal and universal notion of art, warn, but through sheer rhetorical caution, that this notion is a fiction. E. H. Gombrich, for example, begins his *Story of Art*

1.3.

Now perhaps a slightly more philosophical curiosity urges you to wonder about this essence. It might be that you feel the need to give the word "art" an ontological status that would, once and for all, provide its definition. Thus, you make yourself into a philosopher or even a logician—inasmuch as logic has been, ever since Aristotle and Thomas of Aquinas, the main road into ontology—and you return first of all to the empirical definition of your corpus: art is everything humans call art.[6] That this definition, or pseudodefinition, is circular doesn't stop you in the least, because you can already infer from it that art is a name, a predicate common to everything called art, a concept which it is now a matter of defining, both in extension and in intension. If it is exhaustive, your corpus will furnish the extension of the concept of art, allowing the analysis of the class of artistic things into subclasses that supply as many regional concepts

---

with this warning: "There really is no such thing as Art." To which he immediately adds, "There are only artists" (London: Phaidon, 1972, p. 5). But Gombrich is not Vasari, and what he offers is not a history of artists but well and truly a history of "Art." Even more symptomatically for what concerns us here, H. W. Janson, for his part, opens his *History of Art* with a reproduction of Picasso's *Bull's Head* which is a "semi-readymade" composed by a bicycle seat and handlebars, and about which the first sentence of the text asks: "Why is this supposed to be art? How often have we heard this question asked . . . ?" (p. 9). All pedagogy aside, it is a question to which Janson's history of "Art" replies no more than does any other.

6. Thus Richard Wollheim asks, "What is art? Art is the sum or totality of works of art" (*Art and Its Objects* [New York: Harper & Row, 1968], p. 1). It is obvious that the ontological question concerning art can arise elsewhere and need not be posed exclusively from within logic. Thus Heidegger's famous text, "The Origin of the Work of Art," deliberately outflanks and subverts this conceptual frame. But it is a fact that once a theory of art tries to base itself on an ontology, it is often inclined to do so with the help of that distinction prevailing in analytical philosophy between ontology and epistemology, assigning a priority to the first. The question "Under what conditions is something art?" precedes de jure the question "Under what conditions is knowledge of art possible?"

as the general one of art subsumes. In this way, you distinguish the subclass of painted things and the concept of painting, that of musical things and the concept of music, that of literary things and the concept of literature, and so on. What remains is to determine, in intension, under what necessary and sufficient conditions anything whatever can be called a painted thing or a musical thing or a literary thing. In other words, you will have to identify the properties that are common to all the things called painting, music, literature, and so on, then isolate the properties common to all the arts taken together, and finally eliminate those properties which are also present in things not called art at all. Arduous, interminable, it is a task that is also probably in vain. For even if you reached the conclusion, for example, that the presence of pigment on a support is the criterion identifying the members of the class of painted things, this still would not separate paintings, as works of art, from all the painted things that have no claim to the name of art. Thus, you must still discover the criterion that all subclasses composing the class of art-things have in common and that simultaneously discriminates art in general from non-art.

Your task becomes more and more difficult but you don't give up. You abandon an exclusivist theory, whose criterion allows only the intersection of the concepts under consideration, in favor of an inclusivist theory that is satisfied with their reunion. But you are in danger of ending up with the same absurdity. Either the ontological status of the work of art is an empty set, or it is an infinite one; either nothing is art, or everything can be. However, since the logician's ingenuity is unlimited, you leave the level of things for that of theories. Thus, you look for what there is in common between Aristotle's theory, for example, which held that art is imitation, and Collingwood's, which claimed it as expression, and Tolstoy's, which maintained that art is the communication of feelings; and so, from comparison to comparison, you try to produce the theory of all theories. Since the dangers at this level are identical to those at the first level, and since there is the added one of an infinite regress into metatheories, perhaps you now adopt the strategy of counterexamples, chosen or constructed to refute, one by one, the existing theories of art, examples that you will test in all "possible worlds."

And there, having perhaps exhausted your resources but not lacking inventiveness, you probably draw one of the following conclusions: that the ontological status of works of art is, like that of games according to Wittgenstein, nothing but family resemblance; that all attempts to define art must end in either a solipsism or a tautology; that the concept of art is undecidable; that the openness and indeterminacy of the concept are pertinent to any definition of the concept; or finally, either by recourse to a theory of performative speech acts, or through the detour of an institutional theory, that the circularity of the empirical definition "art is everything that is called art," far from being a sophism, constitutes the ontological specificity of works of art. And you will thus, even despite yourself, have brought your scientific grain to the ideological mill that has for quite a long time made the discourse of art history and current opinion go round: art is an autonomous business that is its own foundation, names itself, and finds its justification in itself.[7]

1.4.

Armed with all the certainties acquired over the course of this journey through ethnology, the history of art or of styles, and logical ontology, you finally plunge into your corpus in order to extract a model from it, the embodied proof of your theory, its paradigm. And out of it you pull—indeed, yes—a urinal. This particular one, rebaptized *Fountain* and signed R. Mutt, although everyone knows that its real author is a famous artist called Marcel Duchamp, is reverently kept in a museum, under the name of work-of-art and as part of the cultural patrimony. Its import seems indeed to have reduced the work of art to being the very symbol of this symbolic value that the word "art" confers on the objects of an exchange, whether linguistic, economic, ritual, or sumptuary. Better than

7. Allusion is here made to many theories of art arising from analytical philosophy, some essentialist (DeWitt Parker, Ducasse) or neoessentialist (Beardsley, Mandelbaum), others sceptical and Wittgensteinian (Weitz, Kennick, Ziff), still others conventionalist or "ascriptive" (Danto, Binkley), or finally, institutional (Dickie).

any other work of the cultural patrimony, Duchamp's urinal manifests the magic power of the word "art"; testifies to an almost impertinent freedom vis-à-vis the history of styles, which it appears to summarize and complete without owing it anything; and above all, illustrates the undecidability, the openness, and the indeterminacy of the concept of art, or even its entrenchment in solipsism or its expansion into universal tautology. Further, it is just as much the emblem of a theory of art-as-performative-institution. In fact, it welcomes all theories of art, or disqualifies them all, inasmuch as it is the counterexample to all of them, traversing all "possible worlds" like an absolutely sealed-off monad. This particular urinal has nothing in common with any of the countless things carrying the name of art, except that it is, like them, called art. And nothing distinguishes it from just any ordinary urinal, from non-art, except, once again, its name, *art*. In conclusion, it allows you to administer the striking proof of art's very autonomy, taking the glorious form of a nominalist ontology.

Having arrived at this stage, you are contemplating your paradigm as if it were a marble Aphrodite. It is supposed to sum up all works of art preserved as such on the planet Earth, and to reduce them to their common essence: they are called art by humans. But don't you realize that your theoretical definition of art simply brought full circle the empirical inquiry with which you started? Aren't you sensing the irony and the biting humor of this ready-made urinal? Aren't you worried by the absence of freedom that is the consequence of such an autonomy collapsed into tautology? Don't you feel disgusted or made ridiculous by the idea of accepting that anything whatever be made into the paradigmatic model of art's universality? Aren't you upset at the prospect of seeing so vulgar an object put an end to an entire stylistic heritage? If this urinal has not yet succeeded in instilling in you some sort of suspicion as to the validity of your theory, then you really must be from outer space. Perhaps you affect the detachment of the Martian observer, seeking shelter under the notion of scientific objectivity. In fact, you are either a blind idealist or an inveterate cynic. But if, on the contrary, you feel awkward after all the work you have done since you first imagined yourself as an extraterrestrial ethnologist, when the heterogeneity of your corpus led you to become, successively, a historian of art and a philosopher obsessed with the ontology of art, then your case is different.

If you sense that contemplating a urinal as if it were a marble Aphrodite is either ridiculous or disingenuous, then you are already laughing at yourself in disbelief. If you feel swayed by this urinal's irony, if its corrosive humor has eaten away at your Martian ethnocentrism, your patriarchal arrogance as an art historian, or your confidence in logical rationalism, then its autonomy as art already appears to you as nothing but an act of faith. Suspicion sets in. You realize that when a urinal can be art, then anything can be, provided one believes it. And if your model proves to be merely a matter of faith, then the theory it supposedly demonstrates is bound to be just a belief system. When the ontological definition of art ends up being equated with the empirical description—art is everything humans call art—that was your starting point when you were an honest but outside observer, then the autonomy of art has become of caricature of itself. And when all the disparate things accumulated through the history of styles as the heritage of humanity seem to lead to an institutional definition of art that is deliberately running in circles, then humanity itself must feel dispossessed. And so do you. For after all, in question is *our* culture, not the threshold nature/culture in the abstract, and *our* history, not that of an essence, and *our* performative speech acts, not a self-defining institution. The detachment of the observer—the ethnologist's outsideness, the historian's overview, the logician's neutrality—are unsuitable when the meaning of art, not just its recognition, is at stake. You will have to start all over again.

Act Two: In Which You Share the Plight of Humankind and Ask Yourself "What Should Art Be?"

2.1.

You are no longer from outer space. You are an Earthling. No longer an extraterrestrial ethnologist, you are a sociologist who is implicated in his or her own field of research. In other words, you are someone fired by the desire for scientificity—an observer, but an observer who is also a part of the observed phenomenon (in your case, the society of your fellow humans); moreover, someone who knows and wants this and takes it into account at the theoretical level. By the same token, you are also someone for whom this awareness is upsetting, someone practicing not methodical doubt but methodical suspicion. In other words, you are modern. In abandoning those forms of outsideness that constitute the confidence—or the faith—of the ethnologist, the art historian, or the logician, you have also left all forms of extratemporality behind. And you can no longer say, "Art is everything that is called art by humans . . . by *them*." Nor even, "It is everything humans have called art over the course of centuries, and which they continue to call art." You have to say, and in the present tense, "It is everything *we* call art." What at first rose before you with all the neutrality of a corpus gathered without bias now appears to you as the necessary object of a consensus—a consensus, furthermore, that ought to be universal. In order for art to be identified with everything we as humans call art, all of us would need to agree about it. But this consensus is problematic from the start, if only because it is too obvious that we don't agree. To you, as a sociologist, it is even more problematic, because it implicates and involves you while you seek to maintain scientific objectivity. You cannot nor do you want to neglect the fact that despite its social weight, consensus—in art as in other domains of social life—is always somewhat blurry and unreal; that it is never anything but a statistical distribution of opinions, bunching up around its mean but significant above all in its standard deviation; that it is suspect even when it is that of the majority, because the unequal spread of cultural capital tends to base all polls on art on some cultural poll tax. You are highly aware that the inventory of things constituting *our* cultural heritage does not equally belong to all of us.

For you, implicated sociologist, the notion of consensus remains an expedient, an opaque unsatisfactory concept, which must be demystified. The registration of social accord always requires some factor analysis to penetrate behind appearances and show that currents of convergent opinions merge at the confluence of several competing logics that govern group behaviors, carry social agents along, and seem to strip them of any real power of decision. Because you are a sociologist and because sociology should be a science, you cannot describe artistic consensus in any other way than as a field of forces whose effects are both random in their detail and deterministic in their totality. And because you are implicated, you cannot resign yourself to this mechanistic vision. Not only would it reduce the feeling of your own free will to nothing, but it would also level the meaning of your scientific practice, which in itself constitutes a social commitment. For in seeking to understand society as it is, you want to grant it the means to direct its changes. And while your analytical tools blow apart the zones of agreement that keep the social fabric together, you cannot help hoping that, in the end, they will foster a happier togetherness. As a sociologist, you are bound to be both utterly sceptical and slightly utopian. The uncomfortable position you are in (which is inherent to the practice of "critical" or implicated sociology) forbids you to consider that the relative agreement, through which the society of Earthlings as a whole calls art what it calls art, is the result of the miraculous coming together of the opinions of individual subjects. But it equally forbids you to consider it as the expression of a grand collective subject—that is, *we* humans—acting on design, even should this design remain as unconscious as Adam Smith's "invisible hand." Indeed, consensus is infinitely more mysterious, paradoxical, and difficult for you to understand than is social inertia, on the one hand, or social struggle, on the other. As a sociologist, all you can say is that consensus is the aggregate result of a variable number of social conducts which obey neither individual and subjective intentions nor objective class interests. You will say that consensus comes about just where, fleetingly or enduringly, there converge a certain number of *habitus* that seem teleologically oriented, but which are, in fact, socially acquired dispositions toward transindividual practices, most often unreflected upon although intentional, and objectively orchestrated in a given field. Such would be, in the aesthetic field, the consensus through which we call art what we call art.[8]

---

8. Better than anyone else, Pierre Bourdieu illustrates the position of the *implicated sociologist* who knows that he shares in the society he observes, and so shoulders all the methodological and epistemological difficulties deriving from this. Beginning with *L'amour de l'art* (Paris: Minuit, 1966) and continuing through *La distinction* (Paris: Minuit, 1979), Bourdieu demon-

Having said all this, you are about to stop being a sociologist, for sociology has limits that it recognizes and butts up against. The field it explores is peopled with facts to which it must adapt its tools, under the threat of not being considered as a science. Now, at one end of this field, the fact of consensus, even as something relative, even as something uncertain and problematic, escapes sociology as such. The more it is equipped to take the phenomenon of general assent apart, to analyze it in terms of balance of power, to describe the circumstantial collusions of independent *habitus,* the more sociology is powerless to explain consensus itself. If consensus is an empirical sociological object, it is never a theoretical one, because to analyze it into factors and factions results in,

---

strated an unremitting suspicion toward aesthetic consensus. In *Esquisse d'une théorie de la pratique* (Paris: Droz, 1972), and then in *Le sens pratique* (Paris: Minuit, 1980), he has criticized the objectivist presuppositions of structural anthropology, extolled a *praxeological* knowledge of the social world, and introduced the concept of *habitus* as "systems of enduring and transposable *dispositions,* structured structures predisposed to function as structuring structures, that is, as organizing and generative principles of both practices and representations which can be objectively adapted to their goal without implying either conscious purposes or an explicit mastery of the operations required to achieve them, objectively 'regulated' and 'regular' without in the least being the produce of obedience to rules, and, being all that, collectively orchestrated without being the product of the organizing action of a conductor" (*Le sens pratique,* pp. 88–89; see also *Esquisse,* p. 175). My translation. Later, in *Homo Academicus* (Paris: Minuit, 1984), where he closely observed the social group in which he intimately takes part, Bourdieu went so far as to assume—not without pain or courage—the personal consequences of the demystification of the consensus apparently projected by academics as a class. But in his last book, *Les règles de l'art, Genèse et structure du champ littéraire* (Paris: Seuil, 1992), Bourdieu seems to want to disimplicate himself from the field he is studying by positing precisely the concept of *field*—the literary or artistic field being defined as a belief system capable of *producing* artists as well as works of art. It is with this rather surprising inversion of Marx's infrastructure/superstructure relationship that Bourdieu hopes to regain an objective, scientific status for the sociology of art, or to restore what other sociologists would call "axiological neutrality."

and perhaps aims at, the dissipation of its illusion. This is why the anonymous crowd speaking with a unanimous voice remains an enigma for sociology, an enigma that is made all the more unassailable since sociology refuses to attribute this unanimity to a collective subject or to the sum of individual free wills, but also refuses to make it the epiphenomenon of either a mechanistic determinism or a Brownian motion.[9]

At the other end of its field, sociology also butts up against consensus, not as fact but rather as idea, postulate, or presupposition. Sociology doesn't merely take stock of society's existence; it posits a concept that it calls *the social* and whose unity, constancy, and necessity lie beyond empirical investigations. Sociology postulates that there is an *us;* this is what distinguishes it from ethnology, and also what tinges it—in spite of its striving for scientific objectivity—with a mild but inevitable utopianism. From your previous Martian perch the fact of human accord, when it existed, was attributed to some nature common to all humans, some universal identity among them. And when it did not occur, you interpreted this as a set of differences among humans, whose analysis revealed a structure all the more universal for being more deeply hidden. But at this point, you have descended to earth, a man or a woman among men and women, and what you observe is no longer the human species in its ecological niche but humankind in its social becoming. The differences that structure men and women are in fact the conflicts that divide us, men and women, and the identity

9. Perhaps it is because consensus is by definition a nontheorizable object for sociology that, as soon as it deals with crowd or masses, sociology seems to make way for psychology. The crowd's cohesion is then explained either by emotivity and suggestibility (Le Bon), or by imitation and mass communication (Tarde), or by identification and substitution of the object with the "ego ideal" (Freud), or yet again by the inversion of a phobia against contact (Canetti). All these interpretations converge on the desire for the charismatic leader and not on a postulated common sense. It is the merit of Serge Moscovici's book, *L'âge des foules* (Paris: Fayard, 1981) that it could coolly reread a body of texts that emphasized the fundamental irrationality of a phenomenon that sociology, always dependent on the antipsychologism of Durkheim, has a tendency to avoid.

that cements humanity is more than a biological feature; it ought to be a historical goal.

2.2.

You are once more a historian, but though art is still what interests you, you are not, this time, a historian of art, that is, of style. You no longer draw the progress of the forms you have inherited against the background of an essence that supposedly maintains itself unchanged over the course of history. You are the historian of the becoming-art, that is, of the very movement through which art is produced and progresses in its historical unfolding. You are not dealing with a given corpus but with a problematized consensus. Art, you say, is everything we call art, but the *we* is not a given. You have been to the school of suspicion and know that humans rarely say "I" in unison without having been forced to do so. Consensus, when it exists, is always suspect of not having been spontaneous, a cover for power and its abuses. But when it does not exist it needs to, like a horizon line in the name of which the abuse of power may be denounced. Consensus—whose other name is, after all, peace-on-earth—is always a state of happiness, whether you project it as a religious ideal, a political program or Paradise lost. In all three cases, even in the third, it lies ahead of you. No one would dream of paradise if it didn't promise reunion. The art historian's gaze was retrospective, yours is prospective. The art historian had inherited an inventory of things and he or she ruled over this domain as the distant representative of humanity as it is. You see yourself as the committed emissary of humanity as it will be or should be. You watch over the same cultural heritage, but it is not made up of things; it is made up of practices. The art of the past interests you only insofar as it holds out promise for the future. As a corpus, it simply doesn't exist. The word "art" exists, certainly, but when it signals accord, it is already past. Only when it is in conflict does it make history, when its meaning lies in its being transformed and destroyed as much as created. Like the historian of art, you record the history of styles, but you pay attention only to the leading edge where a style is destroyed to make way for another, and where the becoming-art occurs through negation and breaks the consensus.

You are not a historian of art; you are a historian of the avant-garde. Such is the name of the practices that alone interest you. The name of art and the consensus that it begs are nothing but the retrospective sanction of these practices. It makes them autonomous, and in so doing alienates them; it endorses them, and in so doing drains them of power; it affirms them, and in so doing negates their negating impetus. If the name of art arrests your attention, it does so only slightly. You never use it except for convenience in that larger context you call culture and civilization, or superstructure and ideology. It is the phenomenon of the avant-garde that entices you—its attitudes and practices, its hopes and conquests, its programs and achievements, its excesses and failures. All this mobilizes you, and this mobilization is, in the end, always political. You are a historian of the avant-garde, and the avant-garde sets the direction where history is to go. You want, therefore, to predict and to prescribe more than to tell and to describe.

Notice that for all that you are not necessarily an avant-garde historian. Rather, you are summoned either to advocate the avant-garde or to fight it. You are facing an abrupt alternative that allows for no neutrality. Either you make the values of the avant-garde your own and you become a militant of the political revolution, or at least of the cultural one; or else you castigate and fight these values and you also become a militant, a reactionary or at least a conservative one. In both cases, you place yourself in an agonistic field which is that of the very practices whose historian you are. In both cases, art—that which, as a convention or a concession, you call art—has a symptomatic value of reflection or of premonition of the state of social struggle. And in both cases, these values are essentially constituted through negation. It is the negativity of the avant-garde that stokes the conservative historian's resentment at seeing nothing in it but a vast enterprise of dehumanization. It is the same negativity that enthusiastically bloats the utopian historian's prophecies in seeing in the avant-garde a healthy clearing out before tomorrow's victory celebration. And it is still the same negativity that sharpens the vision of the critical historian in seeing in the avant-garde a resistance to the one-dimensional flattening of "affirmative" culture. These are more or less the political choices open to you, but nothing stops you from pushing them even further by denying them in their turn, as the most recent avant-gardes do. More radical than the frightened conservative, you could pursue antihumanism to the point of bestiality or angelism, or toward the reawakening of the superman. More disenchanted than the former utopian avant-gardist, you could proclaim that alienation is a virtue and that the lack of future is the truth of the *tabula rasa*. More subversive than the theorist of negative dialectics, you could go so far as to negate dialectics and play the game of cynicism, mimetic camouflage, and passivity.

These choices and others still, unforeseen because history does not stop, are open to you, since you, as historian of the avant-garde, are set in motion by the very history you are writing, and since there is no theoretical methodology that is not simultaneously a practical strategy. The only thing from which these choices cut you off is to become what the historian of art had been: the mere historiographer of an essence. They force you to espouse a philosophy of history for which there is no definition of art except the historical process through which art negates itself and comes to terms with its own negation. This process does not have an essence for its ground; rather it has a struggle for its motor. It never constitutes itself as a patrimony but projects the heritage of the past into the future in order to contradict it. When you call this process art, you mean that we, humans, don't need to agree about what art is. On the contrary, we need to struggle for what art should be. Some fight for one conception of art, others for another; yet we all stake a claim to what art ought to be for all of us. When you identify art with avant-garde art and with the avant-garde exclusively, you imply that conflict and contradiction are the very fabric of art. Most contradictorily indeed, you call on the idea of a reconciled humankind to claim that the history of art will end with art's disappearance, while you anticipate the end of history to justify art's premature existence.

Indeed, just as the art historian reflecting upon his or her activity could not fail, sooner or later, to encounter the question of art's origins, as a historian of the avant-garde you cannot avoid asking yourself about the direction of history.

In fact, you have asked yourself this question already, in the very act of becoming this historian. And you have answered it through a wager, which is nothing other than your own commitment. Optimist or pessimist bettor, you have put your money either on progress or on decline, but in any case you have put your interpretations of history on the line. Their truth or falsity awaits confirmation by the future; logic will not settle the question. In other words, in the becoming-art of the avant-gardes, it is the meaning of the word "art" that matters to you, not its truth value.[10]

10. This sketch-like portrait of the *historian of the avant-garde* of course summarizes a far more nuanced reality. In fact, it fits art critics better than art historians, because they take sides in the heat of the history that is being made around them and to which their own writings contribute. On one side, we would find, in 1913 for example, when the "historical avant-gardes" came into being, Royal Cortissoz as the defender of the establishment and, on the other, Roger Fry as the formalist advocate of the new art; or today, now that we hear of various neo-, post-, or transavant-gardes, Hilton Kramer as neoconservative critic and Benjamin Buchloh as post-Adornian theorist. In the meantime, the history of the avant-gardes has been written more often than not by *historians of art* for whom the avant-garde is after all a style and modern art is a cultural heritage. Even the Marxist art historians, who do not always write about modernity but who at least know better than others that they belong to its conflictual field, do not escape from this model of *style*. Such is the case with Arnold Hauser, Frederick Antal, or Nicos Hadjinicolaou, even though for the latter the notion of style has been replaced by that of "visual ideology." One must turn to philosophers–art historians, sometimes to "straight" philosophers, always to theorists, to find this particular form of history-writing which, espousing or castigating the avant-garde, stems from either fervent hope or deep disquiet or both at once, about the future of art and its possible disappearance. Around 1930, for example, when the "historical avant-gardes" had achieved their breakthrough, we would find Ortega y Gasset on the right and Herbert Read on the left. The former redirects against the formalist, "dehumanizing" avant-garde the aestheticizing and elitist prejudice that is in fact his own, while the latter imbues the avant-garde with a revolutionary power through which he hopes to resolve his own personal contradictions as a "bourgeois" aesthetician absorbed by Trotskyist ideas. Besides, the duty to take a political stance for or against the avant-garde, which results from the jettisoning of the concept of art as a historical

2.3.

You are not far from being, once again, the philosopher-logician you were earlier. Like him or her, you say: art is everything that is called art. Like him or her, you infer from this that the word "art" is the name common to everything called art. Like him or her, you deduce in turn that "art" is a common noun. But unlike him or her, you do not treat this noun as a concept. For the sentence "art is everything that is called art" is no longer a logical proposition the minute you add to it the mark of a "subject-of-utterance" that is presumed but necessary: ". . . called art by us." Since *we* are fighting over the meaning of art, the word "art" cannot avoid taking on plural and contradictory meanings. Moreover, since the very fight over the meaning of the word "art" is its most salient meaning when art is equated with the avant-garde, its features can no longer be reduced to logical predicates. So, the question that the logician asked

---

invariant and from the acknowledgment of the fact that the historian is carried along by history, does not necessarily lead to splits between conservatives and progressives. One of the most interesting and fruitful of these splits, the debate between Lukács and Adorno, took place within the Left and even within Hegelo-Marxism. It was the attempt to account for the *alienation* of modern art that led Lukács to opt for realism and Adorno for the avant-garde. Finally, today's cultural situation, after the failure of the "historical avant-gardes" to make the concept of art fade into a revolutionary society or to profoundly change its meaning, leads one to ask whether the position of a *historian of the avant-garde* is still tenable without provoking in those who claim to hold it either painful conflicts or powerful denials of their own value judgments. How could it be otherwise, now that the avant-gardes have become a historical object classed as *art,* while the concept of "avant-garde" still clinches to a sense of history that makes art the dialectical process of its own declassification? These conflicts and denials are very visible, as much in the work of an author like T. J. Clark, who, a careful historian himself, tries to reconstitute the phenomenon of the avant-garde in all its social density before he lets theory intervene, as in the work of an author like Peter Bürger, who, a thorough theorist himself, tries to resolve the problem of correct theorization of the avant-garde before he inscribes historical facts in this framework.

him- or herself undergoes a considerable rephrasing. He or she wondered what all the things humans call art might have in common, and you wonder what we might have in common that predisposes us to agree to call art the same things, whether because the agreement is in effect, or whether, in order for such a desire to grip us, in order for such a dream even to be thinkable, it might be in effect some day. The germ of an answer soon arises: we all have an aptitude for language, for communication—in short, for signs in general. Moreover, this common faculty is also our common fatality. We dwell in language as we do in society or history; it preexists us and constitutes us down to our very unconscious. What works of art have in common is what we have invested in them, driven by our common necessity to produce signs that in turn produce us.

Having said this, you are a semiologist, or better, a semiotician.[11] The word "art" is not the predicate of all the things we call art. It is not a concept; it is a sign. Because it is merely a sign, it takes the place of consensus; that is, it substitutes (itself) for it and signifies it, being the metaphor—and one of the most exalted that humankind has produced—for the accord between humans. Each of the things named by this sign is in turn made up of signs, of so many metonyms of this metaphor begging approval. But because the works of art are condemned to being made of signs and the word "art" to being itself a sign, the universal agreement that art claims as its signified is equally condemned to remain a signifier, ceaselessly running down the chain of signifiers, like an object desired but out of reach, forever pushed under the "bar" of metaphor.[12] For

11. The nuance between semiology and semiotics used to set a telling dividing line among French intellectuals in the seventies. Whereas the "semiologists" strove for objectivity and sought to give their discipline a truly scientific status, they were deemed conservative by the more progressive "semioticians," some Marxists but not all, who thought of their discipline as a linguistic—not metalinguistic—practice transforming its object rather than reflecting it. The way your involvement with and in the history of the avant-garde has led you to raise the issue of the meaning of art naturally turns you into a semiotician more than into a semiologist.

12. The allusion here is to Lacan's theory of metaphor, certainly an adequate intellectual framework for the role of (French) semiotician that you are playing now.

you, as semiotician, signs—and art-signs to a greater extent than those of ordinary exchange—have their own existence; they form a system among themselves, but this system is limitless and overwhelms humans who, thinking to serve themselves by working this system, in fact are worked by it. Once senders and receivers exchange a chain of signs, they cannot prevent them from saying either too much or too little, or from causing their acoustical or graphic substance to generate incongruous resonances that call to mind other signs, or from attesting to the disappearance of the reality they evoke. Consensus, which for your part you call successful communication, is no longer the enigma it was for the sociologist. It is simply the exception, a special case that exists when the message is exceptionally primitive, or the coding exceptionally strict, or the channel exceptionally pure. The rule is polysemy, equivocation, noise, dissemination. The rule is art, poetic language, the text without author, because each of its readers is counted among its producers. Art, all that by this common—and convenient—name we call art, is this infinite "rustle of language" (Roland Barthes) accompanied, assumed to the point of its madness, analyzed for its explosive pulverization, then catalyzed in the name of the impossible consensus it signifies and substitutes for.

Thus, for you there are two types of art since there are two types of consensus. The first, which you deem to be beneath your concern, gathers together the canonical masterpieces of the past and the art made for easy consumption. This consensus is indeed nothing but a *habitus,* or a habit. It is the one that the historian of art exaggeratedly respects because he or she understands it as tradition, that is, as continuity, and of which the historian of the avant-garde is systematically suspicious because he or she sees in it nothing but tradition, that is, nothing but established power. In your eyes, only the contested works deserve the name of art, and these might very well include masterpieces from the past, once they are reread for their power to reactivate dissension. But in this case, you will call even the masterpieces avant-garde works. So for you, as a semiotician, the name of art is the metaphor for the same contradictory and conflictual becoming-art on whose meaning the historian of the avant-garde, which you yourself were just a while ago, was betting. But whereas he or she was making a wager, your job is to make an interpretation. Where consensus about an avant-garde work exists, there is agreement about the fact that disagreement is necessary in order for the name "art" to be invoked and provoked; and where consensus does not exist, it exists negatively, since disagreement is necessary in order to signify that consensus is desired and desirable only when it is impossible. Thus, you have to interpret the identity of contraries that makes of art and non-art an indivisible couple. This is something you will have difficulty doing scientifically, since science dislikes contradiction and its reductionism is too reductive, to your taste, to encompass the proliferation of signs. Rather, you will write, and you will conceive of your own textual practice as something as polymorphous as the art you are interpreting, and from which you expect, on a theoretical level, an effect of isomorphism. The calculated, strategic confusion of practice and theory thus inevitably leads you to some art doctrine.

Because you are a semiotician, artistic signs are likely to present themselves to you, by turns, under the three aspects of signified, signifier, and referent. If you favor the signified, yours is a symbolist doctrine. Since the meaning of art is nothing but the impossible consensus about its name, you make yourself the witness and defender of art-for-art's-sake. And since consensus is impossible and should be so, you call on art against art. With the melancholy of the Décadents or the enthusiasm of the dadaists, you take it upon yourself to give the ruin or destruction of art its meaning of anti-art. If you favor the signifier, yours is a formalist doctrine. In encoding and decoding, in construction and deconstruction, in the abandoning of established conventions and the invention of new ones, you look for the principle of "significant form." And you find it, never better assuming its critical and self-critical power than in formlessness and antiform, just where the lack of semantic meaning opens the way to syntactical significance. Finally, if you favor the referent, yours is a realist doctrine. Yet, this realism must deal with the aura of unreality with which signs, being signs, color their referents. Art's "real" having been put in abeyance, what remains is surrealistic fantasy or superrealistic decoy; it is the assassination of art through quotation and parody. But toward whatever side your doctrine leans, you find yourself defending an ideal of autonomy which can all the less be taken for granted as it realizes itself through its negation. If you lean toward the symbolism of the signified, you will need to submit to derision the self-exaltation of art's meaning; if you lean towards the formalism of the signifier, you will need to somehow dismantle the self-institution of art's formal conventions; and if you lean toward the realism of the referent, you will need to betray the self-reference of art's discourse. Once the autonomy of art is no longer a given but rather allows heteronomy into its own condition, its accomplishment can only be postponed by a practice that breaks with common sense and alienates itself from the majority. The consensus around the avant-garde is always a minority one; otherwise it is not about the avant-garde. It is always forced, since it is a result of force. It is always both alienated and alienating. And it is always anticipated when it is desired and premature when it happens. That is to say, when the other name of art is *avant-garde,* this sign is always caught in the grip of a double necessity—to be the symbol of an impossible consensus and to be the symptom of an inevitable dissension. Thus, in order for humans to someday come to understand each other, we must daily recall the nature of the constitutive slip-of-the-tongue on which the misunderstanding is based.[13]

13. Under the terms "semiologist" or "semiotician" (see above, n. 11), each will recognize his or her own. From the two Saussures (the one of the *Cours* and the one of the *Anagrammes*) to Gérard Genette, from the Russian Formalists to *Tel Quel,* it is in the necessary complicity of a theory wanting to be scientific and a literary practice wanting to be avant-garde that the quest for artistic *essence* has been displaced from art as a given domain to art as generative process, but for all this without ceasing to be an ontological quest, however denied or negated. This is betrayed by notions such as *écriture,* text, textuality or picturality, when they come to replace those of literature or painting. One might say that negation itself has become the essence, for the shift from logic to semiotics implied a switch of philosophies: whereas the logician's roots are in Aristotle and, beyond Aristotle, in Plato—that is, in a philosophy of *being,* of permanence—the semiotician will tend to rely on some philosophy of *becoming*—of change—be it that of Hegel, Marx, Nietzsche, or Heidegger. Thus, it is an ontological necessity for the being of *écriture* or "the text" to include its fading, its negation unfolding in time.

2.4.

Made more than sceptical by this journey through implicated sociology, the committed history of the avant-garde, and disseminative semiotics, you are not going to rely on any expected consensus to find a model to support your theories. You appeal instead to an impossible consensus; you look for provocation; you instigate conflict. And you set before all of us—we who call art everything we call art—a *fait accompli* by producing the very same urinal that you were contemplating as if it were a marble Aphrodite at the end of your journey through ethnology, art history, and philosophy. It is the incarnated proof of the contradictory identity of art and non-art. When it was submitted, pseudonymously, at the 1917 Independents' Show in New York, it completely sundered the a priori consensus of the show's organizers. It revealed in these organizers, of whom Duchamp was one, the various competing aesthetic *habitus* their judgment followed. It projected into an anticipated future the retrospective sanction that would admit it into the cultural heritage, and in so doing, it was a coup making the avant-garde's dialectical law explicit.[14] For this urinal is in our heritage, now, but it is there as a permanent scandal. More radically than any other avant-garde work, it makes clear that the absolute signified and the true dignity of art-for-art's sake is anti-art; that the brutal abandonment of all formal conventions of art has pushed purism to the absolute "significant form"; that reality is

The Barthesian theme of *para-dox,* the Kristevian theme of *signifiance,* the Derridean theme of *différance,* all are in some respect tied to history's lack of self-presence, which is just as formative for them as the suspicion these authors direct toward the consensus over signs, or the fixity of signifieds, or the finiteness of signifiers, or the reality of referents. This is why—even more than for some political alignments that, judged from a distance, look more than embarrassing—French semiotics (or "semanalysis," Kristeva's expression), which started out with scientific goals as semiology, quickly landed on grounds that were either frankly literary or openly ideological (in a sense, after all, more Hegelian than Marxist or Althusserian).

14. More about this in chapter 2.

excrement, exactly what the absolute self-referentiality of art-about-art leaves behind. Paradigmatic manifesto of art as anti-art, Duchamp's urinal makes all this manifest. It is in vain that it rests in a museum and gets added to the cultural heritage. For some, it has not stopped being the harbinger of the happy day when art will finally fall from its pedestal and belong to everyone; for others, it remains the source of resentment and fear of the day when, everything having become art, nothing will be art any longer; and for all of us—in our society where consensus is either incomprehensible or impossible—it is still an object of dissent revealing our common plight. In conclusion, Duchamp's urinal wields the disquieting proof of art's alienation, an alienation that seems definitive to those who read it as evidence of decadence, provisional to those who see it as the premise of renewal, and necessary to those for whom the faculty of negating is what, in the end, promises emancipation.

Having arrived at this stage, you are contemplating your paradigm no longer. You are brandishing it like a banner, and possibly you are throwing it in your opponents' faces, whoever they are. Whether you took sides with or against the avant-garde, Duchamp's *Fountain* is for you the most significant sign—symbol, symptom—of a culture that you deem to be ours and in which negation, dialectical contradiction, counterinstitutional struggle, ideological deconstruction and textual experimentation fill the word "art" with ambiguous and opposite meanings. As such, *Fountain* has the most general value, either as promise or as warning. It proves your theory and upholds your practice; in short, it embodies your doctrine. But aren't you distressed by the reified negativity of this ready-made urinal, now that it is piously preserved like an icon? Aren't you concerned that the dialectical equation of art and anti-art might have congealed into a perverse tautology, now that even the middle class collects its products? Aren't you bored by the phoniness of a good part of Duchamp's legacy? Don't you feel the powerlessness of avant-garde art to elicit indignation from a society that is too liberal but still not free enough, too eager to mask conflict behind pluralism and too anxious to clothe its consent for cultural illiteracy in the rags of dissidence? If you have not yet started to despair about the practical value of your theories, you must really have fled to another planet. Either you are already there, with the philosophers of resentment and the historians of decline who like to watch Rome burn from a distance, or you are in the takeoff lounge with the modern utopianists and no longer within range of the noise coming from the burning metropolis. Or else, perhaps, you persist in not seeing that the main body of the army has never followed the avant-garde; that the motor of contradiction is exhausted; that the step from creative negation to nihilism has been taken; that around anti-art, the impossible consensus has nonetheless been reached out of indifference, and that it is inevitable that suspicion, once you let it start, gnaws down to your very last bit of hope. But if, on the other hand, you despair enough about art, if the feeling of the vanity of anti-art brings you to the point of remembering that the irony of the urinal was baptized by Duchamp "ironism of affirmation," then perhaps you will go all the way beyond suspicion and realize that, in your engagement with the avant-garde, you were not mistaken about practice but rather only about theory. Perhaps then negativity will seem to you like an unfair concept, because it always reduces affirmation to double negation and therefore never allows it to exist in its own right. And perhaps the concept of alienation, whose social reality is undeniable, will seem equally unjust to you, for being proved precisely by its denial. After all, it is your own social responsibility from which you run the risk of alienating yourself when, as an implicated sociologist, you demystify the illusion of consensus; you run the risk of bankrupting your own duty to freedom when, as a historian of the avant-garde, you prescribe a course of history that you describe as unavoidable; you run the risk of depriving yourself of your own obligation to speak truly when, as artist-semiotician, you knowingly confuse signifying practices with theories of signification. The sceptical disenchantments that led you to abandon the illusions of outsideness, metalanguage, and disinterestedness certainly offer great intellectual benefits, but they do us a wrong. Your commitment, your attention to that common accord and above all that common discord, through which we call art what we call art, has led you, like it or not, to speak in our name for all of us. This *us* is an abuse and an alibi. You will have to start all over again.

Act Three: In Which You Have Become Just Yourself and Know What Art You Like and Dislike

3.1.

You are no longer anyone, anyone special that is. You are not a specialist any more. You are just yourself, without particular qualifications, simply an amateur, which means that you are no longer a professional, but also, in the etymological sense of "amateur," that your dealings with art have the nature of a love relationship. You are Mr. or Ms. Everyone, since everyone is an art lover to some extent. So, you are in love. And just as you need no theory of woman to love a woman, or of man to love a man, you need no theory of art to love art. Just as no one falls in love with Woman (or Man) in general, no one falls in love with Art in general. Even Don Juan, who is looking for *the* woman, loves women individually, one by one. You are in love with this or that work, and certainly with more than one at a time, but not with all works. Like your choices in love affairs, your choices in art are free and at the same time compulsive. Something irresistible attracts you. You don't always know what, but you know that you are attracted because you feel it. All you have for knowledge is your own certitude and all you have for certitude is your own feeling. To you it is indisputable; it is its own proof. Your friends, your psychoanalyst if you have one, and you yourself might be endlessly suspicious of this feeling; your social milieu might disapprove of it; the establishment might repress it or forbid its expression. All this would make it more exalted or painful, but would take nothing away from its authenticity. In love affairs, with works of art as with people, your feelings are of course determined by past experience, channeled through the story of your family, conditioned by your belonging to this or that social class, by your sex and your gender, by your education, by your heredity. Obviously, you can only love within the limits of your social determination and of the cultural opportunities that are objectively available to you, but that doesn't stop you from loving. Your taste is indeed an aesthetic *habitus,* but it is yours; moreover, if you didn't feel it to be yours, it wouldn't be a *habitus* but rather the interplay of forces external to you. You have introjected the socially acquired dispositions that produce the love of art; you have let them lie fallow, or you have cultivated them to a greater or lesser extent; regardless, they shape you just as intimately as anything else in your personality.

If at this point someone asks you to define art, it is with your taste and your personal feelings that you will answer. You will say, pointing a finger at your favorite works: art is this, and this, and that. You have been asked for a definition, but since you only have your feelings as a guide, you don't feel entitled to generalize, so in place of a theory you give examples. Each of them you baptize with the name of art, one by one. The phrase "this is art" is the expression of your judgment, arising case by case. And so is the phrase "art is this." In spite of the fact that it sounds like a definition, it is merely a quasi-definition, an empirical one if you like, since it is based on sense experience, but more precisely an aesthetic one, inasmuch as the word "aesthetic" precisely means: that which has to do with a sentimental, not with a cognitive, experience. In baptizing the examples of your taste with the name *art,* you are thus making an aesthetic judgment. Most often of course, as in the case of established masterpieces, you are simply repeating a christening that has long since been performed. Your personal *habitus* confirms a more or less general consensus. But from time to time, you call art something unexpected, or your refuse to call art something too expected. Perhaps you make it a point of showing how original and audacious you are; perhaps you want to mock taste, whether good or bad, and prefer to display eclecticism, mannerism or avant-gardism; perhaps in trying to distinguish yourself from the ruling *habitus* what you really do is entrench yourself more surely in the *habitus* of the ruling class; perhaps you are doing all this because you are a snob. But if you are a snob, you are a fraud. You are cheating with your feelings and are not using the word "art" to christen the works you genuinely like; you are merely using it as a social password. Perhaps, on the contrary, you make it a point of suspecting the general consensus, which seems to you to be manipulated; perhaps you distrust taste, not so much your own but the very concept of taste, which you read as ideology; perhaps you have developed a hatred for the "man of taste" whose distinction simply marks him off from general opinion, and you retaliate by valuing only the most opinionated works that mark you off as well; perhaps you justify this with theory and hide your hatred. But if you do so, you are an ideologue. You can't help but have feelings, yet you won't allow them to speak out. You deny them and you use the word "art" as a social weapon. You are a snob in reverse, and if you are, your social weapon will turn out to be another (anti-) social password. But if, contrary to both the snob and the ideologue, you are sincere when you call art something unexpected or refuse to call art something too expected, then you are yielding to those complex and contradictory feelings that, akin, indeed identical, to those of love, compel you to go beyond your taste and to surrender. Then the word "art" is dictated to you by the objectified force of these feelings forcing you and about which, by a sort of immediate reflexiveness, you precisely feel that they put your taste, your aesthetic *habitus* and habits, in jeopardy. Then, in attributing this name, art, to the object that occasioned this uneasy feeling in you, you are obeying the contradictory injunction of your feeling. In this case, the unexpectedness of the things that you call art is indeed unexpected by general opinion—not insofar as it is the opinion of others (the mass of humans from which you distinguish yourself), nor insofar as it is ours (the class of distinguished people who impose their class consensus), but insofar as it is yours, personally; insofar as, whatever your class, you have incorporated into your taste or anti-taste that classification which classes you.

Such a judgment, which is born out of dissent—that is, literally (dissent meaning dissentiment) born out of the conflict within your own personal feelings—is perhaps no longer a judgment of taste, even though it is an aesthetic judgment. Just as the feeling of love alternates between lightness and gravity, carries one away with joy or plunges one into worry, encompasses passion as well as tenderness, irrepressible sexual attraction as well as attentive companionship, absolute veneration as well as faithful friendship, a blind fixation on the seductive object as well as empathy and compassion, just as it can exhaust itself in possession or forget itself in charity, just as it often harbors savage jealousy or abruptly slides into hatred, just as it is made up of as much suffering as ecstasy, so too the love of art is sustained by an array of heterogeneous feelings and not based, as the notion of taste would have it, on the rather oversimplified opposition of pleasure and pain. The mixture of pleasure and pain, or the oscillation between terror and delight—indeterminate feelings, or rather, emotions, in which Kant and Burke saw the sign of the sublime—are themselves inadequate to supply a word general enough to cover the embattled diversity of the feelings entering the love of art and coinciding, as they doubtless do, with the whole range of human feelings. The sublime emotion is part of them, to be sure, as is the feeling of beauty that is called taste. But the sudden turn of taste into disgust is also part of them, as is the tiny step that carries the sublime into the ridiculous. Love may not seem to be the appropriate name for the assembly of such incompatible feelings, yet it is. It is even the most realistic one for a love so contrary to propriety. And if one must find an apt word to designate the cause, or rather, the occasion for the summons of those incompatible feelings, it is the word "art" that suits the case. It suits it precisely because it is not suitable, being, in that sense, the least idealistic name for things arousing so unsentimental a sentiment.

The semiotician wasn't wrong in reading the word "art" as the negative sign of successful communication, or of a communication that succeeds only when it fails; the historian of the avant-garde wasn't wrong in hearing the word "art" only in the provocation of anti-art or in the distress calls of non-art; the sociologist wasn't wrong in attributing the word "art" only to the practice that dissolves consensus or reveals it as dissolved, already. And you yourself, mere art lover, when you utter the word "art" to refer to that unexpected something that upsets your feelings beyond all appropriateness, you acquiesce to this upheaval, you lay claim to the opposing feelings that shake you, and it is the object that thwarts your love of art and that occasions the sentiment of dis-sentiment in you that you decide to call, reflexively, by the name of art.

Even though your feelings are your own, proven by the fact of being experienced, they are never your property. They are acquired cultural values in relation to which the probability that you experience them—and that you experience them apropos of "this" rather than "that"—obviously depends on your culture. The breadth of your culture is what allows you to recognize the conflict of values competing within and for the cultural field, whether they are closely linked to or far removed from the spontaneous values of the group you belong to. This conflict is what the sociologist called the competition of concurrent *habitus,* the historian of the avant-garde the inherent contradiction between art and anti-art, and the semiotician the dissemination of signs. But it is one thing to recognize values in conflict, and it is another to experience them. Being cultivated and being sensitive are not equivalent. To be sensitive to art is to feel the conflict of values as a conflict of feelings. This sensitivity is something which, far from putting you out of the fray, plunges you directly into it; it is something completely at odds with aesthetic disinterestedness or distancing, and also very different from the flair of the dandy or the snob who samples the conflicting values in order to choose by reflex the one that will shock and mark him or her off from the crowd. The reflexivity of your contrary feelings is not a reflex; it is what condenses their contradictoriness into the feeling of dissension, the sentiment of dis-sentiment. In calling art something conflictual and unexpected, you give your assent to the reflexive feeling of dissent, that is, to the quarreling rather than peaceful coexistence of the cultural values you are able to experience. You give your consent to the felt absence of consensus about this thing, which is only unexpected by others insofar as it is overwhelming for you, and which is only overwhelming for you insofar as it is controversial for everyone; and for this thing you demand the agreement of all others.

3.2.

Along with the number of overwhelming things you love, the incompatibilities among your feelings multiply. Can you possibly love both Wagner and Mozart without recanting? Can you accommodate both Rubens and Mondrian simultaneously? Would you dare name the feeling that might reconcile John Heartfield and Leni Riefenstahl? How would you justify putting Manzoni's cans of *Artist's Shit* in the same museum as Bonnard's *Nude in a Tub*? The question of the unity, of the identity of art, that the logician raised in terms of the common properties of objects and the semiotician in terms of a common inherence in languages, is raised now not in terms of community or even of compatibility but in terms of the passage from one feeling to another. Aesthetic judgment, which unifies nothing, nevertheless administers these passages. Your personal pantheon is more or less crowded, your ideal library more or less vast, your imaginary museum more or less rich, but they exist as a battleground, a babel of tongues, a Borgesian shambles where you ceaselessly pass from one camp, one language, one form to another. Each of the things to be found there is no more than an example of what art is for you; none amounts to a definition, a concept, a theory. When asked for one, all you can say is: "Look, here is some art." Clearly, such gestures are only quasi-definitions, not generalizable. But they claim generality, they execute a passage, they are the index that shifts the general name, art, from one particular work to another among your choices. In order to generalize, you would have to add up example after example and end up with a formula that may look circular, like those of the ethnologist and the sociologist, but that is in fact reflexive. You no longer say, "art is everything humans call art," nor, "it's everything we call art." You do say, you claim to say, "it's everything I call art." You are not basing yourself on a corpus you inventoried but in whose establishment you have had no role; you don't assume a consensus that you really suspect is impossible or illusory; you simply exhibit your own personal collection, real or imaginary.

But in showing, under the name of art, what you have collected, you are no longer a mere art lover. You advertise your tastes, you claim and profess them, you try to get them shared. And if you go so far as to make public your doubts, your uncertainties, your errors of taste, your distastes and even your disgusts by exhibiting—always under the name of art—those things among the cultural products that aroused so many mixed feelings that you judged them to be overwhelming, then you have all the qualifications to be, so to speak, a professional art lover, which is to say, an art critic. Art critics, in the broad sense—chroniclers, specialized journalists, teachers, but also museum curators, art collectors, even art dealers—in other words, all those people who make their aesthetic judgments public, are people who exercise a critical vigilance, not over a corpus of objects or a consensus of receivers, but over the collection of things having aroused in them the feeling that they were confronting art. It is with and about this that they judge and over this that they will be judged. Whatever other things art critics do, whatever criteria come into play when they write, collect, organize shows, buy and sell art, when all is said and done, art critics are public and professional art lovers. The rest is, while not irrelevant, at least accessory. Of course, with this professional status comes power, a platform, an academic authority exerted through teaching or in the media, a real or supposed expertise, a potential charisma, and the possibility of influencing the public and manipulating the market. But power doesn't make a critic (it shouldn't, and in the long run, it doesn't); reputation does. And reputation imposes itself only in exposing itself. Art critics, in publishing their judgments, ask to be judged on their judgments' quality and, whether they like it or not, consign themselves to the verdict of the future.

3.3.

This expression may sound high-flown, but it is the right one: the tribunal of history is what constitutes culture as value. Because history is a court, constantly in session, cultural values are created even while others are destroyed. The historian of the avant-garde wasn't wrong when he or she defined the agonistic value called art as a process. But "process" would have to be read as "trial" rather than as "transformation." And it is because history is a court that cultural values are preserved across a succession of societies that no longer live according to these values. So, the historian of art wasn't wrong either when he or she defined the sedimented value called art as a cultural heritage. But the emphasis should be put on the jurisprudential aspect of the transmission rather than on the cumulative aspect of the legacy. Jurisprudence is the legal memory in which society stores the judgments issued in the past over cases similar to those currently submitted, but which the written law could not have foreseen in their singularity. Judges are invited to consult jurisprudence for inspiration but they remain free to contradict it. The closer a legal system comes to common law and the less it depends on the written code, the more important jurisprudence becomes. The history of art—and even more, the history of the avant-garde, namely the history of modern art—resembles such a judicial system. Artistic culture transmits art just as jurisprudence passes along judgment: by rejudging. None of the rejudged judgments making up the jurisprudential record is entirely determinant for those that will follow, and none has been entirely determined by those that preceded it. There is no more a Last Judgment than there is a first; there is no more a historical determination "in the last instance" (Marx) than there is a court of first instance. The tribunal of history is a permanent court of appeal. The first reader of a book, the first listener to a concerto, the first viewer of a picture already judges the artist's judgment, while the artist had, through provocation, already lodged an appeal against the prejudices of the times.

You have just been an art critic and now, in the act of rejudging, you have become a historian. Let's say you are a somewhat sluggish critic, slow on the uptake, or one arriving too late and judging an event that is already receding in time, or one enjoying the full historical distance granted by those artworks coming to us from the distant past. Perhaps you are simply less sure of your judgments than the talent scout operating in the heat of the moment; perhaps you need a slightly thicker jurisprudence to pass judgment; perhaps you prefer to sustain your own verdict with that of so many past generations. But between your practice as a historian and that of the day-to-day critic, there is neither difference in kind nor any break. You write history in practicing belated art criticism. Like the *historian of art,* you inherit the cultural patrimony, or rather, the jurisprudential record. Like the *historian of the avant-garde,* you take sides in a struggle, or rather, in a trial. As for the historian of art, art for you is a given domain of facts. As for the historian of the avant-garde, art for you is a conflict whose outcome is at stake. But more clearly than most historians of art, you state and take on your responsibilities as judge. Quite possibly this will mean no more than a slight inflection of style, with which you avoid creating the belief that history itself is speaking through your mouth or writing itself through your pen; yet such an inflection of style will be more than the simple scruple or the regret shown by certain art historians—the most honest ones—who admit to the subjectivity of their choices and accountings. It will be both a working method and a moral principle resulting from your knowing that once you admit a recognized work of art into your discourse, it is accompanied by an invisible tag saying "this is art," and that, though the tag is a given, what it says is not a fact. When, as a historian, you write about something that has already been called art by others—historians who preceded you or critics faster than you—you are taking stock of a judgment registered somewhere on the jurisprudential record, but which nothing forbids you to reverse as long as you are not unaware, nor keep your readers unaware, that a judgment had been passed. Jurisprudence doesn't have the force of law, but it carries some weight. Yet no matter how heavy it weighs on your judgments, it is never a criterion that exempts you from having to judge again; it is merely a guideline that you may or may not follow, a record of *prudence* that helps you decide whether you should let the experience of your predecessors nourish your own, but which, in any case, you ought to confront with your actual feelings.

In judging again you take a stand. You write history both in respecting the events as they took place and in choosing the significant events. The history of art is not a discourse torn between the objectivity of science and the subjectivity of evaluation and interpretation. It is false to claim that it records the past as if the events had organized themselves spontaneously, but it is equally false to say that in reading the events as signs it is free to prescribe their meaning and to orient them according to an end. What the historian of art describes as the spontaneous evolution of style actually occurred under the pressure of aesthetic jurisprudence; and what the historian of the avant-garde prescribes as a trend, which he or she claims is that of history itself, is actually visible only in hindsight. Now, what you do is similar to what the historian of art was doing, only with this proviso: that the style of your writing makes it clear that history as heritage is no more than jurisprudence. With this proviso, your attitude is closer to that of the historian of the avant-garde. Like him or her, you know that you are on board the history train and responsible for intervening in it. But unlike him or her, you don't confuse writing and praxis. Yes, you are at war but you are not a soldier; you are more like a war reporter. Yes, you have a stake in the conflicts of history but you are not a militant; you are more like a moralist. You are in fact at once the judge and the court clerk. The conflicts of the avant-garde and the arrière-garde have been entrusted to you through the jurisprudential record, registered in the form of "differends" and litigations.[15] At times, your job is one of rewriting a "differend" in the language of the litigation it has become over time; at others, it is one of reopening a litigation to show that it still hides a "differend." Both tasks require judgment and interpretation. You intervene in history, but you are not rewriting the events that happened so as to make them anticipate what would happen later; you are not extrapolating trends so as to fill them with historical meaning; you are adding to the jurisprudence. This is also translated by an inflection of style. For if you no longer claim that your writing is dictated by facts, neither do you want to suggest that it is done in the name of a cause. You only write to set a precedent, here and now. The least one can ask from an art-historical text is that it carry the date of its composition as explicitly as possible.

Thus, you are a historian, a critic-historian or a historian-critic, and what you do is akin to, with these inflections of style taken into account, what the historian of art and the historian of the avant-garde were doing. However, you are neither the one nor the other. Rather, you are a *historian of tradition.* Even though, on the one hand, like the historian of art, you inherit the word "art" along with the jurisprudential record, you never take it for granted and you never let it delimit a priori the field of your research. You know too well that the word "art" was at issue in each judgment stored in jurisprudence and that it is still at issue when you decide on whom you are going to write, which

---

15. "As distinguished from a litigation, a differend [*différend*] would be a case of conflict, between (at least) two parties, that cannot be equitably resolved for lack of a rule of judgment applicable to both arguments. One side's legitimacy does not imply the other's lack of legitimacy. However, applying a single rule of judgment to both in order to settle their differend as though it were merely a litigation would wrong (at least) one of them (and both of them if neither side admits this rule)." Jean-François Lyotard, *The Differend: Phrases in Dispute* (Minneapolis: University of Minnesota Press, 1988), p. xi.

works you are going to mention, how many pages you are going to grant them, whether you are going to praise or criticize them—all the decisions art historians make when they write history. You neither believe nor postulate that art is an essence that remains permanent throughout the changes in style, form, taste, ideology, and their underlying socio-historical conditions; but you are aware that the name "art" continues to be transmitted through the sequence of rejudged judgments making up the jurisprudence. Well, this transmission is called tradition. And even though, on the other hand, like the historian of the avant-garde, you have a sharpened awareness of the struggles through which art comes into its historical existence, even though you know how much these struggles necessitate the destruction and the negation of traditional art, you never take the negativity of the avant-garde for granted and you never let it structure your own thinking about art. You know too well that all courts pit the prosecution against an accused or a plaintiff, that without a dispute there would be nothing on which to pass judgment, and that the sentence must decide between "this is art" and "this is not." You do not defend the doctrine that art, or avant-garde art, is the dialectical movement that goes from art to non-art, and from non-art to a transformed notion of art, since you are aware that jurisprudence, not dialectics, has settled the identity of the contraries. For sixty years now dadaism has been in the museum and the "tradition of the new" has been in place. You may judge that tradition has been betrayed or that the betrayal has been transmitted, but you cannot ignore the fact, laid down in the trial record of the avant-garde, that "transmission" is now translated into "betrayal." You will not rejudge without knowing that henceforth "betrayal," "translation," and "transmission" comprise the three inseparable meanings of the word "tradition."

3.4.

As a historian of tradition, in this sense, you are no better equipped than the mere art lover when it comes to defining art. You may be infinitely more sophisticated and knowledgeable than the mere art lover, but you are not a theorist, you are a critic, a slow critic perhaps but a critic nonetheless. Thus, you are an art lover yourself, but one who accepts the duty to go public with his or her preferences. By way of theory, all you have is your collection, which you may or may not want to wrap in explanations; the reasons adduced for a judgment never totally account for the sentence pronounced, and certainly, they don't replace it. You have a notion of what art is and what it means to you, and you have standards about what you expect art should be. But to sustain both your notion of art and your expectations from art, you rely on your judgment alone. Pleas and testimonies are of little help in the cultural court; what matters are the exhibits, and whether they pass the test of time. As a historian, you know this for a fact of jurisprudence; as an art lover, you know this from experience.

So, if someone were to ask you whether you could come up with a model exemplifying your theory of art, your answer would be "No," since you have no theory. Still, could you dig out of your collection a work exemplary enough to stand for a paradigm of the whole? Your answer would be: "Let me consult with my feelings." Examples would be summoned, and most probably the first ones to come to your mind would be your favorites. Undisputed masterpieces would be among them, some of which were highly controversial in their own time—Giorgione's *Tempest* for example, or Manet's *Olympia*. Being as familiar with the jurisprudence as you are, you are also aware that the reversals of verdict these works underwent must have influenced your own feelings about them. And it is not so much now your taste that you consult, or the jurisprudential consensus precisely called taste, as your own reversals of taste, the jurisprudence of your betrayals. You look back on your youthful love affairs with Albers and Vasarely and Kinetic Art with embarrassment, yet you would want to save Albers, and Morellet, and certainly early Soto, from oblivion. You remember vividly how the encounter with pop art on your first trip to America violently disrupted the confidence you had in the supremacy of European, abstract art. The Bauhaus had been betrayed, and it took years until you had digested all the consequences. Whenever you hesitate about post-1968 Warhol today, you feel the need to recall the shock his blunt images had been to you in 1964 and to check whether his later work withstands comparison. For a very long time, Warhol and Cézanne were, in your truncated vision of art history, the two poles around which all your favorite art works had to revolve, like two armies facing each other on the battlefield. During all this time, the past of art was there, in the look of the cities you lived in or in the prestigious names you had learned to respect from childhood on, but the past was not available. Having been educated to the idea that architecture started with the Crystal Palace, painting with Cézanne, music with Schönberg, you would remember the silly guilt you felt simply for liking the ruins on the Forum the first time you visited Rome. The discovery of Palladio, of Masaccio, of Monteverdi came later, and there is no way for you to reach into your imaginary collection of art works without acknowledging the helter-skelter order in which they entered it. "Is this legitimate?" you would ask yourself. "Am I not supposed to come up with a model, something that could stand for art at large and be objectively valid, or at least historically relevant?" More grappling with your feelings is called for. Since Rome came to mind, you would think of Florence, and then Venice, and the fondest memories of museum visits would soon overwhelm you with joy. Siena would not be forgotten, and how, in the wake of your discovering Duccio's *Maestà,* all the Sienese *petits maîtres* found their way into your collection. But joy is not enough, and the hard time you had with Tintoretto, the sort of condescension with which you regarded Mannerism (with the exception, perhaps, of Pontormo and that one painting by Beccafumi), should make you think twice. You would still be facing the fact that there is not one single modern Italian artist whom you would want to put in the foreground of your collection, in other words, whom you could make stand for tradition as a whole (and where would tradition come from, if not from Italy?). Not De Chirico, not even Fontana. As to the contemporaries, the Arte Povera and the transavantgarde people, why is it that none of them seems exemplary enough? Clemente has charm, Merz is powerful, Kounellis is intelligent, Anselmo is subtle, Fabro is both distasteful and superbly clever (which might be something), but they are all too elegant and too subdued by the awesome ruins strewn over the Italian landscape. The legacy of Italy is not in Italian art. It was transferred to France long ago, and your acquaintance with the jurisprudence as recorded in art history books tells you that you know this all too well. But your own jurisprudence tells a different story, which by now is also on the record. Why is it that Hartung and Soulages could not durably sustain the enthusiasm of your adolescent years, and that Fautrier had to wait until Schnabel had succeeded in making something out of the exhaustion of American painting à la Pollock to be a plausible candidate for rediscovery? It is an undisputable fact, to you, that tradition crossed the Atlantic at the outbreak of World War II. Pollock is the true inheritor of Cézanne. This conviction took twenty years to affirm itself. You first valued him because he had made such a radical gesture with the invention of drip painting; the result didn't matter as much as the gesture. Then you valued him because the gesture meant so much, in terms of the relationship between the painter's body and the canvas, the decentering of the self, the final abandonment of the Albertian window, and what not? Now you value him simply because he was the best painter of his generation. This is not to say that your previous readings of his work did not contribute to your present conviction, but they would have been thrown overboard as *péchés de jeunesse* if renewed acquaintance with the works themselves had not confirmed your personal jurisprudence.

At this point in your introspection, you are reminded of the moment when you began to feel very strongly that your personal jurisprudence was sustained by that of others, and that you were part of a tradition, no matter how vehemently you still wanted to deny this. Other critics, with other agendas, had reached similar convictions, and in turn, this is what made them convincing. Do you know the extent to which those critics' comments made you look at art through their eyes? No, but does it matter? They are now part of yourself, an ingrained element in your own judgments, if not in your own commentary. You were not around when Pollock became Pollock, but Clement Greenberg was, and his astonishment, his resistance, his coping, his progressive surrender to Pollock's breakthrough are on the record. Born too late even to have had a stake in the violent rejection of Greenberg by the younger generation of artists and art critics, you simply know what you owe him: his tradition is yours. Your allegiance, however, includes further betrayals, as it should. There is no way you can accept that Olitski or Noland are Pollock's heirs, and if Caro's star is rising again and pushes many a Minimalist sculptor into the shadows, it is not thanks to Greenberg or Michael Fried; rather it may be thanks to Richard Deacon—whose achievement, in your eyes, is to allow you to take in Henry Moore and Reinhard Mucha in the same breath. There is a limit, your feelings tell you, and one that is very quickly reached, to the degree that you can let other critics feed you with aesthetic experience by proxy. Though you were not hanging around with them at the time, you grew up with the generation of conceptual artists, and their intellectualism, their sense of strategy, their awareness of the institutional framing of art were things that you shared and from which you learned. In many cases, their works claimed that they could stand for a critical definition of art in general, and so you need to consult with the feelings they elicited then and they elicit now, in order to decide whether it is not indeed one of their breed that you should extract from your personal collection to be the example standing for the whole. But your feelings are quick to answer: it is not the works with the clearest pedagogical value—such as those of Huebler or even of Weiner—that were able to withstand the passage of time, but those of the most idiosyncratic artists—such as Broodthaers or On Kawara. And the fact remains—because for you it is a fact, although you know that it is merely a fact of your own making—that throughout the entire period when conceptual art was productive, the best artists were painters: Ryman and Stella in the States, Richter, Palermo, Polke in Europe. You care for painting, that much is sure. It is more threatened than other arts. Is that why only those painters who distrust painting attract you? Is that why only those paintings that display the extreme vulnerability of painting are able to move you beyond mere enjoyment, and thus withstand the peril? Perhaps. You can't help but feel that they hang in front of a background constituted by the innumerable discourses that have proclaimed the end of painting ever since photography was invented. Yet you can't help but feel also that this background is justified; and you soon decide that no single painting could speak for all the art that is in your collection. No piece of sculpture, either. Boundaries have fallen apart, you know this both from the record and from the ups and downs of your own enthusiasms. And yet, the collapse of boundaries is a background too; it could never be a criterion. Wouldn't you trade the whole of Sol LeWitt's production for a single piece by Eva Hesse?

Thus you would scan your collection; with such a self-examination, you would check with the multitude of sentiments that are attached to the things stored mentally in the memory of your experiences and called, by you but most probably not by you alone, works of art. And you would be at a loss. Still, your interlocutor would press you: "Stop beating about the bush. Tell me of a single work of art that you think eminently deserves that name, and that would be representative of all the art you love." "It's impossible," you would reply. "Each work of art is unique, works of art don't obey the parliamentary logic of representation." And you would add that feelings don't either, that no one image of love could be made to stand for the infinite variety of all its manifestations, as if *Tristan and Isolde* could be substituted for, say, *Othello*. With this example, you would also show your interlocutor how the love of art and the depiction of love in art are inextricably entwined, a problem, in fact, highly symbolic of your ordeal. Choosing a thing from the world of culture on the basis of what your personal acquaintance with culture tells you is like choosing a spouse: it is more a commitment to the future than a result of past experience. There you are. You might find a way out by exclaiming: "Picasso!" Aren't you a *historian of tradition,* and don't most historians—those of modern art but also those of other periods—agree about Picasso's looming presence in the art tradition as a whole? He might even reconcile the *historians of art* with the *historians of the avant-garde.* He did it all: he initiated more than one of the significant ruptures with the past this century has experienced; he broke with himself many times; he could express a wide range of feelings in a variety of media—painting and sculpture, but also collage works, constructions, objects that are neither painting nor sculpture; and, not to be neglected, he was able to recycle the whole of world art history, from Velázquez to African masks, in such a way that after him, the most outrageous breaks with tradition had not only reintegrated tradition but also rewritten it. But choosing Picasso is too easy a way out, precisely for those reasons. His presence in tradition is too well established, too secure. The jurisprudence about him already fills libraries. Historians, critics and art lovers in general may quibble about individual pieces, disagree in their interpretations, rank Picasso's periods differently, but no one would be foolish enough to want to kick him out of the museum; furthermore, no one is afraid that some day humankind might turn about and decide that the twentieth century was crazy to call Picasso an artist at all. And that is the point. Picasso exempts you from judging. Or rather, he allows you to judge by simply letting the prejudices of your time judge in your stead.

The feeling of having it easy with Picasso prompts other feelings, and other examples. Will Malevich's *Black Square* still be regarded as a great painting two centuries from now? You feel that you have to assume responsibility for the tradition that constitutes your personal collection, and that the only measure of this responsibility is the amount of danger to which your collection would be exposed by the choice you are asked to make in selecting a work exemplary of the whole. Such a feeling is quixotic, no doubt. True, as a critic who goes public with his or her preferences, you will be judged on your judgments. You expose yourself, but all you are risking, if the future doesn't judge as you do, is being forgotten. Yet this is not at all what your feelings tell you; though you may be ambitious, to be remembered by posterity is not something that you could decently call a duty. Vis-à-vis your collection, however, your feeling is one of moral duty. You fear, and rightly so, that if your judgments on art were forgotten, so would be the art itself. What matters is not that these judgments be attributed to you, but that they be passed along. But unless you claimed them as your own, they wouldn't be judgments at all. So, you feel that a preposterous investiture is bestowed upon you: the right and duty to claim all the works in your collection as though you, not the artists, were their author. You must burst into laughter at this point: a feeling like this one catches the sublime at exactly the point where it topples into the ridiculous. And at this point, your choice is ripe.

You dig into your collection and bring back Duchamp's urinal. To make sure, you check the feelings it arouses in you against those aroused by the works that enjoy a prominent position in your collection, and especially by those which might have been plausible candidates for the title of *exemplary examples of art at large,* such as Picasso's, for instance. And you decide to stick with this urinal. It has everything Picasso's *Head of a Bull* has in terms of ready-made qualities and surprise effect; it may even have evolved out of Picasso's *Absinth*

Glasses or cardboard and sheet metal *Guitars*. It has formal qualities that evoke Brancusi and Hans Arp, plus a sense of provocation that Arp never conveys. It expresses its time as well as Manet's *Olympia,* and it reaches far into its own future to connect with the works of Johns and Warhol and many others. Indeed, like the joker in a card deck, it is the ever-present signifier in the cross-referenced index of your favorite works of art since Manet. Without it, how would you account for Manzoni's cans of *Artist's Shit* being in the same collection as Bonnard's *Nude in a Tub?* You don't account for that, yet it is a fact of your experience that they are, and that you can pass from a notion of art where Bonnard is a master, and not just one of good taste, to another, where Manzoni is a priest, and not just one of derision. Perhaps it is thanks to Duchamp, who was a champion of passages. For all those reasons, you love this urinal, and though some of these reasons cancel each other out, it doesn't matter. Feelings are illogical: sometimes you are in the mood for Wagner, sometimes for Mozart. Why couldn't this urinal be a beautiful object at times, while at others, it thumbs its nose at the very idea of beauty?

Yet you find as many reasons, and perhaps less illogical ones, to hate the bloody thing. To admit that Bonnard and Manzoni should stand side by side in one and the same collection yields a very unsettling feeling. Even more unsettling is the idea that Duchamp's urinal might have reconciled them. Hasn't it become an object of taste, and a very bland one at that, *ushering in banality*? If sarcasm should account for art, it would be easier to throw Bonnard out than to keep Jeff Koons at bay. But can you cope with the ensuing schizophrenia? Can you hold on to those works in your collection that have the erosive power of the avant-garde, without simultaneously blotting out all the art of the past that gives you so much pleasure and surrendering to art as kitsch? Can you decently, honestly, claim that Duchamp's urinal is exemplary of *all* the art that is in your collection, from prehistory to the present day? Check with your feelings again. They tell you that there are far too many reasons why Duchamp's urinal should be in your art collection, and that there are just as many reasons why it should stay out. It is neither a painting nor a sculpture, nor, for that matter, a poem or a piece of music. It doesn't belong to any of the arts. It is either *art at large* or nothing. It is on the threshold of your collection, undecidable, but if it enters it—so your feeling tells you—then it is exemplary of everything that is in it. All the while, it compels you to call it art, as if you were its author. The teasing is unbearable, and that's what clinches your decision. For if you decided not to call it art, you would still act as if you were its author. You would merely call it non-art. The thing is in every museum, and for you to expel it from your little personal museum would be a very Duchampian gesture: that of proclaiming a "reciprocal readymade."[16] You laugh at the ridiculousness of your entrapment, but then you remember that this was precisely your duty vis-à-vis the whole of your collection: to take responsibility for it as if you were its author. And suddenly, you feel authorized to do so. Your duty has become your right, for in front of this ready-made urinal nothing distinguishes you from Duchamp. You didn't make it but neither did he. He didn't even call it art himself; he let posterity call it art, and though it is now a fact of jurisprudence that posterity did so, jurisprudence doesn't dispense you from judging on your own. So you judge and, pointing at Duchamp's urinal, you say: "This is art; this is the thing I choose to be an exemplary example of everything I call art."

Having arrived at this stage, you are neither contemplating your exemplary example nor brandishing it like a banner; you are pondering it. You can't help but feel that this very ordinary sample extracted from a virtually endless line of mass-produced goods and made to stand for something for which it was absolutely not prepared is a paradigm, a model of sorts. Isn't this what "paradigmatic" means: exemplary? You have the unjustified feeling that this urinal contains a theory of art, of art at large, of art in general. Yet you can't prove it. You can't prove anything by dint of feeling. And with this generalization, you leave your feelings behind; with this reflection, you break with the realm of sentiments and enter that of concepts. Unlike the mere art lover you were earlier who,

16. "Reciprocal Readymade = Use a Rembrandt as an ironing board." Marcel Duchamp, *The Green Box*, in *Salt Seller: The Writings of Marcel Duchamp*, ed. Michel Sanouillet and Elmer Peterson (New York: Oxford University Press, 1973), p. 32; hereafter abbreviated as *SS*.

when asked "what is art?" could only point to examples so heterogeneous that they could never be samples of one and the same concept, you are now on your way to a theory of art. You will not forget the art lover you were and still are, yet you will have to leap into the cool domain of conceptualization and, in a way, start all over again.

Act Four: In Which You Land upon a Theory of Art and Get Ready to Leave the Planet Modernity

4.1.

In fact, you had already leapt when your reflection led you to realize that the feeling you had about Duchamp's urinal containing a theory of art was unjustifiable. For, as far as you are concerned, the urinal became art only with your aesthetic judgment. How could it have "contained" a theory of art prior to your calling it art? It's just a urinal after all. Your judgment was based on your complex, unstable, oscillating love-hate relationship with this thing, on the inextricable ball of twine of the feelings it elicited in you, including, this is true, the feeling that it contained a theory. There is no proof that it does, however, and you are not foolish enough to believe that your judgment provided it with one. There is no theoretical foundation to aesthetic judgment; in other words, there is no basis in theory for the sentimental sentence by way of which you call art what you call art. Having so pondered and reflected, you are now a theoretician of art, otherwise called an aesthetician. For it is by reflecting on the hiatus between feeling and knowledge that you have just come to the conclusion that feelings are never grounded in knowledge and that, conversely, knowledge cannot be grounded in feelings. And this is already a theoretical proposition, albeit a liminal one. It does not say that there is no theory of art, but rather that there is none that could be deduced from the criticism of art, and conversely, that there is no art criticism that is justified by theory. Criticism has no other justification than feeling, which justifies nothing. Or again, it has no ultimate justification, since it is the exercise of judgment, and to justify a judgment another one is required. As for theory, it could not be based on criticism. If St. Christopher carries Christ and Christ carries the world, where does St. Christopher stand?

Here is a second liminal theoretical proposition, then: the theory of art is not based on art. In other words, art is not autonomous. Consequently, art theory must be based elsewhere, on a theory external to the field of art, and on whose truth or falseness it would depend. Conversely, art does not find its basis in theory, since theory is external to art, and to this extent—but only to this extent—art is not heteronomous. From the theory of art to its criticism, the reverse path is no better grounded. The seal between the two registers remains unbroken, so that in this direction also a jump is required. This is a very strange theory, one implying a knowledge that claims to be verifiable, and therefore scientific, but for which truth statements have no predictive value. With regard to a theory of art based elsewhere than on art, it is in fact impossible to produce the case that would verify the theory, and it is even more impossible to anticipate what the next case would be. The sentence "here is some art" produces a case of art, but it is not a case of theory; it is a case of feeling. The experience is not repeatable, which is to say, experimental; it is singular, which is to say, aesthetic.

You have been an art critic or a historian of tradition and you have produced numerous cases of your feelings, positive, negative, and mixed. You have granted particular attention to those things that were able to bewilder and overwhelm you, and you have come to value especially the feeling of dissension, the sentiment of dis-sentiment, that they elicited. You have added them to the collection of things that you have learned to like either because they were easy and pleasurable, or because, being on the record, they were transmitted to you and solicited your approval. You have gathered all these things together with the sentence, "Art is everything I call art." This sentence is reflexive and not tautological, since the generic *art* only adds up the singular cases that you have so named in judging them. From the sum of these cases, the generic is constituted; but from the generic, the singular cannot be deduced. Reflecting as a theoretician on this collecting sentence, you draw something from it that is very close to what the logician deduced from his or her corpus and the semiotician from his or her consensus: that art is the name of everything you call art. Art is a name, and this is its only theoretical status. This name, common to all works of art, was a concept for the logician, a sign for the semiotician. For you, properly speaking it is neither the one nor the other. For it is no longer a common name, or noun; it is a proper name. Why? In assembling your collection in the first person, you no longer have the distance of the extraterrestrial ethnologist nor the alibi of the implicated sociologist. In claiming that art is everything you call art, you take on the responsibility of a quasi-definition that is neither theoretical nor empirical but, instead, critical. In so doing, you ask to be judged on your judgments and you expect to be asked in turn: "What are you talking about? Go on and display your feelings by telling us which are the things that have triggered them. Show us the cases, the instances." The logician would interpret this injunction as an invitation to establish the extension of the concept of art, and the semiotician as a request to tell the denotation of artistic signs. But for you, a critic who will be judged on your judgments, the injunction is a command to produce the referents, not of a supposed general concept of art nor of an unlimited set of artistic signs, but of the sentence as you pronounce it case by case: "this is art." The word "art" is a linguistic sign, no one would deny it. But it is not a logical concept. It is thus not a common noun, even though it is common to all the things you call art. This communality results from the namings you have brought about through your judgments; it is not prior to them in the manner of a linguistic denotation or a conceptual extension. It is of the same order as that which assembles all the Peters, Pauls, or Harrys: they have their name in common, but their name is not a common noun; it is their proper name. They owe the communality of their respective names to the act of baptism through which they were named and not to any mysterious property or meaning they supposedly share.

Just as with Peter, Paul, or Harry, or Catherine, Fanny, or Valerie, the name of art is a proper name. This is a theoretical definition, the only one that can be given to the word "art." Here, then, is a theory at once extremely simple and terribly meager. It rests on a single proposition, a single theorem. You must not forget that you have arrived at it, not through a deduction or an induction, but via the reflection you have made on your own feelings as an art lover, in other words, on the conviction or the certitude (and what is certitude, if not the feeling of knowing?) that you are dealing with art when you express your judgment with the phrase, "this is art." Among certitudes of this sort, the particularly fragile and totally unjustifiable feeling that Duchamp's urinal "contained" a theory of art was the one on which you reflected the most, for this object is the most exemplary, the most paradigmatic of all works of art, inasmuch as it begs you to call it art and does nothing else. With regard to all the other things that convince you that you are dealing with art, of course you could have chosen to express yourself with other formulas, which are apparently not nominative, like "this is beautiful, sublime, extraordinary, sensational, fantastic, tremendous, great, super," with "as art" being implicit. (You could do this with regard to the urinal too, but only after having christened it.) Such formulas reveal their purport as expressive of feelings more clearly than the naked formula, "this is art." The latter, on the other hand, reveals more explicitly than the former ones the antinomy that results when a personal feeling is cast into the form of a predicative proposition with a claim to conceptual objectivity.[17] It is this antinomy that requires the theory you make your own, as being the only one compatible with your experience, a theory made of a single theorem, which says: the word "art" is a proper name. Now, your theory will be a true one, a scientific one, only if it is proved, that is, based on a theoretical grounding itself verifiable, or, as Popper would say, falsifiable. Clearly the theory that will validate or invalidate your theory will not itself be a theory of art, but rather, a theory of proper names.

Since you are a theoretician of art and not a specialist in proper names, you have to turn to an existing theory of proper names and take the chance that if some day the theory you accept is shown to be false, your theory of art will collapse. This is a handicap, perhaps, but it is the rule in scientific work. Just as

17. More about this antinomy in chapter 5.

biochemistry, resting on the achievements of organic chemistry, which in turn relies on inorganic chemistry, runs the risk—at least in principle—of someday being invalidated if its bases are, so it is completely normal and epistemologically healthy that the theory of art should rest on a discipline that can be opened to question from within itself. It's rather the opposite that would be worrisome. Unlike what often happens in the human sciences, where interdisciplinarity is deemed a virtue, it is the declared dependence of the theory of art vis-à-vis the theory of proper names that can assure its chance for objectivity. Moreover, since there is an airtight seal between the theoretical register and the critical one, the theory of art as proper name might even be proven wrong without making it necessary to repudiate critical and aesthetic choices, which in any case are nonjustifiable, being based on feeling. You thus embark on the search for a theory of proper names. There are several, and they all occasion controversies among specialists in the philosophy of language. The situation is thus less comfortable than it was for the biochemist in relation to chemistry, but after all, among the various theories of proper names, there is nothing to prevent you from choosing the one that lends a certain weight to the intuitive conception at which you have already arrived: Peter, Paul, or Harry, even though common to all the Peters, Pauls, or Harrys, are labels that designate this Peter, this Paul, or this Harry, one by one, without presupposing shared qualities for them, without lending them a common sense. Now, this is exactly what was stated by the first explicitly articulated theory of proper names, that of John Stuart Mill.[18]

Mill said that in contrast to general names (or common nouns), proper (or singular) names—meant to single out an individual—have no connotation but only denotation. In Frege's terms, they have no *Sinn* but only *Bedeutung;* or in contemporary terms, they have no sense but only reference. Mill compared proper names to the signs chalked on the houses to be robbed by the thieves in the story of Ali-Baba. Like these signs, proper names designate without describ-

18. John Stuart Mill, *A System of Logic* (1843; reprint, London: Longmans, Green & Co., 1961), pp. 14–29.

ing. In this way, the art lover who is asked for a definition of art and who answers, "art is this," acts like the thief; he or she designates but does not describe. Yet however simple and seductive Mill's theory might be when it is so annexed to art, it raises two problems, and in addition it contains a defect of form. First, the word "art," contrary to Mill's singular names, does indeed possess meaning. It can, for example, signify the excellence of execution or the fact of belonging to one of the fine arts. In fact, the word "art" has at least as many meanings as there are theories of art, perhaps as many as there are private usages of it, even as many as there are circumstances under which it is pronounced. Moreover, it is the quantity of all possible contradictory meanings of the word "art" that has led the logician to abandon attempts to establish its intension, and the semiotician to constitute its significance out of its very swarm of meanings and non-meanings alike. Second, the word "art" is nonetheless a common noun, or what Mill called a general name. It is perhaps analogous to Peter, Paul, or Harry, but these are also general names; they are first names that on their own are not enough to single out an individual. The addition of a family name will not necessarily suffice either. To be sure of knowing exactly of whom one is speaking, it would perhaps be necessary to say something like: "the Peter Johnson born in New York on May 14, 1934, son of Gerald Johnson and Mary Moore." But isn't such a formula already a description? Doesn't it give the meaning, or an elementary meaning, for the name Peter Johnson? In other words, is it really true that proper names have only denotation and no connotation? And finally, there is the defect of form. In the phrase "art is this," and more obviously still in "this is art," it is the deictic *this* that designates without describing, and singles out an individual. To take Mill literally, the only proper names strictly speaking would be pronouns and demonstratives. In the phrase in question, it is not the word "art" but the shifter "this" that would be a proper name, playing the role of the chalk mark in the Ali-Baba story.

This is what Frege and Russell thought, when they proposed another theory of proper names, in contradiction to Mill's. They claimed that proper or singular names have sense, or in Mill's language, connotation; they are really abbreviated or disguised definite descriptions.[19] Thus the meaning of "Aristotle," for example, would be contained in the following descriptions: the Greek philosopher born in Stagira, the student of Plato, the tutor of Alexander, the author of the *Nicomachean Ethics,* etc. Faced with the difficulty of knowing how many of these descriptions the man about whom one is speaking must satisfy, so as to be sure that one is really speaking about Aristotle, Searle, and later, Strawson and others, have amended the theory of Frege and Russell, making it more flexible by introducing the notion of the *cluster concept* in place of the definite description.[20] To be Aristotle, it would be necessary and sufficient that the man of whom one is speaking respond to a certain (never specified) number of the above descriptions. A single one would not be enough (there might be more than one philosopher born in Stagira), but the conjunction of all of them would not be necessary (some day one might discover that Aristotle didn't write the *Nicomachean Ethics* as we now know he didn't write the *Problems*). One could thus be satisfied with their inclusive disjunction. In the main, Frege and Russell, as amended by Searle, find Mill correct about general names and incorrect about proper or singular names.

More recently, Saul Kripke, and through a different route, Hilary Putnam, have criticized this critique in their own turn.[21] Kripke in particular returned to Mill's theory by inverting the argument Frege and Russell made against it. Mill was right, he said, about proper names, but wrong about certain general names

19. Gottlob Frege, "On Sense and Reference," in *Translations from the Philosophical Writings of Gottlob Frege,* ed. P. Geach and M. Black (Oxford: Basil Blackwell, 1960); Bertrand Russell, "Descriptions," in *Readings in the Philosophy of Language,* ed. J. Rosenberg and C. Travis (Englewood Cliffs, N.J.: Prentice-Hall, 1971).

20. John Searle, "Proper Names," *Mind* 67, no. 266 (April 1958): 166–173; and "Proper Names and Descriptions," in *The Encyclopedia of Philosophy,* ed. P. Edwards (New York: Macmillan, 1967), 6: 487; P. F. Strawson, *Individuals* (London: Methuen, 1959), chap. 6.

21. Saul Kripke, *Naming and Necessity* (Cambridge, Mass.: Harvard University Press, 1972); Hilary Putnam, "It Ain't Necessarily So," *The Journal of Philosophy,* 59, no. 22 (1962): 658–671; and *Mind, Language and Reality,* vol. 2 of *Philosophical Papers* (Cambridge: Cambridge University Press, 1975).

like those of measures, substances, natural species, or colors. According to Kripke, just as with proper names in the strict sense, these are *rigid designators,* that is, labels always relating to the same referent, whatever might be the "counterfactual situations" or "possible worlds" in which one could imagine them. Even though rigid designators might have a meaning, and this meaning might consist of a list or cluster of properties, essential or not, what makes them proper names is their use: they serve to fix the reference and not to pronounce a meaning. According to Frege and Russell, the name "Aristotle" and the expression "Alexander's tutor" are synonyms. Kripke doesn't deny this, but he points out that if one uses this synonymy in order to determine of whom one is speaking when one says "Aristotle," and if for example one imagines a possible world where Aristotle had not been Alexander's tutor, a contradiction appears which amounts to saying that the tutor of Alexander was not the tutor of Alexander. Either Aristotle never existed, or one is speaking of someone else. To this, Kripke objects that even though "Alexander's tutor" is one of the meanings of "Aristotle," nevertheless it will still be the same Aristotle one is speaking about—the one who in the real world was Alexander's tutor—when one imagines a possible world where Aristotle would never involve himself in teaching. Once the reference is fixed, it is rigidly maintained across all imagined counterfactual situations. And this led Kripke to turn his attention toward the event that establishes reference, which for most proper names is a baptism, whether performed by means of a description or not, and to become interested in the chain of speakers through which proper names are transmitted to people who "know" of whom they are speaking even when they really could neither describe, or define, the individual so named nor trace the chain of transmission back to the initial baptism.

Without going further into Kripke's theoretical views, this can form the basis for a theory of art, understood as a rigid designator, or rather, as a proper name.[22] The phrase "this is art," as it is uttered by art lovers who use it to judge

22. In spite of grammars and dictionaries, it is preferable to speak of art as a proper name in the narrow sense rather than as a rigid designator (the Kripkean category that encompasses

by dint of their feelings and of the conflict among their feelings, is a baptism. Art lovers may believe themselves to be justified in their judgment; they may have many motivations, some cultural and learned, others emotional and sensual, still others intellectual and even moral; but it is with the affective sum total of all these motivations that they judge, with the feeling they may or may not have that "everything falls into place" in conformity with their expectations or, to the contrary, in spite of them. In baptizing a given thing with the name of art, they express the feeling that it deserves to be so called. The fact that in the

---

both "real" proper names and names of substances, natural species, colors, etc.), because of the essentialism to which Kripke's category ultimately leads, an essentialism for which your art theory has absolutely no need. In two very confused articles ("Defining Art," *The British Journal of Aesthetics* 15, no. 3 (1975): 191–206; and "A Kripkean Approach to Aesthetic Theories," *The British Journal of Aesthetics* 22, no. 2 (1982): 150–157), James D. Carney tentatively tried to make a case for the "rigid designator model" (or the Kripke-Putnam model, as he first called it). In Carney's model, the word "art" is akin to the word "gold" for Kripke. Whereas it is true that a putative piece of gold (like a putative work of art) is identified with reference to a paradigm sample transmitted over time through the linguistic community, it remains possible to call on an intensional definition of gold (atomic number 79) to verify its true nature. Not so with art. Carney, who has an inkling of this but does not see it clearly, is led to oscillate between various theories that are no improvement whatsoever on the essentialist or Wittgensteinian models he set out to criticize (those very models with which you yourself experimented a while ago when you were assuming the position of the logician; see n. 7). His theory alternately requires (1) that all works of art share a "universal property," or if it can't be found, at least a "hypothesized" one or the belief in one; (2) that the "artworld" (George Dickie's concept) knows about art's "universal properties," or if it doesn't, at least agrees on a "favored theory," or if it doesn't, hopes to arrive at one; (3) that some theory, true or false, "serve as the final court of appeal as to whether *x* is art." How one can arrive at such absurdities is explicable, alas, when it is realized that "aesthetics" practiced in this way is a discipline that has currency only on the planet Mars. That's where Carney and his like (see n. 7) obviously live, with the exception of Arthur Danto, whose theory, though false, is witty, and who has at least a foot in the real world and goes out to look at art more often than not. Let Carney have the last word: "I suggest that the reason the rigid designator model can be fruitful to aesthetic theory is that it saves appearances." Indeed.

enormous majority of cases it had been called art already, by others, simply makes judgment easier; it doesn't deprive art lovers of their right, and their duty, to perform the baptism once again. All art lovers are like artists, in this respect, who when they consider the thing they were working on finished decide to call it a work, or like the discoverers of *art naïf* or of *art brut,* when they decide to acknowledge aesthetic qualities hitherto unrecognized as artistic. What matters is that the word "art" expresses a feeling, or a set of feelings, but that it does not mean what it expresses. In fact, it means nothing, or too many things all at once, which amounts to the same thing. Unlike the words "sad" or "enthralling," it doesn't even hint at the "content" or the "quality" of the feelings it expresses. And unlike the words "colorful" or "rhythmic," it says nothing about the objective features of the thing pointed at. Being a proper name, the word "art" is a blank. The question to ask about proper names, Kripke says, is that of their reference, not that of their meaning. To what are you referring, as art lover, as critic, or as historian of tradition, when you show your appreciation of anything whatever in saying: "this is art"? That is the question. Certainly not to *this,* the designated thing, for then the phrase would be tautological. You are referring to all the other things equally designated by you, in other circumstances, by use of the same phrase; with the word "art," you are pointing a finger at all the things that make up your critical collection, your personal, imaginary museum. In calling *this* thing art, you are not giving out its meaning; you are relating it to everything else you call art. You don't subsume it under a concept; you don't justify it by means of a definition; you refer it to all the other things you have judged through a like procedure, in other times and other places.

This is why aesthetic judgments are always comparative, even though it would be useless to try to say precisely what they compare.[23] Not only does

23. Aesthetic judgments are comparative, at least, in the *anthropological* register in which this chapter is deliberately located. The question of whether an absolute aesthetic judgment is possible opens another register, which could be called transcendental. More about this in chapters 5 and 6.

your interlocutor not know that collection to which you refer when you say "this is art," since you are not showing it to him or her, but neither do you know precisely the extent of your comparisons. You might have two or several paintings in front of you, but you cannot listen to two concerts at once; in any event, it is impossible that, in the *hic et nunc* of experience, you could have access to the totality of what you call art. Moreover, what the word "art" expresses to you, what it has expressed each time you baptized something with it, is not accessible to your full consciousness either. Particular feelings once attached to the perception of particular works of art may subsequently have been detached from them, replaced by others or attached to other works. They are buried somewhere in your experience. Thus, the feeling that comes to you in the presence of this thing, here, which beckons you to call it art, is measured by the memory of past feelings. But feelings are rarely something you could say you simply store in your memory. They can prompt or repress remembrance; they are as much the guardians of memory as guarded by it; they are sometimes the affects of forgetting, sometimes the impulse to anamnesis, sometimes a compulsion signaling repressed memories. Nothing is more deformed, betrayed, at times embellished, at times darkened by time, than the memory of a feeling. But it remains that aesthetic judgment compares comparable things when it confronts a present feeling to the reactualization of past sentiments. For the remembrance of a feeling is always a feeling, while the memory of a piece of knowledge is not necessarily a piece of knowledge (one can remember once having known trigonometry but have forgotten it; one can remember having loved and perhaps have forgotten how it felt, but not without at least feeling the melancholy of oblivion and indifference).

But aesthetic judgment does not simply compare feelings with each other. Human experience in general does that too. Moreover, there is plenty of room in human experience for aesthetic judgments unrelated to art. So, if you choose to express your feelings with the sentence "this is art," does this then mean that you are comparing "art feelings" with one another, feelings that have a special "art quality" to them or that only art can elicit? Certainly not. Your experience has taught you that the feelings to be had from art can be had from life as well, and that, conversely, the love of art possibly encompasses the whole range of human feelings. Yet you know an "art feeling" when you feel one, and what you are attaching to *this,* precisely by calling it art, is certainly an "art feeling." This means that your feeling is such that it prompts you to refer the *this* about which you judge at present to all the *thats* of your personal collection, as though comparison were possible. Now, for all that, you do not succeed in comparing things, objects, perceptions, images, or even recollections. You can, if *this* brings to mind *that,* if similarities in medium, form, style, or subject matter, or whatever other intuitive associations, force specific comparisons. You can't, if your "art feeling" is too vague to prompt specific associations. And in any case, there is no way you could bring to mind all the works in your collection, all the occasions that triggered in you an "art feeling" in the past. Yet when you choose to express your aesthetic judgment with "this is art," you claim such a comparison.

Between the inaccessible referents of the word "art" and the referent of the demonstrative "this," that is, between all the past occurrences of your "art feeling" and this one, there are paths, some opened for free association, others blocked by censorship, through which affects are triggered, evoked, amplified, or silenced, and through which comparisons are compelled. You may or may not be able to call the resulting "art feeling" by its name beauty, for example, or ugliness, or awkwardness if you hesitate—but such names are proper names, too, a shorthand for the level of intensity that you expect from art on the basis of your past experience, and also on the basis of your willingness to let a new and unexpected thing overwhelm you, at the very moment when it proposes itself as a candidate for your aesthetic appreciation. Your "art feeling" may give rise to interpretations, just as your interpretations (or somebody else's) may elicit further feelings. The outcome of this is a complex layering of meanings and feelings, which alternate tentative interpretations about what has been felt and feelings experienced about what has been signified. The referents of the sentence "this is art" can thus recede in memory and get buried under stratified sedimentations of thoughts and affects which are very hard to discern, and for that reason, "unconscious." However, these very referents—alienated from one another by being severed from the affective experience that produced them—are grouped together and made autonomous in the name of a call for comparison, which is sometimes seen as a proof of their common property or as a sign of their common meaning, but which in fact is nothing but the shared reference to this name, art, which is their common proper name. It is misleading to say, as the logician does, that this shared reference represents the open-endedness and the indeterminacy of the concept of art, and it is insufficient to speak of intertextuality in relation to it, as does the semiotician. For it is not with regard to definitions of art—which are rationalizations of something irretrievably irrational—that reference is made to the name of art, or at least not directly: open-endedness and indeterminacy are themselves feelings that only someone with a bias toward logic is prone to attribute to a concept. And though texts and signs inevitably call to mind their context and intertext, on its own the interpretive process that runs through them does not account for their gathering under the banner of art, a term that only someone with a bias towards semiotics is prone to understand both as an elusive signified and as the signifier of this very elusiveness. The shared reference that unites, sunders, reassembles, and opposes all the things that you, personally, call art, is not accessible, even to you; yet it is the stuff of your experience of art. It is the accumulated outcome of a quasi-automatic process of comparison that purports to compare things not necessarily comparable in terms of medium, form, style, or subject matter, as though they were comparable, and which feels justified in so doing because the feelings these things elicit precisely offer a basis for comparison, however treacherous. In fact, aesthetic comparison is not direct: it neither simply matches an "art feeling" with another "art feeling," nor simply pits a work of art against another. It is a comparison by analogy, an "as if–comparison." When you decide to enter a work of art into your collection—especially if it is a work backed up by little jurisprudence or even none at all, a thing unprepared to be art on the basis of medium, form, style, or subject matter, but which nonetheless compels you to refer it to all the art that is in your collection, a thing so unsettling that calling it art, art at large, is the issue, a thing that is likely to bring about a "non-art feeling"—you will not do so on the basis of past experience alone. Comparisons fail. Yet it is as though you went through a comparative reasoning, saying:

"This thing, here, which makes me compare it with all the things I value as art, stands for those things from my present collection, as the overwhelming 'non-art feeling' it is the occasion for stands for the feelings my past experience has taught me to expect from art."

There are alternate readings to such "algebra": "This thing, here, which to me is not art yet, stands in relation to the unsettling 'non-art feeling' it yields, as the whole of my art collection stands in relation to my expectations from art." Still another: "The feeling that so upsets my expectations compares with those very expectations as this unexpected thing compares with everything I call art." And still another: "My experience of art is to the things this experience led me to collect what my inexperience in dealing with this new thing is to the thing in question." And so on.[24] If you surrender to your feeling, the outcome is inevitable. You will conclude, although you need not say it explicitly or even consciously: ". . . so that I call this thing art." Your "conclusion" is not a conclusion in the logical sense, however, and the "rationale" through which you reached it is not a rationale. It is literally irrational, since it equates ratios that are not measurable. This "as if–rationale," this comparison by analogy, is what Kant called a reflexive judgment and what Duchamp, quite pointedly, called an *algebraic comparison.*[25] The theoretician you are may find confirmation in this for your theory of art as proper name. But the theoretician in you has not forgotten

24. Let's call the thing that is a candidate to the name "art" X, and the set of things constituting your personal art collection C; further, let's call the unexpected feeling that X elicits fX, and the vague and unspecifiable feeling you have learned to associate with your collection and which "sums up" your expectations from art fC. The four readings you just gave of the "as if–comparison" making up your aesthetic judgment would then translate into the following "algebraic" formulas:

1. $X/C = fX/fC$
2. $X/fX = C/fC$
3. $fX/fC = X/C$
4. $fC/C = fX/X$

25. More about Kant's reflexive judgment in chapter 5, and more about Duchamp's *algebraic comparison* in chapter 2.

the art lover you were, and still are. And as an art lover, you don't need to name or analyze the process that regulates your aesthetic judgments. It is simply confirmed by experience. Time and again, from childhood on, when you began to acquire a personal imaginary collection of works of art, you went through an "as if–comparison" of this kind each time you entered a new work into your collection, gradually increasing the number of referents you gave to the name of art. In this way, you broadened your taste, built a notion of what art is and means to you, and heightened your expectations as to what art should be. As they say, you gave yourself criteria for art. But "criterion" is the wrong word. It suggests that given objective features or given subjective feelings act as grounds for comparisons having the form of logical inference—"if . . . then." Whereas the comparisons by analogy with which you judge aesthetically have a reflexive form—"it is as if . . . so that." What the accumulated experience of art slowly increases and specifies is not a set of criteria but the plausibility of such "as if–comparisons." As your acquaintance with art builds up, this plausibility at once increases and narrows. It increases because the broader your collection, the greater the probability that you will accept into it things that could not possibly have been art to you previously. And it narrows because as your exposure to art augments, so does the intensity level of the feelings, the quantity of surprise, the richness and density of experience, that you expect to be conveyed by works of art. That you would grow to love a work whose medium, form, style, or subject matter seem unrelated to art becomes more and more plausible, while it becomes less and less plausible that you would be satisfied with it if it did not match the quality of the feelings art usually gives you. This plausibility, more or less rationalized, interpreted in various degrees, constitutes your idea of art.

This idea is not a concept, for at least three reasons: it is personal to you and is not generalizable; you are in no position to formalize it, to prove its pertinence, or to argue the "logic" of it in all its details; and most often, you don't know how it came to you nor from whom you got it. Because, of course it is not a question of claiming that, however personal it may be, the idea of art is original with each individual, purely private or sovereignly subjective. This would be falling into solipsism and idealism. Indeed, to the contrary, it is socially, historically, and culturally conditioned. You did not start your personal art collection from scratch. Before you uttered the sentence "this is art," you had heard it spoken. Things of all kinds, perhaps starting with your first teddy bear, were shown to you and given as examples of things to be cherished. Some of those things were indicated as being art, and you learned to associate feelings with objects already collected and valued by others—your parents, your teachers, the museum, the art community, society at large. Your feelings, whether about art or in life, are receptive to influence, and the memory of your feelings is not impervious to the injunctions of society either. Moreover, the feelings society allows or encourages in regard to art are, to a large extent, stored in the jurisprudential record along with the works and their interpretations. Your idea of art is, for the most part, made of aesthetic *habitus,* of incorporated cultural values, of ingrained prejudices, and of received ideas. Still, it is your idea of art, not someone else's, that you acknowledge whenever you publicize your "art-feeling" by designating the things that you call art yourself. If, for this or that social reason, you cheat with your feelings, dress up your true taste in borrowed clothes, appropriate a collection you cannot honestly claim, or uncritically accept as art what the experts call art, you will still not have made their idea of art your own. It is one thing to pay lip service to a social attitude; it is another to judge on one's own. And since you can't help but judge, because you can't help but feel what you feel, it is your idea of art—the plausibility of your own "as if–comparisons"—that is the regulative idea of your judgment.

Everyone and anyone has an idea of art, and even several ideas, simple or complex, unlearned or cultivated, conventional or audacious. Some people, either underprivileged or not very sensitive, cling to the ideas of art they share with their social group or vie with each other to adopt those imposed by the ruling class. These are the conformists. If they are among the rulers, they never doubt the consensus and never question their own right to say "we" when they judge. They do not see the conflict of cultural values, or if they do, they judge it out of place, as if it were itself an error of taste. If they are among the dominated, they suffer oppression, punishing themselves for their "bad taste" and striving to identify with what they take to be the general consensus. Others, whether they are objectively dominated or whether they have taken sides with those who are, revolt. They see hegemony in the apparent consensus and feel the cultural conflicts strongly because their sense of value is struck by them. These are the rebels, sometimes the revolutionaries, often the partisans of the avant-garde. It matters more to them to destroy their opponents' idea of art than to maintain one themselves, unless as a reaction. Finally, there are those very privileged, and conscious of being so, who want to raise themselves above their own sensibility and that of their group, readily publicizing a universal idea of art that they believe to be beyond judgment and taste. These are the civil servants of humankind, the variety of whose cultures they observe detachedly, rarely involving themselves in the conflicts of the moment. As for you, who are aware of the diversity of cultural values and sensitive to their conflicts, you also have ideas of art, several which you feel are socially at war with each other and historically relative, ideas that are made as much of received conceptions and conventions as of the idiosyncrasies of your taste, and above all, ideas that are ready to fall apart and coalesce again differently in the face of a feeling of dissent so strong that its unsettling is precisely the sign by which you recognize the regulative idea of your judgment. You are, above all, an art lover whose idea of art shifts under the pressure of an unexpected feeling that introduces into the tangled memory of your past experiences the reflexive feeling of dissent, the sentiment of dis-sentiment.

4.2.

You have not stopped being this art lover, but you are one after having been, in turn, an art critic and a historian of tradition, and then, through a leap and a reflection, an aesthetician. It is a new reflection, but one that does not imply any leap "backwards," that now leads you back from theory to history, this time under the banner of a theory of history. For you cannot avoid constructing a conception of the historicity of art. In this, you are both close to and very different from the *historian of art,* for whom historicity was given with the concept of style: linearity of evolution, cycles of civilization, discontinuity of periodization, all contingent. Historicity is also given to you, but as jurisprudence: if styles are maintained, it is because the judgments of the past weigh on those of the present, and if they are broken, it is because a judgment contrary to custom has been passed. You inherit all that. You are equally close to and very different from the *historian of the avant-garde,* for whom the dialectical meaning of art, never given in advance, never inherited but prescribed as novelty, was its very historicity. But you do not confuse practice with theory. The practical, or "praxical," dimension of art is something you once again call jurisprudence, but this time in the sense that you make it by setting precedents. Jurisprudence is the historicity immanent in your practice as historian. It has transmitted to you the records in which your predecessors' judgments are stored, and it will transmit the record of your judgments to your successors. But it does not give the theoretical form of historicity as such. Now, the other name of jurisprudence—the one that corrects all at once the notions of style and of the avant-garde—is tradition. Tradition means transmission, translation, and betrayal. What tradition transmits, translates, and betrays are first of all the things called art. In preserving them in museums, it makes those things available to successive generations of viewers; it translates them in whatever art ideology current museology fosters; and in so doing, it inevitably betrays them. In placing these things in museums of *art,* in gathering them together in the name of art, what tradition also transmits, translates, and inevitably betrays, is the name "art," that very name which, on the theoretical level, you have defined as a proper name. So, reverting to this theoretical level, where it is a matter of conceiving the historicity of tradition, you ask yourself just how proper names are transmitted, translated, and betrayed.

By and large, proper names are transmitted in three ways. First, through direct filiation, from father to son if the lineage is patrilinear. A widely accepted notion, which is not on the whole false but which is much too simple, conceives of the name of art as transmitted this way, along with that of artist: from spiritual father to spiritual son, from legitimate master to innovative disciple. Hardly examined, the procedure of transmission is called influence (and rupture); theorized, as by Freud for instance, it is called (resolved) Oedipal conflict. In any case, it is the name-of-the-father that is transmitted along with the title of artist, eventually to be translated and betrayed by the son who takes it on as tradition. Secondly, proper names are transmitted by hearsay, in the same way information in general is propagated. We hear art spoken about as we hear So and So spoken about. One speaks of art as one spreads rumors, without necessarily verifying them, without knowing from whence they originate, without remembering from whom one got them, and without bothering about where they will go. A large part of culture, understood as acquired knowledge, as familiarity, as *habitus,* even as *savoir-vivre,* is woven of such rumors. Proper names posit themselves in this culture in order to maintain systems of references; this is their only function, as Kripke has shown. One knows of whom or what one speaks, even when one wouldn't know exactly what is understood or what is being said. Among proper names in general, cultural rumor circulates names of artists and names of works, to which it attaches the name of art. But rumor is not enough to make a tradition. Not that it lacks a sufficient amount of translations and betrayals, since, to the contrary, noise is the most probable state of all transmission. Rather, de jure if not de facto, the chains of transmission woven by cultural rumor imply no judgment other than the initial baptism. With tradition, which certainly feeds on culture as well as feeding it in return, but which, above all, is nourished by sensitivity and nourishes it reciprocally, things work entirely differently. The name of art rebounds from judgment to judgment, that is, from baptism to baptism, and although none are primal, all are initial. When the phrase "this is art" is an aesthetic judgment and not just a rumor relayed by hearsay, it is never an origin yet always an initiative. Even and especially when it silently accompanies the first word of the novelist, or the first touch of the painter, it is already the fruit of an initiation, but one that creates an event and, if the case arises, produces a new referent for the name: this, here, now. The here and now shift with time, and one can very easily not be in agreement about the "this." Aesthetic experience does not get transmitted, it is not intersubjective. Only the name is transmitted, and it in no way guarantees the identity of the experience. It remains that, in art, there is no judgment by default and no baptism in absentia, and that the deictics of experience (this, here, now) bear witness to a feeling for which the occasion is unique, unreproducible, and nontransferable. The name is transmitted and repeated, but the baptism is renewed each time the named thing comes up for trial before a new occurrence of the feeling.

Now, it is the idea of art that summons the thing to appear. Indeed, it "measures" how plausible it is that this thing, here, be called into court to see its claim to be art checked against the testimonies of all things already called art, and be compared to them by dint of feeling. Your idea of art has been to a large extent transmitted to you along with the name, partially as unchecked rumor, that is, a prejudice, partially as unchallenged social value, that is, as ideology, and partially as rejudged jurisprudence, and this is what matters. It is simultaneously a diffuse idea allowing comparisons among the things you have called art through *habitus* or out of cultural loyalty, and a regulative idea that is formed and enriched by each of the judgments that have set a precedent in the jurisprudence, at least for you. However, it is not certain that the idea is transmitted along with the name. If criteria allow it to be communicated, and if it forms a conception that is received and preserved by you without further trial, then it is. But if, in that case opened by the summoned thing, it is the idea as well that you are judging, then it is not. Each time the sentiment of your dis-sentiment makes you add a new, unexpected, and overwhelming thing to your critical collection, you shake up the set of references to which you have been referring this or that work up until then. You make certain expectations more plausible and others less. And you betray tradition, since what you transmit is not what you have received. But you also translate it, since it is in the same unchanged name of art that you claim the assent of others to an increased dissension. Your idea of art has changed along the way, but it is not the meaning or explanation of this change that you pass along. You are in the debt of interpretation. This may explain why the idea of art has so often taken the form of a question and why inquiry about the meaning of art is so often undertaken out of a sense of obligation, particularly by semioticians, who sense in the dissemination of artistic signs a powerful call for interpretation at the same time that they are loath to meet it. In hunting out the work's intertext, they refuse to cancel the text's debt. Quite to the contrary, the debt is what they transmit to "posterity" as the obligatorily interrogative meaning of the idea of art. This may also explain why critics, who seem to seal off questions of interpretation through the peremptory assertion of their judgments, when they claim to define art by saying "It's everything I call art," pay for this claim, and always to "posterity," with the obligation of having in the final accounting to produce the totality of their aesthetic choices. This claim is arrogance only if there is confusion about—or if they themselves confuse—this responsibility with the right of decree that the public nature of their judgments confers on them. It is an error only if there is confusion about—or if they themselves confuse—the exhibition of their examples of art or the more or less justificatory comments that accompany them with the establishment of a proof. Finally, it wrongs the readers, the artists, or the public, only if it is believed to be authorized—or if they think it is authorized—to violate the rule of separateness that seals off the critical realm from the theoretical, and to slide from the one into the other without taking any leap and reflection. In fact, critics, all critics—even those who abuse their authority in the name of their expertise—from the moment they make their judgments public and even more if they stir up controversy, all critics see themselves called upon by history, sooner or later, to summon the totality of things they call art. They are not so much in the debt of an interpretation as they are held on account for a showing of cases.

As critic or as historian of tradition, you have declared that art was everything you called art, referring all the occurrences of the name to each other. Your culture has the breadth of your collection, your sensitivity the richness of your feelings, and your probity as critic or historian the publicity of your judgments. Thus, you want to be judged on the totality of your choices—each of them, singly—including those, the majority, through which you relay a previous instance of the art-naming procedure and take charge of it. You then appeal to a judgment which, across your personal choices, will judge, if not tradition as a whole, at least a tradition, the chain of transmission of the name of art of which your judgments are a link. Like all chains, this one is only as strong as its weakest link. Tradition is never as sensitive as at that very point where it is in danger of breaking, jurisprudence never as important as where the dispute is not sealed, judgment never as decisive as where it makes a decision in the undecidable, sentiment never as pertinent as where it has the fragility of dissentiment. And so, the tradition you belong to is no different from what others called the avant-garde.

This tradition is yours, but it would not be a tradition if it were yours alone. You share it with everyone responsible for having weakened a link in the chain of tradition. You are in dangerous company and you know it, for not every attack on what the traditionalists call tradition comes down, in the end, as a link in a tradition. Vulgarity is always just this side of kitsch, "bad taste" is often license for a lowering of expectations, and breaking with tradition sometimes results in just that, a break with tradition. Your feelings and your feelings alone can tell you whether the sense of rupture conveyed by a given work stems from resentment, impotence, and disavowed hatred of art, or whether it proceeds from a deep and understanding love for the fragility of the tradition's weakest links. Consulting your feelings is a way of probing the plausibility that similar feelings presided over the making of the work you are judging—although with no guarantees whatsoever, which is, of course, true for all art, since the communication of feelings is indirect, being mediated by an object. But it is particularly true of the avant-garde, because to weaken a link in the chain of tradition means to attach less importance to the successful communication of feelings than to the lack of guarantee for this communication's possible success. Thus, what those artists and art lovers who share your tradition have in common with you is not a given set of feelings, a temperament, or a taste; it is a willingness to let the works they make or collect run against their temperament, an aptitude to let their betrayals of taste rule over their taste, a readiness to surrender to those feelings that promise solitude rather than community. More than anything else, the stuff of the tradition you belong to is the paradoxical sharing of the sense of being alone. What this shared solitude stands for is both the right to judge by yourself and the duty to judge as if you were not alone; and the ability, the "talent" that this calls for is a capacity to read your feelings as if they were objects projected outside of yourself, forces traversing you, social facts. The more a work forbids you to call it art in peaceful agreement with yourself, the more it invites you to increase the plausibility that it be compared with the works that other times, other people, nations, races, social classes, and the other gender might call art. And the more it upsets your idea of art and arouses in you the feeling that the unexpected has arrived, the more you will sense that it has precisely expected you to broaden your expectations. With this reflexive twist, whose signal is the sentiment of dis-sentiment, you are being pulled out of yourself, and your judgment is made so much more anonymous that you find yourself unable to assign to the various social values, whose conflicts you feel, nameable social instances. It is, then, as if you said: "This thing, here, which I personally can't endorse without inner conflict, compares with my personal collection as my personal collection, once enlarged to include the thing in question, would with a radically impersonal one."

So, your tradition is not yours alone; it is the avant-garde but it is not only the avant-garde. A radically impersonal collection would be composed of everything anyone and everyone might call art—not just avant-garde art—in agreement with you. Of course, it is an abstraction, an ideal, a mere idea whose name is "art in general." Even if every man and woman on earth were consulted, such a collection could not be gathered, if only because the most thorough survey would still leave out the dead and the unborn. And if every man and woman on earth could be consulted, it would be even more a mere idea, for disagreement is the rule: conflict, dissent, that is, dis-sentiment. And yet, as an ideal, art in general ought to be the collective possession of humankind; the radically impersonal collection it represents ought to be *ours,* universally. You know this for sure (although this "knowledge" is merely a certitude or a conviction), in spite of the fact that you also know that not all men and women agree on art, far from it, and that the *we* to which you claim to belong doesn't speak unanimously. Your conviction is well founded and legitimate; for it does not rely on any opinion poll, it stems from the reflexive feeling of dissension (yours, not ours) in which you now read the sign that all ideas of art, the most open, the most contradictory and conflicting, the most uncertain, must be admissible within this tradition held together by its weakest links. What is this tradition if not the genealogy through which the name "art" was transmitted and shifted from the works of the past onto those of the avant-garde, when it passed from an era where it meant beauty, perhaps, or perfection in sensitivity, or excellence in skill, to an era where it was at once believed, wished, and feared that it meant the most absolute indeterminacy of sense and its polymorphous opening onto nonsense? It is the avant-garde as tradition betrayed and betrayal transmitted; it is consensus as impossible; it is art as non-art and non-art as art. And thus, there is no better name for it than art, art in general. This paradoxical jurisprudence leads you to recognize, and to judge, that the avant-garde is not only a tradition, but the continuation of tradition *tout court*.

4.3.

Now you look back on this tradition. You take it all in with the necessarily retrospective gaze of the historian who knows that it constitutes simultaneously the history he or she belongs to and the historicity of this history. You were its genealogist; now you also become its *archaeologist*.[26] Asking yourself how proper names are transmitted, you noted that the name of art, which is also transmitted by filiation and rumor, only sets a precedent in jurisprudence when it is relayed by aesthetic judgment, and that the more a precedent is fragile, the more it is crucial. Reflecting on your own jurisprudence, you have sketched the "family tree" along which the proper name, art, was transmitted, emphasizing these

26. Genealogy, here, is to be understood in all senses of the word: as the discipline that concerns itself with the establishment of filiation (in this case, with artistic filiations, which is what most art historians do); as the discipline (actually, the same one) that examines how proper names are transmitted (in this case, the name "art"); and in the Nietzschean sense, especially as interpreted by Michel Foucault. As to archaeology, it should also, of course, be understood in the sense given to it by Foucault, although its traditional connection to art history should be kept in mind.

judgments based on sentiment and dis-sentiment, and whose regulative idea is itself an idea, or a counteridea, of art, or of anti-art, but always an idea, whatever it may be, that has something to do with art. One last reflection makes you realize that once it is regulated by an idea of art, whatever it might be, and not ruled by such and such a criterion of art, this genealogy in its totality must have as its regulative idea nothing but the idea itself of art as proper name.

What does this mean? One should guard carefully against any confusion between the idea of *art as proper name* and the concept of "art-as-proper-name." The latter operates on the level of theory. It expresses the conceptual knowledge acquired through the theorem that defines the word "art" by the (Kripkean) concept of the proper name or rigid designator.[27] But the idea of art as proper name, on the contrary, operates on the level of practice, that is, of judgment, of the aesthetic usage of the word "art." The *concept* is either true or false, the *idea* is either just or unjust. Through a leap and a reflection, you arrived at the concept that the word "art" was a proper name. Reflecting on your personal experience as an art lover, but leaving your feelings behind, you realized that whenever you issued an aesthetic judgment formulated as "this is art," you were baptizing an object that struck you as art with reference to a collection of samples which, to you, were art already. The word "art," in this sentence, was used in the same way that proper names, according to Kripke, are used: to fix the reference and not to convey meaning. The truth or falsity of Kripke's theory of proper names will determine that of your concept of art as proper name. It will neither affect your experience of art, nor threaten your conviction that this concept is the only one compatible with your experience. The idea of art as proper name came about differently, when you reflected on the fact that your judgments on art had to be part of a tradition and this tradition could only have been that of the avant-garde. The idea that the word "art" could have been used, and has in fact been used, in the manner of a proper name is the only one

27. From which it clearly does not follow that the word "art" is a concept, any more than the word "Peter," since proper names are not concepts.

capable of accounting for the facts of jurisprudence that have constituted the avant-garde as a tradition. The idea that it should be so used, moreover, is the only one to do justice to the avant-garde, for it is the only one allowing you to see it as the continuation of tradition *tout court.* This idea cannot be proven even if it finds strong support in the historical record. It presupposes something that experience confirms but that no theory demonstrates: the use of the phrase "this is art" expresses an aesthetic judgment, and this judgment, born out of a feeling, neither states nor communicates the quality or "content" of this feeling. Further, it supposes that everyone is capable of having feelings about what he or she calls art and includes in his or her collection. This was what you supposed and had to suppose to be an art lover. And it is what you still suppose and must suppose in order to say that the regulative idea that summons before whatever feeling, felt by whomever, anything whatever that is a candidate for art, could only be the very idea of art as proper name. This idea constitutes the gist of the tradition to which you must still belong—that is, from within which you judge without theory—in order to be able (but this time theoretically and without judging) to describe it as if you no longer took part in it. You translate it and you betray it; therefore, you transmit it such as it happened in attempting to describe it.

The first statement of this description will be, "Art was a proper name." It is a historical statement that conjugates in the past tense the theoretical statement, "Art is a proper name." It does not invalidate it, it does not refute a theory which, true yesterday, would be false or outmoded today. The definition of art based on the Kripkean theory is not historically contingent so far as its truth is concerned, even though it has a historical correlate so far as its relevance is concerned. "Art is a proper name" is a conceptual or theoretical definition of art. "Art was a proper name," on the other hand, is not a definition of art at all, but rather the beginning of an archaeological description of the tradition regulated by the idea of art as proper name. This tradition, congruent with the history of the avant-garde, is modernity.

Describing it as a historian, or more precisely, as an archaeologist, is above all to periodize it. This you will attempt to do, getting your bearings from this elementary definition: modernity is that period of Western history for which art was a proper name, that period during which aesthetic practice—of artists as well as of art lovers and critics—was regulated by the idea of art as proper name. It began, obviously, when the idea emerged that art was autonomous, and when the practice of art indeed entrenched itself in its autonomy and alienated itself from society at large. It began when the word "art" became the name of an ineffable quality that did not obey preestablished rules, that did not necessarily coincide with the beautiful or the sublime yet was often substituted for them, and that wrenched from the sphere of myth and religion a space of secular spirituality that became the object of a particular intellection institutionalized by the Museum. Provisionally and very roughly periodized, the moment when modernity began was the eighteenth century. In the writings of Roger de Piles and of Abbé Dubos, the notion of taste and the claim of mere art lovers to have the right to judge on the basis of feeling emerged. In the first reviews of the Salons, by Florent Le Comte in 1699, by La Font de Saint Yenne in 1747, by Diderot beginning in 1759, art criticism was constituted as a new literary genre and a polemical mediation between the works of art and their new audience of art lovers, the "public." With Mengs and Winckelmann, the history of art appeared as a new discipline, one that sought to interpret the past chronologically but also surreptitiously set norms for the present. From Vico and Shaftesbury to Baumgarten and Kant, aesthetics was born, first as an appendix to moral philosophy and a reflection on taste, then as a theorization of the kind of perfection that is accessible to the senses, finally as a critique of judgment. In short, the eighteenth century gave birth to each of the modern positions that you yourself have just occupied in turn, positions that you now look back onto in order to construct their archaeology, fully aware that they are neither facts of nature, nor facts of theory, but facts of history.

While the beginnings of modernity are easily spotted, its end, if one there is, is highly problematic. To periodize requires, however, that one be able to mark off a "block" of history at its beginning and end. If the end seems undecidable, it is not just due to a lack of distance. It is also because the end of modernity is almost as old as modernity itself. The period of history that had invented History could not fail to conceive of itself as moved forward by the project of its own accomplishment and self-negation. The negativity of the avant-garde, for which tradition had to mean betrayal, is explained by the anticipated retrospection of the verdict thanks to which avant-garde art would, in the end, be incorporated into tradition precisely for having first betrayed it. Similarly, the avant-garde's pursuit of novelty, its dynamic of constant surpassing, is explained by its aiming at a horizon beyond the modern, which the modern then overtakes in turn. So, modernity seems to be constituted by a forever unending process of ending. That this can be said, however, is an indication that a point in history has been reached where an after-modernity is at least in sight. From within modernity, this could be said only as a prediction, and such a prediction would fail to cancel itself out only if it thought of itself as a driving contradiction. If, since Mallarmé, the ideology of the avant-garde has been massively Hegelian, this is because the end of modernity, the end of the idea of art as proper name, its completion through incompletion, has been the program ever since Hegel's *Vorlesungen über die Aesthetik*. With Hegel, the object of aesthetics is no longer the beautiful or taste; it is art in its autonomy. It is also art in its historical destiny, the necessary alienation that accompanies its "progress," and the project of its disappearance. A century and a half after Hegel, now that the autonomy of art appears as the *autonymy*—or self-nomination—it has really been, it becomes possible to see that the Hegelian dialectic has maintained a systematic confusion of the positions of art lover, critic, historian, and aesthetician. For even the art lover and the critic are forced by Hegel to project themselves, just like the historian and the philosopher, into the speculative position from which they view an already accomplished history of art. Now that it is not art, but rather the period that made art as a proper name into a regulative idea, that seems to reach its end, it becomes possible, and urgent, to turn round on this period's beginnings and to undo the confusion wrought by Hegel.

The roles of art lover (sections 3.1. and 3.4.), critic (3.2.), historian of tradition (3.3.), aesthetician or theoretician of art (4.1.), genealogist or theoretician of historicity (4.2.), and finally, archaeologist (4.3.), can only be played one by one and in that order of entrance. This order represents the historical debt of each of these characters vis-à-vis modernity: they can't play one role without playing or having played the previous ones. And since you yourself played all these roles in turn, this applies to you. You are allowed to be a mere art lover, of course, but it would be absurd and preposterous to call yourself an art critic without being an art lover. It is perfectly honorable for you to do art criticism as a reviewer, without claiming to write history in the heat of the moment, but it would be unthinkable to write the history of an art tradition without judging as a critic and from within this tradition. You can practice art criticism without theoretical ambitions, but conversely, if you sought to produce an art theory without reflecting on the actual activity of the critic, you would be caught in a formal and sterile exercise. Finally, it is entirely legitimate for you to want to add to the jurisprudence by relying on the jurisprudential record, whether immediately or belatedly, but you would fail to grasp the historicity of tradition if you did not reflect as a theoretician on the jurisprudence in which the critic and the historian are, in other respects, immersed. (And how could you so reflect, if you hadn't had the experience of a critic?) Only then, when you have played these five roles in this order, and in full awareness, will you be able to reinscribe them into the period that gave them birth. Only then, looking back to this period called modernity, will you gain an overview of this culture that sustained itself on the idea that art was autonomous and on everything which, of necessity, contradicted that idea. Only then will modernity begin to reveal the fruitful mistake on which it fed: whereas it proceeded from a regulative usage of the idea of art as proper name, it believed or wanted to proceed from a conceptual or speculative usage of the name of art as idea. And this—belief or desire—probably authorized that—regulation and production. Once fruitful, this mistake is so no longer, unless it is recognized as a mistake. It allowed philosophy and art to walk hand in hand for about two centuries, to the point where most modern philosophers have conceived that the search for truth remains incomplete without looping into the domain of art, and where most modern artists have believed that art lacks dignity without philosophical ambition. But the philosophical drive of modern art has lived itself out. Today, it makes way for the obligation to write the archaeology of modernity. The mistake thanks to which modern art, imagining itself as enacted philosophy, came into being is no more than a historical fact to be reinterpreted as such. This is a task for the archaeologist, and probably no longer one for the artist or the critic. With this task, modernity is brought to a close and yields a new injunction: that of the postmodern.

The possible meaning of the word "postmodern" for artists is beyond your grasp as an archaeologist. Even what it might mean for critics is no concern of yours. Noticing that it is on everyone's lips, you just take stock of the fact that it has appeared in recent years. To you, it sounds like a symptom, the symptom that a large part of our culture doesn't want to call itself modern any more. Throughout the era called modernity, *modern* was a value judgment synonymous with the word *art,* to the point where for the jurisprudence that exhumed long-forgotten artists like Bach or Vermeer, or whole cultures long ignored like African art, it was always their "modernity" that was pushed to the fore, as if it contained the ultimate criterion justifying their status as art. But now that growing numbers of people, disappointed with modernism or dispirited by its possible impasses, no longer value the word "modern" and proclaim the advent of the "postmodern" as if it were a magical absolution for the supposed sins of modernity, obviously a periodization of history has been performed, albeit through wishful thinking. To you, as archaeologist, this indicates that these people, whether artists or critics, want to change names. The word "postmodern" is nothing but a proper name, just as both the word "art" and the word "modern" were for the moderns. As John Stuart Mill would have said, it has no connotation but only denotation. People who use it in praise of certain artworks of today simply point to the things they like or value with reference to a collection made of the works they call modern, and which they reject or push into the past. And people who use it disparagingly simply resign themselves to accepting the periodization performed by the former. Both groups denote a body of works, not necessarily the same, with one and the same proper name. And yet to you they also connote something: for the "postmodernists," the wish to leave modernity behind; for the "antipostmodernists," on the contrary, the nostalgia for a set of values which they feel are no longer shared. The "postmodernists" gladly betray modernity, the "antipostmodernists" sadly register the betrayal and possibly fight back. As an archaeologist, you do neither. You simply take stock of the symptom and interpret its connotation: if the word "postmodern" is but a proper name with which to point to certain works of art in negative reference to those called modern, then the word "modern," which was a proper name when modernity was alive and well, is perhaps one no longer. It is in the process of becoming a common name, that is, a concept that can be circumscribed insofar as the period of history so called is ended. Whether modernity has "really" ended or not is irrelevant to you as an archaeologist. The flow of time does not spontaneously cut itself in slices; its periodization is performative and it is performed by words, such as "pre-" and "post-," which people use to delimit a period. The word "postmodern" has appeared, and this is all you need to know to sense that it carries a strong injunction. But to you, as archaeologist of modernity, this injunction is radically different from the one the artist and the critic might also feel. They are likely to confuse the "postmodern" with "postmodernism," which to you appears as nothing more than another "ism" confined within "modernism," that is, within the very ideology that mistook the regulative usage of the idea of art as proper name for the speculative usage of the name of art as idea. To you, "postmodern" is a neutral and literal term, unladen with values; it is a periodizing instrument that says what it does and does what it says and nothing else. If you feel its injunction, it is simply because it posits you in time in a way that makes modernity the terrain of your archaeological investigation and commands you to look at it from a vantage point that no longer takes the modern, or "modernist," interpretation of the modern era for granted. In other words, the injunction you feel so strongly is that of defining, interpreting, conceptualizing the common name that modernity has become. Or still, it is the injunction to rewrite the history of the modern era in such a way that it will be read as a postmodern reinterpretation of modernity. This you already began to do when you defined modernity, neither as the era in which art was autonomous (which would be a modernist interpretation), nor as the era that entertained the illusion or the ideology that art was autonomous (which would be a postmodernist, in the sense of antimodernist, interpretation), but as the era whose practice and criticism of art was regulated by the idea of art as proper name.

In order to write the archaeology of this era, you surely don't need to subscribe to the idea of art as proper name any longer, nor to believe in it, nor to desire it. But you won't deny that it has been a powerful regulative idea. You will certainly have to renounce the modernist reading of modern art, which interpreted its purism as a progressive reduction to art's necessary and sufficient conditions. But you won't forget the works that the striving for purism generated. You will probably need to accuse the project of emancipation carried by the avant-gardes. But you won't relinquish emancipation as a maxim.[28] You will simply translate both the idea of art's autonomy and its inevitable negative, the idea of art's alienation, into that of art as a proper name. For in the ruleless game, or the ruthless struggle, that modern art has been, what was at stake was the name of art. No matter what modern artists did, no matter what rules they followed or abandoned, no matter what conception of art they fought for or against, no matter what style they invented or destroyed, those who won—the game or the struggle—were those who managed to see their work be baptized by the name of art. This became clear with the late modern art, when the "historical" avant-gardes had achieved their conquest and been fully legitimized and the neo-avant-gardes replayed their struggle as petty artworld games. When the idea of art's autonomy came full circle as tautology, formalism, or self-reference, it also began to lose itself body and soul in the heteronomy of the market, as Adorno had feared. Isn't this a sign that, perhaps, the name of art is no longer at stake? If this were the case, wouldn't you be seeing modernity come full circle before your very eyes?

Here, thus, is a set of new tasks, for which the name of art is no longer at stake. An archaeological site has opened up before you. To sift through it doesn't require any loyalty to its programs, any adherence to its values, any feeling. You

28. More about this in chapter 8.

are allowed to look on coldly as the name of art is erased from the surface of culture, in exactly the way that Michel Foucault saw the figure of Man being washed away "like a face drawn in sand at the edge of the sea."[29] Yet as we now know, Foucault the archaeologist was a committed humanist, his enterprise was political, he took sides. And you yourself, for whom the emergence of the word "postmodern" is merely a symptom, you don't lose sight of the fact that in obeying the injunction to reinterpret modernity with clinical coolness, you also have to rejudge it in the fire of criticism. You don't forget how you arrived at a theory of art and a theory of its historicity: through a leap, yes, aloof from judgment and feelings, but also through a reflection. It is in reflecting on the critical quasi-definition you had given to all the art you loved—art is everything I call art—that the concept of art as proper name forced itself on you. Before being a theoretician, you were an art critic. Similarly, before being a genealogist, you were a historian, which is to say, a slow critic, again. And so, it is in reflecting on your own activity as a critic working from a distance or in the turmoil of the present, that you were able to understand that the idea of art as proper name had been the regulative idea of a tradition that is called the modern tradition, or the tradition of the avant-garde. Although you can now describe it as if you no longer took part in it—that is, as if you came from outer space or were ready to take off to another planet and said, "Art was everything modern humans called art," or, "Art was everything we called art when we were modern"—you know from experience that this tradition was yours, that it was the jurisprudence within which you sought to set precedents.

Well, you are still that critic and your tradition is still with you. In order to reflect you had to judge, and if you have judged, if you still do, you won't avoid transmitting your judgments to those who will follow you and who will not fail to situate you in the tradition you transmit and, in so doing, betray. You are modern, without fail. Even if you write on the Middle Ages, your writings bear a date and what you will transmit will be the "modernity" of the Middle Ages. And even if you write on the hottest current events and invoke the postmodern

29. Michel Foucault, *The Order of Things* (New York: Pantheon, 1970), p. 387.

in order to describe and evaluate them, as good or bad, it will still be "modernity" that you will betray and thus translate and thus transmit. When modernity comes full circle in the symptomatic desire to be done with it, it is fated to trap the critic in a double bind. As a critic, there is nothing you can do for the time being but accept this. For if the postmodern was first of all a symptom for you as an archaeologist, a symptom which you then had to interpret and judge as such, for you as a critic it carries an immediate injunction to judge and interpret. Now, this injunction is contradictory, it is a double bind. When works of art appeal to a new name before the tribunal of history, they give the critic notice to grant it to them or not, and to say why. If you grant them the name "postmodern," you will emphasize rupture and betrayal, since to be postmodern a work must break with the modern. And if the break itself has a say in your evaluation of the work, then, ironically, your explanation of it is bound to be modern. If, on the contrary, you refuse the new name and claim the modern tradition for the work, you will still have to say why this value judgment is more modern than the postmodern. As long as the choice you have at your disposal in order to evaluate a work is one between two proper names, "modern" and "postmodern," you will be drawn to attempt a rereading of the whole of modernity when faced with any single work that seems to question its limits. Today's epidemic of historicism is positively a sign of this; it is also a symptom that such rereadings, modernist through denial, do not yet amount to a reinterpretation. Only when you are wearing your aesthetician's hat—when you define art as a proper name or your archaeologist's hat—when you define modernity as this period during which aesthetic practice was regulated by the idea of art as proper name—are you free to savor all the irony of the nominalist alternative between the modern and the postmodern. When you are wearing your critic's hat—and even though you are the aesthetician and the archaeologist too—you remain prisoner of this alternative, which will probably last as long as the historical transition through which our culture is passing, in the process of leaving modernity for something unknown that is postmodern in name only. And so, as a critic, you are left with nothing other than your feelings to rest your judgments on: the feeling that makes you call a given work modern or postmodern, the feeling of the conflicts between the modern and its wish-fulfilling aftermath, and the feeling, stronger than ever, of dissent and double bind.

4.4.

With this uncertain and painful feeling, you judge. Caught in the double bind, you are forever a late modern, an old romantic at once stubbornly loyal to the avant-garde and dangerously seduced by the wish not to be modern any longer. You look at your love affairs with art with a wry smile, unwilling to atone for sins you have not committed. You are modernity's rejected lover, melancholic perhaps, but peaceful in the end; for you understand that when the time comes to look straight into the black hole of the future, the true sign of love is abandonment. The simplistic alternative of pleasure and pain has long been broken, so you know that to sustain your love of art you need to draw on disgust as much as on taste, just as you know that a sense of the ridiculous is the best antidote to those forsaken emotions of the sublime. Irony is the one feeling left to you, yet you have grown to value it only as *ironism of affirmation*. Soon it will make way for humor, that youth of old people. *Freedom of indifference* should now rule over your choices and lead you out of this double bind that has put a mortgage on the future. You remain free to call art whatever you want, and "art" is, after all, a name indifferent to both the modern and the postmodern. There might be some wisdom in not jettisoning it prematurely, and wisdom is not delivered through doctrines and theories; it is displayed by example. What work could you choose as an example to lift the mortgage? What exemplary thing are you going to draw from your collection and make into a paradigm of the historical transition which is our own?

One last time, you produce Duchamp's urinal, this *Fountain* of youth yellowed by its ironic abandonment in modernity's museum-without-walls, this piece of porcelain prominently displayed in the warehouse of contemporary art and yet covered with the dust of indifference. It is forsaken but still new, ready to serve and to splatter its *oculist witnesses* with humor. Without the *illuminating gas,* the *waterfall* remains invisible. Its status as art has not been granted once and for all, in spite of the more established reputation of the rest of Duchamp's oeuvre. Unlike the *Large Glass,* which Duchamp called a *delay in glass . . . as you would say a poem in prose or a spittoon in silver,* this urinal *in* porcelain promises no reconciliation between the *Bride* and *her bachelors.* Instead, *inscribed* as a readymade, it reminds you that *one only has: for female the pissoir, and one lives by it.*[30] Though in her own day she has been called the Madonna of the Bathroom, you can't make her into a marble Aphrodite, can you? Perhaps it doesn't even matter whether this unlikely goddess of love is beautiful, ugly, or simply interesting, or whether her features triggered a violent, contradictory feeling, composed of disgust and ridicule, but also of mad love, despair, vengeance, and jealousy. She was carved as *the figuration of a possible,* which is *only a physical "caustic" (vitriol type) burning up all aesthetics or callistics.*[31] Hers is the *beauty of indifference,* which reminds you that the one question bequeathed by the avant-garde must remain unanswered: *can one make works which are not works of "art"?*[32] Perhaps it doesn't even matter whether the pissoir is an "objet d'art," or an object of non-art, or whether its ambiguous status of *objet-dard* will keep the question open. Too many answers have been given already. *Fountain* is hard to dislodge from the patrimony of avant-garde art, while it has not yet found its legitimate place among the practices of art *tout court.* It remains the weakest link in the chain of the tradition it betrayed and to which it is nonetheless referred. It is up to you to set a precedent in this uncertain jurisprudence. For the day of reckoning is in sight: postmodernity is knocking at the door, and the avant-gardes of tomorrow will have to look to their past for exemplary references. What art should be no longer lies ahead of us, like a promise, which is why *Fountain* is no more postmodern than it is modern. Unlike Picasso's work, it has not become classic either. But an exemplary reference it is, a paradigm. And you judge it as such.

Of what is *Fountain* a paradigm, if not of this transition we are living through, starting from a period when art was a proper name and moving to a

30. *The 1914 Box,* in *SS,* p. 23 (translation slightly modified).

31. *SS,* p. 73.

32. *The White Box,* in *SS,* p. 74.

period for which the regulative idea of art as proper name has become a given? *Given, first, the waterfall, second, the illuminating gas,* no art worthy of the name will be made that ignores or bypasses the weakest link welding the modern avant-gardes to their premodern past. Duchamp's urinal is this link. A number of today's artists, painters mostly, revert to the premodern as if Duchamp's urinal never existed, as if the readymades, the "historical avant-gardes," modernism even, had not threatened to break the chain of tradition for good. Others—contextualists, appropriationists, or simulationists—are under the urinal's spell, but they fail to look further into the past for references against which to check the quality of their work. They often back their work with theory, and claim to have found it in the readymades. You too felt that *Fountain* contained a theory, but this was merely a feeling. Reflection taught you better. Neither does *Fountain* close the definition of art on itself, tautologically or self-referentially, nor does it open it to the essential incompleteness of some "anything goes." When you say, "Art is whatever I call art," you are not, like these artists-theorists, appropriating the readymade. Appropriation is theft, and tradition is nobody's private property. Rather, you are claiming responsibility for the readymade, as though you were its author, and you are guarding your personal collection as though it were everyone's treasure. For you know that the regulative idea that made you choose Duchamp's urinal as the paradigm of our transition, which, in the long run, concerns all of us humans, was an idea about art regulating the baptism of anything whatever in such a way that the reflection is drawn therefrom that any idea about art whatever was precisely what baptized it. The readymade, Duchamp said, *is a kind of rendezvous, like a speech delivered on no matter what occasion but at such and such an hour.*[33] The hour has arrived for its *allegorical appearance* to elicit, here and now, a hitherto unknown feeling: the jubilation that turns the program of modernity inside out like a glove, the paradoxical sense of the future that a deliberately retrospective gaze opens up.

33. *The Green Box,* in *SS,* p. 32.

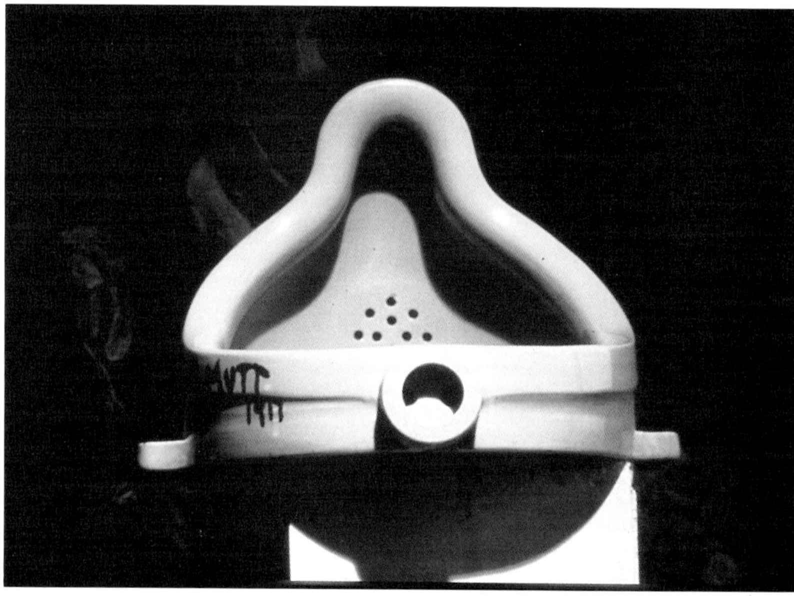

Sturtevant, *Duchamp Fontaine,* 1973, readymade (urinal turned upside down), 36 × 38.75 × 40 cm. Courtesy Galerie Thaddaeus Ropac, Paris.

2

Given the Richard Mutt Case

In philosophy analogies mean something very different from what they mean in mathematics. In the latter they are formulas which express the equality of two quantitative relations, and are always constitutive; so that if three terms of the proportion are given, the fourth is likewise given, that is, can be constructed. But in philosophy the analogy does not consist in the equality of two quantitative, but of two qualitative relations, so that when three terms are given I may learn from them *a priori* the relation to a fourth only, but not that fourth term itself. The relation yields, however, a rule according to which I may look in experience for the fourth term, and a sign by which I may detect it.

—*Immanuel Kant,* Critique of Pure Reason

Preface

The artists and others were having continual discussions about freedom in art, the evils of the jury system. Inevitably there came the idea of holding an exhibition without jury. The Grand Central

> Palace, a huge building, was chosen and the information broadcasted that anyone paying six dollars could send two paintings and have them hung without benefit of jury. Walter [Arensberg] and Marcel [Duchamp] were especially enthralled with the concept, and George Bellows, Walt Kuhn, Rockwell Kent, Walter Pach, John Covert all helped with the bylaws.
>
> The day before the exhibition opened, Walter Arensberg was standing with Rockwell Kent in front of a glistening white object. Both men were violently arguing, and paying no attention as I approached.

These words, written by Beatrice Wood a long time after the events, may not describe them with the utmost accuracy, which is just as well considering the legendary character of the whole story they serve to introduce. She has actually given several versions of the scene that took place, if it did, on April 8 or 9, 1917; in another, George Bellows replaces Rockwell Kent in his argument with Walter Arensberg. But the essential argument itself remains. In this particular version—the most dramatic—she goes on reconstructing the heated exchange between the two men as dialogue:

> "This is indecent!" went on Kent flatly, with red face.
>
> "That depends upon the point of view," said Walter gently.
>
> "We cannot show it," went on Kent flatly, with red face.
>
> "The entrance fee has been paid, we cannot refuse it," blandly added Walter.
>
> "But it is gross, offensive."
>
> "Only in the eye of the beholder."
>
> "There is such a thing as decency, an end to how far a person can go."
>
> Walter said mildly, "But the purpose of this project is to accept anything an artist chooses. It is in our bylaws."
>
> There was an ominous silence, then Kent exploded, "Do you

> mean that if a man chose to exhibit horse manure we would have to accept it!"
>
> "I am afraid we would," answered Walter, with mock sorrow, slowly shaking his head suggesting that all was not as simple as it seemed. . . .
>
> "Someone has sent it as a joke," continued Kent in anger.
>
> "Or a test," finished Walter patiently.
>
> The pristine oval white object on a black pedestal gleamed triumphantly. It was a man's urinal upside down.[1]

Was Duchamp's urinal a joke or a test? Or was it both? Jokes and tests certainly abound in the history of modern art, and they're usually the two sides of one and the same coin. Every futurist prank, dadaist hoax, expressionist farce, or surrealist pun that history has recorded was a way of scoffing at some authority whose liberalism, open-mindedness or resistance to ridicule it put to a test. Duchamp's urinal is no exception. But here the joke was a test in more than one sense, for the testing device was obviously designed to be itself submitted to a test: if the hanging committee of the show at the Grand Central Palace consented to exhibit the gleaming object poking fun at them, they would have to call it art. If they were to pass the test, so would it. They didn't, as we shall see. But it did, and that's the irony of the joke. Who would dare deny, today, that Duchamp's urinal is art? Such is its status in any case or it wouldn't be on the record. What is also on the record is that cohorts of artists registered that Duchamp's joke had passed the test and then went on to play variations on it, pushing the limits of art further and further, probing its boundaries, some jokingly, some in dead seriousness. From surrealism to conceptual art, half of the

1. Francis Naumann, ed., "I Shock Myself: Excerpts from the Autobiography of Beatrice Wood," *Arts Magazine* 51, no. 9 (1977): 135–136. The version with Bellows substituting for Kent is in Wood's autobiography, *I Shock Myself* (Ojai, Calif.: Dillingham Press, 1985), pp. 29–30.

avant-garde played a game on the definition of art in general. (The other half, which is often called modernism, apparently played a different game, confining itself within the specific boundaries of painting or sculpture.[2]) While Meret Oppenheim cloaked a cup and its saucer in fur and Magritte put a painting representing a piece of Brie under a cheese-cover, the surrealists as a group put up a show where myriads of "objets sauvages," redubbed "objets surréalistes," claimed their newly conquered art-status. Later, Yves Klein exhibited the *Void* and Arman the *Full,* while Manzoni sold cans of *Artist's Shit* and balloons of *Artist's Breath.* Warhol produced fake *Brillo Boxes* while Judd and Morris produced boxes. Rauschenberg sent his gallerist, Iris Clert, a telegram stating "This is a portrait of Iris Clert if I say so," and a few years later On Kawara sent his gallerist, Yvon Lambert, a telegram stating "I am still alive." And by the time Ian Wilson could carry on conversations about art and call them art, Robert Barry was able to invite his audience to an (imaginary) round-the-world hopping from one gallery to the next, only to discover that the promised show was to be held the next month in the next gallery.[3] In each of these pieces, subtle humor and deliberate provocation mingled to raise the question of the conditions under which any given thing could be called art. But as the last two examples suggest, an answer, or perhaps two answers, were soon found, which roughly delineate two "theories" of art: something is art because an artist so decided; something is art because the context so determined it. The first theory was already upheld by André Breton, apropos precisely the readymade, when

2. The game is only apparently different. More about this in chapter 4, which investigates an episode of recent art history where the modernist tradition (in Greenberg's sense) and the Duchamp-tradition came to meet.

3. Robert Barry's *Invitation Piece* (1972–1973) consisted of eight invitation cards sent at one-month intervals, where one gallery would announce an exhibition by Robert Barry to be held the next month in another gallery. The piece started with an invitation sent by Paul Maenz in Cologne announcing a show at Art & Project in Amsterdam, and came full circle eight months later with Gian Enzo Sperone in Turin announcing a show at Paul Maenz.

he defined it as "an ordinary object promoted to the dignity of art object simply by way of the artist's choice."[4] Let's call this the *appropriative* theory of art. The second one is the *contextual* theory of art, as it is for instance illustrated by Daniel Buren: "The Museum/Gallery instantly promotes to 'Art' status whatever it exhibits with conviction, i.e., habit."[5] Let's notice in passing that between Breton and Buren and between the time of surrealism and that of conceptual art, dignity sank to the level of status and choice (or conviction) fell into habit. But promotion remained promotion.

The joke really is that both theories are true. They are true in the way tautologies are true, which is hilarious. Lest it should be incoherent, any serious theory of art needs to define "art" and "artist" with the same family of criteria, so we shall assume that these two do. Well, if you say that something has become art because an artist appropriated it, then you must admit that anybody who appropriates something as art becomes an artist. Or else he or she was an artist according to some other theory of art, and then it is not true that something has become art because an artist appropriated it. If you say that something has become art because it was placed in the art context of a museum or a gallery, you must admit that the context is artistic because it contains art. Or else it was instituted as *art* museum or *art* gallery on the basis of some other conception of what art is, and then it is not true that anything it contains and exhibits out of "habit" is art. In both cases, if your theory is true it is circular and if it isn't circular it is false. Moreover, if one is false the other is true, since the success of Duchamp's test—or joke—admits only these two. In fact, they flow into one another in an endless circle, since an artist is someone who is recognized as such by an art institution and since an institution is one of art because it shows what artists do. Thus both theories boil down to a single one, the *institutional* theory,

4. André Breton and Paul Eluard, *Dictionnaire abrégé du surréalisme* (Paris: Galerie des Beaux-Arts, 1938), my translation.

5. Daniel Buren, "Function of the Museum," in *Five Texts* (New York: The John Weber Gallery; London: The Jack Wendler Gallery, 1973), p. 58.

which is true by *petitio principii.* And so did it happen that the joke passed the test.

One imagines Duchamp's pleasure if he had lived to read, under the signature of an eminent aesthetician who, by the way, confesses that "as works of art Duchamp's readymades may not be worth much, but as examples of art they are very valuable for art theory," this definition of art as pataphysically complicated as it is tautologically luminous: "A work of art in the classificatory sense is (1) an artifact (2) a set of the aspects of which has had conferred upon it the status of candidate for appreciation by some person or persons acting on behalf of a certain social institution (the artworld)."[6] We learn in the book of Professor George Dickie, the author of this gem of a quote, that "artifactuality" can itself be a status conferred even on a product of nature, that the aspects of this artifact upon which the status of candidate for appreciation is conferred are simply the aspects submitted to the said appreciation, that this appreciation follows no criteria aside from the conventions which govern the presentation of said artifact in the artworld, and finally that anybody who sees himself or herself as a member of the artworld thereby becomes a member. And so did it happen that the test became a joke.

Dickie's book was published in 1974, but he had issued earlier versions of his institutional definition of art as early as 1969, the very year in which a major proponent of conceptual art, Joseph Kosuth, came up with a definition of art as tautology that is virtually identical.[7] I see no coincidence in this congruence, which is not to say that I accuse either of them of having looked over the other's shoulder. There was tremendous historical pressure at the time in favor of such art theories and it seems, given the recent spectacular comeback of readymades, shelved or not, in today's neoconceptualism, that the pressure is still with us. It should entice us to go back to where it all started and give the Richard Mutt

6. George Dickie, *Art and the Aesthetic: An Institutional Analysis* (Ithaca, N.Y.: Cornell University Press, 1974), p. 34.

7. More about Kosuth's definition of art in chapters 4, 5, and 7.

case a closer look, taking our interpretive clues from Marcel Duchamp himself rather than from a late, crucial but particularly ill-conceived reception of the readymade. Hence the above *Preface* and the following *Warning*:

Warning

> Given, first, the waterfall, second, the illuminating gas, we shall determine the conditions for the allegorical appearance of several collisions seeming strictly to succeed each other according to certain laws, in order to isolate the sign of the accordance between, on the one hand, this allegorical appearance and, on the other, a choice of possibilities legitimated by these laws and also occasioning them.[8]

Taking our interpretive clues for Duchamp's *Warning,* we notice that it sounds like a mathematical theorem, assigning a task to the reader: *we shall determine the conditions . . . in order to isolate the sign of the accordance. . . .* The text, however, is cryptic and calls for an interpretation of the *givens.* Here is one, prompted by many humorous cross-references among Duchamp's works: *given,* first, by way of *waterfall,* a certain famous *Fountain* in the guise of a urinal signed R. Mutt; second, by way of *illuminating gas,* the art institution which illuminates this fountain and gives it its aura and its status, *we shall determine the conditions for the allegorical appearance,* etc.

Duchamp's urinal, as we suspect from Beatrice Wood's story, has vanished. All that remains are the replicas made by Sidney Janis in 1950, by Ulf Linde in

8. Marcel Duchamp, "Avertissement" ("Notice," better translated as "Warning"), *The Green Box,* in *SS,* p. 28. I have actually deleted parts of the text and somewhat collaged it together with the immediately preceding "Preface" (pp. 27–28), to which it is very similar. I have also modified the translation to a certain extent. (Throughout this chapter, italics indicate an expression by Duchamp.)

1963, and by Arturo Schwarz in 1964, and also, of course, the photograph taken by Alfred Stieglitz in 1917. For us, now, this photograph is the *allegorical appearance* of the urinal and the proof that the title *Fountain* once had a referent. With good Duchampian logic, to determine the conditions of an *appearance* is to explain the *apparition which is its mold.*[9] So, *we shall determine the conditions of the allegorical appearance* (or look) of Stieglitz's photograph by explaining the *apparition* (or advent) of *several collisions seeming strictly to succeed each other according to certain laws.*

We are dealing with an organized series of events, each involving the random collision of two independant causal chains, like a succession of chance encounters: the readymade, Duchamp said elsewhere, is *a kind of rendezvous. Fountain* was not the first of the readymades. On the contrary, it was one of the last "unassisted" ones. Nor was this the first time that a readymade had a rendezvous with its spectators. The succession of *collisions* that needs to be explained thus recedes in time, preceding the *Fountain.* And since these *collisions seem strictly to succeed each other according to certain laws,* we must look back in time in order to identify these laws, starting with the one whose appearance (or look) the Richard Mutt case dissipates and whose conditions of apparition (or advent) it reveals.

The law in question, the one that *legitimates and occasions a choice of possibilities,* is simply stated: anyone can be an artist and anything the art institution shows is art. George Dickie was not around in April 1917, at the first exhibition of the Society of Independent Artists, Inc., and it's too bad: he would have saved a lot of time. To all appearances, his pataphysical institutional theory already had force of law. It follows directly though perhaps unwittingly from the bylaws of the Society, founded in December 1916 in New York. Article II, section 3 of

9. *The White Box,* in *SS,* pp. 84–85. In French, *apparition* only occasionally has the meaning of a ghost-like vision. It also, and more prosaically, means the simple fact of appearing, for which the English only employs *appearance* again. In order to maintain the contrast between the French *apparence* and *apparition,* I shall qualify the former as "appearance or look" and the latter as "apparition or advent."

the bylaws stated, "Any artist, whether a citizen of the United States or of any foreign country, may become a member of the Society upon filing an application therefor, paying the initiation fee and the annual dues of a member, and exhibiting at the exhibition in the year that he joins."[10] Sections 4 and 5 specified that the initiation fee would be one dollar and the annual dues five dollars. Notice that the bylaws spoke of "any artist" without indicating how artists are recognized as such—probably by having paid their six dollars and by having exhibited in the year they join. Thus the Society seemed ready, *in advance,* to grant, *with all kinds of delays,* the status of artist to anyone fulfilling those two conditions. Being an artist was cheap enough and exhibiting was no problem.[11] The Society's only rule was a no-rule rule, the slogan "No jury, no prizes." It was not in the bylaws but it was commented upon at length in the foreword to the catalogue of the first exhibition, which opened on April 10, 1917. This stated that the Society was founded "for the purpose of holding exhibitions in which all artists may participate independently of the decisions of juries."[12] This was of course intended to free artists from the extremely conservative juries of the National Academy of Design, until then the only institution in America handing out certificates of legitimacy to anyone seeking the status of professional artist. The Society had no social mandate other than the one with which it was endowed by its members, who, in return, had no proof that they

10. Cited by Clark S. Marlor, *The Society of Independent Artists, The Exhibition Record 1917–1944* (Park Ridge, N.J.: Noyes Press, 1984), p. 81.

11. The press didn't fail to notice this. One journalist ironically commented on the *Big Show,* as the first exhibition of the Society got to be called: "Step up, ladies and gentlemen! Pay six dollars and be an artist—an independent artist! Cheap, isn't it? Yet that is all it costs. You and I, even if we've never wielded a brush, squeezed paint from a tube, spoiled good paint with crayon, or worked with a modelling tool, can buy six dollars worth of wall or floor space at the Grand Central Palace." Quoted in Francis Naumann, "The Big Show, The First Exhibition of the Society of Independent Artists, Part II, The Critical Response," *Artforum* 17 (April 1979): 49.

12. Marlor, *Society of Independent Artists,* p. 7.

were artists other than their membership card. Individually or as a group, the Independent Artists had only the legitimacy they gave themselves through self-proclamation.

The quantitative success of the Big Show in 1917 proves the theory of self-proclamation. Some 2,125 works by 1,235 artists were shown. There is no doubt that given such numbers, the majority of the participants were amateurs or would-be artists whom a jury or a commercial gallery would never have accepted.[13] The list of names tells us nothing, of course, since it consists mainly of names unknown and soon to vanish. But the fact that as many as 414 women were included, compared to 821 men, is a good indicator of the proportion of nonprofessionals, given the hardly advanced state of women's emancipation at the time. The number of related duos—husband and wife, brother and sister, mother and daughter—is another.[14] An unknown among all the unknowns who grabbed their chance to call themselves artists, a certain Richard Mutt from Philadelphia sent in a porcelain urinal entitled *Fountain*, conspicuously signed and dated: R. Mutt 1917. He was in good company, no more and no less talented after all than many a naïve amateur whose display of clumsy craftsmanship embarrassed more than one critic. But Richard Mutt was soon to become famous, while all the others would revert to anonymity. And the paradox is that they had exhibited whereas Mr. Mutt's entry was censured, put behind a partition, surreptitiously stolen, rejected on a technicality by Rockwell Kent, broken by William Glackens or bought away by Walter Arensberg—we'll probably never know, among all the equally fantastic versions of the facts, which is the right one.[15] In any case, *Fountain* was neither seen by the public nor listed in

13. That in itself was enough to infuriate conservative critics like Leila Mechlin, who wrote in the May 1917 editorial of the *American Magazine of Art,* "Naturally a great many of those who became exposed in this instance had not the smallest claim to the name artist." Quoted ibid., p. 10.

14. Ibid., pp. 9, 10.

15. Most versions, including Duchamp's contradictory statements to Rudi Blesh and Pierre Cabanne, are discussed in William Camfield's essay "Marcel Duchamp's *Fountain:* Its History

the catalogue. A press release was issued by the board of directors on the day following the opening, leaving no doubt as to the fate of the controversial object: "The *Fountain* may be a very useful object in its place, but its place is not an art exhibition and it is, by no definition, a work of art."[16] By no definition indeed, except the one following from the very principles that the Society had set for itself and then immediately betrayed at the start of its career. The board of directors must have thought that art can be defined only through comparison, and that a urinal cannot be compared with anything known by the name of art.

Algebraic Comparison

In the *Green Box,* the "Preface" and the "Warning" are immediately followed by a note entitled "Algebraic Comparison." Here it is:

> *a/b, a* being the exhibition, *b* being the possibilities, the ratio *a/b* is in no way given by a number *c* (*a/b* = *c*) but by the sign (/) which separates *a* and *b*; as soon as *a* and *b* are known they become new units and lose their numerical relative value, (or in duration); what remains is the sign (/) which separated them (sign of the accordance or rather of . . . ? . . . look for it.)[17]

and Aesthetics in the Context of 1917," *Dada/Surrealism* 16 (1987): 65–94. For an expanded version, see William Camfield, *Marcel Duchamp, Fountain* (Houston: The Menil Foundation and Houston Fine Art Press, 1989). He does not mention, however, what I believe to be the most probable (in any case the least farfetched) version, that told by Rockwell Kent in his autobiography, *It's Me, O Lord* (New York: Dodd, Mead & Co., 1955), p. 316, in which he says that after a heated discussion, the board of directors finally found a way to refuse *Fountain* on the basis of a technicality: the entry card had not been filled in properly.

16. Quoted in Francis Naumann, "The Big Show, The First Exhibition of the Society of Independent Artists, Part I," *Artforum* 17 (February 1979): 38.

17. *SS,* p. 28 (translation slightly modified).

A and *b* are known, a *being the exhibition,* b *being the possibilities.* For the multitude of nobodies who seized their chance to proclaim themselves artists, the ratio *a/b* represents the relation between what they exhibited—in principle, anything—and the possibilities of exhibition offered to anyone. The ratio *a/b* expresses that formula through which the Society performed its self-legitimation. It is the relation of the founding exhibition of 1917 to the "No jury, no prizes" statutory law that it gave itself. In short: *a/b* equals "anything to anybody." But, as we read in the "Algebraic Comparison," *as soon as* a *and* b *are known they lose their value in duration.* Indeed, this verdict is ironically confirmed by the fact that after the first exhibition of 1917, which was a great success, never again would the Society of Independent Artists, which remained in existence until 1944, produce an event worthy of remaining in the history books of modern art. By contrast, it is when *a* and *b* are unknown—unknown, that is, to their contemporaries, since to us they are given—that the ratio *a/b* retains its value in duration; *a,* this time, which I'll call *a′*, being the *extra-quick exhibition capable of all the eccentricities*[18]—in this case that of exhibiting a urinal—and *b,* which I'll call *b′*, being *the possibilities* that the Society denied to the only individual who took the formula of its self-legitimation literally, the mysterious R. Mutt. Indeed, this verdict has been confirmed by history, with all the required *ironism of affirmation.*

I have just said "by contrast." I could have said "by comparison." In itself, the ratio *a/b* does not yet constitute an *algebraic comparison,* even in "amusing algebra."[19] But we know from other sources what the canonical Duchampian

18. The *extra-quick exhibition capable of all the eccentricities* is a phrase I left out of Duchamp's *Warning.* Duchamp uses it as synonymous to the *allegorical appearance* and, in the *Preface,* to the *instantaneous state of Rest.* (*SS,* pp. 27–28; translation modified.)

19. It is most likely that in Duchamp's mind at the time the notion of *algebraic comparison,* which he invented, was his response to that of *arithmetical proportion,* then in favor with his brothers and cubist friends, all members of the group *La Section d'Or.* When Duchamp maintains that *the ratio a/b is in no way given by a number c (a/b = c),* he is refuting a complete aesthetic theory based on the mystique of the golden section. Indeed, the golden section formula,

formula is for the amusing algebraic comparison: *"Arrhe est à art ce que merdre est à merde."* (Arrhe is to art what shitte is to shit.)[20] Duchamp even put it in an explicitly algebraic form:

$$\frac{\text{arrhe}}{\text{art}} = \frac{\text{merdre}}{\text{merde}}$$

The general formula thus reads: $a/b = a'/b'$. And here is one concrete implementation of it: by way of "arrhe" any object shown at the Independents', for example *Nice Animals* by Rockwell Kent, Jr., aged eight;[21] by way of "art" the art institution called Society of Independent Artists when it respects the liberal principle legitimating it; by way of "merdre," *Fountain,* of course; and by way of "merde" the same institution when it fails to abide by the same principle. The relation a/b, which in 1917 was legitimate in the eyes of the Society, is equivalent to the relation a'/b', which was not but which has since become legitimate, *with all kinds of delays.* This now remains to be demonstrated.

THE FACTS: RICHARD MUTT AND LOUIS EILSHEMIUS

Today everyone knows that the mysterious R. Mutt was none other than Marcel Duchamp, and that he enjoyed a prominent institutional position in the Society. His name is among those of the twenty founders, on whom he no doubt exercised a determining influence. He is said to have proposed that the works be hung in alphabetical order, starting with a letter drawn out of a hat,

---

$a/b = b/a + b = c$, assigns a constant *numerical value* to c: 0.618 . . . In this case, the *numerical relative values* of a and b are *known:* if $a = 1$, then $b = 1.618$ . . . , etc.

20. *Boîte de 1914,* translation in *SS,* p. 24.

21. Rockwell Kent incited his family to participate: not only his son, Rockwell, Jr., but also his sister Dorothy, who was a violin player and an amateur watercolor artist. Cf. Kent, *It's Me, O Lord,* p. 316.

which earned him the nomination as chairman of the hanging committee, assisted by Rockwell Kent and George Bellows. Exactly one year before, Duchamp had exhibited two (unidentified) readymades in the "Exhibition of Modern Art" at the Bourgeois Galleries, and in the "Four Musketeers Show" at the Montross Gallery he had shown the "assisted" readymade *Pharmacie,* 1914. On the whole, the press had been silent and the readymades received no public notice.[22] Bellows, Glackens, Kent, and company had probably not visited

---

22. Lack of source material and unreliable recollections make the identification of the two readymades shown at the Bourgeois Galleries (listed in the catalogue under No. 50 simply as "Two Readymades") unfortunately very hazardous. In perhaps the only press report mentioning the readymades ("Exhibitions Now On," *American Art News* 14, no. 27 [1916]: 3), two readymades are cited, but not identified. Rudi Blesh, probably relying on conversations he had with Duchamp, says that "Duchamp submitted the shovel, the typewriter cover, and the clothes hanger to the Bourgeois Gallery in New York" (*Modern Art USA* [New York: Knopf, 1956], p. 80), whereas Robert Lebel (*Marcel Duchamp* [New York: Grove Press, 1959], p. 40), who also cites three readymades, replaces the shovel with the hat-rack (*Porte-chapeaux*). Both accounts are at odds with both the number of readymades listed and the date (1917) generally admitted for the clothes hanger (*Trébuchet,* or *Trap*). Arturo Schwarz (*The Complete Works of Marcel Duchamp,* 2d. ed. [New York: Abrams, 1970], p. 463), who thinks that only two readymades were shown, believes that they were the typewriter cover and the (now vanished) weather vane entitled *Pulled at 4 Pins,* whereas Jindrich Chapulecky ("Les symboles chez Marcel Duchamp," *Opus International* 49 [March 1974]: 41) thinks that the weather vane was accompanied instead by the snow shovel. Based on information received from Man Ray, Marcel Jean asked Duchamp in 1952 to confirm the presence of *In Advance of the Broken Arm* (the snow shovel) and *Traveller's Folding Item* (the typewriter cover) in the Montross Gallery show. In his response, Duchamp accurately corrected him on the location (the Bourgeois rather than the Montross gallery) but misplaced the event in time (1917 instead of 1916). He also failed to address the question of identification, neither confirming nor denying the presence of the snow shovel and the typewriter cover. But he provided an interesting piece of information, which might explain why the two readymades went unnoticed: he said that they were exhibited in an umbrella stand at the entrance of the show (*Marcel Duchamp: Letters to Marcel Jean,* Munich, Silke Schreiber Verlag, 1987, p. 77). To Calvin Tomkins (*The Bride and*

those shows; otherwise a year later they would have guessed who was the culprit. It seems that in April 1917 even the organizers of the Independents' show were unaware of who was hiding behind R. Mutt. Upon learning the fate of Mr. Mutt's entry, Duchamp immediately resigned from the board of directors, but even his resignation aroused little or no suspicion among the organizers. He had resigned on a matter of principle and out of solidarity with an unjustly ostracized fellow artist. Perhaps he had embraced Mr. Mutt's cause with too quixotic an enthusiasm, but he had done so in good faith.[23] In spite of the press

---

the Bachelors: Five Masters of the Avant-Garde, 2d ed. [New York: Viking Press, 1969], p. 40), Duchamp said a similar thing: that he had hung three readymades from a coat rack in the entrance, not saying which, and adding that they went unnoticed. The similarity with the story about the urinal being behind a partition is striking. Moreover, it may very well be that it was not Duchamp's decision to put the readymades in the entrance. In the unpublished interview he gave to William Coldstream, Ron Kitaj, Richard Hamilton, Robert Melville, and David Sylvester for the Arts Council of Great Britain on June 19, 1966, Duchamp replied to Richard Hamilton, who had asked him whether the hat rack had not already been exhibited as a work of art at a commercial gallery before the urinal: "The director of the gallery said yes if I gave him a painting to show. I said, 'I will give you a painting to show but let me have my readymades also.' He said 'all right' and then put them in the entrance where you put your hats." A natural place indeed, should the readymades have been the clothes hanger and the hat rack. (I am indebted to André Gervais for having drawn my attention to the inconsistencies of some of these accounts, and to Dennis Young for having provided me with the unpublished Arts Council interview.)

23. The issue of good faith lies behind the embarrassment of several of the directors, as is made extremely clear by a letter, dated April 26 (more than two weeks after the opening of the show), from Katherine Dreier to William Glackens, in which she congratulated him for having "cleared the atmosphere with one stroke" in proposing that both Duchamp and Mutt be invited to lecture at the Society, the former on his readymades, the latter on his theory of art. Whereas she was convinced that Richard Mutt was a joker (see n. 33 below), she had an unwavering and rather naïve trust in Duchamp's "absolute sincerity." If Mutt, who had so severely tested the Independents' principles, refused to be tested in turn and "to show whether he was sincere or did it out of bravado," then Duchamp would have to accept that he too

release, the newspapers remained silent, by and large. The rare accounts of an inside scandal occurring at the Indeps—as the press familiarly called the Independents—mentioned an unspecified "bathroom fixture" or "a familiar article of bathroom furniture," with not even a hint at who its author might have been, even though Duchamp's resignation over it was taken up as juicy gossip by at least two reviewers.[24] If the journalists had known what exactly this "bathroom fixture" was, if they had learned or even guessed Mr. Mutt's identity, they would certainly have reveled in that piece of news. In fact, there was no public scandal. Duchamp himself took great care to see that nobody except his immediate accomplices would be informed, even to the point of writing to his sister Suzanne, on April 11: "One of my female friends under a masculine pseudonym, Richard Mutt, sent in a porcelain urinal as a sculpture."[25] Though some

---

had been the victim of a hoax and should retract his resignation. On the other hand, if Mutt accepted, then it would prove Duchamp right, and Glackens would be the one who should reconsider. Certainly Dreier had little feeling for irony and a typically Germanic common sense, but her willingness to envisage Mutt's rehabilitation not only shows the extent to which Duchamp was able to conceal his strategy from even such close friends; it also shows that, in the end, she was right in her evaluation of the moral implications of the Richard Mutt case. The way she imagined a countertest reveals that she had neither understood the nature of the test nor guessed who was responsible for it, but when, in the same letter, she said of Duchamp, "The very fact that he does not try to force his ideas on others but tries to let them develop truly along their own lines is in essence the guarantee of his real bigness," she is right on target and goes way beyond the "sincerity-of-the-artist defense" (which is the argument Camfield retains in "Marcel Duchamp's *Fountain*," p. 74, where Dreier's letter can be found, as well as other evidence of Mutt's concealment of identity).

24. See ibid., pp. 67–68, and Naumann, "The Big Show, Part II," p. 50. One reviewer even reported that "The Fountain" was "described by those who saw it, as a painting of the realistic school" (*The New York Herald,* April 10, 1917). (I am indebted to Francis Naumann for sharing with me some of the press clippings he collected in the course of his research.)

25. Francis Naumann, ed., "Affectueusement, Marcel: Ten Letters from Marcel Duchamp to Suzanne Duchamp and Jean Crotti," *Archives of American Art Journal* 22, no. 4 (1982): 8.

were shown in 1916, the readymades began their paradoxical public career only at the Independents' Show, where nobody saw R. Mutt's ready-made urinal. More subsequent *collisions seeming strictly to succeed each other according to certain laws* would be necessary for that career to really surface. Meanwhile, there was another paradoxical effect: in spite of the urinal's invisibility, or rather thanks to it, the Society was able to retain its legitimacy. With the readymades' public appearance remaining underground—an *apparition*—the Society was spared open ridicule. And, more importantly, the betrayal of its principles was kept safe from public critique. Thus, the liberation of all the artists, known or unknown, serious or spurious, who were until then oppressed by the juries of the National Academy, was real. In the days following the United States' declaration of war, no troublemaker was going to cast doubt on the way America obeyed President Wilson's watchword, "The world must be made safe for democracy."

Duchamp's tact, here, was both exquisite and cruel. He graciously avoided posing as a martyr and provoking a "Salon *du* refusé."[26] But he made sure that others did it for him, at the dénouement, when the show's success was secure and the organizers' righteousness was no longer in peril. His politeness was matched only by his revenge, and the coup was carefully planned. On the day of the opening, or perhaps a few days later, the first issue of a small satirical magazine entitled *The Blind Man* came out. It was announced as the "Independents' Number" on the cover, and it was adorned with a caricature by Alfred Frueh representing a blind man guided through a painting exhibition by his

26. He considered doing it, but the prospect of being alone at his Salon des refusés and the ironic awareness that the Independents' Show already was one held him back. In his letter to Suzanne on April 11, he went on to say: "It was not at all indecent—no reason for refusing it. The committee has decided to refuse to show this thing. I have handed in my resignation, and it will be a bit of gossip of some value in New York. I would like to have a special exhibition of the people who were refused at the Independents—but that would be a redundancy! And the urinal would have been *lonely*." Ibid.

dog.[27] The sarcasm was mild, yet the cover seemed to say that the public is blind to modern art, an opinion echoed in the magazine by the poetess Mina Loy, who stated, "Only artists and serious critics can look at a greyish stickiness on smooth canvas" (p. 7). This opinion apparently reflected that of the professional critics, most of whom considered the general public incapable of making sound judgments and took the absence of a jury, even worse, the hanging in alphabetical order, as a denial of their mission. As Francis Naumann remarks, one of their frequent rationales in discrediting the Indeps was the following: what would happen if magazines accepted everything submitted to them for publica-

27. *The Blind Man* (or *The Blindman,* depending on how one reads the graphic design on the cover), no. 1, is dated April 10, 1917, the day of the show's opening. Henri-Pierre Roché, Duchamp's writer friend from Paris who had arrived in New York in November 1916, signed the editorial, within which he enthusiastically embraced the cause of the Indeps, quoting at length from the Society's program: "The great need, then, is for an exhibition, to be held at a given period each year, where artists of all schools can exhibit together—certain that whatever they send will be hung and that all will have an equal opportunity." All contributions to *The Blind Man* sincerely rejoiced at the prospect of "equal opportunity" given to artists of all schools, even to those, as Roché said, "who might as well never have painted at all" (p. 5). The tone of sincerity that runs through the magazine is important, because it is precisely sincerity that was invoked to forgive in advance every possible extravagance and clumsiness (as it would still be, after the event, what might excuse Richard Mutt in the eyes of Katherine Dreier). (See Camfield's discussion of Dreier's letter to William Glackens, dated April 26, in "Marcel Duchamp's *Fountain,*" p. 74.) Roché made it very clear: "Never say of a man: 'He is not sincere.' Nobody knows if he is or not. . . . Rather say: 'I do not understand him.' The Blind Man takes it for granted that all are sincere" (p. 6). However, given the irony implied by the magazine's title and Frueh's caricature, one wonders whether one should not apply to Roché himself the warning he gave to his readers: "Nobody knows if he is [sincere] or not." I think not. Like everybody else in his milieu, Roché was genuinely thrilled at the sudden freedom granted to artists. But he might have been ironic when, quoting from the Society's program again, he said: "For the public, this exhibition will make it possible to form an idea of the state of contemporary art." Whereas the artists were assumed to be sincere, the public was assumed to be blind.

tion?[28] With this remark as background, R. Mutt's sweet revenge begins to appear. *The Blind Man,* Independents' Number, had been concocted by a merry threesome nowhere identified as such: Henri-Pierre Roché, Beatrice Wood, and Marcel Duchamp.[29] Significantly, however, the readers were called upon to make the next number. This "notice" (or was it a "warning"?) was printed on the cover: "The second number of The Blind Man will appear as soon as YOU have sent sufficient material for it." And Roché's editorial explained what the procedure was to be: "The Blind Man's procedure shall be that of referendum. He will publish the questions and answers sent to him He will print what the artists and the public have to say. He is very keen to receive suggestions and criticisms. So, don't spare him" (p. 4). The editors would exert no selection on the articles. Just as anyone having paid his or her six-dollar dues would become an artist in the Society, so—as Beatrice Wood recalls in her memoirs—anyone having contributed four dollars toward the budget of *The Blind Man* would become an art critic.[30] The second issue came out around May 6, when the show closed, and this time its editors were identified on the cover, but with three initials as cryptic and pseudonymous as the "R." in R. Mutt: P. B. T., standing for (Henri-) Pierre (Roché), Beatrice (Wood) and Totor, diminutive of Victor, the nickname Roché had given to Duchamp. On the cover, there was a reproduction of Duchamp's *Chocolate Grinder,* which the hanging committee would certainly have accepted, and inside the magazine (pp 4–5) an unsigned contribution entitled "The Richard Mutt Case" revealed the mysterious R. Mutt's first name. Though it was probably Beatrice Wood who wrote

28. Naumann, "The Big Show, Part II," p. 50.

29. No editor's name appeared on the cover. For reasons of legal liability, however, the last page carried the information, "Published by Henri Pierre Roché," in spite of the fact that Roché, not being an American citizen or an immigrant, was in no position to be legally liable. In the trio's initial project, Beatrice Wood was to stand alone as publisher but was forbidden to do so by her father, infuriated at the prospect that she would put her name onto "such filth."

30. Naumann, "I Shock Myself," p. 136.

the piece more or less under Duchamp's dictation (and rather more than less),[31] it was supposed to have been written by "a reader" (thus, by a visitor to the show), who was blind, since he or she had not been able to see the urinal, but who nevertheless authenticated Mr. Mutt's signature by completing his first name, thereby making the hitherto unknown artist into an unrecognized artist.[32]

---

31. Wood, *I Shock Myself,* p. 31. According to other sources, it was Arensberg who wrote "The Richard Mutt Case" (see Alice Goldfarb Marquis, *Marcel Duchamp: Eros, C'est la Vie, A Biography* (Troy, N.Y.: Whitston, 1981), pp. 163–164). When asked in writing, Duchamp was very cautious not to reveal the identity of the editorial's writer, referring simply to "the editors," as for example in his response to one of Serge Stauffer's questions (Marcel Duchamp, *Die Schriften,* ed. and trans. Serge Stauffer [Zurich: Regenbogen-Verlag, 1981], p. 280). But the oral interview for the British Arts Council is very telling. Sylvester and Hamilton really grilled him, insisting that the editorial's style and syntax read like his and not like somebody's whose mother tongue is English. "Oh, sure," Duchamp kept answering, rather mockingly. The interviewers wanted to know who really formulated the idea, "He chose it." Duchamp: "It's the writer who said that, 'He chose it.'" Hamilton: "You say you didn't write it, you say it was by an editorial board, but it has your language, even has your accent." Duchamp: "Oh sure, I agreed with it of course, he chose 'I chose it,' yes." Sylvester: "But that answer was not written by you?" Duchamp: "We were doing the magazine together. I did not actually write it, no. I would have said 'I chose it' and instead I said 'He chose it.'" This is marvelous proof that concealment and humor can make someone produce the most revealing slips of the tongue: if the sentence "He chose it" was itself chosen by the editorial's writer, then it was a readymade, and so, who could the writer have been, if not . . . Richard Mutt? Hence: "he chose '*I* chose it,' yes," and: "instead *I* said 'He chose it.'" A little further down in the interview, Duchamp finally said, "it was Louise Varèse who wrote it in fact." Especially in view of the sudden gender transformation of the editorial's writer, one really has the impression that he gave his interviewers the first plausible answer that came to his mind simply to get them off his back. Louise Varèse (Louise Norton, at the time) was a likely candidate, since it is she who wrote the article "Buddha of the Bathroom," which starts right under the editorial.

32. The first name Richard was of course known to all the insiders who had seen the urinal, since it was written in full on the entry card attached to the object (and visible in Stieglitz's

So, someone apparently knew this R. Mutt from Philadelphia. *The Blind Man's* readership learned that his name was not Ralph or Robert but Richard. Whereas very few people knew or even guessed that Mutt was in fact Duchamp, quite a few people had made the association with the famous cartoon characters Mutt and Jeff and had drawn the conclusion that the urinal must have been a joke.[33] But now the joker became somebody, acquired an identity, proved that he had friends and defenders among the readers-writers of *The Blind Man*. More and more, his case resembled that of Louis Eilshemius, who was showing two paintings at the Independents', entitled *Supplication* and *The Gossips*.[34] Eilshemius was quite a character in the New York artworld. Born in 1864 into a wealthy family, this skilled painter in the Hudson River tradition, influenced by Corot, Innes, and Ryder, gradually fell into pathetic dementia and delusions of grandeur following a tragic love affair in his youth. In spite of promising débuts in 1887 and 1888, thereafter he was systematically turned down by the National Academy. By 1910–1912 he was poor; his style had become hallucinatory and repetitive, his subject matter obsessed with impotent

photograph); it had also made its way into a few of the press reports that had mentioned the existence of an inside scandal at the Indeps. However, not only were these reports rare in number, the majority of them had Mutt's identity misspelled altogether as "J. C. Mutt," one even as "Jeff Mutt." (See Camfield, "Marcel Duchamp's *Fountain*," p. 88 n. 16.)

33. With her characteristic lack of humor and her eagerness to rehabilitate R. Mutt, should he prove his sincerity, Katherine Dreier complained about this in her letter to Glackens: "I told Covert and Arensberg that in my judgment Richard Mutt caused the greatest confusion by signing a name which is known to the whole newspaper world as a practical joker. 'Mutt and Jeff' are too famous not to make people suspect, if their name is used, that the matter may be a joke." (Quoted by Naumann, "The Big Show, Part I," p. 39 n. 16.)

34. Both paintings are dated 1916. *The Gossips* was bought by the Musée du Jeu de Paume in Paris following Eilshemius's one and only European show at Durand-Ruel's in 1932. *Supplication* (which will come under discussion here) is an oil on cardboard, 61 × 40.5 in., representing a chunky female nude, presently in the collection of Mr. Roy R. Neuberger, New York. Its full title, *Rose-Marie Calling (Supplication),* has an amusing Duchampian ring.

eroticism, and his technique crude and uncontrolled. With sometimes surprisingly fresh directness, he began painting his deranged visions on roughly cut pieces of cardboard, lids of cigar boxes, and the like, unaware of the vague kinship of his work with the recent experiments of fauvism and cubism. After being rejected from the Armory Show in 1913, his previously mild paranoia took a more aggressive turn, and he soon became a celebrity of sorts, notorious for touring the New York galleries, hurling invectives at anything they were showing, especially modern art, and handing out extravagant pamphlets in which he claimed his unrecognized genius. Self-proclaimed "painter, poet, musician, inventor, linguist, mystic, educator, prophet, etc." (as one of those pamphlets stated), he was constantly bombarding the critics, especially Henry McBride at the *New York Sun,* with complaint letters, of course to no avail. Everybody gossiped about him, nobody took him seriously, no gallery was showing him.[35] With the Independents, he was at last given a chance to proclaim himself an artist to the entire universe and to demonstrate his mighty talents. He grabbed it twice, since he participated in the show and since *Supplication* was reproduced in *The Blind Man.* Moreover, truthful to Roché's promise that *The Blind Man* "will print what the artists and the public have to say," the editors granted him an interview. He was at last vindicated.

But Eilshemius's interview in *The Blind Man* demands closer attention. It was published under the French title "Pas de commentaires! Louis M. Eilshemius," and it strikes a note quite different from everything else in the magazine. The "reader" who sent it in was Mina Loy, the poetess, occasional painter (she had a piece at the Indeps), and mistress of Arthur Cravan. She was close to the editorial group, P. B. T.—perhaps, after all, no closer than Louise Norton or Clara Tice, but still her role seems to have been more pointed than that of other "readers." She had been the only contributor to the first issue of *The Blind Man* beside P. B. T. themselves; in a very interesting piece, she had protested against

35. See Paul J. Karlstrom, *Louis Michel Eilshemius* (New York: Abrams, 1978); see also William Schack, *And He Sat among the Ashes* (New York: American Artists Group, 1939).

"Education . . . [which] demands an art that is only acknowledgeable by way of diluted comparisons," and she had advocated "pure uneducated seeing" as the only vital—alas, only remotely probable—meeting point between "The Artist" and "The Public" (p. 7). In the second issue she conducted the interview with Eilshemius and wrapped it in some critical comments of her own, the title "Pas de commentaires!" notwithstanding. Not surprisingly, what she sees in Eilshemius is a true "naïf" blessed with "pure uneducated seeing": "He is so virginally the way a picture must be painted by one unsullied by any preconception of how pictures are painted, so direct a presentation of his cerebral vision, that . . . his pictures, if one may say so, are instantaneous photographs of his mind at any given moment of inspiration" (p. 11). Yet the very construction of her text belies this seemingly genuine enthusiasm. Her flattering comments are abruptly interlarded with excerpts from the interview in such a way that Eilshemius, whom she compares to an American Douanier Rousseau, appears grossly naïve indeed. The text continues with the artist boasting to her: "'I am very broad-minded,' said Eilshemius, 'I like everything that is nice, everything,' smiling benignly, 'that is *nice* you understand. I can paint anything, anywhere, beautiful pictures on your hat or your dress, if you like!'" When we bear in mind that "anybody being allowed to paint anything, presumably anywhere, and to show it" was precisely the formula *a/b* of the Independents' self-legitimation, we tend to think that Eilshemius is here being quoted for no purpose other than to prove the ridiculousness of such pretensions, and that *Supplication,* which *The Blind Man* reproduced, presumably, as an "instantaneous photograph" of the artist's "mind at any given moment of inspiration," is here being framed—in both senses of the word—as an ironic proof of comical self-indulgence. It is hard not to read Mina Loy's article as if her pen had been at times held by another hand, almost sarcastic in a deadpan fashion. Consider the following passage, in which Eilshemius's mad ambition is simply sandwiched between two admiring lines by Mina Loy as if nothing peculiar had happened: "Hopefully inspired by the granite simplicity of the painter's speech I asked him if he ever wrote. 'Don't you know who I am?', he gasped. 'Louis M. Eilshemius, M.A., Supreme Protean Marvel of the Ages. The Peer of all who create

Painting, Literature and Music.' As I am used to do in reading I found by intuition the finest passages while skimming the volumes handed to me" (p. 11). And she goes on to cite these "finest passages," one bland poem after another, until, with no transition whatsoever, she abruptly concludes her piece with this line: "Anyhow, Duchamp meditating the levelling of all values, witnesses the elimination of Sophistication" (p. 12).

This is quite a comment with which to end a piece entitled "Pas de commentaires," and there is little doubt in my mind as to whose very sophisticated hand was guiding Mina Loy's pen when she wrote it. She virtually acknowledged his identity in her conclusion. Eilshemius's rehabilitation was the exclusive and cruel work of Marcel Duchamp, who had announced on opening night that, together with Dorothy Rice's *Claire Twins, Supplication* was the best painting in the show. I said "cruel" and perhaps I should qualify this. From all historical accounts, it seems that it was in all honesty and without guile that Duchamp, apparently joined in his opinion by artists as diverse as Lachaise, Stella, Demuth, and Walkowitz, "declared the paintings of this artist to be delightful and comforting in their simplicity."[36] The fact that Duchamp gave Eilshemius the very

36. This is not a verbatim account. It is taken from an unpublished obituary of Eilshemius, written right after his death, in December 1941, by Marsden Hartley. It is worth quoting at length, for it shows that the effect of Duchamp's praise of Eilshemius, whether sincere or not, was objectively albeit indirectly cruel:

> The fallacy, to my mind, and I may be completely wrong—in the Elshemius [sic] case—came in at the moment when Duchamp—quite harmlessly and surely without pose—declared the paintings of this artist to be delightful and comforting in their simplicity. It is quite reasonable—all this—in view of the all but exhausting hair-splitting of the eclectics in Paris, that this quiet and unpretentious art should have so appealed to the weary intellect of this important modern painter who turned several lesser careers away by his forceful personality and left them stranded. . . . Those who overheard Duchamp speak of the charm and quiet distinction of Elshemius' output took the simple and natural remark and made it into a comme il faut snobbism. A cult grew up—

first one-man show at the Société Anonyme in 1920, and a second one-man show in 1924—a unique event in the history of the Société—apparently confirms his initial praise. But such generosity makes Duchamp's judgment on Eilshemius in 1917 appear like aesthetic admiration only in hindsight. It was uttered on the spur of the moment, amidst the brouhaha of the opening, and on the very day of his resignation over the Richard Mutt affair. I cannot help but think that it was tinged with derision and revenge. By 1920, Eilshemius was already the victim of the fad that had seized his work and for which Duchamp was mainly responsible. I suspect that there is more remorse than admiration entering his strangely unabated support of the poor Eilshemius from then on, and also the awareness, which only supreme artists can reach, of how thin is the line between genius and self-delusion. More than anyone else, Duchamp understood how to convert personal failure into authentic artistic success, and he must have wished that Eilshemius, who obviously lacked it, had the same understanding. The steady public support of an artist who so blatantly had the wrong mixture of naïveté and ambition from an artist who clearly had the right one is incomprehensible without that background of remorse and, by 1920, of genuine compassion. In 1943, two years after Eilshemius's death, in the sober notice he wrote on the artist for the catalogue of the Société Anonyme, Duchamp said: "In Eilshemius we face a tragedy which, although comparable to

---

> which continued until the day of Elshemius' death—and it quite possibly may go on with always something of an arrogant aroma about it. It would probably have been better if Elshemius had not heard this praise—as it did more harm than good and most likely settled once and for all Elshemius' Jehova complex about himself. (*Louis Elshemius* [not an uncommon misspelling], autograph manuscript by Marsden Hartley, The Yale Collection of American Literature, Beinecke Rare Book and Manuscript Library, Yale University)

I am indebted to Patricia C. Willis for allowing quotation of this excerpt. My very special thanks go to Jerry Ferguson, who is a connoisseur of both Eilshemius and Duchamp. A long conversation with him convinced me that careful psychology was needed to understand the evolution of Duchamp's sentiments for Eilshemius over time and not betray them.

that of many artists, nevertheless takes an acute form for us, helpless witnesses to his long struggle."[37] The remorse can still be read between the lines, veiled by a slight hypocrisy. But there is true empathy as well. The erotic mythology behind Eilshemius's work is not unlike that behind the *Large Glass,* and one senses that Duchamp is acknowledging kinship: if he had just been blessed with ever-adolescent naïveté rather than cursed with a keen sense of irony, Eilshemius's tragic destiny might have been his own. But this is 1943, long after Eilshemius's downfall into squalor, physical handicap and a lonely death.[38] In 1917 Duchamp could not have anticipated the extent of the tragedy. But he could have—and in my opinion, had—understood that Eilshemius, despite and perhaps because of his unreflexive authenticity, was not equipped to make art of real ambition. Yet his inflated pretensions were well-known, and when Du-

---

37. *SS,* p. 148. Whereas Duchamp's remorse is veiled, other people, notably Henry McBride, who had received more self-advertising *supplications* than any other critic, made their belated recognition of Eilshemius quite public. After visiting his second show at the Société Anonyme, McBride wrote (in the *Evening Sun,* April 19, 1924) an absurdly overcompensating confession in which he said: "Eilshemius's work already takes a place ahead of both Fuller and Blakelock. This, I must confess, is both a pleasure and a shock to myself for when I realize that when I accuse the public of neglect of this genius . . . I accuse myself also. . . . Suddenly, like another Saint Paul, I see a great light, and the scales drop from my eyes. The pictures in the Anonyme gallery are completely lovely." ("The Société Anonyme Discovers Eilshemius," quoted in Karlstrom, *Louis Michel Eilshemius,* pp. 35–36.)

38. Following his two shows at the Société Anonyme, Eilshemius enjoyed a short-lived artistic success. For the first time in his life, a dealer, Valentine Dudensing, gave him a one man-show in 1926, and another one in 1932, which earned him the honor of being exhibited at Durand-Ruel's in Paris and of being praised by Matisse as "un artiste avec vrai talent." But that very same year, he was struck by a car and left paralyzed from the waist down. From then on, he could not leave his room and his decline was steady. Though the Metropolitan Museum bought a canvas in 1933, he was more often than not robbed by cynical collectors who plundered his studio and paid him barely enough to pay the gas bill. He died on December 29, 1941, twelve days after having been transferred to the psychiatric section of Bellevue Hospital.

champ proclaimed that *Supplication* was the best painting at the Indeps, equal only to Dorothy Rice's *Claire Twins,* it was a cruel and ironic compliment. One need only glance at the grotesque *Claire Twins* to be convinced of this. In the climate of worship surrounding him Duchamp's verdicts were oracles, so that thanks to him Eilshemius got his fifteen minutes of fame and became a footnote in art history books. The poor Eilshemius was being manipulated, and it was Richard Mutt, alias Marcel Duchamp, who was pulling the strings.

In 1917, and only then, the Independents published two catalogues, one illustrated, the other not. For the price of four dollars—the same sum required for publication in *The Blind Man*—all members could have one of their works on view reproduced in the illustrated catalogue, and thereby make history. Sure enough, Eilshemius saw to it that *Supplication* was reproduced. Thus it was shown three times: in the show, where the painting was claimed to be art by the painter; in *The Blind Man,* where it was "selected" by the critics; and in the catalogue, where it was posing for posterity. *Fountain,* the work sent in by R. Mutt, was ushered out of the show and was not cited, let alone reproduced, in the catalogue. Everything was done to prevent it from making history. Word went around but the press didn't bother to really investigate, and the show ended without incident. Only with the epilogue did *The Blind Man* open "The Richard Mutt Case." But the party was over and a scandal at the Indeps would have been stale news, if it reached the press at all. The circulation of the little magazine was confidential and its distribution inefficient; its content smacked of jokes and its editors were not credible. Duchamp, who even then still concealed Richard Mutt's true identity, graciously remained aloof from the whole affair. He knew that his "bathroom fixture" would not land in the dustbin of history. He had arranged that "The Richard Mutt Case" be accompanied by a photographic reproduction that revealed what kind of bathroom fixture it actually was. To make sure the photograph referred to *Fountain by R. Mutt,* it was captioned as *The exhibit refused by the independents*, and duly credited to its author: *Photograph by Alfred Stieglitz.*

More Facts: Richard Mutt and Alfred Stieglitz

The manipulation of Eilshemius was merely cruel, but that of Stieglitz was a stroke of genius. The Stieglitz gang and the Arensberg gang didn't mingle much at the time; Duchamp was not on such good terms with Stieglitz; and from Duchamp's circle, only Picabia was a close friend of the photographer. Nevertheless, not only did Stieglitz take a photograph of the *Fountain,* but he also contributed a letter to *The Blind Man,* dated April 13, where he maintained that all entries to the Independents should be anonymous, and on the 19th he wrote to Henry McBride, the *Sun's* critic: "I wonder whether you could manage to drop in at 291 Friday some time. I have, at the request of Roché, Covert, Miss Wood, Duchamp & Co., photographed the rejected Fountain. You may find the photograph of some use. It will amuse you to see it. The Fountain is here too."[39] Apparently McBride didn't take his cue, nor did he react to a similar letter from Charles Demuth, who had tried to attract the critic's attention to the Society's betrayal of their principles and had given him other important clues, namely Duchamp's and Richard Mutt's (actually Louise Norton's) telephone numbers.[40] All this confirms that not only McBride but also Stieglitz were unaware of Richard Mutt's real identity.[41] Beatrice Wood recalls that Stieglitz agreed to photograph the *Fountain* "at Marcel's request," but it was probably thanks to her intervention, for she recorded in her diary entry for

39. Quoted by Naumann, "The Big Show, Part I," p. 39, n. 22.

40. "A piece of scultor [sic], called: 'a Fountain,' was entered by one of our friends for the Independent Exhibition now open at the Grand Central Palace. It was not exhibited. 'The Independents,' we are now told have a committee, or jury, who can decide, 'for the good of the exhibition . . .' If you think you could do anything with this material for your Sunday article we would appreciate it very much. . . . P.S. If you wish any more information please phone, Marcel Duchamp, 4225 Columbus, or, Richard Mutte [sic], 9255 Schuyler." (Demuth to McBride, quoted by Camfield, "Marcel Duchamp's *Fountain,*" p. 72.)

41. Camfield, citing an unpublished letter from Stieglitz to Georgia O'Keeffe, adds that "Stieglitz was also led to think that the urinal had been submitted by a young woman, probably at the instigation of Duchamp" (ibid., p. 91, n. 39).

April 13: "See Stieglitz about 'Fountain.'"[42] In any case, "Duchamp & Co." appear only last on the list of names Stieglitz mentioned in his letter to McBride. His complicity in the Richard Mutt case is all the more startling when we remember that, at the time, he tended to consider Duchamp as a charlatan. But according to Beatrice Wood, again, he "was greatly amused" and "felt it was important to fight bigotry in America. He took great pains with the lighting, and did it with such skill that a shadow fell across the urinal suggesting a veil."[43] As William Camfield has demonstrated, he photographed the urinal in front of a painting by Marsden Hartley entitled *The Warriors*, setting its smooth curve against a similar ogival shape and flanking it by two flags in the painting, a mise-en-scène certainly meant to symbolize his fight against "bigotry in America."[44] The surprising thing about this photograph is not so much that Stieglitz annexed the urinal to his own aesthetics of symbolist correspondences—he did that even with the works he was showing at 291—but that Duchamp let him do it. And when, thanks to that photograph, the piece was redubbed "Buddha or Madonna of the Bathroom"—associations hardly congenial to Duchamp's own aesthetics and in any case quite alien to the testing of the Independents' liberalism, which was the real purpose of the urinal—he didn't bat an eye. He could afford to let "the viewers make the pictures" and Stieglitz turn a urinal into a Buddha, since his own strategy was of a very different nature. Stieglitz was to play a quite involuntary role in it.

Why did Duchamp go to the trouble of calling on Stieglitz for a photograph in the first place, when the natural thing to do, if he simply wanted a

42. Ibid., p. 74. Wood's recollection that Stieglitz agreed to photograph the *Fountain* "at Marcel's request" is in *I Shock Myself*, p. 30.

43. Wood, *I Shock Myself*, p. 30.

44. Though the question is open as to whether or not it also meant to convey indirectly Stieglitz's secret pro-German sympathies. A few days after America's entry into the war, the choice of a painting entitled *The Warriors*, done by Marsden Hartley—who had pro-German sympathies of his own (he had been homosexually involved with a German officer and had expressed his fascination with German insignia in his paintings)—hardly seems coincidental.

photograph, was to go to Man Ray? Man Ray was then making a living photographing works of art for various artists, and he had already photographed some readymades for Duchamp. But this is precisely the point: Duchamp needed someone to take a picture of the urinal who didn't know who its author was, and Man Ray had probably been Duchamp's accomplice all along in this affair, together with Arensberg. Perhaps it was he who took the only two photographs of the urinal besides Stieglitz's that we have, and in which we see it hanging in Duchamp's studio. Anyway, Duchamp didn't call on his friend. Neither did he turn to just any photographer. The photographer had to be Stieglitz for another reason: he was the owner of The Little Galleries of the Photo-Secession, otherwise known as Gallery 291. Located at 291 Fifth Avenue, Stieglitz's gallery, which he had opened in 1905, was far more than just another commercial art gallery, and its owner was not a mere photographer, admittedly even a famous one. In the early days of the Photo-Secession and of its magazine, *Camera Work* (which he had founded in 1903), Stieglitz had launched a number of major photographers such as Edward Steichen, his friend and associate, Gertrude Käsebier, and Clarence White, and had done a lot for the recognition of photography as an art form, deliberately alternating shows of photography and of painting. He had introduced America to Rodin's watercolors and to Matisse's drawings and had exhibited, among other European masters, Cézanne, Toulouse-Lautrec, and Rousseau. He had discovered the new, modernist, Europeanized and "post-Armory Show" generation of American artists: Alfred Maurer, Marsden Hartley, Max Weber, and his favorites, the "Big Three": John Marin, Arthur Dove, and his future wife, Georgia O'Keeffe. When Duchamp turned to him, in 1917, he had just discovered Paul Strand, whose "machine aesthetics" might very well have prepared him to look at a urinal with an unprejudiced eye. In any case, one can be certain that if Duchamp addressed Stieglitz, it was not just to obtain a photograph. The photograph had to be signed, and what better signature than that of Stieglitz, the artist, the maker of the American avant-garde, the former honorary vice-president of the Armory Show, the prestigious and irascible guru of 291, which one admirer had called "an oasis of freedom, a rest when wearied, a stimulant when dulled, a negation of preconceptions, a forum for wisdom and folly, a safety valve for repressed ideas"?[45]

Stieglitz agreed to take the picture, and his defense of Richard Mutt proved to be absolutely candid. He was sincerely shocked that the Independents were betraying the principles they had set for themselves, and when he leaked the information to McBride, he enjoyed repaying them in their own coin. For Stieglitz believed in the independence of the Independents. He was participating in the show with two already famous photographs, *The Steerage* and *The Hand of Man,* and his complete gallery stable was accompanying him: John Marin, Charles Demuth, and Arthur Dove, as well as Marsden Hartley and Georgia O'Keeffe, whose initiation fees he had paid himself. Stieglitz was elitist and purist when it came to his own gallery, but he was a libertarian when it came to group shows. On the aesthetic level he didn't expect much from them, but he had already learned from the Armory Show that they were beneficial to the cause of modern art in America. The letter he contributed to *The Blind Man* one or two days before he was contacted by "Roché, Covert, Miss Wood, Duchamp & Co." (the only letter, by the way, that appears to have been a straight and earnest response to Roché's invitation to comment on the Indeps) is extremely telling. When he asked whether it wouldn't "be advisable next year during the exhibition, to withhold the names of the makers of all work shown" (p. 15), he was stating his ethics, not defending his aesthetics. For the latter he had *Camera Work* and 291. In his gallery he was a dealer and the defender of a certain taste. Here he was a moralist: "In thus freeing the exhibition of the traditions and superstitions of names the Society would not be playing into the hands of dealers and critics, nor even into the hands of the artists

45. The admirer was the financier Eugene Meyer, Jr., who contributed in 1914 to an issue of *Camera Work* entirely devoted to people's comment about what 291 meant to them. (Quoted in Sue Davidson Lowe, *Stieglitz, A Memoir/Biography* [New York: Farrar Straus Giroux, 1983], p. 157.)

themselves." In such an anonymous system, he seemed to imply, a Richard Mutt affair would not occur. An artist relying on pseudonyms and jokes in order to stir up a scandal would be as unlikely as an artist banking on his already acquired fame. Rather, "each bit of work would stand on its own merits. As a reality. . . . The Independent Exhibition should be run for one thing only: The independence of the work itself." And he concluded his piece by thus completing the Independents' motto: "No jury—no prizes—no commercial tricks."

How ironic! This was written on April 13. The next day or the day after, Stieglitz fell prey to a particularly shrewd institutional (if not commercial) trick, one that far from freeing the unknown R. Mutt's entry from the "superstition of names" would bestow on it the authority of the photographer's—and art dealer's—own name and fame. Stieglitz understood no more than Eilshemius that Duchamp was using him. By photographing the *Fountain,* by inviting McBride to come to see it in his gallery, he was actually endorsing it in a roundabout way, as though it had been exhibited at 291, as though Duchamp had been among his protégés instead of compromising himself with minor artists such as Rockwell Kent or teaming up with clowns such as Arensberg and Man Ray.[46] Though Stieglitz was amused at the prospect of sanctifying the rejected *Fountain,* turning it into a Buddha or a Madonna, he didn't realize that in doing precisely that he was giving it the aura of a full-fledged work of art and that, by veiling the urinal with his own symbolist taste, he was shifting his defense of Richard Mutt from ethical to aesthetic ground. Stieglitz didn't understand that the function of the urinal's photograph was not to feed an immediate press scandal but to put *Fountain,* whose very existence could be doubted were it not for this photograph, on the record for subsequent art history.

46. Carl Van Vechten went even further. In a letter to Gertrude Stein, he actually said that "Stieglitz *is exhibiting* the object at '291' and he has made some wonderful photographs of it." (Quoted in Camfield, "Marcel Duchamp's *Fountain,*" p. 75; emphasis mine.)

DEMONSTRATION?

There it is, on the record, in art history books. Stieglitz's photograph concludes the transformation of the Richard Mutt case into a *fait accompli*. A/b and a'/b', in and by themselves merely two *collisions* between an object and an institution, two encounters which in *appearance* cannot be equated to each other, are tied together in the equation of their *apparition:* $a/b = a'/b'$. This equation shows itself to be true, provided one notices that it is established only through the intervention of *several collisions seeming strictly to succeed each other according to certain laws* or rather, according to a single law, which is nothing but the *algebraic comparison* itself. Let us envisage the following chain of *collisions*. Since the editorial board of *The Blind Man* mimics and parodies the democratic rule of the Independents' hanging committee, Eilshemius's painting, *Supplication,* as shown in the exhibition, is equivalent to its reproduction as shown in *The Blind Man*. Both relations are legitimate in the eyes of their respective committees. The formula of the first *collision* would thus read:[47]

$$\frac{\textit{Supplication}}{\text{N.Y. Indeps}} = \frac{\textit{Reproduction of Supplication}}{\text{The Blind Man}}$$

Since *The Blind Man* prints the reproduction of *Supplication* and the photograph of *Fountain* on equal footing, as well as, by the way, Joseph Stella's *Coney Island* and Marcel Duchamp's *Chocolate Grinder,* the respective relations of both reproductions to their medium are equivalent. Thus, the formula of the second *collision* would be:

$$\frac{\textit{Reproduction of Supplication}}{\text{The Blind Man}} = \frac{\textit{Photograph of Fountain}}{\text{The Blind Man}}$$

47. In the formulas, objects shall be in italics, institutions in roman characters.

Since Stieglitz, who is the author of the photograph, falls into the trap and more or less unwittingly endorses Richard Mutt, the legitimation of the object "Photograph by Alfred Stieglitz" by P. B. T., the editorial board of the magazine, is equivalent to that of the object that is its referent, *Fountain,* by Gallery 291. So we would have:

$$\frac{\textit{Photograph of Fountain}}{\text{The Blind Man}} = \frac{\textit{Fountain}}{291}$$

It follows, in algebra (even in "amusing" algebra, $a/b = a'/b'$ can be rewritten as $a/a' = b/b'$), that *Supplication* by Louis Eilshemius is to *Fountain* by Richard Mutt what the Society of Independent Artists is to the Gallery 291:

$$\frac{\textit{Supplication}}{\textit{Fountain}} = \frac{\text{N.Y. Indeps}}{291}$$

Such is the *algebraic comparison* that, in the eyes of history, legitimates the difference between putative Art and provocative "non-art," between a self-proclaimed genius and the great *anartist* of the century, between Eilshemius, who claimed that "the artist . . . requires no instructor, no critic, no public, to certify that the result of his efforts is Art"[48] and Duchamp, who said, "it's the viewers who make the pictures." Such a difference, however, is beyond formal or "retinal" appearances. Why would a urinal be better art than a fat nude, even clumsily painted? On its own it is not art at all. Only in its *allegorical appearance* is Richard Mutt's urinal art, and there is no allegory that doesn't refer formal appearance back to the *apparition which is its mold.* And there are differences in the "molds" too—the difference for example between a Society of independent, that is, self-proclaimed, artists and a small, very selective modernist gallery run by a man who is a prominent modernist artist himself. Yet this difference

48. Quoted in Schack, *And He Sat among the Ashes,* p. 222.

on its own is no guarantee either. Why would a democratic grouping of free individuals produce art of ipso facto inferior quality to that which has been screened by the trained eye of a dealer less interested in commerce than in purist aesthetics? The *algebraic comparison* requires that all four elements of the equation be balanced against each other, and this comparison is anything but "diluted," as Mina Loy had said in her diatribe against education. To acknowledge *Fountain* as (good) art is not to compare it visually to the art of the past, and to reject *Supplication* as bad painting is not to despise "pure uneducated seeing." Rather, it is to take stock of differences in strategies: that of Eilshemius is wishful thinking blown up to the dimension of a social event from which it hopes to profit; that of Duchamp is cunning manipulation shrinking to the size of a ready-made photograph in which it finds a repository. The difference legitimated by the algebraic comparison is the split between tradition and the avant-garde, when the historical context (to which the institutions, but also the psychological destinies, belong) is such that tradition can only deteriorate and lay itself open to ridicule, and that the avant-garde can be significant only when it takes it upon itself to show precisely this. The algebraic comparison does not compare aesthetic objects to one another, and it does not simply switch contexts. It refers the objects to the contexts and vice versa, and it points to a difference that is one of objects in contexts, and that can be attributed neither to the objects (a and a') and their visual properties nor to the contexts (b and b') and their institutional determinations. Such a difference is beyond naming, yet it is articulated on either side of a pure signifier of difference, the one that the *Green Box* called *the sign (/) which separates a and b, the sign of the accordance*. What is not beyond naming, or description, however, is the strategy through which the split between tradition and the avant-garde found its legitimation in the equal sign (=) that forces comparison between incomparable objects by contriving a substitution of institutional contexts. The foolish Eilshemius was made a fool and Stieglitz was fooled. As a result, *Fountain* passed the test. The presence of *Supplication* at the Indeps ridiculed tradition and made it look like a joke by contrast—or comparison—to that of *Fountain* at 291, which, conversely, entered a joke into tradition and made it look like art: $a/b = a'/b'$. Which was to be demonstrated.

Still More Facts: Richard Mutt and the Ash Can School Alumni

Well, not quite yet. It is not logically correct that the enigmatic *sign of the accordance* should be one of separation, and it is not morally right that it should be read out of a fool's bargain. One should distrust any *fait accompli*. It is always the result of a bid for power. Perhaps the law of the strongest is always the best, but it is not, for all that, the most legitimate. When written like this, the history of the avant-garde would merely be the history of the victors. How many smartasses in Duchamp's wake have not banked on that, at the expense of how many Eilshemiuses who were deserving of better? Now, there's been a coup: Duchamp was all trick, guile, and irony. He put everyone in his pocket, and he could afford to. After all, he was not merely the anonymous R. Mutt, he was also Totor, or Victor, an institution unto himself. As Henri-Pierre Roché recalled in his memoirs, "At that time, Marcel Duchamp's reputation in New York as a Frenchman was equalled only by Napoleon and Sarah Bernhardt."[49] All exaggeration aside, it remains that Duchamp enjoyed a reputation far out of proportion with what people knew of his work. It had actually preceded him: when he arrived in New York in June 1915, he was already, even for the general public ignorant of his name, "the man who had painted the *Nude Descending a Staircase*."[50] The painting raised a scandal and drew considerable success at the

---

49. Henri-Pierre Roché, "Souvenirs of Marcel Duchamp," in Lebel, *Marcel Duchamp,* p. 79.

50. Pierre Cabanne: "Did you think about what you represented at that period for Americans?" Marcel Duchamp: "Not very much. The tiresome thing was that every time I met someone, they would say: 'Oh! Are you the one who did that painting?' The funniest thing is that for at least thirty or forty years the painting was known, but I wasn't. Nobody knew my name. In the continental American sense of the word, 'Duchamp' meant nothing. There was no connection between the painting and me." P.C.: "No one connected the scandal and its author?" M.D.: "Not at all. They didn't care. When they met me they said, 'Well, fine!' but there were only three or four who knew who I was, whereas everyone had seen the painting or reproductions, without knowing who had painted it. I really lived over there without being bothered by the painting's popularity, hiding behind it, obscured. I had been

Armory Show in 1913: it was mocked and caricatured by the press; it was hailed and stigmatized as the last word in cubism and futurism combined; and it became the emblem of the extravagances of modern art as a whole. It is this celebrity that earned Duchamp an institutional position in the Society and from which the twenty founders hoped to benefit. John Sloan, Maurice Prendergast, and William Glackens had brought to the Society the already stale prestige of the Ash Can School, to which Rockwell Kent, George Bellows, and Charles Prendergast could add reputations consolidated in its wake. The dedicated Walter Pach contributed, with his undisputed role as the great mediator in the organization of the Armory Show; John Covert had a modest fame as a cubist and the privilege of being Arensberg's cousin; Joseph Stella held the prestige of being the only American futurist; and John Marin, one of the first American painters to have been given a one man-show at 291, was the favorite among Stieglitz's "Big Three." Jacques Villon had been enrolled in his absence (if at all) by his brother, and Albert Gleizes, the only European with Duchamp and Picabia to have been actively involved in the foundation of the Society, represented the orthodox cubism of the Puteaux group.[51] In fact only Duchamp and the friends under his influence, Picabia, Man Ray, and to some extent Morton Schamberg, held promise for the future.

At the root of the Society's creation, there are extremely ambiguous motivations. It was a coalition against the National Academy, and coalitions as always are fraught with all sorts of dissent. It was everyone's desire to perpetuate the

---

completely squashed by the 'Nude.'" P.C.: "Didn't that correspond perfectly to your idea of the artist?" M.D.: "I was enchanted." Pierre Cabanne, *Dialogues with Marcel Duchamp,* trans. Ron Padgett (New York: Viking, 1971), p. 45 (hereinafter indicated as *PC*).

51. This is based on the list counting twenty founders published by Marlor, *Society of Independent Artists,* p. 58. The list, published in the initial notice at the time of the Society's incorporation, counted seventeen founding members, to whom "the three French artists, Gleizes, Picabia and Villon, were added at Marlor's initiative because they were involved in the planning of the Society." (Camfield, "Marcel Duchamp's *Fountain,*" p. 87, n. 10. Camfield cites the complete list and says that he owes this additional piece of information to Marlor himself.)

Armory Show. But what this meant differed radically depending on the various factions involved. Arensberg, who had received the shock of his life there, and his circle, wanted to restage a big hullabaloo. Possibly they hoped that the Richard Mutt case would provide them with such an opportunity. Stieglitz and his circle wanted to give to American cubism and futurism the dignity of high art, in other words, of European art, on a par with Cézanne and Picasso. The Ash Can School alumni—forming the core of the Society's promoters, they were the ones who would reject the urinal—wanted to recuperate, institutionalize, academicize, and repatriate the Armory Show. In 1913, they had been caught unaware and outflanked on their left, so to speak, by the massive invasion of the European avant-gardes. They still resented it in 1916, and it was not without chauvinism that they sought to endow those artists who claimed a moderate and specifically American modernism with the platform denied to them by the even more conservative National Academy. In this context, Duchamp's presence among the founding members was obviously desirable as a display of liberalism, a guarantee of cosmopolitanism, and a token of avant-gardism.[52] There was no better way of perpetuating, in other words, of neutralizing the Armory Show than by trying to secure the imprimatur of the author of the *Nude Descending a Staircase,* presenting him with the presidency of the hanging committee, and hoping that he would honor the show with his participation. The founders, no doubt, expected him to come up with something that would send back an attenuated echo of the *Nude's* scandal at the Armory Show, something surprising but not really shocking, like the *Chocolate Grinder,* for instance.[53] Instead, there came a urinal.

52. "Every school is represented at this salon, from the most conservative to the most radical. . . . [T]he . . . result is assured by the presence among the founders of the Society of distinguished artists who represent every important tendency in contemporary art and who will participate in its exhibitions." From the foreword to the catalogue, quoted by Marlor, *Society of Independent Artists,* p. 8.

53. Or a painting entitled *Tulip Hysteria Co-ordinating,* according to a rumor possibly spread to mislead intentionally and compounded by the press. No entry by Duchamp is listed in the

Duchamp had shown cruelty in manipulating Eilshemius and genius in manipulating Stieglitz, and here he revealed himself to be diabolic. They wanted to trap him; he would make them trip on their own trap. Eilshemius was not the only one to practice wishful thinking. The whole mechanism of self-legitimation of the Society of Independent Artists, Incorporated, was a colossal wish, as if one could, even collectively, proclaim oneself an artist by decree. For the Society was still lacking true legitimation, that is, recognition by others besides its own members. It was torn between two desires that were also two necessities: to see itself legitimated by the past—tradition—but also by the future—the avant-garde. It sought to force the National Academy to recognize it or at least to acknowledge its existence. As with the Armory Show, the adopted strategy was numbers and publicity. But it was also seeking approval from the small purist avant-garde that did not expect anything either from the past or from exchange with the general public, the one on which Stieglitz for example conferred dignity. Here the founders made a gross miscalculation. They could have tried to get Stieglitz more deeply involved—we have seen that he had sympathy for their project—or to enlist Marius de Zayas, Stieglitz's ex-associate and now director of the new Modern Gallery, or perhaps Robert Coady, whose little magazine, *The Soil,* followed a modernist-nationalist line more in tune with their own ideology. Instead, they turned to Arensberg and Duchamp. And in so doing, they laid their demand for legitimation at their feet. What did Duchamp do with this fearsome power? They wanted him to

catalogue, and none at all under that title by any artist (although a certain Ellen Anderson submitted a painting entitled *Tulips* and a certain Rosalie Clements a painting entitled *Early Tulips*). However, it seems that a painting indeed bearing the title *Tulip Hysteria Co-ordinating* was actually shown, since it was reviewed by Jane Dixon in the *New York Sun* as "the most hysterical tulips I ever saw in my life." (See Camfield, "Marcel Duchamp's *Fountain,*" pp. 68, 88 n. 16, and Naumann, "The Big Show, Part I," pp. 37, 39 n. 15.) It is possible that the rumor about *Tulip Hysteria Co-ordinating* was spread by Duchamp, but to me such a title evokes Picabia much more than Duchamp.

cover up an enterprise that smacked of conservative intentions. With his usual courtesy, he bowed to their demand. Even better, he graciously played the role of the eccentric but harmless troublemaker they expected him to play. As we remember, it was he who proposed that the works be hung in alphabetical order. There he was playing the eccentric. But it was also he, so it seems, who had first suggested the motto "No jury, no prizes," which he would soon submit to a drastic test. Here he was preparing his not so harmless revenge: they wanted him to be avant-garde, all right, his alter ego R. Mutt would be avant-garde. But—and here he was diabolically generous, yes, diabolic and generous—in suggesting the motto "No jury, no prizes," he offered to the Indeps the guarantee of tradition, rather, of a tradition. The Society's slogan did not appear out of thin air. Since 1884, "Ni récompense ni jury" had been the motto of the Paris Société des Artistes Indépendants, an institution that was no longer, to say the least, a temple of extravagance in 1917. And so the respectable legitimacy that the New York Independent Artists acquired is not the one they gave themselves but the one they received, through Duchamp, from the Paris Indépendants. The founders were reassured. Actually, they made a point of establishing their pedigree in their founding act, explicitly modeling the newborn institution on its French equivalent, even calling on the authority of Ingres and Renoir. The fact that the pedigree was unabashedly borrowed didn't seem to bother them. Didn't they have Duchamp (and possibly Picabia, Gleizes, and Villon) among them to establish their claim to filiation? The fact that the borrowing itself was a strategy and that they were wearing it on their sleeve didn't bother them either. They didn't even try to conceal that it was primarily institutional, not aesthetic, legitimation that they were after, and commercial, not artistic, success that they sought. Their pamphlet stated: "The latter Society [the Paris Independents], whose salon is the oldest in France, has done more for the advance of French art than any other institution of its period. A considerable number of the most prominent artists of the present generation and the preceding one established their reputations at its annual exhibitions. It has more members, sells more works and is on a firmer financial basis than any other of the four great salons."[54] Being the true Americans they were, the founding members were probably hoping, not entirely wrongly, that quantity would somewhere along the way convert into quality. When the a priori legitimation of this hoped-for conversion was being offered to them by Marcel Duchamp, they eagerly seized the offer. And so the relation a/b, which was founding the Society (and which a while ago I expressed in short through the formula "anything to anybody"), was neither self-legitimated nor self-legitimating; it was inherited from a tradition which, by 1917, had grown more than venerable.

As always, art is legitimated solely by comparison: $a/b = a'/b'$. The substance of the founding act is this: anything that will be shown at the New York Independents is declared in advance to be on a par with everything that was shown at the Paris Indépendants throughout their career. This time the equality of the two relations is blindingly obvious, since the denominator is common. In b, we have "No jury, no prizes," in b', "Ni récompense ni jury." The guarantee of this common denominator, guaranteed in turn by the avant-garde personified by Duchamp, is precisely what led the founders of the Society to believe that they were allowed to conclude in advance that $a = a'$. Richard Mutt would prove them wrong. Comparison is not equality and b is in fact not equal to b'. Only in *appearance* do both slogans translate into one another, and then only if one fails to consider that between their *apparitions* (or advents) thirty-three years had passed, during which the Paris Indépendants had become a very academic institution. Duchamp could not have offered the founders of the Society a better vanguard alibi for their true conservatism. Token avant-garde is what they wanted, token tradition is what they got: the tradition of the avant-garde gone academic. Institutional legitimation is what they wanted, mere institutional legitimacy is what they got: on the aesthetic level the test lay ahead of them. Meanwhile, Duchamp had it behind himself. He knew from

54. From the foreword to the catalogue, quoted by Marlor, *Society of Independent Artists,* p. 7. The same excerpt is also cited by H. P. Roché in the first issue of *The Blind Man* (p. 4), and taken up by at least one reviewer of the show (*The Springfield Republican,* April 15, 1917).

experience that, no matter how much the Independents, in Paris or in New York, had done or would do "for the advancement of French—or American—art," social liberalism is for the true artist just another aesthetic constraint. In other words he knew that, despite the maxim "No jury, no prizes," which seems to forbid aesthetic comparison, the true law of artistic legitimation remains the *algebraic comparison,* which he also knew should not be allowed to bypass the series of *collisions seeming strictly to succeed each other* that articulates it. We must now see this series regress in time in order to then see it fall back onto the Richard Mutt case, by *commissioned symmetries.*[55]

Had Duchamp not actually gone through the experience of the Richard Mutt case, but in a reversed chronological order? He knew better than anyone to what kind of circus he owed his nomination as chairman of the hanging committee. And he knew what scandal means, too. At the Armory Show, the crowd was pouring in to see his *Nude.* An even larger crowd knew the painting only from the press, from hearsay, from gossip. Never since Manet's *Olympia* had a painting been more reproduced, and above all more caricatured in the papers. Not only is it "the viewers who make the pictures," but in this case blind viewers, who have never seen it! Duchamp knew all this and would remember it when the time would come for *The Blind Man.* There is also something else that he would remember very well, for he had felt it as a bitter failure: the *Nude* had first been refused by the hanging committee of the cubist room, which included his own brothers, at the Paris Indépendants in March 1912. The Independents had already betrayed their principles. The Richard Mutt case had already taken place. For Duchamp, when he arrived in New York, as for us today, it is *given.* And the demonstration may be taken up again from that vantage point.

55. The very complex notion of *symétries commanditées,* translated in *Salt Seller* as *subsidized symmetries* and for which I propose *commissioned symmetries,* can give way to several interpretations, not mutually exclusive, among them one that invites the reader to imagine a symmetry axis in time rather than in space, so that the flow of time would fold back on itself round this axis, *as if* time ran backward.

DEMONSTRATION?

Let $a/a' = b/b'$. In translation: *Fountain* is to *Nude Descending a Staircase* what Society of Independent Artists is to Société des Artistes Indépendants. Let $a/b = a'/b'$. In translation: the relation of *Fountain* to its real exhibition conditions at the New York Independents is equivalent to the relation of the *Nude* to its real exhibition conditions at the Paris Indépendants:

$$\frac{\textit{Fountain}}{\text{N.Y. Indeps}} = \frac{\textit{Nude}}{\text{Paris Indeps}}$$

Indeed, the two works were rejected by institutions that had identical goals. The above formula now shows the negation wrought by the New York Indeps' legitimating principles, thus expressing the formula for their betrayal and their possible delegitimation.[56] They had declared that anything they would show

56. The risk of delegitimation was so real that, even to the present date, all the protagonists in the Richard Mutt affair more or less involved in the censorship of *Fountain* have cloaked the episode in embarrassed silence or downright travesty. In his autobiography, *It's Me, O Lord,* Rockwell Kent didn't give the affair more than ten lines; William Glackens's biography, written by his son Ira Glackens (*William Glackens and the Ashcan Group: The Emergence of Realism in American Art* [New York: Crown Publishers, 1957], p. 188), travestied the facts and tried to have the laughs on the censors' side; in 1937, John Sloan, president of the Society from 1918 to 1944, wrote an apologetic letter to Alfred Barr, Jr., then director of the Museum of Modern Art, in which he claimed that the hanging committee did not act as a jury, since a jury "is a body that passes on aesthetic merits," and that, therefore, the committee was not "in the position of rejecting an exhibit offered as a work of art when, as you know, we were dealing with a matter totally unrelated with art" (cited by Marlor, *Society of Independent Artists,* pp. 37–38). The taboo is apparently so strong that 67 years after the events, and 40 years after the disappearance of the Society, its "official" historian, Clark S. Marlor, still showed the greatest reluctance in recognizing the affair's historical importance and a rather disingenuous

would be on a par with everything their Paris counterpart had shown. It follows that the one thing they refused to show was also on a par with the one thing the Indépendants had rejected. But from the vantage point of December 1916, when the Society was founded, *Fountain* still lay in the future while the *Nude*'s rejection was a thing of the past. It had already been triumphally rehabilitated at the Armory Show.[57] When Duchamp disembarked from the *Rochambeau*

---

laziness in trying to establish the facts with the help of firsthand sources. (See Francis Naumann's review of Marlor's book in *Archives of American Art Journal* 26, no. 2–3 (1986): 36–40.)

57. To be true to all the facts, it should be noted that when Walter Pach selected the *Nude* for the Armory Show in November 1912, it had just been rehabilitated already. It was shown in October at the Salon de la Section d'Or, organized by the very same orthodox cubists, led by Marcel's brother, Jacques Villon, who had rejected it form the Indépendants in March and were now only too eager to amend. But this first rehabilitation remained, in more than one sense, a family affair played out from within the cubist brotherhood. The "fathers" of cubism, Picasso and Braque, stayed away from all Salons and showed only contempt for institutional legitimation. Not so with the "sons," Gleizes and Metzinger in particular, who attached great value to the incorporation of cubism into the great tradition and insisted on group discipline as a strategy of penetration. Marcel, the "prodigal son," would thus be reintegrated into the co-opted (i.e., self-proclaimed) avant-garde of orthodox cubism. The irony is that the Duchamp family was split on this occasion: while Raymond Duchamp-Villon showed at the Salon d'Automne, Jacques Villon, who was on its committee, resigned in protest against their hostility toward cubism and replied with the Salon de la Section d'Or, held simultaneously. And Marcel, not surprisingly, showed in both Salons but didn't care. He already had the kind of "structuralist" understanding of the issue of artistic legitimation that is at the bottom of his *algebraic comparisons:* neither rejection from one Salon nor admission into a counter-Salon is pertinent in isolation, since both Salons form a couple leaving the public on the sidelines. True legitimation—or, in the case of the *Nude,* rehabilitation—would have to involve the public. And this is what happened at the Armory Show. One more fact, which seems to complete the interplay of *commissioned symmetries:* in April 1912, right after the Indépendants and months before the Salon de la Section d'Or, the *Nude* was included in a cubist group show and sent to Barcelona where it didn't raise an eyebrow, just as the first readymades shown in 1916 at the Bourgeois and Montross galleries would go totally unnoticed. We would be

in June 1915, he was preceded by his scandalous success, *like a comet having its tail in front.*[58] And so the pissoir too was rehabilitated, but *in advance.* One only needs to fold the *commissioned symmetries* round their axis, the *Nude* at the Armory Show in 1913, to see everything fall into place and to understand that Duchamp's wager (for he didn't know yet what the fate of *Fountain* would be) was diabolically strategic on the aesthetic—not merely on the institutional—level, while on the ethical level it was strategically generous (for he was determined to eschew public scandal and not reveal the Society's actual delegitimation). Just as the *Nude* was rejected in Paris in the spring of 1912, so *Fountain* would be rejected in New York in 1917:

$$\frac{\textit{Nude}}{\text{Paris Indeps}} = \frac{(\textit{Nude})}{(\text{Armory Show})} = \frac{\textit{Fountain}}{\text{N.Y. Indeps}}$$

At both ends of this chain of *algebraic comparisons* folded around a loud, successful scandal, there are two suppressed scandals. In 1912, out of affection for his brothers but also out of real bitterness, Duchamp withdrew his painting and hushed up. In 1917, out of courtesy but also out of a strategic calculation and supreme revenge, he got the "Richard Mutt Case" on the historical record but saw to it that it remained muffled. It is here that Duchamp's strategy proves inextricably diabolic and generous. The *Nude*'s scandalous success at the Armory Show is precisely what the Ash Can School alumni among the Society's founders sought to repress with their desire to academicize and repatriate the Armory Show (hence the parentheses in the above formula). Yet it is also precisely what they appropriated when they invited Duchamp to chair the hanging

---

pushing our luck if, for the sake of *commissioned symmetries,* the two readymades shown at the Bourgeois proved to have been *In Advance of the Broken Arm,* the snow shovel, and *Emergency in Favor of Twice,* a lost object whose title seems to have been *symmetrically commissioned* by that of the shovel. (See above, n. 22.)

58. *The Green Box,* in *SS,* p. 26 (Translation slightly modified.)

committee and begged him to bestow on them his perhaps dubious prestige. The coup of the urinal is the planned return of the repressed, and in order to be at once effective, significant, and just, in a way it had to be repressed, too. The absence of a scandal at the Indeps at once renders Duchamp's success with the Armory Show conspicuous and puts it into the background. For if R. Mutt had been an anonymous wisecracker, the Society could have afforded to censor him without risking open delegitimation. If, on the other hand, Duchamp had revealed the true paternity of the urinal, the Society might have been forced to endorse him, running the risk of letting the Big Show as a whole appear as a farce. In the end R. Mutt was censored, but not without Duchamp sticking his neck out by resigning from the board of directors, and not without his reputation as a troublemaker being whipped up again.

We can be sure that the coup was long fomented; it was, in any case, deadly on target, and it would prove to be just. It was ripened in workshop solitude, developed in bachelor chemicals, gently lit by the enlightening gas of meditation much more than it was concocted in the social fever of the Arensberg Salon. From the very first day that Duchamp had set foot on American soil and Walter Pach drove him to the Arensbergs to become drunk with success, he knew that having its tail in front is not the normal anatomy of a comet. That is not how history is made. Success and scandal, success as scandal, are nothing. With the plans for the *Large Glass* tucked under his arm, he had already decided to *use "delay" instead of picture.*[59] Soon he would use "readymade" instead of delay too. Like the definitively unfinished *Large Glass* (called a *delay in glass* by Duchamp) in Jean Suquet's admirable demonstration, the "delay in porcelain" that he was fomenting represented the moment "before."[60] Before scandal, before success, before the moment when it would be proclaimed to be art by *The Blind Man,* or men.

---

59. *The Green Box,* in *SS,* p. 26.

60. Jean Suquet, "Possible," in Thierry de Duve, ed., *The Definitively Unfinished Marcel Duchamp* (Cambridge, Mass.: MIT Press, 1991).

The urinal's art status was obtained through impeccable, shrewd, and merciless strategy. Once on the record, the Richard Mutt case has proven impossible to erase. It has been written into the art history books, which means that it has been registered in the jurisprudence of modern art. The legal vocabulary is more than appropriate here, since we are dealing with legitimacy in general, with the legitimation of *Fountain* in particular, and with the possible delegitimation of a group of putative artists who could not cope with the test to which their own statutory law was submitted. On trial in 1917 was the Society of Independent Artists, whose members, all of them, Eilshemius as well as Stieglitz, Rockwell Kent, Jr., as well as Rockwell Kent, Sr., were acquitted with Richard Mutt's vindication. If *Fountain* is art, then *Supplication* is art and the little boy's *Nice Animals* is art too. But *Fountain* is still on trial. And so is *Supplication* for that matter, as is the product of the child's "pure uneducated seeing," his father's name notwithstanding. From institutional legitimation—or art status—it does not follow that aesthetic legitimacy—or art quality—is secured once and for all. The urinal is still awaiting further trial. Like the *Large Glass,* it ought to maintain itself in this expectation, definitively unfinished. And it is in relation to expectation, to the interplay of expectations, that we must take up the demonstration one last time and find the missing link tying together two chains of *algebraic comparisons*. The first chain, as we recall, was summarized by the following equation: *Supplication* by Louis Eilshemius is to *Fountain* by Richard Mutt what the Society of Independent Artists is to Gallery 291. Or, if you prefer: *Supplication*'s presence at the Indeps is equivalent to *Fountain*'s presence at 291:

$$\frac{\textit{Supplication}}{\text{N.Y. Indeps}} = \frac{\textit{Fountain}}{291}$$

This chain is made of bids for power on the artists' part and disappointed expectations on the institutions' part. For *Supplication* is not exactly what the Society's founders were expecting or hoping for, as far as talent scouting goes.

No more is *Fountain* what Stieglitz was expecting or fostering, as far as quality in modern art goes. If there is any kind of legitimation in this equation, it is forced: Richard Mutt's coup is equal to Eilshemius's self-promotion, only wittier. We may admire the ruse, we might even think we are laughing with Duchamp, but it would be at the expense of those who listened to him. Eilshemius paid that price, and it was high enough. We would endorse a conception of the avant-garde that sees art in terms of institutional strategy and nothing else; a sad conception, proud of deceiving all expectations and which depends on the delegitimation of tradition for its own legitimacy, as if Eilshemius could be called an artist only because he let the Hudson River tradition of landscape painting go crazy in his hands, as if Duchamp's manipulation of Stieglitz automatically meant that he was making fun of Georgia O'Keefe and systematically practiced *negative ironism dependent solely on laughter.*[61] The second chain was summarized by this equation: *Fountain* by R. Mutt is to *Nude Descending a Staircase* by Marcel Duchamp what Society of Independent Artists is to Société des Artistes Indépendants. Or, if you prefer: *Fountain* being submitted to the New York Indeps is equivalent to the *Nude* being submitted to the Paris Indeps:

$$\frac{\textit{Fountain}}{\text{N.Y. Indeps}} = \frac{\textit{Nude}}{\text{Paris Indeps}}$$

This chain is made of betrayed expectations on both the artists' and the institutions' part. For the least we can say is that neither *Fountain* nor the *Nude* met the expectations of the two societies, respectively. It's not that the works were not on the level, they were an act of treason, and as such they were rejected. What Gleizes, Le Fauconnier, and the Duchamp-Villon brothers ex-

61. It is to this *negative ironism* that Duchamp opposed the *ironism of affirmation* ("General notes for a hilarious Picture," *The Green Box,* in *SS,* p. 30). Georgia O'Keeffe was showing at 291 at the time of the Independents' Show.

pected from Duchamp in 1912 should rather have been entitled *Portrait of Chessplayers* or something similar; when they were met with a painting which, though cubist in appearance, bore a title incompatible with the orthodoxy of the Puteaux group, they felt betrayed. And what Kent and Bellows expected from Duchamp in 1917 should rather have resembled the *Chocolate Grinder;* they were ready for a fancy title, this time, but not for an object whose appearance they could not compare with anything artistic. They felt their liberalism was taken advantage of and put to an unfair test. On the side of the artist, however, this symmetry is broken: the later event is *commissioned* by the earlier one. Whereas in 1912 Duchamp sincerely expected his *Nude* to be welcome in the cubist room, in 1917 sincerity was no longer the issue: Duchamp knew he was putting the Indeps to a test when he fabricated an unknown self-proclaimed artist whose supposed expectations he expected to be betrayed. We may admire his gesture, we might even thumb our nose at the Indeps and think we are grinning with Duchamp, in 1917; we would soon be led to think that in 1912 the *Nude Descending a Staircase* was not a painting but also a gesture, whose avant-garde value was to force the hanging committee to betray either their taste or their principles. We would endorse an equally sad conception of the avant-garde, as if it were only satisfied with the far-out and relied on provocation and escalation, as if rejection were the only proof of artistic validity and nihilism the true source of creation, as if radicalism vis-à-vis the institution, not aesthetic quality, were the sole criterion of art. Both chains of *algebraic comparisons* leave us with strategy for the sake of strategy, success for the sake of success, or art for the sake of non-art. Following either of them leads to writing the history of the avant-garde as that of the victors, and what the victors have won is sheer negativity.

Another scenario ought to be envisaged, one in which the issue of the avant-garde's legitimacy would be dealt with—as it should be—in juridical rather than military terms. Let's take sides with the defeated for a brief moment and ask what the *algebraic comparisons* would have looked like if the Paris and the New York Independents had not been forced to betray their principles, if Duchamp had complied with their desire and respected their sense of tradition.

Let's thus replace the chain of betrayed expectations, as it actually happened, with the chain of fulfilled expectations, as it should have happened in order for the two institutions to have retained their self-respect. *Chocolate Grinder* being submitted to the New York Indeps would then be equivalent to *Portrait of Chess-players* being submitted to the Paris Indeps:

$$\frac{\textit{Grinder}}{\text{N.Y. Indeps}} = \frac{\textit{Chessplayers}}{\text{Paris Indeps}}$$

Now, the *Grinder* was reproduced on *The Blind Man*'s cover, whereas *Supplication* and the *Fountain*'s photograph were printed inside the magazine. Since, as we remember, the editorial board of the magazine parodies the hanging committee of the Independents, the former mimics the scale of preferences of the latter and shows where the latter's real desire for legitimation goes: that rather than attracting slightly paranoid individuals such as Eilshemius, the Big Show would be honored with Duchamp's presence. So we may substitute the *Grinder* for *Supplication* in the chain of bids for power and disappointed expectations, thereby nullifying not only Eilshemius's embarrassing claim to genius but also Duchamp's contemptuous declaration that *Supplication* was the best painting in the show. We would be bringing Eilshemius's participation down to the level where he is equal to all other participants, while elevating Duchamp's to the level where his prestige was eagerly awaited. We would thus ease out all coups and bids for power vis-à-vis the Society, while remaining sure that we would fulfill its desire:

$$\frac{\textit{Grinder}}{\text{N.Y. Indeps}} = \frac{\textit{Fountain}}{291}$$

The coup is now directed solely at Stieglitz. The Society might be more pleased with the *Grinder* than it was with *Supplication,* but Duchamp's offhand enlisting of Stieglitz still makes him a pawn in Richard Mutt's game. Yet in order to dissolve this last abuse, one need only let the *algebraic comparison* do the work. It is, after all, the law *legitimating a choice of possibilities* and *occasioned* by them. The last equation and the one above are solved together in the following, which links the two chains:

$$\frac{\textit{Chessplayers}}{\text{Paris Indeps}} = \frac{\textit{Fountain}}{291}$$

This would be the new chain of fulfilled expectations, the one that shows where Stieglitz's true desire for legitimation goes. Stieglitz might now be satisfied that the presence of *Fountain* in his gallery is as legitimate as that of the *Chessplayers* would have been at the Paris Indépendants. He might be very surprised to learn that what was being forced into his avant-garde gallery with his involuntary blessing is now on a par with a European avant-garde (the orthodox cubism of the Puteaux group) legitimized to the point of having become academic; but this is after all what he wanted for the art he was willfully promoting. In substituting *Fountain* for the *Grinder* that the Indeps expected, Duchamp also substituted, through *algebraic comparison,* one institution awaiting its legitimacy from the future (291) for one that had received its legitimacy from the past (the Indeps). In *using "delay" instead of picture,*[62] Duchamp would thus have under-

62. "*Employer 'retard' au lieu de tableau ou peinture*" ["Use 'delay' instead of picture or painting."] *Retard* has two meanings: "delay" and "lateness." Just as the Indeps are slow when they expect what has already happened, so Stieglitz's true, unconscious desire is running ahead of the schedule set by his conscious expectations. From the vantage point of Duchamp, the urinal is a "delay in porcelain" for everyone. But the Indeps will always lag behind whereas Stieglitz will eventually compensate for his "lateness." After 1920 he will change his mind about Duchamp "the charlatan," to the point of calling the *Large Glass* "one of the grandest works in the art of all time not excluding Egyptian, Chinese, or even French." (Herbert J. Seligmann, *Alfred Stieglitz Talking* [New Haven: Yale University Press, 1966], p. 110.) But when he asked Duchamp for his opinions on photography, probably expecting some support from this artist who had abandoned painting, what he got for an answer was another "delay" pinpointing his own lateness (*SS,* p. 165):

stood and fulfilled in advance Stieglitz's true desire: to see the future receive the sanction of the past, to see modern art enter the museum. There it is, and as one historian of American art noticed: "It is also not too farfetched to consider the opening of the Museum of Modern Art in New York in 1929 as another outgrowth of the pioneering Stieglitz activity."[63]

Such is the way Victor, alias Duchamp, rendered unto Caesar what belonged to Caesar. He forced Stieglitz's hand, but Stieglitz—whose activity was declining in April 1917, and who would close down 291 two months later—was to enter history proudly, endowed not only with the prestige of having successfully supported his own protégés, but also with the more discrete fame of having lent his authority to the maxim "No jury, no prizes" in which the unknown R. Mutt found the authorization that led him to illuminate with the gaslight of the name "art" the *allegorical appearance* of a waterfall. *Fountain by R. Mutt* is this waterfall's referent, *Photograph by Alfred Stieglitz* is its *extra-quick exposure* and its *instantaneous state of Rest.*[64] But what happened to *THE EXHIBIT REFUSED BY THE INDEPENDENTS*? It has vanished. The Independents too have vanished. They disappeared in 1944, but their prestige had waned long before. The "Richard Mutt Case" saves them from oblivion and generously restores to them the true legitimacy that they had betrayed and that they almost lost, and

---

> Dear Stieglitz,
> Even a few words I don't feel like writing. You know exactly how I feel about photography. I would like to see it make people despise painting until something else will make photography unbearable. There we are.
> Affectueusement,
> Marcel Duchamp
> (N.Y., May 22, 1922)

63. Sam Hunter, *American Art of the 20th Century* (London: Thames & Hudson, 1973), pp. 63–64.

64. Given the photographic context, here I choose to translate *exposition extra-rapide* as *extra-quick exposure* rather than *exhibition*. The French can mean both. See above, n. 18.

that they would have lost if *Fountain* had been conjured away for good. The true expectation of the French Indépendants and their American carbon copy is that history should render them justice and legitimate this unheard-of principle, which was the bottom line of all the utopias of modern art but also their true condition of emergence: everyone and anyone can be an artist. Everything harks back to the year 1884, when the Société des Artistes Indépendants was founded around Seurat, whom Duchamp admired more than Cézanne. There and then we observe for the first time that an art institution claimed to found its own legitimacy on the mandate it had received from its members rather than on the continuity of a tradition guaranteed by a jury.

But this was wishful thinking. The reality is that art is legitimated only through comparison and that comparison can be made only with what is already legitimate. Legitimation comes from the past alone. The moderns, those utopianists, those *comets having their tails in front,* asked that the future grant their demands. The avant-gardes wanted time, whose iron law is to be irreversible, to flow backward. The Richard Mutt case does not fulfill their wish but does them justice through *ironism of affirmation*. Making avant-garde art of true significance means anticipating a verdict that can only be retrospective. It means delivering the unexpected in lieu of the expected in such a way that betrayed and disappointed expectations show themselves, in the end, to have been fulfilled. Because it is in the nature of expectations not to depend on factual verification for their truth as expectations—that is, as projected scenarios—the scenario that I have described as the chain of fulfilled expectations proves to be the right one. Indeed, let's reestablish the facts: instead of the *Chessplayers,* the Paris Indépendants were presented with the *Nude Descending a Staircase,* and they rejected it; instead of going directly to Stieglitz in order to gain avant-garde legitimacy for *Fountain,* Richard Mutt went to the Independents, and they rejected it. The last formula, the one that happily linked the two chains of *algebraic comparisons,* translates back into one that is familiar:

$$\frac{\textit{Nude}}{\text{Paris Indeps}} = \frac{(\textit{Nude})}{(\text{Armory Show})} = \frac{\textit{Fountain}}{\text{N.Y. Indeps}}$$

We may now remove those parentheses. The *Nude* at the Armory Show is the axis of *commissioned symmetries* around which the interplay between the expectations that are betrayed *in advance* and those that are fulfilled *with all kinds of delays* is being unfolded. Let's put ourselves in Duchamp's position in March 1912. He is already recognized as a cubist painter, his work is already legitimated by the (immediate) past extending into the present. Yet he experiences rejection, and his decision, which is aesthetic, not to modify the *Nude Descending a Staircase* but to await future rehabilitation, has the shape of prospective, straightforward anticipation. It is as though he had wagered that the relation of the *Nude* to the Paris Indépendants, where it has just been rejected, would some day be equal to the relation of this same *Nude* to the Armory Show, where it would triumph. He is acting like an avant-garde artist and the future will prove him right. Let's now put ourselves in his position at the time of the Society's foundation, in December 1916, or a little later. He has already experienced both a kind of Richard Mutt case and its vindication, and it is as though he were wagering something quite different, which has the shape of anticipated retrospection: the relation of *Fountain* to the New York Independents, where it is most likely going to be rejected, will have been equal to the relation of the *Nude* to the Armory Show, where it has triumphed. Duchamp is still an avant-garde artist, projecting legitimation into the future, but with the awareness that such legitimation will have to come from comparison with the past. The comparison involved is not merely aesthetic in any formal sense: strategies intervene that address institutions. On the other hand, as a strategy, a move like Duchamp's anticipated retrospection is not merely institutional; it is aesthetic, for it allows the reconstitution of a chain—two chains, actually—of expectations that are aesthetic, the satisfaction and dissatisfaction of which are framed in an institutional context precisely made of what is already aesthetically legitimate in the eyes of the protagonists at any given moment. The comparison involved is the *algebraic comparison:* it is itself beyond the formal or "retinal." But it is also beyond the merely contextual. The *Nude* at the Armory Show is the missing link in the interplay of expectations and satisfactions, the time and place of an immediate gratification, of an *instantaneous state of Rest.* It is fulfilling everyone's desires and wishes: those of Duchamp who erases a failure, those of the European artists whose flag the *Nude* has become, those of the American artists whom its audacity is liberating, those of the public who is bursting into healthy laughter at the sight of the best joke in the show. And herein lies the real test. The Armory Show was everyone's business, and that is rare enough in the history of the avant-garde. A party was going on at the Armory, people were dancing round an *a/b* ratio that *is in no way given by a number* c *but by the sign (/) which separated* a *and* b, *the sign of the accordance.* Scandal, usually a combat weapon, a pretext for repression, the locus of dissent and separation, was, for once, the *sign of the accordance.* Which was to be demonstrated.

Well, not quite. Nothing is demonstrated. In art, you can show but not prove. You don't deconstruct the *allegorical appearance* in order to strip bare, once and for all, the *apparition which is its mold.* You err between the appearance of apparitions and the apparition of appearances and you compare analogically: *a* is to *b* what *c* is to *x*. *Merdre est à merde ce que arrhe est à art.* You will never know what art is, for as Kant said, "the analogy does not consist in the equality of two quantitative, but of two qualitative relations."[65] You won't know but you judge; you say, "this is art," speaking of a quality, not of a status. In order to judge, all you have is "a rule according to which you may look in experience for the fourth term"—the rule of *algebraic comparison*—and "a sign by which you may detect it"—the *sign of the accordance.* And now that you have judged, where will your conviction come from that you have judged well, that you have done Richard Mutt justice, if not, reflexively, from the assuaging feeling that you have judged according to the accordance, a sign which to you is its own proof?

65. Immanuel Kant, *Critique of Pure Reason,* trans. Max Müller (Garden City, N.Y.: Doubleday, 1966), p. 147 (translation slightly modified). For the full quotation, see the epigraph of this chapter.

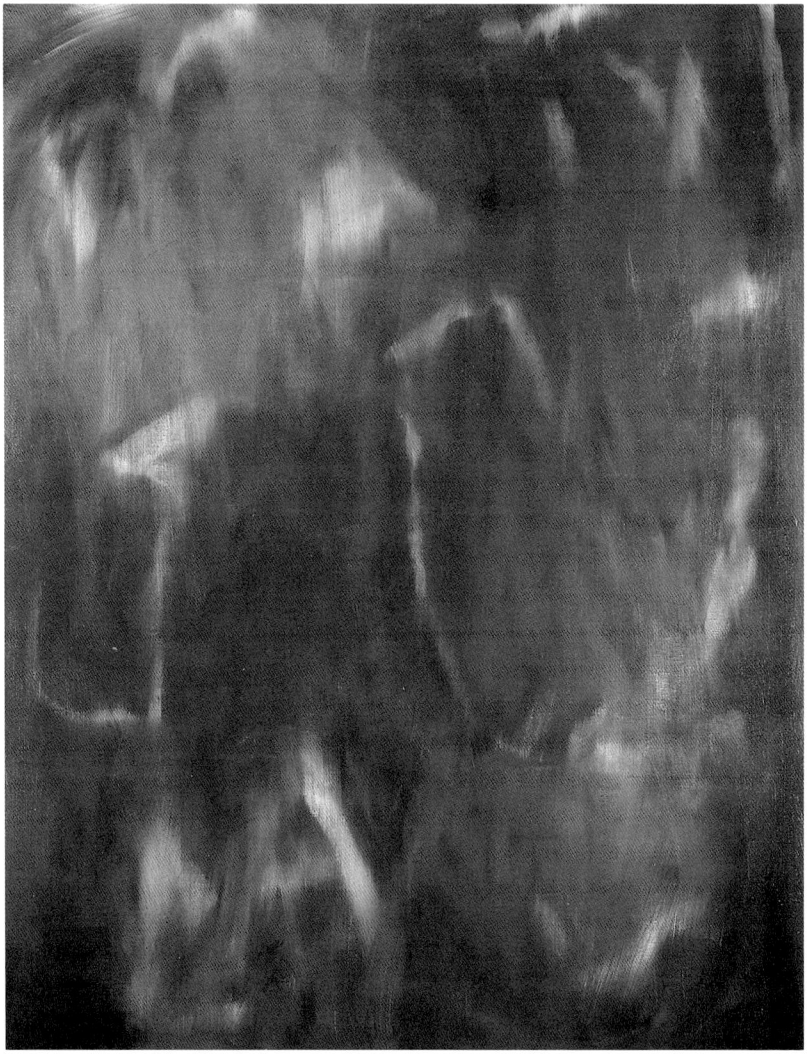

Gerhard Richter, *Red-Blue-Yellow, No. 333/5*, 1972, oil on canvas, 251 x 200 cm. Crex Collection, Hallen für neue Kunst, Schaffhausen.

Part II:

The Specific and the Generic

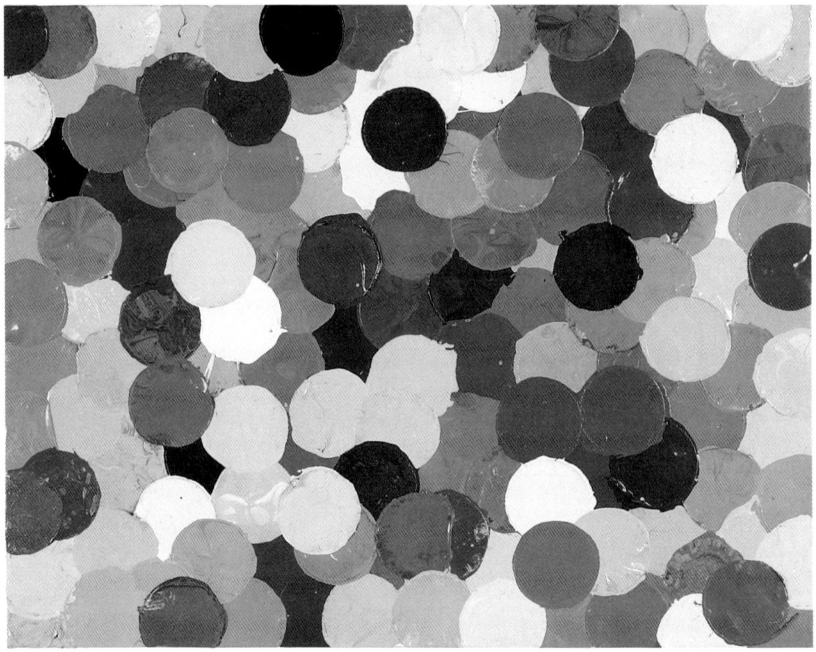

Bernard Frize, *Suite Second (15 No 1),* 1980, alkyd-methane lacquer on canvas, 50 × 65 cm. Collection Galerie Chantal Crousel, Paris (Photo Kleinefenn).

3

The Readymade and the Tube of Paint

The finest colors can be bought ready-made at the Rialto.

—*Tintoretto*[1]

The Missing Link

It took Marcel Duchamp exactly one year, from *Sonate* (Sonata) in August 1911 to *Mariée* (Bride) in August 1912, to make his way through cubism. He had been a rather eclectic painter until then, seemingly uncommitted and not too gifted, either. But the production bracketed by those dates displays an extraordinary and enigmatic concern for painting, cubist in appearance, yet invested with an irony and an eroticism absent in orthodox cubism. It is as if, quite suddenly, a compelling desire to establish his identity as a painter had set in, and as if he understood, albeit unconsciously, that cubism was both the mandatory path

1. Such, in about 1548, was Tintoretto's response to Aretino, who reproached him with not considering color as the ultimate purpose of painting, as did Titian. Quoted in Hans Tietze, *Tintoretto* (London: Phaidon, 1948), p. 43. Jacopo di Robusti's nickname, Tintoretto, came from the fact that he was the son of a dyer.

toward his own identity and a transitional style that avant-garde art would soon abandon, and that he would have to betray at the same time as he adopted it.

Painted in Munich right before the painting entitled *Mariée* and right after the two drawings both called *Vierge* (Virgin), *Le Passage de la vierge à la mariée* (The Passage from Virgin to Bride) signals a crucial point of passage in Duchamp's life and work. It is by far his best canvas (*Mariée* is good too, but slightly more contrived), the only one that measures up to what Picasso and Braque were doing at the time yet borrowing virtually nothing from them. With it, Duchamp accomplished his desire to become a painter worthy of the name while, by the same token, something was revealed to him about painting's loss of historical significance. If you're not a "born painter," if the smell of turpentine doesn't lure you naturally and easily into the studio every morning, as it did Renoir or Picasso, then you have to labor hard toward being born as a painter. But once you're born, once you have witnessed your own birth-to-painting, have taken a revenge against uneven talent and asserted your name as a painter, why do it again? Wouldn't you repeat yourself, "stupid as a painter" (as Duchamp used to say), and indulge in a craftsmanship altogether obsolete as such? For it may well be that in industrialized society, the specialized craft called painting has become useless. Mechanization and division of labor have replaced the craftsman in most of his social and economic functions, so why would they spare the painter? Indeed, to cite but the most blatant specific impact of industrialization on painting, from the moment photography was invented, painters had lost their job as purveyors of resembling images. Their skill had lost its social utility; the pleasure they could take in their work became private enjoyment; the product of their labor had to compete with a cheap ready-made substitute. If you are aware of all this but don't want to renounce the ambition to push painting beyond its loss of social functions and have it carry on a meaningful tradition, then you are bound to feel that it has become impossible to continue trusting your own skill. You might want to acknowledge that the art of painting is dead and switch to something else. The hackneyed issue of the death of painting is inseparable from both the objective conditions that have made painting useless as craft and the subjective feeling that has made it impossible as tradition. If you persisted while ignoring those conditions and denying this feeling, you would do no more than yield to the solitary pleasure that Duchamp called "olfactory masturbation."

Unless, of course—but you don't have to be a born painter for this, Cézanne certainly wasn't—what you do is reinvent painting, give it a new meaning by acknowledging the crisis it is in and give the *idea* of painting, not the craft, new birth with each canvas. You would paint, certainly, but what would you paint? Ideas are not visible; they have neither form nor color. Perhaps you would try to paint the fact that when the machine has supplanted the artisan and the photograph has provided the public with ready-made resemblance, then resemblance can no longer fill the canvas with significant subject matter, then craft can no longer point at referents in the world. But how would you paint that fact, and make that loss visible? You would renounce resemblance and empty the canvas of all concrete references. You would paint reflexively, not transitively. You would conceive of a *Gegenstandslose Welt,* inhabited with forms and colors whose purposiveness is to make visible that, when you paint, you are being guided by the idea of painting as *pure visibility.* Suprematism was the practice of that idea, and so was neoplasticism, so were orphism, simultanism, synchromism, amorphism, unism, and purism in general. The switch to abstract painting comprised the crucial step in the recognition of painting's demise as craft and its instant rebirth as idea. For most of its early practitioners, this switch occurred late in 1912 or early in 1913, and after a passage through cubism, which was also a resistance to it.

Exactly at the same time, in the same cubist context, with the same awareness of the cultural challenge of industrialization and the same mixed feelings about the fate of painting, Duchamp, instead of abandoning figuration, abandoned painting altogether. No sooner had he come back from Munich, in October 1912, than he told himself, "Marcel, no more painting, go get a job."[2]

2. Interview with James Johnson Sweeney, 1956, in *SS,* p. 133. I am aware that Duchamp did not toally abandon painting in 1913, but he certainly abandoned it in a modernist sense. *Tu m',* 1918, is actually his last oil on canvas.

Two months later, with *Erratum musical* and then with the *Stoppages-étalon* (Standard Stoppages), he started to rely on chance as a substitute for craftsmanship. By the end of 1913, he had almost completely sketched out the project for the *Large Glass* (1915–1923) and had invented his first readymade, the *Bicycle Wheel*. The readymades (and to some extent the *Large Glass*) are the other side of Duchamp's abandonment of painting. If he had relinquished every artistic ambition when he renounced painting, no one would speak of him today. Obviously the readymades are, among other things, Duchamp's way of registering his abandonment of painting, of getting it on the record. If only for this reason, they belong to the history of painting and not, for example, despite their three-dimensional appearance and qualities, to that of sculpture.[3] Duchamp was never a sculptor, but he had been a painter when he quit painting, surrendering, after all, to a pressure that was not different in nature from the pressure to which all the modernist painters before him had yielded when they abandoned history painting, one-point perspective, Euclidian space, or figuration itself. However, though the pressure was similar, the outcome was not, and it may seem far-fetched to claim that the readymades, which clearly are not paintings, show more than negative dependency with regard to the historical sequence they left behind. Duchamp found a way out of painting after having discovered that he was not too gifted, but also after having painted his best two canvases. One may judge that Duchamp's escape is mere escapism, or that it is the sign of his supreme intelligence. However, one would hardly conclude from his abandonment of painting that it establishes a paradoxical link with the history and the tradition with which it breaks. Yet this is what I wish to show. The readymade, on many counts, ought to be reinterpreted today in connection with painting.

3. Their only historical link with sculpture is that they may, in part, stem from the cubist practice of collage. But from the vantage point of 1913, that link is really with the future of sculpture—with Constructivism or *Merz,* for example; they themselves are offspring of cubist *painting*.

Such a reinterpretation by no means exhausts the historical significance of the readymade. But it is a key issue right now, in the face of an artworld in which every five years or so painting alternately agonizes and rises from its ashes. This swing of the pendulum has repeated itself many times in the last thirty years, and each time that the final demise of painting has been announced, the comeback of the readymade or of one of its avatars has been heralded too. Once again these days, an avant-garde strategy, sometimes dubbed "appropriation" and openly indebted to the idea of the readymade, is pitted against a return to painting that equally appropriates the past (though not the same one perhaps) while it disavows the precedent of the readymade.[4] This swing of the pendulum is a symptom. Not only does it indicate that some hidden solidarity must exist between these two trends which apparently negate each other; it also calls for a reexamination of the art-historical context in which the readymade appeared, as an offspring of Duchamp's abandonment of painting. The birth of abstract painting is the relevant context, and as such, it is theoretical and aesthetic as well as art-historical. It revolves around the issue of specificity—or purity—attached to the word "painting."

Although the issue of specificity has presented itself in every art practice during modernity, nowhere has it been more acute than in the practice of painting, where it also presented itself sooner. Modern literature and poetry have sought to isolate and define "the literary" and "the poetic"; modern music has gone after pure "musicality"; modern theater, even, has come to think of itself as the enactment of sheer "theatricality." But it was in painting that this self-referential (better called reflexive) striving for purity became both the exclusive

4. The reception history of the readymade shows several episodes where the idea of appropriation was claimed by some artists and critics to oppose the continuation of the painting tradition. It was called "sovereignty of choice" by André Breton, and in the heyday of conceptual art it was often referred to as "decontextualization" and "recontextualization." But it is in the pop art episode, and especially in its French equivalent, Nouveau Réalisme, that the word "appropriation," thanks for the most part to Pierre Restany, came to be equated with "the readymade strategy."

object of aesthetic theory and the all-encompassing subject matter of practice. In other words, it was in painting and nowhere else (not even in sculpture, which merely took it over from painting), that the idea of abstract art came into being. With abstract *art* emerging around 1912–1913 from cubist (and expressionist) *painting,* a radically new set of aesthetic principles was born, whose ideological justifications were complex and not at all homogeneous but—and this is what matters here—whose claim was that they were generalizable, as a form of thought about art in general rather than as a skill confined to a specific craft. There is a profound paradox in this. For when the early abstractionists spoke of *pure painting,* they understood its specificity to mean that which defines painting *qua* painting, transhistorically and universally: some essence that they supposed to be common to all paintings, regardless of style or period, and apt to distinguish a painting from everything that is not a painting. They also prescribed that the painters' task was to make this essence visible by purifying painting of everything that was not specifically pictorial. They sought the essence of painting—which is merely an idea, a *cosa mentale*—in painting itself, technically, as if it were hidden deep in the structure of matter and had to be purified by narrowing the field of painting technique so as to extract from it some elements, some "pictorial atoms" accounting for its being art. The paradox is thus that such a reduction would open onto the broadest generalization, whose name was abstraction in general. Only when this generalization was achieved in painting did sculpture turn abstract. Perhaps it could have been the other way around (although I doubt it), but it so happens that abstraction was invented by painters. Since then, we have spoken of abstract art, in the singular, as though abstraction as an aesthetic principle had uncovered an essence that was not peculiar to painting but was present in all the arts. Better still, we seem to imply that the various arts, in the plural, are reducible to a single essence called art in general, art at large, as though this essence were not specific but generic. Again, the comparison with what happened in the other arts underlines not the uniqueness of this paradox but that of painting's privilege in this paradox. Though purism in literature may be said to have started with Mallarmé, it is only much later, in the work of Blanchot, Barthes, and Derrida, that "the poetic" got generalized way beyond the boundaries of poetry and became "the text." Though the search for the "musicality" of music may be said to have started when Schönberg dismantled traditional harmony and invented twelve-tone music, it is only with John Cage that "sound" in general became both a musical object and the subject matter of the composer's practice. And though "theatricality" had been a topic of reflection for many modern playwrights and directors including Brecht, Artaud, and Stanislawski, it is only with the advent of "happenings" and "performance art" that one sought a generalization that would lead outside the tradition of theater. (Interestingly enough, it also came from outside, namely from painting and sculpture.) As names, "the text," "sound," and perhaps "happening" (less so "performance") indicate the same desire for generalization, paradoxically grounded in the striving for purity, as that encountered in the history of painting. They also indicate the same desire to expand what is considered artistic and to annex mundane, nonartistic matter, while reducing their own field to some specific and irreducible "essence." But for innumerable reasons, the names they secured for those paradoxical reductions/expansions remained specific. If, for example, "sound" in general is now regarded by many musicians as a legitimate definition of their domain, if some musicians, even, prefer to call their work "sound" rather than "music," no musician would claim that what he or she is doing is "art" and nothing but "art."[5] The readymades, by contrast, are "art" and nothing but "art." Whereas an abstract painting reduced to a black square on a white background is art only when you accept seeing it as a painting, a urinal is a sculpture only when you accept seeing it as art. Otherwise it simply remains a urinal. The generic seems to precede the specific

Genus and species are names, proper names.[6] You don't call a black square a painting in the way you would call a table a table; you baptize it a painting

5. This may not be entirely true. La Monte Young is still considered a musician, but Max Neuhaus is regarded as an "artist who works with sound." There are other such cases, and they always concern people whose career developed within the "artworld," not the musical word. The legitimation for this state of things can be traced to John Cage and from Cage, of course, to Duchamp.

6. See chapter 1.

out of aesthetic conviction. You call Malevich an artist through the same judgment that makes you call him a painter. Logically, if not chronologically, he is a painter first. With the legitimation of Duchamp's readymades, a very different situation was seemingly made legitimate, a situation about which, I believe, one should never stop wondering and perhaps worrying: you can now be an artist without being either a painter, or a sculptor, or a composer, or a writer, or an architect—an artist at large. What has made this situation plausible? To answer that Duchamp liberated subsequent artists from the constraints of a particular art—or skill—is either begging the question or failing to take responsibility for endorsing this "liberation." You might as well accept that anything goes. The plausibility in question has to be a regulative idea authorizing "as if–comparisons" between things that are out there, in the world at large, and things that were already plausible candidates for the title of art, because they partook in a specific craft conventionally recognized as an art form. It is again a matter of what Duchamp called an "algebraic comparison," like the one that allows us to judge *Fountain* in reference to the *Nude Descending a Staircase*. In other words, to justify the plausibility of someone deserving to be called an artist, without being a practitioner of a given art, is to show that somewhere there hides a missing link between the generic and the specific, between art in general and one or more of the arts in particular. Where shall we look for this missing link? The historical evidence points not at music, nor at literature, nor even at sculpture, but rather at painting. Duchamp himself was a painter before he became an "artist." Lest he be accused of being a fraud, his work ought to reveal the hidden link between *painting* and *art*.

Pure Color Is to Pure Painting What Abstraction Is to Art in General

Specificity or purity was painting's major regulative idea when it switched to abstraction. Regulative ideas should not be confused with rules or criteria. Just as imitation, for example, was a regulative idea for classical painting and not simply a rule to abide by or to transgress, so abstraction, pure visibility, integrity of the picture plane, faithfulness to materials, "less is more," and so on, have been major regulative ideas for modern painting. Now, a very wide array of painted artifacts—belonging to different times, done in different techniques, partaking in different cultures, and proceeding from regulative ideas as different and opposed as imitation and abstraction—still have in common that they have been judged worthy of bearing the same name, painting, and in the eyes of modern Westerners this is what makes them belong to the same specific tradition. The history of painting is the jurisprudence that passed on the name "painting" along with the objects so called, in spite of all the breaks that have occurred in this tradition—called by some revolutions, by others paradigm shifts, but which are better described as major changes in regulative ideas. What emerged with modernity is that the practice of painting gradually became more and more regulated by the idea of its own specificity, or purity, or autonomy, in a reflexive application of the idea of painting upon its name. This tendency peaked with the foundation of abstract painting, when a whole generation of painters all of a sudden had the strongest feeling that they were dropping all their conventions at once, to leap into an unknown territory where comparison with the past was no longer possible. At that moment, calling their work by the name of painting, and even of "pure painting," explicitly became the key issue of the artist's (and the viewer's) aesthetic judgments—explicitly, yet to some extent unconsciously. What occupied the consciousness of the various founders of abstract painting was the ideas regulating their judgments and the feelings through which these ideas were themselves evaluated. Fondness for design and color, a sense of respect for the flat surface, the joy of discovery and exploration were certainly among those feelings, but a much stronger incentive was fear and hope: fear that a craft reduced to the mere coating of a surface bearing no resemblance to the outer world would no longer deserve its name, and hope that it could be redeemed if it could only prove meaningful. Thus, what occupied the mind of the first abstractionists was their anxiety to prove that a surface, covered with colors, that had abandoned every readable link with nature was nevertheless "readable," that it was a language of sorts. Hence, for example, Mondrian's attempts to establish the universal linguistic value of his vertical/

horizontal symbolism or, more significantly, of his triad of primary colors. For Mondrian and for virtually every founder of abstract art, primary colors, or color itself, in the singular—pure color, as it was called—became the basic signifier of the new language, the "essential," "natural," metonym for pure painting. Whether an act of faith or a profession of hope, the idea that there is such a thing as pure color—as transcendental foundation authorizing the plurality of all empirical colors—was what set purism, as a regulative idea, into motion. So the search for the essence of painting comprised its own "as if–comparison," at once substituting a new, unknown territory for the one mapped by all the painting of the past and authorizing a generalization which would sweep through all the arts: pure color is to pure painting what abstraction is to art in general. Further, the interpretation of pure color as the elementary signifier of a new visual language offered itself to most pioneers of abstraction as the best available rationalization of this "as if–comparison" and, by the same token, as the best legitimation ensuring that the new language be called painting in its own right, in other words, that it be art.

Thus Kandinsky, anticipating the advent of abstract painting as early as 1904, boldly prophesied:

> If destiny will grant me enough time I shall discover an international language which will endure forever and which will continually enrich itself. And it will not be called Esperanto, its name will be *Malerei* [painting]—an old word that has been misused. It should have been called *Abmalerei* [non-painting, counterfeit]; up till now it has consisted of imitating. Color was seldom used for a composition (or, if so, it was used unconsciously).[7]

It is obvious from this passage that color, used consciously and outside the conventions of imitation, was intended to be the cornerstone of a new international

7. Quoted in Hans K. Roethel and Jean K. Benjamin, *Kandinsky* (Oxford: Phaidon Press, 1979), p. 13.

language that would at last deserve the name of painting. In *Über das Geistige in der Kunst* (On the Spiritual in Art), written between 1909 and 1911 and published late in 1911, Kandinsky, who kept postponing the actual passage to abstraction out of fear that it might be confused with decorative art, nevertheless proceeded to lay down the theoretical—or ideological—bases upon which abstract painting was to be grounded as, to quote the title of chapter 6, "the language of forms and colors." His argument starts with a color's name: "When one hears the word red, this red in our imagination has no boundaries. One must, if necessary, force oneself to envisage them."[8] It then proceeds to link this very abstract work of the imagination with the formal and material conditions that could make it into the basic element of an immanent pictorial language: "If, however, this red has to be rendered in material form (as in painting), then it must (1) have a particular shade chosen from an infinite range of different possible shades of red . . . ; and (2) be limited in its extension upon the surface of the canvas, limited by other colors that are there of necessity."[9] Linguists would say that what Kandinsky does in this passage is establish the paradigmatic and syntagmatic conditions of pure color as a language. It is as if he had read Roman Jakobson and had posited the linguist's axes of selection and combination as the linguistic transcendentals that, in his mind, would soon constitute the objective foundation for a universal language deserving to be called *Malerei,* not Esperanto.

Looking back, as early as 1913, upon his foundation of the abstract language of pure painting, Kandinsky stressed the subjective aspects of his passage to abstraction, aspects much more important to him, even, than the "objective" or "linguistic" ones, because without them the language of abstract painting would forever lack "inner necessity," like Esperanto. In *Rückblicke* (Reminiscences), he recalls a few intense aesthetic experiences that he sees in hindsight were endowed with enough inner necessity to have justified his

8. Wassily Kandinsky, *On the Spiritual in Art,* in *Kandinsky, Complete Writings on Art,* ed. Kenneth C. Lindsay and Peter Vergo (Boston: G. K. Hall & Co., 1982), 1:162.
9. Ibid., p. 163.

passage to pure painting. One of them, dated from adolescence, is described as follows:

> As a 13- or 14-year old boy, I gradually saved up enough money to buy myself a paintbox containing oil paints. I can still feel today the sensation I experienced then—or, to put it better, the experience I underwent then—of paints *emerging from the tube.* One squeeze of the fingers, and out came *these strange beings,* one after the other, *which one calls colors*—exultant, solemn, brooding, dreamy, self-absorbed, deeply serious, with roguish exuberance, with a sigh of release, with a deep sound of mourning, with defiant power and resistance, with submissive suppleness and devotion, with obstinate self-control, with sensitive, precarious balance, living an independent life of their own, with all the necessary qualities for further, autonomous existence, prepared to make way readily, in an instant, for new combinations, to mingle with one another and create an infinite succession of new worlds.[10]

Lyrical as it is, and written in hindsight, this text roots the very foundation of the abstract language in a personal—undoubtedly mythified—aesthetic experience that links the naming of painting to that of color. Color is thought of as a strange living being, autonomous and rich with all its pictorial potential. In Kandinsky's memory, it is also seen as bursting out of the tube, virgin, as it were, yet propelled by "inner necessity." The text presents the tube of paint, then the palette,[11] next the virgin canvas,[12] and finally the brush, not as the tools

10. *Reminiscences,* ibid., pp. 371–372 (my italics).

11. "Praise be to the palette for the delights it offers; formed from the elements defined above, it is itself a 'work,' more beautiful indeed than many a work." Ibid., p. 372.

12. "At first, [the canvas] stands there like a pure, chaste maiden, with clear gaze and heavenly joy—this pure canvas that is itself as beautiful as a picture." Ibid.

of the painter, as one might expect, but as metonyms of potential yet accomplished paintings. But the tube of paint, the palette, the canvas and the brush are also the protagonists of an erotic saga which the rest of the text then unfurls, with a dubious lyricism infused with machismo and colonialism: "And then comes the imperious brush, conquering [the canvas] gradually, first here, then there, employing all its native energy, like a European colonist who with axe, spade, hammer, saw penetrates the virgin jungle where no human foot has trod, bending it to conform to his will."[13]

The Readymade Is to Art in General What the Tube of Paint Is to Modern Painting

To an eye more skeptical and less enthusiastic than Kandinsky's, the passage to abstract painting thus appears to be of the kind ironically referred to in Duchamp's *Passage from Virgin to Bride.* No artist could be more diametrically opposed to Kandinsky than Duchamp. His own brand of colonialism ("*Le nègre aigrit, les négresses maigrissent . . .* ") resembles that of Raymond Roussel in *Impressions d'Afrique* (1910). And his own brand of self-defeating machismo ("*On a que: pour femelle, la pissotière et on en vit*") would leave the "rapist" a bachelor keeping his hands busy with "olfactory masturbation." For Kandinsky's abstract expressionism, for Malevich's suprematism, for Mondrian's neoplasticism and for all the purisms that sprang between 1912 and 1914 from the idea of pure color, Duchamp substituted eroticism, which, as he very seriously explained to Pierre Cabanne, he wanted to turn into a new artistic "ism."[14] And when he was asked to define eroticism, he answered with a comparison and an example.

13. Ibid., pp. 372–373.

14. "I believe in eroticism a lot, because it's truly a rather widespread thing throughout the world, a thing that everyone understands. It replaces, if you wish, what other literary schools called Symbolism, Romanticism. It could be another 'ism,' so to speak. You're going to tell me that there can be eroticism in Romanticism, also. But if eroticism is used as a principal basis, a principal end, then it takes the form of an 'ism,' in the sense of a school." *PC,* p. 88.

Not by chance, and just as in Kandinsky's recollection, this example was the tube of paint: "Eroticism is close to life, closer than philosophy or anything like it; it's an animal thing that has many facets and is pleasing to use, as you would use a tube of paint, to inject into your production, so to speak."[15]

Duchamp painted *Le Passage de la vierge à la mariée* in Munich, where he could have met Kandinsky. It is unlikely that he did so, but there is some evidence that he bought *Über das Geistige in der Kunst* in Munich, in the second edition dated May 1912, and that he annotated it in the margins, trying to translate some passages. Even if we had no biographical support at all, it would still be obvious, I believe, that *Le Passage de la vierge à la mariée* has everything to do with the passage of a whole generation of painters into abstract art. The dates coincide perfectly. As far as the Parisian painters are concerned, Duchamp's transit through cubism is congruent with that of Delaunay, Mondrian, and Herbin, and it seems unbelievable that Duchamp would not have been taking note of what was happening around him. Moreover, Kupka's studio was next to his brothers' house. And as far as Munich is concerned, it is very possible that the issue of pure color, repressed in the Parisian cubist context but highly visible in the context of the Blaue Reiter group, triggered an intuition at the same time very close to that founding Kandinsky's "language of forms and colors," and yet diametrically opposed to it. In *Le Passage de la vierge à la mariée,* and especially in its title (titles were, as Duchamp always said, a way of adding to the painting "a color which had not come out of a tube"), one already recognizes a typically Duchampian way of handling *allegorical appearance.* In seeing color burst out of the tube, or in discovering one of his figurative canvases lying on its side in the twilight of the studio, Kandinsky underwent a spiritual revelation authorizing the coming into being of abstract painting. He deferred acting on this revelation, but he had understood, very early on, that what was at issue in the passage to abstraction was that painting would at last

15. "Marcel Duchamp Speaks," interview by George Heard Hamilton and Richard Hamilton, London, BBC, 1959; published in *Audio Arts Magazine* 2, no. 4, (1976).

deserve its name, *Malerei*. What Duchamp got out of *Le Passage de la vierge à la mariée* was the same revelation with an ironic, sceptical twist: indeed, the tradition of craftsmanship that had been called painting until then, and that Kandinsky called *Abmalerei,* was no longer viable. Indeed, what was at stake if painting wanted to survive was that it once again deserved its name, *Malerei*. But did it deserve to survive at all? And could it survive if one didn't first acknowledge whence the death sentence had come? In any case, to allow painting to survive was not to dream that it be born again, springing from a brand-new tube of paint like Venus from the ocean, as though before the advent of pure painting there had been only *Abmalerei*. It was not to succumb to the fatal attraction of the virgin canvas and to rape it, nor to construct a yet unspoken language on a tabula rasa. If painting was a *bride,* painters were her *bachelors*. Separation between the lovers had to be recognized first, as the condition of *eroticism,* humorously understood as a new artistic "ism," along with *ironism, oculism* and, as we shall see, *pictorial nominalism*. First of all, the name of painting had to be recorded in such a way that it significantly referred its degraded tradition to the very conditions that had made it objectively useless and subjectively impossible to pursue.

In the aftermath of Munich came Duchamp's abandonment of painting and, a little later, his invention of the readymade. Only many years later, when the readymade had left its indelible imprint on modern art history and Duchamp had achieved the reputation of the world's most influential artist, did he, tongue-in-cheek, give "little explanations" of the readymade that are absolutely luminous when read literally. In an interview with Georges Charbonnier in 1961, Duchamp stated:

> The word "art," etymologically speaking, means to make, simply to make. Now what is making? Making something is choosing a tube of blue, a tube of red, putting some of it on the palette, and always choosing the quality of the blue, the quality of the red, and always choosing the place to put it on the canvas, it's always choosing. So in order to choose, you can use tubes of paint, you can

> use brushes, but you can also use a ready-made thing, made either mechanically or by the hand of another man, even, if you want, and appropriate it, since it's you who chose it. Choice is the main thing, even in normal painting.[16]

If the word "art" means making, and if making means choosing, then we are left to draw the most general conclusion possible: art means choosing. But what is striking, in regard to this level of generality, is the extreme particularity of the chosen example: "Making something is choosing a tube of blue, a tube of red . . ." It is as if art in general could stem only from choices specific to painting. "Choice is the main thing, even in normal painting." Through an analogy Duchamp invites, one is led to think that the readymade is a sort of abnormal painting. Of pictorial descent, it would be the generic offspring of choices that engender art only if they are specific. In an interview with Katherine Kuh in May 1961, Duchamp, playing ingénue, inverted this kinship: before color engenders "normal" painting, it is born out of a ready-made tube. And so the choice of a readymade is analogous to that of a tube of paint, because the tube of paint was a readymade in the first place:

> Let's say you use a tube of paint; you didn't make it. You bought it and used it as a readymade. Even if you mix two vermilions together, it's still a mixing of two readymades. So man can never expect to start from scratch; he must start from ready-made things like even his own mother and father.[17]

Nothing is *sui generis,* and likewise, no art can be made on a tabula rasa. Just as no one can avoid carrying the Oedipal weight of "mother and father," so the

---

16. Marcel Duchamp, interview by Georges Charbonnier, radio interviews, RTF, 1961 (my translation).

17. Interview by Katherine Kuh, in *The Artist's Voice Talks with Seventeen Artists* (New York: Harper & Row, 1962), p. 90.

painter too bears the burden of tradition. And just as mother and father are "ready-made things," whose heredity one has received, so is tradition. It has been handed over to the painter, as though encapsulated in a ready-made tube of paint. And again, the analogy is inverted: if the painter has inherited a tradition that is already made, then no matter what he does, even "normal painting," he will end up doing a modified readymade. At the Symposium on the Art of Assemblage, in October 1961, Duchamp concluded:

> Since the tubes of paint used by the artists are manufactured and ready-made products we must conclude that all paintings in the world are "readymades aided" and also works of assemblage.[18]

Here is the reason why the whole tradition of painting now amounts to one large readymade. Just as the prerequisite of the painter's work is a manufactured product, so "all paintings in the world" now partake of an industrial culture. An artist who has stopped painting but now chooses a readymade thus belongs to the same tradition as the painter, because the fact that colors are produced industrially both annihilates this tradition and sets up its new conditions. Painters have been dispossessed of their tradition by the paint manufacturers, as Duchamp wittily implied in an interview with Francis Roberts in October 1963:

> A readymade is a work of art without an artist to make it, if I may simplify the definition. A tube of paint that an artist uses is not made by the artist; it is made by the manufacturer that makes paints. So the painter really is making a readymade when he paints with a manufactured object that is called paints. So that is the explanation.[19]

18. "A propos of Readymades," in *SS,* p. 142.

19. Marcel Duchamp, "I Propose to Strain the Laws of Physics," interview by Francis Roberts, *Art News* 67 (December 1968): 47.

Indeed, as in Edgar Allan Poe's *The Purloined Letter,* the explanation stares us in the face. The analogy had to be read literally. Not that from now on we are to take all paintings for "readymades aided," or the readymades for "unaided" paintings. But the clue was certainly there to be picked up, all the more so since Duchamp, of course, carefully refrained from ever producing a tube of paint as a readymade. Asked for a definition of the readymade, Duchamp answered with an example instead. Asked about a generality, he answered with a singularity. Asked how he would justify the existence of an art that would no longer be either painting or sculpture or anything specific, but instead simply generic, he replied with an analogy establishing an *algebraic comparison* between the specific and the generic: what the choice of a "tube of blue, a tube of red" is to painting, the choice of a bottle rack or of a snow shovel is to art at large. One cannot help but see in this *algebraic comparison* an ironic mimicry of the modernist regulative idea: pure color is to pure painting what abstraction is to art in general. Duchamp's timely response to the birth of abstraction was an object of pictorial extraction. For Duchamp as for Kandinsky, the tube of paint is the locale of an initial choice in which the making of a painting is grounded. But where for Kandinsky it is an origin, for Duchamp it is a given. For both artists the tube of paint refers to pure color. But for Kandinsky, pure color is the elementary signifier of a pictorial language reduced to its essence; for Duchamp, it is the unmixed pigment whose purity has been determined by the manufacturer, not by the painter. For both artists, the tube of paint is charged with erotic potency. But the lyrical eroticism with which Kandinsky saw color burst out of the tube, burgeoning and inseminating the canvas, is here castrated: not only does Duchamp's tube remain sealed, it also remains concealed in every readymade, as a secret example of choices that of course the artist never acted out, and of which snow shovels and bottle racks are the *allegorical appearance.* It is not the tube of paint that inseminates the canvas as if it were erotic in and of itself; it is eroticism that "is pleasing to use, as you would use a tube of paint, to inject into your production, so to speak." And so the allegory works both ways: as much as it is true that "all paintings in the world are 'readymades aided,'" it is equally true that all readymades are offsprings of painting, once painting has been abandoned for its objective uselessness and its subjective impossibility.

Nowhere is the difference in ideology between Kandinsky and Duchamp more visible than in the opposition of these two descriptions of pure color: Kandinsky's "strange beings . . . which one calls colors" are Duchamp's "manufactured object that is called paints." Pure color was a regulative idea in Kandinsky's practice, and he felt obliged to justify it by giving it the ontological status of a living being; but for Duchamp, it was flatly a thing, already made, a dead commodity. And what the one called "colors," the other called "paints." When Duchamp abandoned painting, he did a lot more than just renounce the craft and the skill for which he realized he was, after all, not too gifted. He switched from one regulative idea to another by giving that of his colleagues, the early abstractionists, an additional reflexive twist which turned it into a referent for his own idea. Their regulative idea was the specifically pictorial; his was *about* the specifically pictorial. Theirs was geared to establish their craft's name, *Malerei;* his was a philosophy *about* that name, *a kind of pictorial Nominalism.*[20] In pure color liberated from imitation, in elementary forms, they sought the conditions for "an international language which will endure forever." Instead, he *referred* to those conditions and provided an ironic commentary on their utopian quest for a language that would have, as Lévi-Strauss put it in *Le cru et le cuit,* only one level of articulation. "Conditions of a language: the search for 'prime words' ('divisible' only by themselves and by unity)."[21] Proper names

20. The note from the *White Box,* "*Une sorte de* Nominalisme pictural (*contrôler*)," is dated 1914 (*SS,* p. 78). The word "nominalism" appears in two other notes: note 185 (also dated 1914) and note 251 (undated), published posthumously in M. Duchamp, *Notes,* presented by Paul Matisse (Paris: Centre Georges Pompidou, 1980).

21. *SS,* p. 31. To understand how Duchamp's regulative idea could take Kandinsky's as a referent is again (see chapter 2) a matter of linking two "algebraic comparisons": there is the same relation for Kandinsky between the name of a color and its purity ("When one hears the word red . . .") as there is for Duchamp between his "prime words" ("the colors one

satisfy these conditions, but whereas for the founders of abstraction what mattered was that the proper name of painting be maintained in its ambition and dignity, even though it had ceased to refer to anything but a mere surface covered with pure colors and basic forms, what was at stake for Duchamp was to assert that the proper name of art—or of *arrhe*—be given to a practice that no longer *was* painting, but that was *apropos* of painting.

L'impossibilité du fer

Thus, the readymade is art about painting even before it is art about art. The art of painting means making, said Duchamp, thereby quoting a very traditional definition of art as skill and craftsmanship. But if craftsmanship has been rendered objectively useless by industrialization, then skillful making must also be subjectively felt as impossible by the sensitive artist. This is, "even in normal painting," that "inner necessity" which drove Kandinsky and the other early abstractionists toward the abandonment of almost every traditional convention of painting, and Duchamp toward the abandonment of the craft itself. Gone is the making, what remains is the name. Gone is the skill, the talent, what remains is the genius, the wit. Asked by Denis de Rougemont to define genius, Duchamp replied with a pun: "*l'impossibilité du fer*" (the impossibility of the iron / *l'impossibilité du faire,* the impossibility of the making).[22] Since making means choosing, the implied syllogism leads to the conclusion that genius lies in the impossibility of choosing. And since the privileged example of such an impossible choice is "a tube of blue, a tube of red," then genius must lie in the impossibility of choosing one's colors, of opening a tube, of beginning a canvas, of painting. Where impotent talent forces the painter to quit, the genius

speaks about," he says elsewhere) and the "purity" of the color still in its tube. Both relations set "the conditions of a language." But Duchamp's is a "metalanguage": it is *about* Kandinsky's.

22. Denis de Rougemont, "Marcel Duchamp, mine de rien," *Preuves* 204 (February 1968): 45. (Written in 1945 but not published before 1968.)

of impotence takes over! There is an undeniable element of retaliation—of *talionism* (another artistic "ism"), as Duchamp used to say—in *pictorial nominalism.* Duchamp knew that he would never equal Picasso or Matisse even when he painted his best two canvases in Munich in August 1912. He didn't renounce his ambition for that. In quitting painting, he showed his extreme intelligence, his extreme pride, certainly, but also his extreme humility. He didn't dissuade other artists from holding on to painting. Some would do so, having an understanding of painting's impossibility at least equal to his (I am thinking of Pollock, mainly). His *talionism* was directed only against his own failure. But his *ironism* was such that painting after Duchamp, as if nothing had happened, became precisely impossible to anyone who had the ambition but perhaps not the talent of Picasso or Matisse. To paint after Duchamp means to paint in the hostile conditions set up by industrialization. Duchamp cannot be made responsible for those conditions; he simply showed them, and herein lies his genius.[23] But he would have shown nothing had he not succeeded in recording the *impossibility of the making* by making something nonetheless; and he would not have evoked genius—albeit the genius of impotence—had the double entendre in the pun, *the impossibility of the iron,* not incited those who could hear it to look for some object with which to pry open to interpretation this *Witz* (joke) made of iron and irony.

At least two of Duchamp's readymades are "three-dimensional puns" (as Arturo Schwarz said, perhaps quoting Duchamp) made of iron. *Trébuchet* (Trap, 1917) is a coatrack nailed to the floor so that one stumbles (*trébucher*) on it.[24] And *Peigne* (Comb, 1916) is an iron comb whose interpretation reveals, I believe, the

23. This is the genius we spontaneously recognize when we speak of "art after Duchamp" being different from "art before Duchamp." Such periodizations of art history by way of a proper name are not accounted for by the art-historical notion of influence.

24. When Duchamp had a replica of *Trébuchet* made by the Galleria Schwarz, Milan, in 1964, he specified on the blueprint, "*Fer ordinaire clair, pas cuivre*" (Ordinary light iron, not copper). The blueprint is reproduced on the inside cover of Walter Hopps, Ulf Linde, and Arturo Schwarz, *Marcel Duchamp, Ready-Mades, Etc. (1913–1964)* (Milan: Galleria Schwarz, 1964).

full implications of genius understood as *l'impossibilité du fer.* It is similar to those combs used by the cubists to paint fake wood, aware that they were introducing into the noble craft of painting a practice that was of a very different social origin. The cubists' comb is to Kandinsky's brush what the house-painter is to the artist-painter. It is unfit to be erected into a metonym of pure painting but, on the other hand, perfectly suited to act as a signifier for the plight shared by both the house-painter and the artist-painter, since they are both craftsmen threatened by mechanization. Painting fake wood by hand was already obsolete in 1912, as Braque and Picasso demonstrated by juxtaposing in their collages pieces of ready-made woodgrained wallpaper and hand-made *trompe-l'oeil* skillfully imitated by means of an iron comb. As to Duchamp's comb, nobody ever used it to paint. Once chosen as a readymade, nobody would use it as a comb either. Born out of the cubist collages, *Peigne* is a "three-dimensional pun," in the shape of a comb, referring to the collages and their pictorial origin. In French, the name of the object reads as a *Witz* on painting. Indeed, *Peigne* is the subjunctive mode of the verb *peindre* (to paint), either in the first or in the third person. It could be read as "*qu'il peigne!*" (let him paint!) and might be referring to Picasso who, not lacking wit himself, had used a comb to paint the hair and the mustache of his *Poet,* a painting from 1912. Such a reading would be confirmed by the fact that to Picasso's painted/combed *Poet,* Duchamp apparently replied with an enameled one. It was to be *Apolinère Enameled,* an assisted readymade made towards the end of 1916: a can of paint in her hand, a little girl paints a bed frame that looks as fantastic with regard to perspective as does Picasso's cubism. Duchamp, who had ceased to paint, merely chose a small poster advertising Sapolin pigments, a French brand of paints manufactured in the United States by Gerstendorfer Brothers.[25] Yet he scribbled, by

25. We owe it to André Gervais (*La raie alitée d'effets* [Montreal: HMH, 1984], p. 116) to have discovered that the two lines (in the lower right-hand corner) whose letters were modified by Duchamp in order to compose the cryptic phrase ANY ACT RED BY HER TEN OR EPERGNE were to be read originally as MANUFACTURED BY GERSTENDORFER BROS. As to the title itself,

mirrorical return, the shuffled hair of the little girl in a corner of the mirror, as if he wanted to underline that it needed some combing. And likewise, he scribbled other hairy appendages onto a reproduction of the Mona Lisa two years later. Countless are the works by Duchamp in which his witty genius took as referent the impossible act of painting/combing, varying on the act and the pilosities it acts on: he wore a star-shaped tonsure; he got himself photographed with shampoo on his head; he shaved the Mona Lisa's mustache as well as the Bride's crotch. This is enough, I believe, to verify in his work the resonance of a *Witz* that, on February 17, 1916, was perhaps no more than a Freudian slip betraying his regrets.

For *Peigne* is dated. It is the only readymade for which Duchamp obeyed the rule that he had given himself in a note from the *Green Box* where he defined the readymade as *a kind of rendezvous.*[26] In this note he planned, *for a moment to come (on such a day, such a date, such a minute), to "inscribe a readymade,"* adding this instruction: *naturally inscribe that date, hour, minute, on the readymade, as information.* Date, hour, minute—*FEB. 17 1916 11 AM*—are indeed inscribed on the comb, which would be the only strict enactment of the *rendezvous* he had set himself with a readymade, if *Peigne* had not been inscribed eleven days, exactly, after he did another readymade, equally inscribed with the date, hour, minute, and precisely entitled *Rendez-vous du 6 février 1916 à 1h.3/4 après-midi.* It is a literary work, and one might call it a poem, though Duchamp called it a readymade. In any case, it is a text, typewritten on four postcards and addressed to Walter Arensberg, who was then heavily involved in deciphering cabbalistic poetry. It was painstakingly composed through the following method: Duchamp decided that he would write sentences, grammatically correct but making no sense at all, not even nonsense. An impossible task if ever there was

---

Apolinère Enameled, it is of course both a modification of the original advertisement, *Sapolin Enamels,* and a pun on the name of the French poet Apollinaire.

26. *SS,* p. 32. The note itself is undated, but too many coincidences lead me to believe that it was written a few weeks, perhaps a few months, prior to *Peigne.*

one: having chosen the first word of the sentence, Duchamp would then proceed to choose the next, scratching every choice until he was satisfied that no meaning was produced but an *abstract* one.[27] Such a method is both close to and diametrically opposed to André Breton's automatic writing. (Moreover, it anticipates the surrealist technique.) Whereas Breton, thinking that he could let the unconscious flow into his poems simply by obeying the Freudian principle of free association, never achieved much more than a display of the preconscious and its resistances, Duchamp, practicing "overcensorship" (*surcensure:* his word), forced himself to put the most drastic constraints on his associations, to the point where virtually every word that slipped through could be said to be significant, like an overdetermined lapsus. And in the text that is the product of this contrived "impossibility of the making," we find this sentence, which is anything but abstract: "*Conclusion: après maints efforts en vue du peigne, quel dommage*" (Conclusion: after many efforts toward the comb, what a pity).

Eleven days later, this slip of the tongue became a "three-dimensional pun." The proximity of the two works leaves no doubt that what is referred to in *Peigne* is an intricate set of feelings towards painting, involving joy, irony, and revenge but also nostalgia, jealousy, and impotence. Perhaps Duchamp had Picasso and his *Poet* in mind when he let the pun in the comb's name be read as "*qu'il peigne!*" But he was certainly addressing himself too, and "*que je peigne!*" is a more likely and a more profound reading. Its best translation would be something between "I ought to paint" and "If only I could paint." The slip of the tongue (by then, probably a feigned one) was a stroke of genius—genius, whose Duchampian definition, pun included, lies in *l'impossibilité du fer.* Painting has become impossible, the *Witz* seems to say: the verb "to paint" can no longer

27. "There would be a verb, a subject, a complement, adverbs and everything perfectly correct, as such, as words, but meaning in these sentences was a thing I had to avoid. . . . The verb was meant to be an abstract word acting on a subject that is a material object; in this way the verb would make the sentence look abstract." Quoted in Schwarz, *Complete Works,* p. 457.

be conjugated in the indicative, but rather is alluded to in the subjunctive, a verbal mode that in French also acts as a hypothetical imperative.

But painting has not become impossible. The fact that industrialization has bereft painters of their traditional social function as purveyors of images—the fact, for example, that photography has taken over the market for portraits and other representations—does not in the slightest make the practice of painting objectively impossible. It makes it useless in regard to this traditional function, but it does not forbid it nor does it ipso facto suppress its know-how or repress the desire to paint. On the contrary, it can be argued that economic progress has made it possible for many more people to find the leisure to paint than was ever the case prior to the industrial revolution. The impossibility of painting is merely a feeling, the subjective signal accompanying the awareness of its objective uselessness in a society where the production of images has been mechanized and from which painting has withdrawn, like a relic from an obsolete artisanal past. Though merely a feeling, the impossibility of painting is a mandatory feeling, however, a quasi-moral one, a feeling that should be felt by any artist who is sensitive to his or her time, to the inventions that propel it towards economic progress, to the ideas that carry the hope of social progress, to the technologies that upset the cultural status quo. It is, in other words, the feeling of any artist who, like Duchamp, around 1912, understands or senses that there is more art in photography or cinema than there is in painting because these new cultural forms, far from being deprived of social function, allow a glimpse of the possibility of a truly popular art. Thus, *l'impossibilité du fer* is not at all a logical modality; it does not entail the negative necessity of that which cannot happen. Rather, it connotes the moral imperative of that which should not happen. The melancholic feeling of impotence the sensitive artist must feel in the face of painting's objective uselessness forbids him or her to paint, but it is not as if one could no longer paint. Rather, it is as if one should not paint yet. Painting may be doomed by industrialization, but as long as the desire, the drive, or the impulse to paint survives, to abandon painting means to postpone actual work. The tubes of paint remain sealed and the canvas remains blank, and as such, they retain their potential. Duchamp's *Peigne*—both the object and the pun in its title—is the work in which he recorded his abandonment of painting and made it significant. Referring to cubism and to its abstract aftermath, it is the most extraordinary allegorical condensation of the two main *topoi* of pictorial purism, the tabula rasa and the last painting. Duchamp refrained from painting so that painting, in its potential, unactualized state, would forever remain possible.

La figuration d'un possible

Thus, Duchamp speaks of "*the figuration of a possible* (not as the opposite of impossible nor as related to probable nor as subordinated to likely); the possible is only a *physical "caustic"* (vitriol type) burning up all aesthetics or callistics."[28] *Peigne* is the "figuration" of just such a caustic (or, in Duchamp's French, "*un mordant physique,*" something that bites), as is suggested by his humorous aphorism, "*Classer les peignes par le nombre de leurs dents*" (Classify combs by the number of their teeth).[29] This particular comb refers to painting as being both impossible and possible. On the one hand, it is the offspring of the "impossibility of the making," that is of choosing, in exactly the same way that the tube of paint is the offspring of the uselessness of making, once making has been replaced by choosing. On the other hand, and again exactly like the tube of paint, this comb has as a possible offspring a painting that is potential and should remain so. The analogy with the tube of paint is not gratuitous. It was brought up by the "little explanations" that Duchamp gave late in life each time he was asked to explain the genesis of the readymades; and it led to a reading of the one comb he actually chose, as an *allegorical appearance* of the tube of paint he never actualized. But the analogy should be verified, and the reading of the comb as the *figuration of a possible* (which is another name for the *allegorical appearance*) should be traced back to the tube of paint as an "explanation" of this very

28. *SS,* p. 73.

29. *SS,* p. 71.

thin potential or possibility. Some twenty years after his *rendezvous* with the comb, Duchamp once again called in the tube of paint as an example: "The possible is an infra thin. The possibility of several tubes of paint becoming a Seurat is the concrete explanation of the possible as infra thin."[30]

Apparently we are brought back to where Kandinsky had left us: to the enthusiastic experience of seeing "these strange beings . . . which one calls colors" emerge from the tube, ready "to mingle with one another and create an infinite succession of new worlds." Yet there are three differences. (1) The tubes remain sealed, and therein lies their possibility as "infra thin."[31] Only if their potential to become painting is never actualized do they retain it. (2) If the tubes were to be opened, they would not yield an "infinite succession of new worlds," they would "become a Seurat." They do not enthusiastically announce the birth of a universal language whose name would be *Malerei;* they point to a singular example of painting signified by a proper noun. (3) This example belongs to the past, not to the future. It has already happened, yet it is presented as not happening yet. Seurat's tubes were opened long ago and the painter himself, who died young, disappeared before his potential could reach full bloom. Yet he is here fictionalized as a would-be painter. His paintings are presented as if they were not yet even begun, kept prisoner in "several tubes of paint," which have not yet inseminated a single canvas. The infra-thin possibility that these tubes of paint—or the *Comb,* or all the readymades retain is not that of painting again. It is not offered to the painter, only to the historian. It is no more than an invitation to look back. As in a parody of Kandinsky's *Rückblicke,* the

30. Duchamp, *Notes,* note 1. The note is undated, but it is probably from the late thirties. The oldest dated text relative to the infra thin is note 35, dated July 29, 1937.

31. "Infra thin" is not a noun but an adjective, says Duchamp (*Notes,* note 5), although the *sign of the accordance* might be the perfect exemplifcation of the infra thin made into a noun. Even as an adjective, "infra-thin" never qualifies a thing or an experience, but rather the difference between two things or experiences. This difference is at its thinnest when those two things are the same.

history of modern painting is melancholically looked at in hindsight as if it still had its future, while its achievements already belong to the past.

Now the question raised by this "explanation" is, why Seurat? Why not "the possibility of several tubes of paint becoming a Duchamp," for example, or "becoming a painting" in general? Why is this particular name recalled for the potential it entails? Isn't it an invitation handed over to us, the posthumous readers of Duchamp's note and the posthumous spectators of Seurat, to reinvestigate the history of modern painting as if it still had its future? Doesn't it suggest that although modernism might be over, it still retains a potential future in the form of a postmodern rereading of modernism? Inasmuch as hindsight forces us to recognize that the "program" of modernism was accomplished in the very brief time span that separates Seurat from Malevich's *Black Square,* doesn't Duchamp's note invite us to reinterpret this "program," not through the grid of its own regulative ideas—pure visibility, pure color, pure painting—but through Duchamp's idea of *pictorial nominalism,* as it takes the modernist regulative ideas as its referent? Doesn't it compel us to take a second look at the feeling of impossibility that has propelled the history of modernism and to relocate that feeling in the objective conditions that have made painting useless? Why not start, then, by relocating Duchamp's feelings for Seurat in those objective conditions? We would see that Seurat's relation to the tube of paint is also Duchamp's link to Seurat. "The greatest scientific spirit of the nineteenth century, greater in that sense than Cézanne is Seurat, who died at the age of thirty-two."[32] Subjectively speaking, the link between Duchamp and Seurat, their common feeling, is their equal contempt for the hand, *la patte.* As early as 1886, Félix Fénéon commented to that effect upon Seurat's *Un dimanche après-midi à la Grande Jatte* (A Sunday Afternoon on the Grande Jatte, 1886): "Here indeed is *la patte* useless and trick effects impossible; there is no place for bravado; let the

32. Marcel Duchamp, "A Complete Reversal of Art Opinions by Marcel Duchamp, Iconoclast," *Arts and Decoration,* September 1915; reprinted in *Studio International* 189, no. 973 (1975): 29.

hand be clumsy but let the eye be nimble, perspicacious and well learned."[33] What Duchamp admired in Seurat was the "scientific spirit" who abandoned "the devilish convenience of the brush" (as Delacroix already said) and mechanized it within the codes of divisionism. It was this abandonment of handicraft that Duchamp amplified to the point where he abandoned painting itself:

> From Munich on, I had the idea of the Large Glass. I was finished with cubism. . . . The whole trend of painting was something I didn't care to continue. . . . There was no essential satisfaction for me in painting ever. And then of course I just wanted to react against what the others were doing, Matisse and all the rest, all that work of the hand. In French there is an old expression, *la patte,* meaning the artist's touch, his personal style, his "paw." I wanted to get away from *la patte* and from all that retinal painting.[34]

Duchamp's admiration for a painter as "retinal" as Seurat is rooted in their common indictment of *la patte,* and this in turn offers the possibility of a new reading of early modernism, which, far from taking the positivistic naturalism of neoimpressionism at face value, relates it to one of its most important technological conditions, the tube of paint.

The Divisionist Division of Labor

Although tin or copper tubes were already in use in England at the end of the eighteenth century for the preservation of watercolor, it was only around 1830–1840 that tubes of oil paints began to be available on the market. The American painter-turned-paint-manufacturer John Rand is believed to have

33. Félix Fénéon, "*Les Impressionnistes en 1886,*" in *Au-delà de l'impressionnisme* (Paris: Hermann, 1966), p. 66; my translation.

34. Quoted in Tomkins, *The Bride and the Bachelors,* p. 24.

been the first to produce oil paints in tin tubes on an industrial scale. The impact of this simple technological innovation upon the future of painting is considerable, and it would be wrong to read it as mere practical progress and to believe that it simply liberated painters from a slavery external to their art. Together with the invention of photography—with which it is contemporaneous—the spreading of the tube of paint represents one of the two specific points of industrialization's penetration into the painters' practice. Like photography, it was thus threatening painters most directly in their artisanal tradition: certainly the tube of paint freed them from a tedious and mechanical task, but it also introduced division of labor into a professional activity that had always sought to maintain as much control as possible over the whole production process. What is called modernism in painting, and which began then, is perhaps nothing but the history of the obstinate—and to this day, continued—resistance that painters opposed to the division of labor with which industrialization was threatening them. Competition with photography was the most obvious threat; competition with the pigment industry was a more insidious but no less crucial one and, by the way, linked to the first. Historians usually agree to date the beginnings of modernist painting from the moment landscape painters abandoned the artifices of workshop practice to seek daylight. In submitting their skill to the constraints of on-site production, of course, the *plein-air* painters entered into explicit competition with photography. The camera was the principle mechanizing device that the painters had to reclaim, which they did by mimicking it and behaving as if their eye and their hand, coupled to their canvas, constituted a light-recording machine. They sought to give their craft a reprieve by "internalizing" the technology threatening it and by "mechanizing" their own body at work. Whereas this strategy of resistance was still implicit in impressionism ("Monet is but an eye," said Cézanne), it was made explicit by Seurat's divisionism, which was simultaneous and parallel to the invention of "autochrome" color photography by the Lumière brothers. Since Van Eyck, color and light had been one and the same thing for the true painter. With impressionism, they began to split: the instantaneous imprint of light is what Monet tried to capture in his *Rouen Cathedrals* or his *Haystacks*. Color, on the other hand, became the means to an end. And it could do so because, being readily available in tubes, it had become a commodity whose supply was abundant and devoid of mystique. As long as painters had to grind and mix their pigments themselves, *plein-airism* was a technical impossibility. For Constable or the Barbizon painters to leave their studio and paint outside, directly from nature, the availability of ready-made oil paints in easy-to-carry containers was a prerequisite. One cannot imagine them carrying along the bulky equipment that the preparation of paint on the premises would involve. Out of *plein-airism,* the palette of the impressionists developed as an aesthetic doctrine already reflecting upon this new state of things. It was limited to the colors of the prism, and thus it excluded black. Although the justification for this exclusion was naturalism—there is no black in nature—what the doctrine really did was to organize the act of painting as a series of choices within a standardized logic of colors. The divisionist (or, loosely called, pointillist) technique first developed by Seurat rationalized this production even further, explicitly turning the hand of the painter into a clumsy machine that operated in steps and rejected the blending continuity of handicraft.

As it did in regard to photography, divisionism resisted the threat wrought by the tube of paint in mimicking it. Since division of labor had already entered the painter's trade, painters now being consumers of the pigment industry, it became a matter of accepting this and of shifting the division of labor further down the production process, so to speak, while transposing it on the aesthetic level where it would be meaningful (and where divisionism, in the double sense of the word, would truly deserve its name). The deliberate "industrialization" of the painter's hand resulted in a displaced division of labor, which was no longer simply technical but rather aesthetic, and which the divisionist doctrine recognized and promoted: not only was the hand severed from the eye, but also the maker from the author, with, as a result, an altogether new solidarity between author and spectator. In classical aesthetics the function of authorship was a combination of skill and culture: form and content meshed into one another through artisanal craftsmanship. The author was the maker. The spectator's function was to be in a state of passive receptivity—that state which classical aesthetics called disinterestedness or contemplation—and to exert taste, to evaluate the degree of excellence in skill and culture displayed by the maker.[35] Divisionism set up a new aesthetic division of labor: authorship now included spectatorship and excluded, as far as possible, the simple mechanical task of making. The maker (the hand) remained passive inasmuch as it simply obeyed, "clumsily" and automatically, the commands of the eye already encoded in the ready-made discriminations provided by the paint manufacturers' color charts. The spectator, on the other hand, was asked to blend the pointillist encoding of the colored image on his or her retina, and became an active partner to the artist (who is of course also the first spectator of the work). Aesthetic reception was no longer contemplative and could no longer be disinterested. Even taste, as innate faculty or acquired culture, didn't matter as much as the injunction to synthesize the image on the retina and, through a reflexive movement of the mind, "nimble, perspicacious and well learned," to constitute its phenomenological status. Despite the positivistic intent of divisionism, this is not to say that there was no room left for aesthetic judgment. But the aesthetic judgment was not exclusively a judgment of taste anymore, and it no longer merely appreciated how the author/maker succeeded in meshing skill and culture. It became, so to speak, a second-degree judgment, the reflexive movement of the mind that took the beholder's retinal task as a springboard and produced a phenomenological object that, in itself, was not retinal at all, but rather the mental outcome of a critical choice. Is this what Duchamp had in mind when he said, in conversation with Alain Jouffroy, "I believe there is a difference between a kind of painting that primarily addresses itself only to the retina, to the retinal impression, and a painting that goes beyond the retina and uses the tube of paint as a springboard to something further"?[36] Perhaps not quite. For he added:

---

35. Disinterestedness and contemplation are essential to any aesthetics of taste. To arrive at a critique of aesthetic judgment that is not necessarily an aesthetics of taste, but that allows for it as a particular case, is a central concern of this book. See chapters 1, 4, and 5, in particular.

36. Alain Jouffroy, *Une révolution du regard* (Paris: Gallimard, 1964), p. 115; translation by Rosalind Krauss.

"This is the case of religious artists of the Renaissance. The tube of paint didn't interest them." The context of the conversation was one of those frequent occasions when Duchamp would pit "gray matter" against "retinal painting," a theme, by now a cliché of Duchamp scholarship, that has lingered too long and has allowed too many art critics who systematically oppose painting, or modernist painting, to cover themselves with Duchamp's authority in order to proclaim that painting as a whole is definitively obsolete (that's the "leftist" version), or that modernist or abstract painting is doomed and should revert to literary values (that's the conservative version: Jean Clair's defense of *peinture lettrée* is typical). But in his conversation with Jouffroy as in many others, Duchamp took great care to dissociate himself from literary painting—surrealism discreetly included. So that when he mocked what he called the "physical preoccupations" of "impressionism, fauvism, cubism, abstraction," it is the exceptions that deserve attention: "Some men like Seurat or like Mondrian were not retinalists, even in wholly seeming to be so."[37]

So, when Duchamp said, "It's the viewers who make the pictures," he took stock of the redistribution of the traditional division of labor within aesthetics accomplished by divisionism. When he equated art with making and making with choosing, he gave this redistribution ethical value, conferring on the viewer a share in the responsibilities of aesthetic choice. When he mentioned "a tube of blue, a tube of red" as an example of making (that is, of choosing) and systematically offered the tube of paint as an "explanation" of the readymade, he referred the readymade to those technological conditions that were already underlying *plein-airism* and which divisionism acknowledged. When he identified genius with the impossibility of making (that is, of choosing, that is, of painting), he granted the viewers their share of genius, provided they would refer their aesthetic choices to the abandonment of an attitude of pure contemplation, in the way the divisionist painters referred theirs to the abandonment of craftsmanship. And finally, when he found precisely in this abandonment the

37. Ibid., p. 111.

"possibility of several tubes of paint becoming a Seurat," what did he do if not hand over to us, viewers of Seurat as well as of Duchamp, the responsibility of reinterpreting, in the face of the readymade, that portion of the history of modern painting that goes from *plein-airism* to divisionism, so as to posit the historical and aesthetic importance of Seurat in the technological conditions that had made the practice of painting objectively useless, subjectively impossible, yet possible nevertheless?

The readymade's potential to allow a rereading of modern painting as if it still had its future does not stop with Seurat and divisionism. It extends into the very context in which it appeared in 1913, the birth of abstract painting. The tube of paint was Duchamp's ironic response to what was *the* question at issue in the genesis of abstract painting, the question of pure color. The concern with pure color is, in fact, a century or so older than abstract painting itself, and has its roots in two different and very opposed traditions. The first, which is psychological and symbolist, starts with Goethe's *Farbenlehre,* published in 1810, and makes its way in the history of nineteenth-century painting and painting theories, mostly German and Central European, through Runge, Friedrich, and the Nazarenes, the German romantic aesthetics of the sublime, subsequent *Farbenlehren* such as Bezold's, and the announcement of an abstract ornamental art in Viennese Sezession circles at the turn of the century (Karl Scheffler, Arthur Roessler, Adolf Hoelzel). It eventually leads to Kandinsky's theorization of pure color as an elementary signifier of pure painting. Kupka's own passage to abstraction equally owes much to this tradition, although it is also, and very significantly, indebted to the second tradition of pure color, which is essentially French and has its origins in Chevreul's researches on simultaneous contrast.[38] First published in 1839 and republished in 1889, Chevreul's memoir, which is a complete, scientific and systematic theory of color, had already inspired Delacroix when, in a climate of both symbolism and positivism, it became the

38. Eugène Chevreul, *De la loi du contraste simultané des couleurs et de l'assortiment des objets colorés considéré d'après cette loi* (Paris: Pitois-Levrault, 1839).

theoretical grounding for divisionism. The new doctrine was laid down in writing by Signac, who soon became the leader of the neoimpressionist movement, even before Seurat's death, in 1891. He defined the "basic principles of neoimpressionism" in terms of works "painted only with pure hues, separated, balanced and optically mixed according to a rational method," adding what historically speaking is perhaps the first definition of purism in painting: "Like the impressionists the neoimpressionists find on their palette nothing but pure colors. But they absolutely forbid themselves all mixing on the palette. . . . Each brushstroke is taken pure from the palette and remains pure on canvas."[39]

Toward the end of the century, Signac's theoretical justification of an art "guided by tradition and science" was no longer believed in. The symbolist interest in irrationality had outgrown the positivistic confidence in scientific rules, and the objective naturalism inherent in impressionism gave way to the subjective concerns of expressionism. Yet there is a formal continuity between the practice of Signac, Luce, Cross, or Van Rysselberghe and that of early fauvism. Between 1904 and 1906, Matisse, Marquet, Manguin, Vlaminck, and Derain were all painting in a loosely pointillist manner, decorative and devoid of theoretical claims.[40] Moreover, many of the artists who would a little later

39. Paul Signac, *D'Eugène Delacroix au Néo impressionnisme* (1899; reprint, Paris: Hermann, 1964), pp. 89, 91; my translation.

40. Of course, especially in the case of such a great painter as Matisse, things are more complex. Following Catherine Bock (*Henri Matisse and Neo-impressionism, 1898–1908* [Ann Arbor, Mich.: UMI Research, 1981]), but differing in interpretation, Yve-Alain Bois reminds us that Matisse went through two divisionist phases, one in 1898, in which "he is completely engrossed in trying to put Signac's principles in practice," and one in 1904, culminating in *Luxe, calme et volupté,* in which he in fact prepares his complete break with divisionism demonstrated by *La joie de vivre* (1905–1906). Signac's rage when he saw this last painting at the Salon des Indépendants led him to write to Charles Angrand that it "evokes the multicolored shopfronts of the merchants of paints, varnishes and household goods" (Yve-Alain Bois, "Matisse and 'Arche-drawing,'" in *Painting as Model* [Cambridge, Mass.: MIT Press, 1990], p. 18.) An interesting accusation, in the context of a discussion of the tube of paint, and one that makes

become the cubists had a corresponding pointillist period at the same time: Braque, Derain, Delaunay, Metzinger, even Mondrian in his "luminist" vein. Indeed cubism, especially the dogmatic cubism of the Puteaux group, was a reaction against the superficial decorativeness of fauvism and neoimpressionism and an attempt to provide painting with a new set of theoretical tasks. Partly thanks to new reception conditions that had put Cézanne's reputation far above Seurat's, the issue of pure color was momentarily abandoned and even repressed. Hence the general dullness of palette in cubist painting. But it emerged again, toward 1911–1912, in the practice of Mondrian, Kupka, and especially Delaunay, coinciding with the advent of abstract painting. It involved a new reading or a new reception of Chevreul's theories, made possible by a new intellectual context—the combination of symbolism and positivism had given way to that of simultanism and structuralism.

In poetry, the interest in simultaneity, indeed the passion for it, as evolved by Apollinaire, Cendrars, and Barzun, was itself a late offspring of symbolism. In painting, it developed as an aspect of the ongoing speculation on the fourth

---

me wonder whether the "quantity-as-quality-equation"—"One square centimeter of any blue is not as blue as a square meter of the same blue," which Bois convincingly posits at the root of what he calls "the Matisse system" and its break with "the Signac system"—does not represent another regulative idea, distinguished both from the "pure-color-as-language-idea" promoted by the early abstractionists and from Duchamp's *pictorial nominalism,* an idea moreover a lot less idealist than the former and a lot more compatible with the latter. This is a major issue for any historical rereading of modern art. It perhaps allows one to escape the forced choice between the Duchamp-lineage and the "modernist painting"–lineage à la Greenberg. It is difficult to make room for a Matisse-lineage that would not take the road of abstract, modernist painting (Kelly being the major figure), yet, if you think of Warhol's enigmatic statement, "I want to be Matisse," in connection to what he actually did with drawing, color, and "cutting in color," you begin to think that the figurative Matisse has had at least one magnificent, and very unforeseen, heir, one who was definitely a *painter* in the guise of an *artist.* And of course, the road from the ready-made tube of paint to both the *Brillo Boxes* and the "paint by number" canvases is straight.

dimension among the cubists and on speed among the futurists. It was left to Delaunay to bring this rather loose concern together with Chevreul's theory of simultaneous contrast, and to produce in his work and in his writings a new doctrine of painting, which he called simultanism. The issue of pure color no longer worked in the service of an aesthetics of imitation (as it did for Chevreul himself and to a large extent for the neoimpressionists); it was fully translated into a new aesthetics borrowed from poetry and whose outcome was, in Delaunay's words, "the ABC of expressive methods that derive from the physical elements of color creating new form."[41] Here again, in Delaunay's reference to the "physical elements of color," we encounter the profound paradox at the root of the impulse toward abstraction: in the depth of matter lies a language. Delaunay's writings actually provide us with the most elaborate rationalization for the switch to abstract painting. While the elements he posits as a groundwork for abstraction may be "physical," like atoms, they are also and above all linguistic or semiotic: "the ABC of expressive methods." Chevreul's system was no longer read as an application of physics to the realm of perception psychology (a typically positivistic bias), but as the establishment of a linguistic system through which color could "speak" without reference to the representation of nature. Numerous parallels, starting with the prevalence given by both to synchronicity over diachronicity, can be drawn between Chevreul's theory of colors and the new, structuralist theory of language developed by Ferdinand de Saussure in precisely those years preceding the birth of abstract painting. Of course, none of the pioneers of abstraction had read Saussure at the time, and structuralism became an "ism" only fifty years later, when the work of Saussure became the grid for various reading strategies applicable to virtually every "signifying practice," painting included.[42] But what in the sixties became a matter

41. Arthur A. Cohen, ed., *The New Art of Color: The Writings of Robert and Sonia Delaunay* (New York: Viking Press, 1978), p. 16.

42. The starting signal for this might be seen in Roland Barthes's "reversal" of Saussure, when, in *Eléments de sémiologie* (1964), he suggested that semiology should be seen as being part of linguistics rather than linguistics as being part of semiology.

of deconstruction was first a matter of construction. What was at stake around 1913 was not the analysis, or the ideological critique, of the "pictorial language," it was its synthesis, the ideological legitimation of abstract painting justified as a language.

Both Delaunay and Kupka openly acknowledged Chevreul and Seurat as their sources. Duchamp, as we know, also acknowledged the importance of Seurat (and thus indirectly of Chevreul). The same interview where he rails against *la patte* ends with this conclusion: "The only man of the past whom I really respected was Seurat, who made his big paintings like a carpenter, like an artisan. He didn't let his hand interfere with his mind. Anyway, from 1912 on, I decided to stop being a painter in the professional sense."[43] To become, I suppose, a painter in the *nominalist* sense, since all around Duchamp in 1912, what was unconsciously at stake for all those painters who sought to establish the "ABC" of an "international language which will endure forever" was that its name would not be Esperanto but *Malerei*. Well, for Duchamp *Malerei* spells out *Peigne:* the infra-thin slip of the tongue that hides the potential "I ought to paint" in the name of a ready-made object which it is impossible to call a painting.

LE CÉLIBATAIRE BROIE SON CHOCOLAT LUI-MÊME

The feeling of painting's impossibility must have been the subjective signal accompanying the awareness of its objective uselessness, that is, of the painter's idleness in an industrial culture. With industrialization, the painter was replaced by the machine. The camera, of course, come readily to mind, but here again the consequences of the newly available tubes of paint should not be overlooked. The fact is that the bachelor no longer grinds his chocolate himself. Duchamp spent eight years on the *Large Glass,* meticulously transferring its elements—the *Bride* in her domain, up there, the *Bachelor Machine,* of which the *Chocolate Grinder* is the central piece, below—from sketches and preliminary works. This magnificent painting on glass—better, painting under glass—was

43. Quoted in Tomkins, *The Bride and the Bachelors,* pp. 24–25.

the tireless labor of a craftsman, and even if the result shows no resemblance at all to the modernist painting done in the period, still, it is a painting. Duchamp could not have relinquished the painter's slow, artisanal activity without ceaselessly mourning it and recording the process. The bachelor's (i.e., the painter's) impossible desire for the Bride (i.e., painting) is not only encapsulated in the ready-made objects that infinitely postpone its fulfillment. The *Large Glass* also tells its story, and it is the story of scopophilia, of the desire to see the Bride stripped bare, of seeing painting reduced to its naked appearance of pure painting. With the same ironic twist that made him want to see eroticism transformed into an artistic "ism," Duchamp was mocking the idea of pure visibility. Redubbed *oculism,* the regulative idea of abstract painting became the object of a narrative fantasy. In retrospect, this may very well be what the history of abstract or modernist painting was. All the same, the desire to paint was still there, and Duchamp didn't fail to melancholically refer the chocolate grinder's "adage of spontaneity: the bachelor grinds his chocolate himself,"[44] to the objective uselessness of the old grinding machine. "The 'useless' of the chocolate grinder must be the brush stroke over some invisible spots that the bachelor secretly maintains."[45] With all its onanistic connotations referring to painting as "olfactory masturbation," the *Bachelor Machine* is a self-portrait in disguise, whose very personal meaning also resonates with the historical conditions that led Duchamp to officially record his abandonment of painting in the readymade, on the one hand, but also to "secretly maintain" the cherished activity of a painter-bricoleur, on the other. The *Grinder* portrays the painter jobless and useless, since the "basic elements" of his craft, the fabrication of pure color, had been taken over by industry. Painters no longer grind their own colors, they buy them in tubes. But the *Grinder* also portrays the painter as he mimics this industrial process, taking on the guise of a color-grinding machine. Duchamp, like John Rand, planned to turn himself into a paint manufacturer: "For the final colors, make up all the colors of the picture before using them and *put*

44. *The Green Box,* in *SS,* p. 68.

45. Duchamp, *Notes,* note 115.

them in tubes, with labels (for being able to correct, retouch, etc.)."[46] The project is ironic, of course, and the *Grinder* is an allegory, which is why it is the color of chocolate, brown, the most impure of all colors, that in Duchamp's allegory stands for pure color—in the singular. He calls it molecular, natural, and native, as in a pastiche of Delaunay's "physical element": "There is *one* single native chocolate color which serves to determine all chocolates."[47] And when, years later, in *Moonlight on the Bay at Basswood,* 1953, he used actual chocolate for pigment, the irony of the *Chocolate Grinder* came full circle.

The fact that painters no longer grind their own pigments may seem merely an obvious consequence of the availability of industrially processed tubes of paint. Yet this fact is crucial to an understanding of the cultural changes that disrupted the tradition of painting and that made the modern tradition a sort of anti-tradition leading to the demise of painting as craft and its instant rebirth as idea. In the old days of painting, the grinding of colors, along with the making of stretchers, the gessoing of the canvas and other preparatory practices, was not considered a subordinate activity. Cennino Cennini prescribed it as an important, almost amorous process in which the echoes of Duchamp's "olfactory masturbation" can already be heard:

> Start grinding color by color: take a porphyry slab, not too polished, half an arm long on each side. Take another porphyry stone to hold in hand, flat underneath, in the shape of a bowl, and smaller, so that the hand can grip it firmly and steer it here and there as it wishes. Pour your oil on the color and grind it for about half an hour, an hour, as long as you want, for if you ground it a whole year long the color would only become better and better.[48]

---

46. Ibid., note 80.

47. *SS,* p. 85.

48. Cennino Cennini, *Il libro dell'arte,* (New Haven, Conn.: Yale University Press, 1932), 1:21. (Written *ca.* 1400.) See also Xavier de Langlais, *La technique de la peinture à l'huile* (Paris: Flammarion, 1959), pp. 332–333.

Despite the increasing intellectualization of painting from the Renaissance on, the humble, mechanical task of grinding colors remained an important part of the painter's know-how, endowed with alchemical prestige, and jealously protected as a secret knowledge. Moreover, in the days when young painters still had to learn their skill in apprenticeship to a master, the transmission of the workshop recipes played a considerable role in keeping the continuity of tradition. It was a symbolic gesture, a sort of passport to autonomous professional life that the master handed over to the apprentice only when he judged him worthy of it. As academic training began to replace workshop apprenticeship, of course the grinding of colors lost some of its secrets, and the passing on of the grinding recipes some of its symbolic value. By the time of the industrial revolution, it had long ceased to be a privileged procedure in the transmission of tradition. But interestingly enough, the more it lost its real importance, the more it was idealized by those traditional artists who, witnessing the industrial revolution, were afraid for art's survival, and whose only answer to the new challenge was to seek to revive the golden age of guilds and corporations. From Ruskin and the Pre-Raphaelites down to the foundation of the Bauhaus, and all the way through the Arts and Crafts movement and the evolution of the *Kunstgewerbeschulen* in Germany, the same nostalgia for handicraft can be felt, accompanied, as far as painting is concerned, with a fixation on the most manual aspects of the trade. In most cases, the concern for painting technique went hand-in-hand with a frightened refusal of industrialism and a more or less avowed hatred of modernism. In most cases also, this refusal and this hatred focused on a certain fetishization of the grinding of colors, proportionate to the importance it once had in the transmission of tradition. It is therefore not surprising that as late as 1921, almost a century after the invention of the tube of paint, such a leading authority on painting technique as Max Doerner, in his book *Malmaterial und seine Verwendung im Bilde,* would start his chapter on oil paint with this sentence: "It is recommended that the painter grind his own colors."[49]

49. Max Doerner, *The Materials of the Artist* (London: Granada Publishing, 1977), p. 143 (a translation of *Malmaterial und seine Verwendung im Bilde,* 1921). Doerner was a very academic

Absurd and pathetic as it sounds in retrospect, Doerner's admonition to painters to grind their own colors is highly symptomatic, and quite understandable from the academic standpoint that he maintained. His book is not a neutral treatise on technique, it is a surreptitious sermon against modernism:

> The painter of today must become more conscious of his responsibility for the permanency of his work than is unfortunately the case. Many a painter of today lives to see his own handiwork go to pieces in his lifetime because he abused his materials. Before one can become a master, one must first have been a disciple. Those who do not believe this will pay the penalty sooner or later. There is no shortcut to becoming a good painter, to quote Reynolds.[50]

What is at stake is duration, tradition, and continuity. No makeshifts, no shortcuts should be allowed in discipline and apprenticeship. Even relying on ready-made pigments is not innocent and would lead painters to abuse their materials. When one considers the general contempt among modernist painters for *la patte,* durability, and other overvaluations of sheer technique in the light of Doerner's reactionary defense of tradition, one comes to think that this contempt was neither accessory to their stylistic innovations nor simply and deliberately provocative. It is not as if Mondrian and Malevich, whose work, technically speaking, indeed didn't pass the test of time too well, had no other

but prominent character on the Munich art scene while Duchamp was there. He was *Dozent* at the Royal Bavarian Academy and chairman of the *Deutsche Gesellschaft zur Förderung rationeller Malverfahren,* a society that had been founded in 1884 in order to mediate between the paint manufacturers and the painters. A few weeks after Duchamp's departure from Munich, Doerner, who thought of himself, so to speak, as the Ralph Nader of the painters, began giving a series of public lectures on painting technique. One wonders whom these lectures could actually have reached. Obviously, Doerner was pursuing the dream of rallying the scattered community of painters back to tradition.

50. Ibid., p. 316.

claim but the destruction of the painting tradition as it hitherto existed and didn't seek to transmit their own work to future generations. Quite the contrary. But what they felt had to be passed on was much less an object than an attitude, a sensitivity, an ideal. Someone else could redo their paintings if they fell to pieces, or better still, make new ones, working from the example they had set. What they actually understood and worked for, and what Doerner stubbornly refused to acknowledge, was that the mode of transmission of culture that constitutes a tradition had been radically changed. The time is long gone when artistic culture and know-how were transmitted from one painter to the next in the private space of the workshop, and the apprenticeship contract that bound together two generations of painters is a thing of the past. There have been many attempts during the nineteenth century and since to reconstitute, often in esoteric and always in nostalgic forms, craftsmen's and painters' guilds modeled after the corporations of the Middle Ages, but none of them succeeded. The Academy itself could no longer control access to the profession of painter, which is why its teaching, ever on the defensive, degenerated into academicism. Reynolds was the last great pedagogue-academician and David, the revolutionary painter, did not succeed in being one: the Revolution had put an end to the monopolistic claims of the Academy, which in any case had been threatened since its very inception by the rise of another competitive and public institution, the Salon.[51] Modernity starts with Salon painting, and this means that a modern painting is addressed to the layman even before it is conceived, because it is destined to land in the marketplace from its outset. The avant-garde was born out of the controversies around Salon painting, and the core of the phenomenon of the avant-garde is that from then on, painters had joined the crowd, laymen among laymen, partly because their means of production, tubes of paint among them, were in the marketplace already, available to anyone.

51. See Thomas E. Crow, *Painters and Public Life in Eighteenth-Century Paris* (New Haven, Conn.: Yale University Press, 1985).

No padlock restricts access to the profession of modern painter. The politics of the Salons, the very inadequate conversion of the Academy into Ecoles des Beaux-Arts, the economics of the marketplace—all these phenomena that evolved under the impulse of the general process of industrialization—conspired to fuse art's conditions of production with its conditions of reception. With the Salons, anyone, even deprived of taste and culture, was granted the right to judge painting, and was even invited to do so. With the decline of academic art into academicism anyone, even uncultivated and "primitive," could claim the title of pioneer, in spite of the Beaux-Arts. With the market as sole regulator of practice and arbiter of taste, anyone, even untalented and unskilled, could try painting. Like the adolescent Kandinsky, all they needed to do was buy a box of oil paints and try their luck. The story that Kandinsky remembers with so much lyricism in *Rückblicke* is emblematic on more than one count. The gist of the modern utopia is to have enthusiastically embraced the conditions set forth, if only symbolically, by the tube of paint. Out of it sprang pure color, but in Kandinsky's fantasy pure color meant pure painting already: a brand-new form of painting, without past, without apprenticeship, without tradition. Plebiscite would replace the masters as soon as humankind would speak the same universal language. It would not be called Esperanto but painting. With this act of faith abstraction was founded, and everything had to be done anew: new teaching methods would relinquish the models provided by the *Abmalerei* of the past and rest, instead, on "the language of forms and colors"; a new regulation of artistic supply and demand would correct mercantilism and restore art's use value; a jurisdiction of taste more democratic even than the Salons, and legitimated by the people, would set in. Kandinsky spared no effort to make this utopia, which was pedagogical throughout, into a reality. He would teach at the Bauhaus and write the "grammar of forms" he had already projected in *Über das Geistige in der Kunst,* which he entitled *Punkt und Linie zu Fläche* (From Point to Line to Surface). Itten and later Albers would do the same for the language of colors. Klee would look to nature and its organic laws to find his Organon; Malevich would write a semiotic history of painting starting with Cézanne; Mondrian, El Lissistzky, Van Doesburg, all would write, teach, broadcast their ideas as much as their art. Since the constitution and the transmission of a modern tradition were now in the hands of the public at large, the world would become a vast art school. And so painting would rise from its ashes.

Transition

This utopia failed. This pedagogy, this policy, this ideology failed, and if it were true that aesthetics is irredeemably tied to the ideals informing it, we would have to say that the art generated by the modernist utopia failed too. The Bauhaus produced very few great artists and the Bauhaus model, adopted by innumerable art schools around the world, either perpetuated a formalism of the most sterile kind or entered a deep crisis. The world does not speak the Esperanto of abstract art; the public at large has not learned to regulate its aesthetic judgments through the idea of pure visibility; and the professional artworld has retreated into a specialized culture analogous, but only analogous, to scientific culture, when it has not simply surrendered to the market. No new tradition has been founded on the basis of an elementary universal language made, for example, of red squares, yellow triangles, and blue circles. Instead, we have had "the tradition of the new." It has not replaced tradition in the old sense. The pessimist and conservative Max Doerner had more insight than Kandinsky when he said: "Today most artists work independently of one another, but in the days of old masters each artist was a link in a chain, a part of tradition. . . . Today every artist is expected to turn out a new hit each season in the manner of a vaudeville performer."[52]

Doerner was right: as the chain of tradition has been broken, "artists work independently of one another." When temporal filiations are cut, spatial ties become undone; when the dead don't speak to the living anymore, then the living cease to communicate with each other. Once the community of peers with whom artists speak across time has dissolved, there remain only social

52. Doerner, *Materials of the Artist,* p. 315.

values on which to shape their ambitions. When there is no authority to distinguish between artist and non-artist, then the very definition of art becomes a public matter settled by the vox populi, with the obvious risks of yielding to fashion and demagogy. Doerner saw this, but what he refused to admit was that this condition of the painter of modern life, which Baudelaire had grasped with so much more clear-sightedness, was irreversible. No corporatism, no defense of craftsmanship, no admonition telling the bachelors to grind their own chocolate, would make them cease to be bachelors. If Duchamp and his readymade prove Kandinsky wrong, and empty the tube of paint of its promises, they do not prove Doerner right; they explain him. They reopen the file on pure painting; they investigate the archaeology of pure color; they provide the historian, or the "archaeologist," with a thread to be followed backwards, from Kandinsky's tube, from Kupkas "planes by color," from Delaunay's simultaneous *Windows,* to Seurat's divisionism where, for the first time, a new aesthetics, inherent in his canvases, took stock of a new division of labor attributing execution to the bachelor machine and authorship, together with spectatorship, to the alienated crowd in the midst of which artists and non-artists alike work "independently of one another."

It is around Seurat and Signac that the Société des Artistes Indépendants, whose motto was "Ni récompense ni jury," was founded in 1884. It is the Indépendants who gave divisionism a home, who propagated the theories of Chevreul, Ogden Rood, and Charles Blanc, who showed Dubois-Pillet, Angrand, Luce, Cross, and also Pissarro in his divisionist period. It is the Indépendants who stood for anything progressive in French art in the latter part of the nineteenth century. Signac, who saw himself as invested with Seurat's legacy and who, like Seurat himself and like Pissarro, had sympathy for the anarchists, had sketched a program that would not be disclaimed by any of the subsequent pedagogical enterprises, such as the Bauhaus, which counted on the education of the eye to free modern painters from their alienation and given them the broadest social basis: "When the eye is educated, the people will see more than subject matter in paintings. When the society we dream of exists, when the workers, rid of the exploiters who drive them stupid with work, have the time to think and to learn, they will appreciate the manifold qualities of works of art."[53] Here, better than anywhere else, the foundation of the Société des Artistes Indépendants reveals its social dream, and the theme of pure color reveals its fundamental utopianism. The fact that artists work "independently of one another" was a premise to the Société's foundation but by no means its last word: when the workers' eye would be educated, artists would have reintegrated their community; but it would no longer be the community of their peers, it would be the whole of society. To educate the workers' eye does not mean turning them into bourgeois connoisseurs; it means teaching them to do consciously what they already do spontaneously: discriminate colors and recompose them optically. Perhaps it is the utopian socialism underlying modernism that explains why it settled for pure color even more than for "basic form," when it purported to lay the grounds for a universal access to art. The combat of drawing and color is a very old one, and even at the time of the quarrel between the "Rubénistes" and the "Poussinistes," the conservatives were on the side of drawing and the progressives on that of color. Le Brun, who played such an important role in the creation of Colbert's Academy and would become its first director, seemed to be echoing Max Doerner in advance when he said, in 1672: "The grinders would be ranking with the painters if drawing didn't make the difference."[54] A century later, Diderot apparently agreed, only to play unwittingly into Signac's hands: "Only masters of art are good judges of drawing; anybody can judge color."[55]

Signac's utopia translates as follows: when pure color is legitimated as the true foundation for painting, then anyone will be a judge of painting as well. In this lies the Indépendants' legacy to the founders of abstract painting. Meanwhile, however, the Indépendants didn't live up to their utopian ideal. They

53. P. Signac, quoted in Germain Bazin, *L'univers impressionniste* (Paris: Somogy, 1981), pp. 152–153. (My translation.)

54. Quoted in André Richard, *La critique d'art* (Paris: P.U.F., 1968), p. 23. (My translation.)

55. Denis Diderot, *Traité du Beau* (Verviers: Marabout, 1973), p. 69. (My translation.)

hosted the progressive academization of divisionism and allowed the doctrine to freeze, until it became no more than a pretext for decorative pointillism. It is at the Indépendants that the grand pedagogical utopia of modernism first failed and that pure color was betrayed. Do I need to insist on the reasons for the myth's failure? It suffers from a contradiction that has accompanied the whole of modernity: on the one hand, only "when the society we dream of exists" will the new division of labor promoted by divisionism cease to alienate professional painters from the people. On the other hand, only "when the eye is educated" will the people erase the differences setting them apart from the professionals. Art was given the task of reforming society. Needless to say, it failed. In twenty years, the Indépendants lost their illusions: Pissarro abandoned divisionism grumbling at ideological painting, Signac and Luce took refuge in Saint-Tropez. They began dreaming of Arcadia once again, and the time when Seurat had the social classes rubbing shoulders on the banks of the Seine was long gone. Signac was named president of the Société in 1908, after the fauvist explosion, as if the authority of an old-timer had been required to properly welcome the young blood and to warrant the continuity, which is formally evident but which is merely formal, between *La Grande Jatte* and *La Joie de Vivre.* The fireworks would soon die out. The discovery of Cézanne overshadowed Seurat. Cubism repressed color, and when the Indépendants reluctantly made room for cubism, in 1911, it was for the orthodox cubism of Gleizes and Metzinger. Braque and Picasso refused to participate. By 1912, the Indépendants were an academy and had rejected Duchamp's *Nude Descending a Staircase.*

Five years later, at the New York Independents, Duchamp put his abandonment of painting on the record. *Fountain* spoke of art, or prompted people to speak of art in connection with it. We have passed from the specific to the generic, and this passage is a switch of names. Exit the painter, enter the artist, the artist in general. His name was Richard Mutt, that is, anybody, since anybody could be an artist at the Independents, even a manufacturer of bathroom fixtures whose corporate name was The J. L. Mott Iron Works. That is the height of *ironism:* Mutt's piece of porcelain came out of the workshop of a manufacturer dealing in iron, the substance of *Witz* and genius, the substance of the previous year's *Comb*. This comb would return in 1937 in the shape of a photographic reproduction adorning the cover of the magazine *Transition*, designed by Duchamp. The layout is extremely subtle: at first sight, the comb seems to float in space, seen at an angle and in perspective, like some of Malevich's figures. The title is in italics and is set so as to appear to be on the same oblique plane as the comb. The background is an edge-to-edge expanse of green—the color of the *Green Box*, but also the one color Mondrian had banned from abstract painting. Under the title, a slightly undulating trace, as if executed with watercolor by a trembling hand, alters the pure monochromy of the page and hinders fixed accommodation of the eye. Once you notice it, you can no longer read the title as if it were in continuity with the comb's perspective, but you can't plunge your gaze into the expanse of green either. With superb economy of means, Duchamp has created an image that simultaneously thwarts the flatness of the support and disturbs perspectival identification, as if he had called on both the pre-modern and the modern regulative ideas, the illusion of depth and the integrity of the picture plane. This is a figurative image, not an abstract one; it is the cover of a magazine and not a painting; but "the brushing stroke over some invisible spots that the bachelor secretly maintains" at least alludes to painting, and the reflexion that inspires it no doubt refers to the ideas regulating modernism—pure painting, pure color, pure visibility—and takes them as referents. Finally, it is a very conscious quotation of the key work in which the artist recorded his abandonment of painting, and this quotation is in turn recorded by the title: *Transition*. As if by "commissioned symmetry," it thus refers to the *Passage from Virgin to Bride* where it all started, and it sheds retrospective light on the context out of which the readymades were born: on the passage to abstraction by a whole generation of painters who rediscovered Seurat's pure colors as they moved out of cubism. Duchamp's response to their passage from figuration to abstraction would be his transition from painting to art in general.

Are we done with "the possibility of several tubes of paint becoming a Seurat"? Yes, if we simply mean that Seurat is dead. But if we think—as the reception history of the readymade proves it was thought all too often—that in abandoning painting for readymades Duchamp assassinated painting, we would be misinterpreting the facts and perpetuating an injustice. We should not forget that, although the stroke of genius in the readymade, its *Witz,* rested in "the impossibility of the making," this was no more than a feeling, a quasi-moral feeling already at work in Seurat's painting, whose "concrete explanation" is "the possible as infra thin." It is not with promises that Seurat's tubes were filled: the progressive academization of divisionism into merely decorative pointillism has shown the failure of the modern utopia that had linked together the existence of industrially produced tubes of paint, a scientific theory of pure color, a new aesthetic division of labor, and the promise of a society that the eye's education would free from alienation. But in another sense, Seurat's tubes were not empty of promises; his paintings fulfilled them. The tube of paint—this readymade that Duchamp maintained in the *possible* state—allows a rewriting of that history which goes from Seurat to the fauvists and from the fauvists to abstraction, as it happened, but freed both from the utopia and from its failure. It lifts a mortgage that has weighed all too heavily on the way art history is written, when works are kept as hostages of ideologies whose failure is blatant. It rehabilitates the only judgment that counts, the aesthetic judgment that makes us rank *La Grande Jatte* and *La Joie de Vivre* side by side among the masterpieces of modern painting, and thus, of painting *tout court*.

There remains only one question: can we rank Duchamp's urinal, or his comb, alongside both *La Grande Jatte* and *La Joie de Vivre* as a masterpiece of art *tout court*? Perhaps not. But do we need to? Duchamp has done the "algebraic comparison" for us. We can put the comb in the rubric *art* and Matisse's canvas in the rubric *painting* and keep the rubrics separate. With the tube of paint providing us with the missing link, we are equipped to evaluate art in general on its own merits. Pure visibility will not help, that's for sure. But then it will not help us evaluate Rodchenko's red, yellow, and blue triptych either. Anyone can judge color. That doesn't prove one judges well.

Robert Ryman, *Versions VIII,* 1991, oil and graphite on fiberglass, with nails, 15 × 15″. Hallen für neue Kunst, Schaffhausen.

4

The Monochrome and the Blank Canvas

> The American vanguard painter took to the white expanse of the canvas as Melville's Ishmael took to the sea.
>
> —*Harold Rosenberg*

Some Interpreted Facts

> I wanted to get the paint out of the can and onto the canvas. . . . I tried to keep the paint as good as it was in the can.
>
> —*Frank Stella*

In December 1959 a virtually unknown painter named Frank Stella, aged twenty-three, was invited to participate in one of the prestigious shows staged at MoMA by Dorothy Miller throughout the fifties, whose purpose was to promote the new American art. Entitled *Sixteen Americans,* the show was a strange yet interesting mixed bag: it included second-generation Abstract expressionists like Alfred Leslie, James Jarvaise, and Richard Lytle, as well as the "hard-edge" abstract painters Ellsworth Kelly and Jack Youngerman and the "proto-pop" artists Robert Rauschenberg and Jasper Johns. Among them was Stella, whose work contrasted strongly with that of his colleagues. He presented four huge canvases painted mechanically with a regular, repetitive pattern of black stripes executed with commercial enamel on raw cotton duck with a flat, 2½-inch-wide housepainter's brush. Their stretchers were thicker than usual, approximately as thick as the brush's width, and the sides of the painting had been left unpainted so as to visually detach the painted surface from the wall and to project it into the room. The contrast with the exuberant expressionism of most of the other participants could not have been more striking. By comparison, even Johns's *Flags* and *Targets* must have looked "painterly" and Kelly's Matissian compositions rather "arty."

Stella's self-presentation in the catalogue also stood in striking contrast to that of his fellow artists. Whereas the majority had been photographed in the studio, clad in the usual artist's attire and surrounded by the usual paraphernalia, Stella showed a deadpan image of himself wearing a tie and a dark gray suit, as if he were floating against an all-white, shadowless background reminiscent of Manet's *Fifre.* The photograph was taken by Hollis Frampton, then a close friend of Stella and a photographer, later to become one of the most interesting experimental filmmakers of the times. And whereas most other participants in the show either accompanied the reproductions of their work with an "artist's statement" or with the usual laudatory comment of a well-known art critic, Stella asked his friend Carl Andre, soon to become a leading minimalist sculptor, to speak on his behalf. Here is Andre's laconic statement:

> Preface to Stripe Painting
> Art excludes the unnecessary. Frank Stella has found it necessary to paint stripes. There is nothing else in his painting. Frank Stella is not interested in expression or sensitivity. He is interested in the necessities of painting. Symbols are counters passed among people. Frank Stella's painting is not symbolic. His stripes are the paths

> of brush on canvas. These paths lead only into painting. Carl Andre.[1]

The show, followed a few months later by a show of all-aluminum shaped canvases at the Leo Castelli gallery, had an enormous impact on Stella's generation of artists. Though it may be an overstatement to say that minimal art sprang from this show, it is clear that the show crystallized a new sensibility which had hitherto expressed itself only negatively, as a sheer lassitude with Abstract expressionism. It also offered the possibility of rereading Abstract expressionism, and Pollock's "all-overness" in particular, in formal rather than existential terms. Harold Rosenberg's concept of "Action Painting" became suddenly trite and hopelessly romantic, whereas Clement Greenberg's understanding of "American-type Painting" in terms of formal results, historical conventions, and flatness of the medium gained momentum and credibility. Indeed, Greenberg's *Art and Culture* became a bestseller among artists as soon as it came out in 1961.[2] And his best known essay, "Modernist Painting," also published in 1961, instantly became a sort of aesthetic Organon for a whole generation of artists, even for those who rejected it.[3] It offered a bold yet simple reading of the history of modern painting, one that gave painting renewed intellectual credibility and the avant-garde a new sense of direction. In the forties and the fifties, there was a revival of the late-romantic cliché of the artist as instinctive

1. Carl Andre, "Preface to Stripe Painting," in *Sixteen Americans,* ed. Dorothy C. Miller (New York: The Museum of Modern Art, 1959), p. 76.

2. Clement Greenberg, *Art and Culture* (Boston: Beacon Press, 1961).

3. In fact, Greenberg's "Modernist Painting" was first broadcast and published as a pamphlet by the Voice of America in 1960, but it remained rather confidential until it was issued, unrevised, in the *Arts Yearbook IV,* 1961. Since then it has been republished several times (for the complete list of republications, see John O'Brian, ed., *Clement Greenberg, The Collected Essays and Criticism,* vol. 4, *Modernism with a Vengeance, 1957–1969* [Chicago: University of Chicago Press], 1993, p. 93).

resource of creativity, with no ties to history and no cultural function beside his (never her) sacred vocation. The refreshing and cleansing effect of Greenberg's text was to eliminate that image and to provide instead a coherent aesthetic and historical rationale for professionalism in painting. The romantic image of the artist as the Bohemian or the social rebel was no longer plausible in the face of the academization of Abstract expressionism and its commercial success. The extended series of abandonments, destructions, or deconstructions of pictorial conventions that Greenberg described as building up the history of modernist painting were no longer presented as revolts or subversions, but rather as the establishment of a secure area of competence. This could only appeal to a generation of artists who needed to shake the Oedipal weight of their Abstract expressionist elders while also realizing that they had to compete with them, both professionally and for the same market.

In that context, Carl Andre's *Preface to Stripe Painting* appears utterly Greenbergian. It shares the same ontological assertion that painting is defined by its minimal, formal, and material "necessities" or conditions, which exclude any symbolic subject matter. Stella's black paintings themselves bear witness to this paragraph from "Modernist Painting":

> The essential norms or conventions of painting are also the limiting conditions with which a marked-up surface must comply in order to be experienced as a picture. Modernism has found that these limiting conditions can be pushed back indefinitely before a picture stops being a picture and turns into an arbitrary object; but it has also found that the further back these limits are pushed the more explicitly they have to be observed.[4]

---

4. Clement Greenberg, "Modernist Painting," in *The New Art,* ed. Gregory Battock (New York: Dutton, 1973), pp. 72–73. I shall, throughout this chapter, assume that Greenberg's definition and descriptions of modernism, of modernist painting, and of its history are correct, granted that modernism is not congruent with modernity and that modernist painting is not

Yet Stella's black paintings don't seem to have received Greenberg's stamp of approval. What Greenberg had in mind when writing "Modernist Painting" was a view of the history of painting's reduction to flatness, a history in which the works of Manet and Monet, Matisse and Picasso, Pollock and Newman were acknowledged landmarks, and in which the most recent examples supporting his view were Morris Louis's *Veils* and Kenneth Noland's "circle paintings," but not Stella's black paintings. Why? "They were not good enough" is his most probable answer, and there is no arguing with that.[5] But why are they "not good enough," since "Modernist Painting" reads as if it had been written in support of them? Greenberg has always insisted that "Modernist Painting" was a neutral account of history, that it was descriptive and did not in the least seek to establish criteria for judgment. Still, it is informed throughout by its author's taste, which seems to have evolved under the same pressure as modernist painting itself. Thus, one would expect to see his taste surrendering in front

the whole of modern painting. My concern is to somewhat disentangle the intricacies of a particular episode—indeed, the beginning of a pivotal crisis—in modernist art and formalist criticism alike. It is an episode in which, whether correct or not, Greenberg's views literally shaped the work of so many artists—especially of those, ironically, who rejected them—that they made history, although they may not have described it adequately or judged it fairly. With some inevitable simplifications, the Greenbergian doctrine and its success, the controversies it raised and the countertheories it gave rise to in the work of some artists, are here all taken as facts, to be interpreted from the viewpoint of a historian or an "archaeologist," not to be criticized from the viewpoint of a critic, an aesthetician or an art "theorist." However, the critical reinterpretation I shall offer in the last part of this chapter will, I hope, "reformat" the episode under scrutiny, and even some of its antecedents and consequences, in such a way that it will show on which crucial works and issues my judgment and my interpretation differ from those of both Greenberg and his opponents. The implications of this, for aesthetics and art "theory," provide the substance for the next chapter.

5. Since I wrote this, I have had a chance to ask Greenberg the question. This was his reply: "As for Stella's black paintings: they're plausible, but not good enough; his aluminum ones are better, but still not good enough." (Letter to author, 23 January 1987.)

of Stella's black paintings, since these observe so explicitly the limiting conditions that "can be pushed back indefinitely before a picture stops being a picture and turns into an arbitrary object." Yet Greenberg's taste stopped short of including Stella's black paintings. Is it perhaps because they transgressed this ultimate limit and became "arbitrary objects"? But it would then mean that this limit could not "be pushed back indefinitely" and that the history of modernist painting might be terminated. Or is it perhaps because the black paintings so conveniently illustrated "Modernist Painting," converting its historical account into a theory of sorts, and thus threatening free aesthetic judgment? By compelling the viewer who finds them "good enough" to see them as ultimate paradigms of modernist painting, the black paintings would make Greenberg's historical description prescriptive, even normative; they would make the minimal condition of flatness into a maximal one.

This is exactly what the young painters who were soon to become the minimalists must have felt. The impact of Stella's black paintings on them was tremendous, as was the aura of Greenbergian criticism. They must have felt that it was impossible to be a significant artist without being a painter and at the same time that it was impossible to pursue modernist painting without going beyond the monochromatic literal flatness of Stella's black and aluminum paintings. At that point, they would cease to be painters and would merely produce "arbitrary objects." At that point, they would also have to break with Greenberg, lest Greenberg break with them first. Both have happened, of course, and it is quite ironic that the central debates concerning the art of the sixties and the seventies should have revolved around a critical doctrine that sees itself as retrospective and descriptive, yet becomes prospective and prescriptive in the very works of those artists who took it for granted and who therefore had to reject it in order to create. In any case, most minimal artists (among them Dan Flavin, Sol LeWitt, Donald Judd, Michael Steiner, Ronald Bladen and John McCracken) started out as painters around 1960. Their early work stems directly from Stella's black paintings, acknowledging their monochromatic flatness, mechanistic look, and extra thickness. Consider, for example, Dan Flavin's *Icon V* (*Coran Broadway Flesh*) of 1962, a square masonite panel uniformly painted in a flesh color and framed by a series of lighted bulbs; or Donald Judd's *Light Cadmium Red Oil and Sand, Black and White Oil and Galvanized Iron on Wood* of 1961, a rectangular wooden panel painted in red to which a cornice of galvanized metal has been attached on both the top and the bottom sides; or Sol LeWitt's *Wall Structure, Black* and *Wall Structure, White,* of 1962, two monochrome canvases, one white, the other black, in the center of which a protruding wooden parallelepiped has been affixed. These works—and there are many others—depart from the two-dimensionality of painting by adding a three-dimensional element to it. They deliberately seem to transgress the limit where, according to Greenberg, *a picture stops being a picture and turns into an arbitrary object.* Moreover, they claim this arbitrariness as a quality in itself.

All this happened thirty years ago and seems far removed from current preoccupations. Meanwhile, the advent of minimal art was followed by that of conceptual art, Land Art, performance art, and, more recently, various "appropriation" practices often referred to as neoconceptual. Varied as they are, all these movements have one thing in common: they pit themselves against painting, and sometimes against sculpture as well. What they have retained from the sixties is the authorization to produce *generic* art, that is, art that has severed its ties with the *specific* crafts and traditions of either painting or sculpture. Meanwhile, the artworld has also seen an overwhelming return of painting, but in the form of figurative and neoexpressionist painting, whose specificity is defended with the most conservative arguments: a revival of craftsmanship, traditional authorship, the quality of oil or the smell of turpentine, and the like. What has been sacrificed in the process is modernist painting in the Greenbergian sense, whose specificity was defined by its particular history, that very history which dispensed with, one by one, virtually every convention of painting and ended up in Stella's back paintings or in monochrome painting in general. The pendulum swings back and forth with predictable regularity, and it may be fascinating for those who like predictability to watch the recent trend of Neo-Geo supplant that of neoexpressionism in a parody of Greenbergian modernism. For those who expect unpredictability from art, it is a saddening sight. The time has thus come to shift one's attention from the pendulum to the fulcrum where the pendulum is attached. And there lies a question in need of factual, then critical, interpretation. It is a question pertaining to the relation of painting in particular to art in general, in other words, between the specific and the generic. The question is art historical, critical, "theoretical," and, ultimately, ethical. Art historically, it is as old as modernity itself and, as you realize, it is the same question as the one posed by the birth of abstraction, with abstract *art* emerging from cubist *painting*. But there is another episode that deserves particular analysis, and in many respects it is a repetition of the cubist/abstract episode. It certainly overdetermines the present situation even more and draws us back to the issue of the monochrome in the early sixties in New York and to the case of "Modernist Painting" versus minimalism.

Some Factual Interpretations

> It remains that Modernism in art . . . has stood or fallen so far by its "formalism." Not that modernist art is coterminous with "formalism." And not that "formalism" hasn't lent itself to a lot of empty, bad art. But so far every attack on the "formalist" aspect of modernist painting and sculpture has worked out as an attack on Modernism itself because every such attack developed into an attack at the same time on superior artistic standards.
>
> —*Clement Greenberg*

In Greenberg's view of modern art, the relation of painting to art is equated with that of modernist painting to modernism at large. But "modernism at large" is an elusive concept for which Greenberg never offered more than an elliptic definition:

> I identify Modernism with the intensification, almost the exacerbation, of this self-critical tendency that began with the philosopher Kant. . . . The essence of Modernism lies, as I see it, in the use of

> the characteristic methods of a discipline to criticize the discipline itself—not in order to subvert it, but to entrench it more firmly in its area of competence.[6]

Rigorously speaking, there is no "modernism at large" since the self-critical tendency characterizing modernism can apply only to a given discipline from within that discipline. Modernism doesn't allow for interdisciplinarity. Specificity is thus essential to modernism, and modernism in the arts proceeds from their strict separation:

> Each art, it turned out, had to effect this demonstration on its own account. What had to be exhibited and made explicit was that which was unique and irreducible not only in art in general but also in each particular art. . . . It quickly emerged that the unique and proper area of competence of each art coincided with all that was unique to the nature of its medium.[7]

What is this nature of the medium with regard to painting?

> Flatness alone was unique and exclusive to that art. . . . Flatness, two-dimensionality, was the only condition painting shared with no other art, and so modernist painting oriented itself to flatness as it did to nothing else.[8]

This is the best-known aspect of Greenberg's doctrine of modernist painting. It states its specificity in positive terms. Stated in negative terms, this specificity would be made of the residue of all the conventions that pre-modern painting

6. Greenberg, "Modernist Painting," p. 67.

7. Ibid., p. 68.

8. Ibid., p. 69.

shared with the other arts (above all, "literature") and which modernist painting had to relinquish, one by one, so as to assert its own "area of competence."[9] But the more modernist painting pushed back the limiting conventions of its medium, the closer it came to its immediate neighbor, sculpture, and the more explicitly it had to trace a borderline between sculpture and itself so that, defined negatively, the specificity of modernist painting became equated with strong antisculptural qualities:

> Three-dimensionality is the province of sculpture, and for the sake of its own autonomy painting has had above all to divest itself of everything it might share with sculpture.[10]

Modernism is thus defined as specific and, in the case of painting, as a tendency toward flatness or "non-sculpture." In that sense, there is no modernism at large.

But in another sense, there is. The retrospective historical account that Greenberg gives of modernist painting privileges the Lessing–Wölfflin–Roger Fry lineage, that is, a *formalist* tradition of criticism.[11] It is not devoid of value judgments, hierarchies, and exclusions. They may in part stem from intellectual preferences; they certainly correspond to a series of judgments of taste that also privileges a modernist tradition of artists, precisely that which progressively uncovered painting's minimal and essential convention of flatness. Thus, the ten-

9. In Greenberg's early writings, where he was defending the superiority of abstract art, the word "literature," which meant not only narrative content but also "ideas," every sort of psychological subject matter and even "the ideological struggles of society," encompassed everything that painting had to dispense with so as to be "pure." See Clement Greenberg, "Towards a Newer Laocoon," in *Clement Greenberg, The Collected Essays and Criticism,* ed. John O'Brian, vol. 1, *Perceptions and Judgments, 1939–1944* (Chicago: University of Chicago Press, 1986), pp. 23–38 (p. 28 in particular). First published in *Partisan Review* 7, no. 4 (1940).

10. Greenberg, "Modernist Painting," p. 70.

11. See Thierry de Duve, "Clement Lessing," in *Essais datés I* (Paris: Editions de la Différence, 1987), pp. 65–117.

dency toward flatness, of which Greenberg takes stock as a historian, shows itself to be inseparable from a tropism toward aesthetic value, which Greenberg judges as a critic:

> Modernism defines itself in the long run not as a "movement," much less a program, but rather as a kind of bias or tropism: towards esthetic value, esthetic value as such and as an ultimate. The specificity of Modernism lies in its being so heightened a tropism in this regard.[12]

Aesthetic value is the outcome of a judgment of taste; it is neither an objective property of the works nor an a priori criterion or norm. The aesthetic value of a given work is what makes up its *content* for a given viewer, who can of course be the artist him- or herself:

> The quality of a work of art inheres in its "content," and vice versa. Quality is "content." You know that a work of art has content because of its effect. The more direct denotation of effect is "quality."[13]

Quality or content, also paraphrased as "gist, meaning, what works of art are ultimately about,"[14] must be carefully distinguished from "subject matter," which, in modernist art, is the medium itself:

> In turning his attention away from subject matter of common experience, the poet or artist turns it upon the medium of his own craft.

12. Clement Greenberg, "Necessity of Formalism," in *Contemporary Esthetics,* ed. Richard Kostelanetz (Buffalo: Prometheus Books, 1978), p. 207.

13. Clement Greenberg, "Complaints of an Art Critic," *Artforum,* October 1967, p. 38.

14. Ibid.

> The nonrepresentational or "abstract," if it is to have aesthetic validity, cannot be arbitrary and accidental, but must stem from obedience to some worthy constraint or original. This constraint, once the world of common, extraverted experience has been renounced, can only be found in the very processes or disciplines by which art and literature have already imitated the former. These themselves become the subject matter of art and literature.[15]

The medium in its specificity is not simply a matter of physical constituents; it comprises technical know-how, cultural habits, working procedures and disciplines—all the conventions of a given art whose definition is throughout historical—even more so that the self-critical (or self-referential, but better called reflexive) tendency of modernism is to take those conventions for subject matter and to test their aesthetic validity. This means that the conventions of a specific art such as painting are never a given. They are the momentary and fragile state of a consensus that is bound to be broken before it is reconstituted elsewhere. The individual work of art—more precisely, its *form*—embodies this call for a new consensus. Form is what translates into visual, describable appearance the state of the conventions of modernist painting as they are incorporated in a work at a given moment in the history of painting. In other words, the *form* of a work is what makes its *subject matter* visible and offers access to its *content* or quality. It is a constraint that puts pressure on the artist's (and the viewer's) aesthetic judgment and that the work respects or transgresses, modifies or displaces and, in any case, remodels. In this sense, Greenberg can say, but only in retrospect, that modernist painting's tendency toward flatness ran hand in hand with its tropism toward aesthetic quality, so that:

> Quality, aesthetic value originates in inspiration, vision, "content," not in "form. . . ." Yet "form" not only opens the way to inspira-

15. Clement Greenberg, "Avant-Garde and Kitsch," in *Art and Culture,* p. 6.

> tion; it can also act as means to it; and technical preoccupations, when searching enough and compelled enough, can generate or discover "content. . . ." That "content" cannot be separated from its "form."[16]

Readers of Greenberg have often confused "formalism" with "modernism." Greenberg himself is partly responsible for this, because he never explicitly distinguishes the two terms. They are indeed intimately intertwined because modernism—contrary to both premodern art and non-modernist tendencies within modern art—ascribes the aesthetic judgment not to imitation, expression, or imagination, but to the state in which artists leave the conventions they have inherited after having tested them. Whereas modernism simply appears as a tendency, to which works belong or not, formalism involves the way in which the aesthetic judgment, moved (or unmoved) by the *content* of a given modernist work, is compelled to approve (or disapprove) of the *form* in which the work remodels its historical conventions:

> Reflection shows that anything in a work of art that can be talked about or pointed to automatically excludes itself from the "content" of the work. Anything . . . that does not belong to its "content" has to belong to its "form. . . ." The unspecifiability of its "content" is what constitutes art as art.[17]

Thus "art as art," that is, art as value, is not specifiable. If it were, it would mean that the conventions of a given art could restrict aesthetic judgment a priori and that one would have to judge according to those conventions, whereas it is clear to Greenberg that what modernism compels us to do is judge those conventions themselves. Art as art cannot and may not be specific; it has to

16. Greenberg, "Necessity of Formalism," p. 174.

17. Greenberg, "Complaints of an Art Critic," p. 39.

give the works of modernism a generic content that is, so to speak, perpendicular to its specific form and subject matter. In other words, the sentence "this is art (as art)" is never trivial for Greenberg, but conveys an aesthetic judgment:

> It remains: that when no aesthetic value judgment, no verdict of taste, is there, then art isn't there either, then aesthetic experience of any kind isn't there. It's as simple as that.[18]

The word "art" evaluates quality, which is not to say that it is synonymous with quality. Greenberg has repeatedly said that the word "art" was not necessarily an honorific appellation. Indeed, the passage just quoted doesn't presume the direction in which the value judgment is to go. A negative aesthetic judgment is still an aesthetic judgment, and an unsatisfactory aesthetic experience is still an aesthetic experience. Thus bad art is art as much as good art. (Greenberg took issue with Croce on this.) As we shall see, it may turn out to be not "as simple as that." But the reasons things get problematic have everything to do with the events I shall recapitulate and interpret. In the meantime, what remains on the level of doctrine is that when it expresses an aesthetic judgment the sentence "this is art" is never trivial. It would be trivial if it meant, for example: "this is a painting—that is, it obeys the conventions of painting—therefore it is art." The word "painting" would refer to a socially accepted set of norms and the word "art" to a category of human activity of which painting is a subcategory. The sentence "this is art" would merely take notice of a certain state of the social consensus; it would not judge it. But when there is an aesthetic judgment (and let us, for the sake of clarity, suppose that it is a positive one), it has to be the other way around: "this is art—that is, my taste, sufficiently acquainted with and pressured by the historical state of the conventions of the medium, tells me this is good—thus it is a painting worthy of the name." This

18. Clement Greenberg, "Seminar Seven," *Arts Magazine* 52 (June 1978): 97.

is what it means to say that "the unspecifiability of its 'content' is what constitutes art as art."

"This is good (or bad)," "this is beautiful (or ugly)," or "this is art (as art, good or bad)," expresses an aesthetic judgment. It is nonspecific and unspecifiable. Yet it has validity for modernism only insofar as it refers to—and exerts itself on—the specific set of conventions making up the historical state in which a given work leaves its medium. It can only mean something like "this is a good painting" or "this is beautiful within sculpture," or "this is bad poetry," or "as a piece of music this is art." Between content and form, between the generic value judgment and the specific self criticism of the particular medium, there has to be a mediation, but one that doesn't allow for a deduction. If it did, it would mean that content—aesthetic value—could be inferred from the state of the medium. Conversely, it would mean that the medium could be deliberately manipulated so as to produce content or quality, thus allowing for what Greenberg called "concocted" art. The judgment of taste, in the first instance that of the artist, is obviously the mediation we are looking for. It expresses the quality of the work as it is felt; better still, it *is* this quality:

> Aesthetic value or quality *is* affect; it moves, touches, stirs you . . . it does that in being value and in compelling you to like it more or less, or not like it more or less. . . . Aesthetic value, aesthetic quality can be said to elicit satisfaction, or dissatisfaction. . . . Satisfaction or dissatisfaction is "verdict of taste."[19]

Satisfaction and dissatisfaction are affects or feelings, and a feeling cannot be feigned, or it ceases to be a feeling. Thus verdict of taste—or aesthetic judgment—is passive and involuntary:

> Aesthetic judgment is not voluntary. . . . Your aesthetic judgment, being an intuition and nothing else, is received, not taken. You no

19. Clement Greenberg, "Seminar One," *Arts Magazine* 48 (November 1973): 45.

> more choose to like or not like a given item of art than you choose to see the sun as bright or the night as dark.[20]

As to the modernist artist's aesthetic judgment, it has to be suggested, inspired, provoked by or received from the medium itself, for the medium is the only subject matter of modernism and the locus of the artist's aesthetic constraints:

> The artist receives judgments-decisions—inspiration, if you like—from his medium as he works in it.[21]

As a result, it is also from the medium, indeed from the *form* it takes in a particular work, that the spectator receives his or her aesthetic judgment. Although there is a generic meaning to "modernism," there can be no modernism at large. Conversely, although the conventions defining a given medium historically are specific by definition, their specificity may not be taken for granted but ought to be judged "generically." The name of the necessary mediation between genericity and specificity is *formalism*.

The sentence "this is beautiful" or "this is art (as art)" expresses, formulates, *formalizes* in language the affect or feeling of quality constituting the aesthetic judgment, as if quality were a property of the work in its visual appearance, in its *form*. As a methodology of art criticism, formalism means that form and subject matter are the only things one can talk about. It certainly doesn't mean that it values form for the sake of form. To say that it values form for the sake of content would be closer to the truth. But, since "anything in a work of art that can be talked about or pointed to automatically excludes itself from the 'content' of the work," content is the one thing that never acquires discursive existence in formalist criticism. Content is ineffable because it is a feeling and because feelings do not get communicated by talking about them. In a way, art critics cannot write about "art as art"; they can write about painting, sculpture,

20. Ibid.

21. Clement Greenberg, "Seminar Five," *Studio International* 189–190 (May–June 1975): 191.

poetry, or music, that is, about the medium, and treat the medium as the only subject matter of art, even if the artist didn't. In this case they are modernist, even if the work is not. They are formalist if "art as art"—that is, their aesthetic judgment, their feeling of quality—is what makes them speak of a given work, whose form alone they can describe in language. This doesn't make their feeling of quality an objective or even linguistic property of the work's form, yet doesn't simply imply that beauty—or quality—is in the eye of the beholder. The paradox—actually built into sentences such as "this is beautiful" or "this is art"—is that the feeling of beauty, or of art, is formulated as if it were a noticeable fact ascribable to the form of the work. One recognizes in this paradox the antinomy of taste established once and for all by Kant.[22] It is not particular to formalist criticism. What complicates the issue, tangles up formalism and modernism so closely and accounts not only for their confusion, but also for the false impression that formalism values form for the sake of form, is the fact that the specific conventions of the medium are, in modernism and in modernism alone, the only subject matter that indeed matters for the verdict of taste. Though formalism considers that its discourse cannot speak of content, it can speak of subject matter. But "once the world of common, extraverted experience has been renounced," there remains only one subject matter, to "be found in the very processes or disciplines" of a given, specific medium. And though the medium is specific, it is still a generality; only individual works can be appraised aesthetically. In other words, the self-critical tendency that Greenberg calls modernism, and which is specific, yields individual *forms* whose generic art-*content* is appraised *as if* it were a function of their *subject matter*. When judged successful, a given modernist painting is experienced *as if* its success "measured"

22. More about Kant's antinomy of taste in chapter 5. Meanwhile, let's notice that the aesthetic judgment according to Greenberg is the Kantian judgment of taste (i.e., about beauty), not the judgment about the sublime. The parts that I left out in the above quotation distinguished "affect" from "emotion," and elsewhere Greenberg has linked emotion to the sublime and the sublime to "concocted art." See his *Avant-Garde Attitudes* (Sydney: The Power Institute of Fine Arts, University of Sydney, 1969), p. 12.

the outcome of the aesthetic test to which it put the conventions of the medium. The mediation between form and content hides in the necessary "as if"–structure of this judgment expressed, however, by the simple sentence, "this is art."

For the sake of simplicity, from now on I shall reserve the name "modernism" to designate modernism as specific self-criticism and I shall use the name "formalism" to designate modernism as generic quality (art as art). As far as painting is concerned, "modernism" thus refers to its specific tendency to assert the flatness of its medium, and "formalism" refers to its tropism toward aesthetic value as such. Neither modernism nor formalism can be willed. That the two tendencies or tropisms converge in the properties of the medium and in the passivity of the aesthetic judgment is a result of the history of modernist painting and, as such, can only be recognized retrospectively. It was never a deliberate intention or a program set forth by the painters. Yet it seems to have been, very early on, Greenberg's conviction that the two tendencies had to converge, as is confirmed by his use of the word "surrender" in his major early essay, "Towards a Newer Laocoon," to describe the history of modernist painting (or of avant-garde painting, as he was still calling it then): "The history of avant-garde painting is that of a progressive surrender to the resistance of its medium; which resistance consists chiefly in the flat picture plane's denial of efforts to 'hole through' it for realistic perspectival space."[23]

Some Reinterpreted Facts

> I remember that when Stella was doing his black paintings, Motherwell told me: "It's very interesting, but it's not painting."
>
> —*William Rubin*

From Manet to Stella, modernist painting has progressively surrendered to the resistance of its medium, to the point where very little was left beside its

23. Greenberg, "Towards a Newer Laocoon," p. 34.

flatness itself. Accompanying a portion of this history, from Pollock to Morris Louis, the critic's taste has equally surrendered. Yet it stopped short of acknowledging Stella's black and aluminum paintings, judging perhaps that they had turned into *arbitrary objects*. Battling Greenberg on his own turf, the early minimalists pushed their paintings into the third dimension, where they became objects indeed. It is of course not the first time that monochrome or quasi-monochrome painting appeared in the history of modern art. In each case, its advent has spelled out the zero degree of painting. For some (like Rodchenko) it meant its death, for others (like Malevich) it meant its birth or rebirth under a new name, for others still (like Tarabukin) it meant its birth and its death all at once. In each case one of the answers was a leap into the third dimension. As early as 1940 Greenberg had shown awareness of this:

> Sculpture hovers finally on the verge of "pure" architecture, and painting, having been pushed up from fictive depths, is forced through the surface of the canvas to emerge on the other side in the form of paper, cloth, cement and actual objects of wood and other materials pasted, glued or nailed to what was originally the transparent picture plane, which the painter no longer dares to puncture—or if he does, it is only to dare. Artists like Hans Arp, who begin as painters, escape eventually from the prison of the single plane by painting on wood or plaster and using molds or carpentry to raise and lower planes. They go, in other words, from painting to colored bas-relief, and finally so far must they fly in order to return to three-dimensionality without at the same time risking the illusion—they become sculptors and create objects in the round, through which they can free their feelings for movement and direction from the increasing ascetic geometry of pure painting.[24]

24. Ibid., p. 36.

This paragraph from the "Newer Laocoon" might describe the advent of minimal art, if it were not for a few crucial differences. Far from freeing themselves "from the increasing ascetic geometry of pure painting," the minimalists claimed it and projected it into real space. Although some of them became sculptors or were sculptors already, indeed practicing a kind of sculpture that "hovers finally on the verge of 'pure' architecture" (think of Tony Smith, who began as an architect), others started out as painters, like Hans Arp. But unlike Arp, they would never be content to call their work "colored bas-relief." As we shall see, what to call it was very much an issue.[25] The minimalists would have felt most uncomfortable to see their practice linked to the tradition of bas-relief, a tradition that is at least as old as easel painting and goes back to Ghiberti or even to Nicola Pisano, a tradition, also, that straddles painting and sculpture and that, therefore, cannot be modernist in the Greenbergian sense because it is interspecific rather than specific. This shows to what extent minimalism depends on Greenberg's doctrine, and all the more so since it rejected it. Its history is thus written three times: in the works themselves, of course, but also in the "theories" offered by the artists in justification of their works, and finally in Greenberg's resistance to both the works and the theories. I shall start with the

25. It is this issue that is new and particular to the minimalist episode. Arp had no objection to calling his works "reliefs"; quite the contrary. And to shift contexts, one remembers that in England, in the early fifties, relief had become a category in itself for the "constructionists" gathered around Victor Pasmore, especially for Mary Martin, who quit painting in favor of relief in 1951. Like the minimalist one, this episode was governed by the feeling, spread by Charles Biederman, that abstract painting could not "go any further." When you think that it was in 1951 that Fontana did his first pierced monochromes, Rauschenberg his seven white panels, and Kelly his white reliefs, you come to think that there is another crucial episode here, on an international scale, in the recursive history of the monochrome. As always, it was an attempt at finding a way out of a crisis in abstract painting by jumping into the third dimension. But unlike what happened in New York in the sixties, this episode was not overdetermined by a doctrine of specificity which excluded from modernism the hybrid tradition of relief or bas-relief.

latter. Its "theoretical" stumbling block is the issue of the monochrome repeating itself in particularly sensitive conditions of reception. The irony is that those conditions are set by the success of Greenberg's account of the progressive surrender of painting to its own specificity, and that the last chapter of the history so described appears to be, with the historical distance we have, that of the critic's progressive surrender to art's genericity.

This last chapter is written between the lines of Greenberg's writings throughout the decade that saw the advent of minimal art. We will have to follow his surrender and his struggle to resist it step by step. In 1958, a year or so before Stella's show at MoMA, Greenberg is still confident that modernist painting has a bright future. In "American Type-Painting" he writes:

> Though it may have started toward modernism earlier than the other arts, painting has turned out to have a greater number of *expendable* conventions imbedded in it, or at least a greater number of conventions that are difficult to isolate in order to expend. It seems to be a law of modernism—thus one that applies to almost all art that remains truly alive in our time—that the conventions not essential to the viability of a medium be discarded as soon as they are recognized . . . Painting continues, then, to work out its modernism with unchecked momentum because it still has a relatively long way to go before being reduced to its viable essence.[26]

In 1961, after Stella's two seminal shows, Greenberg feels compelled to keep his guard up. Although he still boasts in "Modernist Painting" that the limiting conditions or conventions of painting "can be pushed back indefinitely before

26. Clement Greenberg, "American Type-Painting," in *Art and Culture,* p. 208. An earlier version of "American Type-Painting" had appeared in *Partisan Review* in the Spring of 1955. See John O'Brian, *Clement/Greenberg, The Collected Essays and Criticism,* vol. 3, *Affirmations and Refusals, 1950–1956* (Chicago: University of Chicago Press, 1993), pp. 217–235.

a picture stops being a picture and turns into an arbitrary object," he feels the necessity of fencing off the excessive literalness of Stella's examples of modernist painting. A hesitation appears in the text that undermines his confidence, and a new line of defense is traced around what can be called residual illusionism, the very same illusionism for which he will praise Jules Olitski's spray paintings a few years later:

> The flatness toward which modernist painting orients itself can never be an utter flatness. The heightened sensitivity of the picture plane may not permit sculptural illusion, or *trompe-l'oeil,* but it does and must permit optical illusion.[27]

Published in October 1962, "After Abstract Expressionism" subtly articulates this new line of defense. With a rapid and tactical oscillation of "give and take" designed to dismiss the alleged dogmaticism of his doctrine, Greenberg grants Hoffman's "behind-the-frame" pictures, de Kooning's and even Johns' "homeless representation" or Fautrier's "furtive bas-relief" some positive qualities, which he nevertheless deems insufficient, the better to present his case in favor of Still, Rothko, and Newman with concepts drawn from Wölfflin, such as painterliness and openness of form. It is thus, thanks to a nimbler historical narrative and a stronger theoretical apparatus, that he can regain confidence in modernist painting and reassess aesthetically its limit or essence:

> By now it has been established, it would seem, that the irreducible essence of pictorial art consists in but two constitutive conventions or norms: flatness and the delimitation of flatness; and that the observance of merely these two norms is enough to create an object which can be experienced as a picture: thus a stretched or tacked-

27. Greenberg, "Modernist Painting," p. 73.

> up canvas already exists as a picture—though not necessarily as a successful one.[28]

But only two months later, in December 1962, he publishes under the aggressive title "How Art Writing Earns its Bad Name" an angry defense of his formalism, in which he is forced into a retreat of a new kind:

> Art turns out to be almost inescapable by now for anyone dealing with a flat surface, even if it is mostly bad art.[29]

What happened in between these two texts? The case under scrutiny is a hypothetical one, but one that the very history of modernist painting has made plausible: the blank canvas, the empty flat surface. In October it was called a picture, "though not necessarily a successful one"; in December it was called art, "even if it is mostly bad art." The change in formulation may seem trivial: if something is a picture then it is art, and if it is an unsuccessful picture then it is bad art. But let's remember that formalism doesn't allow that kind of deduction. Nothing can be called a picture—certainly not a blank canvas—unless it is called art (as art) first or by the same token. A blank canvas, such as you would find at the artists' supply store, is a mere object, a worldly thing destined to be painted on; it is neither a painting nor a work of art as yet. The brash assertiveness of the October text hides an almost fatal surrender, and one that is not (or not exactly; more about that later) of the same nature as that of the critic's taste in front of a chronologically arranged series of paintings which, from Pollock to Stella, have observed the convention of flatness more and more explicitly. With the hypothetical case of the blank canvas, Greenberg didn't simply surrender his taste to the resistance of the medium; he came very close to

28. Clement Greenberg, "After Abstract Expressionism," *Art International* 6, no. 8 (1962): 30.

29. Clement Greenberg, "How Art Writing Earns Its Bad Name," *Encounter* 19 (December 1962): 69.

surrendering his aesthetic doctrine—which precisely articulates a doctrine of taste (formalism) with one of specificity (modernism)—to his minimalist opponents. Once an unpainted canvas can be called a picture or a painting, then it is automatically called art. With the dismissal of the very last *expendable convention* of modernist painting— that the canvas be painted at all—the specific surrenders to the generic. The consequences branch out into two possibilities. Either (this would be the left branch of the alternative) the making and the appreciation of art require nothing but a mere identification predicated on the conceptual "logic" of modernism, and aesthetic judgment is no longer necessary; formalism would have to be betrayed; or (this would be the right branch of the alternative) aesthetic judgment is still necessary. But the pressure that the conventions of painting had put on its practice is now nil, and one is forced to allow for an art that is no longer the outcome of its specific history, a generic art. Modernism, this time, would have to be abandoned. Although reluctantly and to a great extent unconsciously, Greenberg chose the right branch of the alternative, which is why the line passing between a picture and a successful one had to be redrawn between art and good art. In the process the aesthetic judgment has been saved, but specificity had to be sacrificed. There is still room for quality, but purism or reductivism is no longer tenable. Formalism is redeemed at the expense of modernism.

Some Factual Reinterpretations

> The young artist of today need no longer say "I am a painter." He is simply an artist.
>
> —*Allan Kaprow*

The door to generic art is now open, which is tantamount to a blanket authorization for minimal art. Yet Greenberg, who will not surrender formalism, is not ready to surrender modernism that easily. Minimal art may have been legitimized by the history that led modernist painting to the threshold of the blank canvas, but in order to be judged convincing, it needs to pass the test of aesthetic experience. Some works may pass it while others may not. All works, however, need to be linked to their specific history in order to be plausible candidates for aesthetic appreciation; this is why a 1967 article entitled "Recentness of Sculpture," in which Greenberg severely criticizes minimal art, significantly starts with a long recollection of his first reactions to monochromatic painting:

> Advanced sculpture . . . worked out as badly as it did in the forties and fifties because it was too negatively motivated, because too much of it was done out of the fear of not looking enough like art. Painting in that period was much more confident, and in the early fifties one or two painters did directly confront the question of when painting stopped looking enough like art. I remember that my first reaction to the almost monochromatic pictures shown by Rollin Crampton in 1951 was derision mixed with exasperation. It took renewed acquaintance with these pictures to teach me better. The next monochromatic paintings I saw were completely so—the all-white and all-black paintings in Robert Rauschenberg's 1953 show. I was surprised by how easy they were to "get," how familiar-looking and even slick. It was no different afterwards when I first saw Reinhardt's, Sally Hazlett's, and Yves Klein's monochromatic or near-monochromatic pictures. These, too, looked familiar and slick. What was so challenging in Crampton's art had become almost overnight another taming convention. . . . A monochromatic flatness that could be seen as limited in extension and different from a wall henceforth automatically declared itself to be a picture, to be art.[30]

This paragraph reiterates the process that had led Greenberg in 1962 to accept that a blank canvas be called a picture and thus art, and now conflates the two

30. Clement Greenberg, "Recentness of Sculpture," in *Minimal Art, A Critical Anthology,* ed. Gregory Battcock (New York: Dutton, 1968), pp. 180–181.

appellations: "to be a picture," "to be art," are now one and the same thing. But this perfect overlapping of the specific and the generic is not concluded from a hypothetical case; this time, it is arrived at through "renewed acquaintance" with concrete examples. Seeing the practice of monochromatic painting as an ultimate test of confidence and, in retrospect, relying on his negative aesthetic judgment on Rauschenberg, Reinhardt, and Klein, Greenberg once again concludes that painting (the specific) has ultimately surrendered to art (the generic). In the process, the word "art" has lost whatever honorific status it may have retained when applied to Crampton's quasi-monochromes. The sentence "this is art" is now automatically inferred from "this is a picture," itself an automatic deduction from the perceptual phenomenon of monochromatic flatness. At this point the aesthetic judgment is shunned and shunted. For if the word "art," or "art as art," had retained its evaluative meaning of aesthetic quality—or lack of quality—as such, never would a monochromatic flatness have automatically declared itself to be art. But is it not an ironic paradox that the short-circuit of the aesthetic judgment should be the outcome of one ultimate, negative aesthetic judgment, the one that declares all but Crampton's monochromes "familiar and even slick"? And is it not another, even more ironic paradox that these paintings could not have appeared familiar and slick to an eye untrained and unacquainted with modernist painting's progressive "surrender to the resistance of its medium" down to Crampton? So that in fact the ultimate test of confidence to which the next monochromes—Rauschenberg's all-white and all-black paintings—have put modernist painting had to be passed successfully before they could be called a failure. In other words, they had to be judged as bad paintings before they could automatically be called art. Around this paradox the whole case of "Modernist Painting" versus minimalism revolves. There is no need to suspect that the account Greenberg gives of his aesthetic judgments in front of Crampton's residual illusionism is disingenuous[31] (although it

31. Especially since he has warned us against this: "But it is one thing to have an aesthetic judgment or reaction, another thing to report it. The dishonest reporting of esthetic experi-

is true that he had a tendency to pull virtually unknown names out of a hat so as to make them appear as the victims of everybody else's poor taste), in order to see that he is rescuing Crampton so as to retrieve a future for painting, while he is downplaying Rauschenberg, Reinhardt, and Klein so as to condemn the "recentness of sculpture," that is, minimal art.

Greenberg's rejection of minimal art is well known. There is no point in arguing on aesthetic grounds. Every art critic, after all, grows up with this own generation of artists, and I don't believe that the case "Modernist Painting" versus minimalism can be settled by a forced choice between Crampton and Rauschenberg or between Olitski and LeWitt. But a critical reassessment of the art doctrines implied on both sides is called for. Minimal art was a threat to Greenberg's aesthetics. Or rather, the success of minimal art was sensed by Greenberg as a threat to high standards in art. It soon became pointless for him to try to fight back by declaring minimal art illegitimate so that, from the mid-sixties on, he had to live with the fact that there is an art around that calls itself minimal, that sometimes claims to be sculpture but never painting, and that relies on the perceptual experience of the "real" or the "literal," an experience, that is, unmediated by the conventions of a specific medium and hence not submitted to the strict constraints of modernist history. If two-dimensionality is the last specific refuge of painting, three-dimensionality is the domain of this new generic art. Highly aware that most significant (and some insignificant) changes in modernist art first appeared with the look of non-art—which simply means, as in the Rollin Crampton story, that it takes "renewed acquaintance" to judge otherwise—Greenberg seemingly grants minimal art a major concession when, in "Recentness of Sculpture," he writes:

> Given that the initial look of non-art was no longer available to painting, since even an unpainted canvas now stated itself as a picture, the borderline between art and non-art had to be sought in

ence is what does most to accustom us to the notion that esthetic judgments are voluntary." Greenberg, "Complaints of an Art Critic," p. 38.

> the three-dimensional, where sculpture was, and where everything material that was not art, also was.[32]

The concession is apparently a huge one, since it means that art-making outside the specific conventions of either painting or sculpture is now recognized as valid. But validity or legitimation is nothing. Art-status is not aesthetic quality. The former can be willed and contrived, the latter ought to be the involuntary outcome of an aesthetic judgment:

> In idea, mixing the mediums, straddling the line between painting and sculpture, seemed the far-out thing to do.[33]

Though the far-out might be valid in idea, in actual aesthetic experience it has to be convincing. Inasmuch as modernism is tied up with specificity, it may be over, but the duties of formalism cannot be shed. Taking minimal art more seriously than he does "other forms of Novelty,"[34] Greenberg then makes his choice of convincing artists from the bulk of the minimalists he more or less openly despises. Very few artists pass the test. Not surprisingly, Anthony Caro is among them. Less expected is the choice of Anne Truitt, who is the only artist whose work Greenberg discusses:

> It was hard to tell whether the success of Truitt's best works was primarily sculptural or pictorial, but part of their success consisted precisely in making that question irrelevant.[35]

Greenberg's endorsement of Anne Truitt is strategic but certainly no less sincere than was his endorsement of Rollin Crampton. It is actually crucial

32. Greenberg, "Recentness of Sculpture," p. 182.

33. Ibid., pp. 182–183.

34. Ibid., p. 186. Greenberg often opposes "novelty" to "newness."

35. Ibid., p. 185.

because it provided him with a passageway between the specific and the generic, between the conventions of either painting or sculpture and the wide open domain of art at large. Whereas the works of most minimalists, in straddling the line between painting and sculpture as "the far-out thing to do," "ideate" art status and shun aesthetic constraints, Truitt's works address the conventions of both painting and sculpture. What makes them relevant and successful is precisely that they compel the critic to deem their specific identification irrelevant. Greenberg's discussion of her work is not merely a strategic countermove in his dealing with minimalism. It also reveals how reluctant he was to abandon modernism and to surrender specificity, forcing us to fine-tune our interpretation of his struggle with generic art. Strictly speaking, a work that is stranded in the no-man's-land between painting and sculpture is freed from the constraints of both media and is thus unspecific. In that sense it cannot be modernist, since modernism does not allow for interspecificity. But this may be too rigid an interpretation of Greenberg's modernism, and one that does not take into account his prejudice for the pictorial, even in sculpture. Had Greenberg been as consistent a proponent of purism in sculpture as he was in painting, he would have made a point of following a tendency in the history of modern sculpture toward the "essential conventions" of the medium equivalent but opposite to that which he deemed prevalent in painting. He would then have closely watched the reduction of the sculptural practice to questions of matter, tactility, mass, and weight, which are as "essential" to sculpture as flatness is to painting. Had he done so, even sceptical as he was with regard to the kind of minimal art that had its origins in monochrome painting, it is probable that he would nonetheless enthusiastically have endorsed the art of Carl Andre or of Richard Serra. But he hasn't. Leaving singular aesthetic judgment aside, the reason is probably that Greenberg has always been convinced that sculpture never had to fear its proximity to painting in the way that painting had, for its own survival, "to divest itself of everything it might share with sculpture." If sculpture had anything to fear, it would more likely have been its excessive proximity to architecture; this is why, according to him, the tradition of the monolith was driven to its ultimate conclusion by Brancusi, after whom the best of modernist sculpture (David Smith and Anthony Caro included), far from fencing off the pictorial, incorporated openness of form, textural effects, color, and, more generally, the opticality that also characterizes the best of modernist painting.[36] With this bias of Greenberg in mind, it is easy to see why Truitt's work would be spared the minimalist limbo. Its redeeming quality is akin to the residual illusionism he advocates in Olitski and which he opposes to the utter flatness of the straight monochrome.[37] In another article on Truitt, the argument of interspecificity is repeated; it is also more focused:

---

36. Greenberg's preference for the optical over the "haptical" in sculpture is rooted in his interpretation of cubist collage. See his "Review of the Exhibition *Collage*," *The Nation,* 27 November 1948, reprinted in *Clement Greenberg, The Collected Essays and Criticism,* ed. John O'Brian, vol 2, *Arrogant Purpose, 1945–1949* (Chicago: University of Chicago Press, 1986), pp. 259–263; "The Pasted Paper Revolution," *Art News* 57, no. 5 (1958): 46–49, 60–61; "Collage" (1959), in *Art and Culture,* pp. 70–83. Greenberg understands the cubist collage works as an episode of the history of painting where the flatness of the pictorial plane was momentarily made to identify literally with that of the support. The emphasis is on "momentarily." The outcome of collage is, according to him, an increased awareness that illusionism had to be turned against itself in order to be maintained. So he sees Synthetic cubism and abstract painting as consequences of collage (hence opticality and residual illusionism), whereas, with some exceptions (e.g., Arp and Schwitters), he ignores its dadaist and constructivist consequences (which some minimalists will, on the contrary, claim as a source of influence). Moreover, he relies on collage in order to make "construction-sculpture" or "drawing-in-space-sculpture," notably that of González, depend on pictorial opticality. From there, the road leading to David Smith and Anthony Caro is straight. It can be walked by reading "The New Sculpture," "Modernist Sculpture, Its Pictorial Past," and "David Smith," all three in *Art and Culture.*

37. One gets an idea of the complex subtlety of Greenberg's debates with himself when it comes to painting/sculpture relationships if one notices that he grants Olitski's spray paintings, precisely, a "grainy surface" offering "tactile associations hitherto foreign, more or less, to picture-making," only to add that "together with color, it contrives an illusion of depth back to the picture's surface; it is as if that surface, in all its literalness, were enlarged to contain a world of color and light differentiations impossible to flatness but which yet manages not to violate flatness." (Clement Greenberg, "Jules Olitski," in *XXXIII International Biennial Exhibi-*

> It was hard to tell, in Truitt's art, where the pictorial and where the sculptural began and ended. Had they been monochrome, the "objects" in Truitt's 1963 show would have qualified as first examples of orthodox Minimal Art.[38]

So, despite the doctrine of modernist specificity, it seems that a hybrid of painting and sculpture is permissible, and that it can even be convincing, provided it is polychrome. Rather than an outright abandonment of modernism, what we have is an expansion of formalism taking advantage of a disparity in Greenberg's attitudes toward painting and sculpture. It may be that the monochrome, and certainly the blank canvas, set the limit beyond which "a picture stops being a picture and turns into an arbitrary object." But if this object can claim some acquaintance with a tradition of sculpture itself indebted to the opticality of painting, then it is not totally arbitrary. In other words, it is not free of constraints, and the judgment of taste can apply itself to it, significantly. Modernism, narrowly speaking, is jeopardized, but the essential thing is that

---

tion of Art [Venice, 1966], p. 38.) Here we would have a belated version of the benefit that Greenberg grants the cubist collage works (Pollock's *drips* offering the link), namely, anti-illusionistic tactility turned against itself, this time more highly abstract and "micrological" since it is inscribed at the level of the "grainy surface" that the technique of spray painting achieves. Rosalind Krauss ("On Frontality," *Artforum,* May 1968) has pushed this micrological analysis of the grain as tactile opticality into almost absurd refinements. Generally speaking, the fact that Olitski, who nowadays appears as a sumptuously decorative painter but not much more, was a "test case" for all the critics whom Judd nastily called the "Greenbergers," has to do, it seems to me, with the extreme doctrinal importance that the sort of oxymoron represented by "tactile opticality" had for the formalist/modernist approach. It has left its imprint on the writings, besides those of Greenberg himself and Rosalind Krauss, of Michael Fried (*Three American Painters,* [Cambridge: Fogg Art Museum, 1965]), Darby Bannard ("Quality, Style and Olitski," *Artforum,* October 1972), and Kenneth Moffet (throughout his monograph *Jules Olitski* [New York: Abrams, 1981].)

38. Clement Greenberg, "Anne Truitt, An American Artist Whose Painted Structures Helped to Change the Course of American Sculpture," *Vogue Magazine,* May 1968, p. 284.

formalism is maintained. In order to be probatively called art (as art), an object, any object, needs to be (either) painting or sculpture. An overlapping of the two specificities is now allowed under certain conditions. If the object in question stems from the tradition of modernist painting—as do Stella's black paintings, the monochrome in general and even the blank canvas—then no overlapping is allowed. The "either painting or sculpture" is the latin *aut;* the disjunction is exclusive. If, on the other hand, the object in question stems from the tradition of modernist sculpture, even if it steps out of it (Anne Truitt's objects certainly do so more than Carl Andre's), then hybridization is allowed and even welcome. The "or" is the latin *vel;* the disjunction is inclusive. In this way (and although a major concession has been made to minimalism), room is provided for a particular kind of unorthodox minimal art—generic, yes, but multispecific rather than unspecific. It is both painting and sculpture.

MORE REINTERPRETED FACTS

> What puzzles me is, why do we always find ourselves arguing painting, when we set out to talk about sculpture?
>
> —*Carl Andre*

The major "theoretical" manifesto of minimal art is a text published in 1965 by Donald Judd entitled "Specific Objects." It starts with this sentence:

> Half or more of the best new work in the last few years has been neither painting nor sculpture.[39]

This statement applies to a great variety of works, among which Judd discusses those of Lee Bontecou, Claes Oldenburg, John Chamberlain and Stella. He also

39. Donald Judd, "Specific Objects," in *Complete Writings 1959–1975* (Halifax: The Press of the Nova Scotia College of Art and Design, 1975), p. 181; first published in *Arts Yearbook VIII,* 1965.

cites Yayoi Kusama, H. C. Westermann, Richard Smith, even Yves Klein and many others. The article is lavishly illustrated with works by Johns, Rauschenberg, Flavin, Artschwager, Morris, Stella, and with one of Judd's own works, which he modestly claims the editor has included, not he. Modesty notwithstanding, it is clear that the text is a manifesto in favor of his own conception of art. Some of the works Judd mentions definitely belong to painting, some to sculpture, most of them to an indeterminate realm straddling both. Many of his own works, for example, are colored and hang on the wall like paintings, but protrude into the third dimension like sculptures. The strange thing is that Judd claims for them a rather paradoxical status: although they combine qualities of both painting and sculpture, they are said to be neither. The paradox, however, becomes intelligible when one understands that Judd's justification for minimal art is absolutely overdetermined, albeit *a contrario,* by the Greenbergian doctrine. Judd seeks to secure legitimation for generic art, more precisely (as we have seen from the example of his early work, as well as that of LeWitt and Flavin), for an art that deliberately oversteps the limit beyond which "a picture stops being a picture and turns into an arbitrary object," in other words, an art that stems from and steps out of painting rather than sculpture. On Greenberg's terms, it ought to obey and even defend its own specificity. This it precisely refuses to do; it leaps into the third dimension "where sculpture was and where everything material that was not art also was," and it proudly claims this arbitrariness.

As I have tried to show above, the influence of Greenberg's doctrine on Judd's generation of artists was so strong that the double bind they must have felt when confronted with Stella's black and aluminum canvases left them with no alternative other than to pursue the modernist tradition even beyond the literal monochrome where it actually meets its end. The consequences are manifold and in direct opposition to Greenberg's views on minimalism, to the judgment with which he saves Anne Truitt's work from the minimalist doom, and to the arguments with which he backs it up. This is of course no surprise, since Judd's and Greenberg's rationales developed in dialectical opposition to each other. The arbitrariness Judd claims for his "specific objects" is precisely what makes them condemnable in Greenberg's eyes: they are neither painting nor sculpture, that is, they are not accountable to the tradition of either modernist painting or modernist sculpture. Hence, they can be "ideated" instead of judged aesthetically. The formalist judgment that would call them art (as art) is lost in a limbo where confrontation with the constraints of a specific tradition can be avoided and where no aesthetic experience of significance can be had. The experience of such objects is merely phenomenal, says Greenberg, and Judd agrees. What we have is generic art with only logical, not aesthetic, ties to history.

Yet Judd's manifesto is not entitled "Generic Objects"; its title is "Specific Objects." This, more than anything else, shows the extent to which his thinking is indebted to that of Greenberg. But he takes the other branch of the alternative set by Greenberg, and quite systematically so. It is essential to Judd that modernism should be allowed to progress beyond the limit set by the literal monochrome. Since the essence of modernism lies "in the use of the characteristic methods of a discipline to criticize the discipline itself—not in order to subvert it, but to entrench it more firmly in its area of competence," Judd is bound to claim, for the area where painting overlaps with sculpture, a competence or specificity of its own, which would thus be severed from the traditions, or areas of competence, of both painting and sculpture. Within the generic domain of art and non-art alike—since by now virtually anything is readable as art[40]—the works of the minimalists struggle to assert their unique specificity while having to acknowledge the genericity of their own conditions of production. Judd is aware of this double task:

> One of the important things in any art is its degree of generality and specificity and another is how each of these occurs. The extent and the occurrence have to be credible. I'd like my work to be somewhat more specific than art has been and also specific and general in a different way.[41]

---

40. "Minimal works are readable as art, as almost anything is today—including a door, a table, or blank sheet of paper." Greenberg, "Recentness of Sculpture," p. 183.

41. Judd, *Complete Writings,* p. 181. The statement was originally printed in Barbara Rose, "ABC Art," *Art in America,* October–November 1965.

A new "species" of art is born, for which the risk of confusion with non-art is greater than it has ever been. Hence the importance of its name. There is no end to the string of names that the critics and sometimes the artists coined for the new species: Minimal Art, Literal Art, ABC Art, Primary Structures, Art of the Real, Post-painterly Relief (this last one surely of Greenbergian ascent) and many others, the prize in barbarian neologism going to *Sculptecture*. The new hybrid discovered by the artworld's natural scientists is a monster born out of the most improbable genetic manipulations. I am being ironic. What is crucial here is not to decide whether this or that name is better suited, but rather to figure out what this frantic naming activity reveals: in order to secure some legitimation for minimal art, as it was cut from the traditions named (from the traditional names of) "painting" and "sculpture," it was vital to see that a specific name, preferably new, brought it under the generic name "art" as a brand new art devoid of tradition, but as an art in its own right.[42] Donald Judd chooses

42. Do I need to underline the extent to which this phenomenon accompanied the whole of modernity? From Courbet's realism to Breton's surrealism, through impressionism, expressionism, divisionism, cubism, fauvism, futurism, constructivism, neo-plasticism, not counting all the other "neos" and all the "posts" since Signac or Roger Fry, and leaving aside bizarre things such as rayonism, synchromism, orphism, amorphism, vorticism, and others, never in the whole of art history did an epoch coin more "ism-names"—which, even when coined by their detractors, always carry a desire for legitimation and periodization—than modernity. But most "isms," unless they express a sensibility running through all the arts (like romanticism), qualify one art in particular. Not by chance, it is painting that was granted the greatest amount of "isms." A new phenomenon appeared after World War II—with pop art actually—which I believe to be a major symptom of the fact that what overdetermines the art of the postwar era is the passage from the specific to the generic: the invention of "isms" gets stifled (whereas that of "neos" and "posts" appears at the horizon) and a new naming activity beings, which gets hold of the generic name "art" and adds to it an adjective meant to respecify it. So we have had pop art and op art, kinetic art, body art, minimal art, conceptual art, land art, narrative art, and many others. The fact that this phenomenon begins with pop art—i.e., with neo-Dada, as it was sometimes called—seems to me highly significant. Equally

the appellation "Specific Objects," to which he ascribes the task of crossing the categories of pop art, minimal art, and a few others, as his choice of artists in this text shows. If one absolutely had to choose a name, this one would be the most intelligent, no doubt, and the one that most clearly indicates what was at stake: to conquer, inside the generic name "art" now deprived of its aesthetic ambition, a nonetheless qualitative "area of competence." Stated in positive terms, the specificity of the works that Judd defends comprises a set of qualities that seek to affirm as strongly as possible the individuality of a given piece, so as to set it apart from all that is not art and, at the same time, establish a "family resemblance" among those works making up the new breed. Both Judd and Robert Morris have insisted on the nonrelational, noncompositional forms adopted by minimalism, on the wholeness, compactness and objectness of their Gestalt, on the reality of the time and space in which their presence is experienced, and on the obdurate literalness of their materials.[43] The word "specific" is meant to convey all these qualities:

> The characteristics of three dimensions . . . may persist, such as the work's being like an object or being specific. . . . [44]

> Materials . . . are specific. If they are used directly, they are more specific. . . . Also, they are usually aggressive. There is an objectivity to the obdurate identity of a material.[45]

---

significant is the fact that it is only in the work of the postwar artists and art historians who legitimized Dada (Motherwell's book was published in 1951), that this name "Dada," which the artists had chosen because it was a perfectly absurd anti-name, was turned into "dadaism."

43. See Robert Morris, "Notes on Sculpture, Part I," *Artforum,* February 1966, and "Part II," *Artforum,* October 1966; reprinted in Battcock, *Minimal Art,* pp. 222–235.

44. Judd, "Specific Objects," p. 184.

45. Ibid., p. 187.

Just as Greenberg had to define the specificity of modernist painting in negative as well as positive terms and oppose its flatness to the three-dimensionality of sculpture, so Judd finds it easier to define the specificity of the new art by what it is not:

> Painting and sculpture have become set forms. A fair amount of their meaning isn't credible. The use of three dimensions isn't the use of a given form. There hasn't been enough time and work to see limits. . . . Since its range is so wide, three-dimensional work will probably divide into a number of forms. At any rate, it will be larger than painting and much larger than sculpture. . . . Because the nature of three dimensions isn't set, given beforehand, something credible can be made, almost anything.[46]

The tone of this paragraph is programmatic, if not prophetic. It probes the future and makes promises. But it also seeks to deny the past and it fails, quite symptomatically. The obsessiveness of Judd's disavowal of the painting tradition out of which his own art and many other "specific objects" emerged is indeed a symptom. Despite his claim that they have severed their ties with both sculpture and painting, the link with painting keeps creeping back into his text, sometimes as a plain admission:

> The new work obviously resembles sculpture more than it does painting, but it is nearer to painting.[47]

Or, sometimes as a rhetoric fighting back the shadow of painting that looms over the new work:

46. Ibid., p. 184.

47. Ibid., p. 183.

> Three dimensions are real space. That gets rid of the problem of illusionism and of literal space. . . . Actual space is intrinsically more powerful and specific than painting on a flat surface.[48]

Or, sometimes as a denial of painting's future:

> The rectangular plan is given a life span. The sense of singleness also has a duration, but it is only beginning and has a better future outside of painting. . . . The plane is also emphasized and nearly single. It is clearly a plane one or two inches in front of another plane, the wall, and parallel to it. The relationship of the two planes is specific; it is a form.[49]

What is much harder to deny than painting's future is its past, especially the recent past of modernist painting, which led to the monochrome and in particular to Stella's black canvases, the shock of which was so seminal for the advent of minimal art. The way Judd eschews calling Stella's work painting in order to annex it to his "specific objects" is rather amazing, but there is no more need to see intellectual twisting in this than there was to see disingenuousness in Greenberg's judgments on Rollin Crampton or Anne Truitt. The surprise effect of Stella's canvases at the time was so strong that it was indeed difficult to see them as paintings. However, Judd knows that Stella himself wanted his work to be considered as painting. Yet he writes:

> Frank Stella says that he is doing paintings, and his work could be considered as painting. Most of the works, though, suggest slabs, since they project more than usual. . . . The projection, the absence of spatial effects and the close relation between the periphery and

48. Ibid., p. 184.

49. Ibid., p. 182.

> the stripes make the paintings seem like objects, and that does a lot to cause their amplified intensity.[50]

Again, apropos Stella's aluminum paintings:

> It is something of an object, it is a single thing, not a field with something in it, and it has almost no space.[51]

And again, apropos Stella and Flavin:

> Although they exclude painterly art, their work is decidedly art, and is visible art.[52]

---

50. Donald Judd, "Local History," in *Complete Writings,* p. 153; first published in *Arts Yearbook VII,* 1964. Between the lines of Judd's interpretation is the fact, often remarked upon, that the black canvases, the aluminum canvases, the *Copper Paintings* and the purple canvases with a hole in their middle, from 1963–1964, have an unusually thick stretcher, of the same thickness, apparently, as the stripes' width. Extending the picture on its side, this gives the painted surface the look of a three-dimensional object. Stella always rejected this interpretation, saying that he does not consider the stretcher's thickness as a function of the painting's module and that, for him, the shadow cast by the stretcher on the wall (another argument, particularly strong in the case of the hollowed out canvases), far from turning the painting into an object, was meant to emphasize its two-dimensionality. See Bruce Glaser, "Questions to Stella and Judd," in *Minimal Art,* p. 162; see also William Rubin, *Frank Stella* (New York: Museum of Modern Art, 1970), p. 15, p. 151 n. 16.

51. Donald Judd, "In the Galleries," in *Complete Writings,* p. 91; first published in *Arts Magazine,* September 1963.

52. Donald Judd, "Nationwide Reports: Hartford," in *Complete Writings,* p. 119; first published in *Arts Magazine,* March 1964. Who would say today that Flavin "excludes painterly art," when the most striking effect of his fluorescent tubes is to reestablish—literally, indeed—the identification of color and light that the ancient painters, at least since Van Eyck and Bellini, took for granted, an identification that had been split in two—either color or light—

More Factual Reinterpretations

> "Non-art," "anti-art," "non-art art," and "anti-art art" are useless. If someone says his work is art, it's art.
>
> —*Donald Judd*

There is no doubt that in calling Stella's work "visible art," Judd is uttering a judgment. He is evaluating, even praising the work. The question is: is this judgment aesthetic? To be honest, I don't believe that Judd would have denied that it is, or that it was. But in the context of the times, he could not have acknowledged it. It is a matter of consistency: his Greenbergian anti-Greenbergianism left him no choice other than to opt for modernism against formalism. Indeed, the terms of the alternative are set by the Greenbergian doctrine. Generic art is permissible, either because it is in fact interspecific—it allows for the traditions of both modernist painting and sculpture to put pressure on the artist's and the critic's taste, in which case a judgment of taste is called for, conveyed by the sentence "this is art"; such is the right branch of the alternative—or because anything is permitted and everything that is neither painting nor sculpture is encouraged. Once even a blank canvas can be called a picture, anything visible can be called art, in which case art has lost its aesthetic import and taste is not called for. The sentence "this is art" is a convention. Historical knowledge alone is required to make and judge art, some intellectual curiosity or interest for the "logic" of modernism, some strategic desire or interest to see it further extrapolated and tested on mere institutional grounds. Art fades into "art theory." Such is the left branch of the alternative. It is all too easy to see that minimal art and the movements that were to follow, conceptual art espe-

by the beginning of abstract art with, as an (almost immediate) consequence, of course, flatness and monochromy? I would see the disjunction take place in Delaunay especially, between the *Windows* and *The First Disk,* but the seeds had been planted by Seurat. See chapter 3.

cially, chose the left branch, expressed in a nutshell by Judd's most famous assertion from "Specific Objects": "A work needs only to be interesting."[53]

Donald Judd was too much of an artist to be really convinced of what he said there. And Greenberg was too intelligent not to have seen that the strategic extrapolation of the "logic" of taste pervades taste itself, and that it has played its provocative role with every significant leap in modernism. I believe that Judd and Greenberg could still have argued with each other. Things get more dogmatic with the epigones, Michael Fried and Joseph Kosuth. In view of their further development, it may be a little unfair to pit them against each other as mere epigones of Greenberg and Judd respectively, but it has the advantage of giving the debate additional clarity. In the mid-sixties, Fried was not yet the fine historian and phenomenologist of art he subsequently became. Although he claimed to have departed from Greenberg's essentialism, he was in a way more Greenbergian than Greenberg. His much praised and much attacked 1967 article, "Art and Objecthood" nevertheless still remains by far the best analysis done on minimal art at the time. Better than anyone else, Fried has sensed what threat minimalism posed to formalism, and his counter-attack is right on target.

Fried states the necessary link between formalism and modernism—that is, between the value judgment that puts a given work to the test of being compared to the best work of tradition and the very tendency of this tradition to identify itself with the testing of the conventions of its medium—in terms that are stronger and more doctrinaire, even, than Greenberg's:

> The concepts of quality and value—and to the extent that these are central to art, the concept of art itself—are meaningful, or wholly meaningful, only within the individual arts. What lies between the arts is theatre.[54]

---

53. Judd, "Specific Objects," p. 184.

54. Michael Fried, "Art and Objecthood," in *Minimal Art,* p. 142; first published in *Artforum,* June 1967. The same argument can be found in "Shape as Form: Frank Stella's New Paint-

Although the generic value judgment expressed by the word "art" (or "art as art" or "art as such" or "good art as such")[55] is of course still possible and indeed required, it simply cannot be convincing outside the individual arts. The objectness (which Fried calls "objecthood") of the minimalist works (which he redubs "literalist") is acknowledged for what Judd claims it to be, neither painting nor sculpture; but for that very reason it is denied both its specificity and its aesthetic validity:

> It is as though objecthood alone can, in the present circumstances, secure something's identity, if not as non-art, at least as neither

---

ings," *Artforum,* November 1966. Commenting on this passage, Fried later added that "the conviction of quality or value is always elicited by putative paintings and sculptures and not by putative works of art as such." Michael Fried, "How Modernism Works: A Response to T. J. Clark," *Critical Inquiry* 9 (1982): 223.

55. Let us remember that "art as such" and "good art as such" are not synonymous for Greenberg: formalism requires that the word "art" convey an aesthetic judgment, not that the judgment be positive, which is why, in his views, once the irreducible essence of painting has been revealed by the blank canvas, a shift of question occurs. A few lines after having said, in "After Abstract Expressionism," that "a stretched or tacked up canvas already exists as a picture—though not necessarily as a successful one," Greenberg goes on to say, apropos Newman, Rothko, and Still: "The question now asked through their art is no longer what constitutes art, or the art of painting, as such, but what irreducibly constitutes good art as such." In a footnote from "Art and Objecthood," Fried takes issue with this: "But I would argue that what modernism has meant is that the two questions—What constitutes the art of painting? And what constitutes good painting?—are no longer separable; the first disappears, or increasingly tends to disappear, into the second" (p. 124). So that for Fried, "art as such" and "good art as such" are synonymous, though of course valid only for painting (or for sculpture), i.e., "within the individual arts." My own views on the question of "art" and "good art" are different from both Greenberg's and Fried's. Paraphrasing Fried, I would argue that what modernism has meant (notice the past tense in Fried's text as in mine) is that the two questions "what is painting?" and "what is good painting?" *were* not separable (the past tense is not in Fried).

> painting nor sculpture. . . . Here the question arises: What is it about objecthood as projected and hypostatized by the literalists that makes it, if only from the perspective of recent modernist painting, antithetical to art? The answer I want to propose is this: the literalist espousal of objecthood amounts to nothing other than a plea for a new genre of theatre; and theatre is now the negation of art.[56]

Fried's case against "literalism" is strong on the interpretive level, if not necessarily on the level of judgment. In calling the interspecificity of what falls in between painting and sculpture "theatre," he not only accounts for a number of phenomenological qualities of minimalist works, such as their "presence," their involvement of the beholder and their existence in duration; he also hints at an explanation of the new practices that came about in the wake of minimal art and, most significantly, of the new names such as "Performance art" and "Installation art" that they secured for themselves.[57] Interpretation aside, Fried's judgment, when he dumps minimal art into the limbo of "theatre" or non-art, is in line with most non-art judgments uttered—mostly by academic critics—throughout the history of modernism since Courbet: it is a refusal to judge aesthetically, and it means "literalism doesn't even deserve to be called art." But Fried is not an academic critic like those who a priori refuse to take into account anything that doesn't seem to fit the fixed rules of a genre. Like Greenberg, even more than Greenberg, he is far too aware that modernism has ceaselessly put those "fixed" rules to the test of aesthetic experience, and in so doing, has abandoned or displaced them. And like Greenberg, he feels obliged to show that he is able to select a counterexample which, though situated in the same generic no-man's-land as the rest of literalism, would deserve to be called art.

56. Fried, "Art and Objecthood," p. 125.

57. See my essay, "Performance Here and Now: Minimal Art, a Plea for a New Genre of Theatre," *Open Letter* (Toronto), no. 5–6 (Summer–Fall 1983): 234–260.

Among the happy few is Anthony Caro again. Anne Truitt is not mentioned, but a particular work by Jules Olitski receives a great deal of attention. Entitled *Bunga 45,* it is one of the first sculptures ever made by Olitski, in 1967, and consists of a cluster of ten-foot-high aluminum tubes spray-painted in the same not quite monochrome manner as his canvases. It is highly probable that Olitski, if not induced, was at least encouraged by Greenberg to move into sculpture, especially this kind of sculpture, which seems really contrived to be formalism's response to minimalism. At any rate, *Bunga 45* is fairly unique in the production of Olitski, who shortly after went to work in Caro's studio in England and fell strongly under his influence. Here is Fried's comment on *Bunga:*

> It amounts to something far more than an attempt simply to make or "translate" his paintings into sculptures, namely, an attempt to establish surface—the surface, so to speak, of *painting*—as a medium for sculpture. The use of tubes, each of which one sees, incredibly, as *flat*—that is, flat but *rolled*—makes *Bunga's* surface more like that of a painting than like that of an object: like painting, and unlike both ordinary objects and other sculpture, *Bunga* is *all* surface. And of course what declares or establishes that surface is color, Olitski's sprayed color.[58]

The tone, emphasis and argument of this paragraph betray this piece of writing as a paragon—or a cliché—of formalist criticism. As with Greenberg's defense of Truitt, color and subtle polychromy (described at length a little earlier in the text), to which Fried has added the rather farfetched category of "rolled flatness," are invoked to ensure that *Bunga* be saved from the literalist limbo. Not that Fried's description of his aesthetic experience is wrong or unfaithful. But in electing Olitski, he is unfair to what he excludes. After all, Fried could have looked at Chamberlain in very much the same way he looked at Olitski (indeed

58. Fried, "Art and Objecthood," p. 139.

he was tempted to), instead of resting his estimation of Chamberlain's work on a rationale that is neither his own nor the artist's but that of Judd. Fried never challenges the paradoxical claim that Judd had made for the works he advocated as "specific objects." He never underlines that Chamberlain's work, or Judd's for that matter, could be seen as both painting and sculpture rather than as neither. No, they are "theatre" or "non-art." Rather than using his own eyes as formalism recommends, Fried is taking Judd at his own word. In a way, though, he is right, and his reasons have less to do with opting for the exclusive rather than the inclusive status given the indeterminate domain straddling painting and sculpture, than with the invitation, handed out by Judd, not to judge his (or Chamberlain's) work aesthetically. What is allegedly new in the sixties (in fact, it is as old as dadaism) is a situation where the refusal to judge aesthetically—a tactic typical of academic critics since Courbet—is claimed by the artists themselves so that, as Fried says, "what non-art means today, and has meant for several years, is fairly specific."[59] There is thus a specificity of non-art (i.e., of non-painting/non-sculpture) that Fried is forced to recognize yet rejects, not by way of a concrete aesthetic judgment, but in the name of aesthetic judgment at large—and thus in the name of art, generically speaking. Hence his mockery of Judd's assertion, "A work needs only to be interesting":

> Judd himself has as much as acknowledged the problematic character of the literalist enterprise by his claim "A work needs only to be interesting." For Judd, as for the literalist sensibility generally, all that matters is whether or not a given work is able to elicit and sustain (his) interest. . . . Literalist work is often condemned—when it is condemned—for being boring. A tougher charge would be that it is merely interesting.[60]

To which, of course, Judd replied:

---

59. Ibid., p. 123.

60. Ibid., p. 142.

> I was especially irked by Fried's ignorant misinterpretation of my use of the word "interesting." I obviously use it in a particular way but Fried reduces it to the cliché "merely interesting."[61]

Although somewhat unfair to Judd, whose understanding of the works made by Stella, Flavin, or himself clings to "visible art," Fried's charge against the "merely interesting" is certainly valid when directed at the productions of conceptual art, especially at those with an explicit theoretical claim. But it is only valid, the conceptualists argue, within the formalist discourse that the theory of conceptualism precisely claims to invalidate and that its practice seeks as much as possible to render without object. Under Judd's strong influence, Joseph Kosuth issued in 1969 a widely publicized manifesto entitled "Art after Philosophy," in which no effort was spared to prevent, not only the aesthetic judgment in the formalist sense, but also the judgment of "interest" or "interestedness" as sought by Donald Judd. Beyond taste and interest alike, there remains only a circular proposition to define art (as art):

> A work of art is a tautology in that it is a presentation of the artist's intention, that is, he is saying that that particular work of art is art, which means, is a definition of art. Thus, that it is art is true a priori.[62]

Therefore, specific formal qualities such as the flatness of a painting or the holistic Gestalt and obdurate materials of a "specific object" are superfluous. Ideally, one would have to dispense with the object altogether in order to foreclose the possibility of any judgment other than logical or conceptual:

---

61. Donald Judd, "Complaints: Part I," in *Complete Writings,* p. 198; first published in *Studio International,* April 1969.

62. Kosuth, "Art after Philosophy I and II," in *Idea Art,* ed. Gregory Battcock (New York: Dutton, 1973), p. 83; first published in *Studio International,* October and November 1969.

> It comes as no surprise that the art with the least fixed morphology is the example from which we decipher the nature of the general term art.[63]

Consequently, Kosuth claims for art a condition beyond objectness, linguistic in character:

> Works of art are analytic propositions. . . . One begins to realize that art's "art condition" is a conceptual state. . . . In other words, the propositions of art are not factual, but linguistic in character—that is, they do not describe the behavior of physical or even mental objects; they express definitions of art, or the formal consequences of definitions of art. Accordingly, we can say that art operates on a logic.[64]

Since art is a tautology, there is no specificity to this logic, neither in terms of a medium nor in terms of a new, specific "area of competence" severed from, and added to, those of painting and sculpture. Kosuth's conceptualism allows only for generic art:

> Being an artist now means to question the nature of art. If one is questioning the nature of painting, one cannot be questioning the nature of art. . . . That's because the word art is general and the word painting is specific. Painting is a kind of art.[65]

This is why the "kind of art" called painting ought to be banished, made illegitimate and obsolete by the new generic conceptual art. But the more radically

63. Ibid., p. 89.

64. Ibid., pp. 83, 84.

65. Ibid., p. 79.

the generic is severed from the specific, the more insidiously the link with modernist painting, especially with Stella's black and aluminum canvases, creeps back into the text, in the shape of a disavowal akin to that of Judd:

> Johns and Reinhardt are probably the last two painters that were legitimate *artists* as well.[66]

To which he adds, in an appending footnote that has the ring of a Freudian slip:

> And Stella too, of course. But Stella's work, which was greatly weakened by being painting, was made obsolete very quickly by Judd and others.

Even more than his "theory," Kosuth's disavowal makes it clear that conceptual art was not a linear development from minimal art but an even more radical reworking of the aporia, born out of the question of the monochrome, that forced many artists who had been brought up on the Greenbergian doctrine and who, with or without reason, felt that they could not possibly go on painting after Stella, to separate modernism and formalism and to bank on the logic of the former the better to refute the latter. In "Art after Philosophy," Kosuth relentlessly attacks Greenberg, whom he accuses of being "the critic of taste," which is true, and rejects his formalism, which he accuses of accepting "a definition of art resting solely on morphological grounds," which is unfair, since Greenberg has no definition of art. Kosuth, in fact, took his own "definition" of art as tautology from yet another painter of quasi-monochromes, Ad Reinhardt, who, with Johns, was the last painter whom he was ready to recognize as being also a legitimate artist. But he took it from Reinhardt's writings and attitude more than from his paintings. And one imagines that Reinhardt's "*art in art*" as "*art as art*" so easily became Kosuth's "*art as idea as idea*" because

66. Ibid., p. 100.

drawing from a text allowed him to bypass the pictures. The denial of the specific is as obvious vis-à-vis Reinhardt as it is vis-à-vis Stella.

Conceptual art is thus another response to the same double bind that every would-be painter must have felt in New York in the early sixties, standing in front of Stella's black paintings with *Art and Culture* in his pocket. With the exception of the members of the English group Art-Language, in the early seventies Kosuth was the only proponent of hard-core conceptual art, the kind he himself called TCA (theoretical conceptual art), as opposed to the more poetic brand he disparagingly called SCA (stylistic conceptual art). Yet even among the representatives of conceptual art who didn't share Kosuth's theoretical inclinations, the number of ex-painters is remarkable. Between 1966 and 1968, in New York and elsewhere, Robert Huot, John Baldessari, Robert Barry, Jan Dibbets, Mel Ramsden, Lawrence Weiner, and others produced their "ultimate" monochrome or acted out a variation on the blank canvas before they switched to conceptual art. Their conceptual works are intelligible and can be appraised only in reference to the abandoned craft and medium of painting, which, unfortunately for those artists, is precisely what they sought to escape, since they predicated their works on the "logic" of modernist painting while refusing to let them be aesthetically evaluated with respect to painting. Sometimes, as in Weiner's distinction between his *Specific Statements* and his *General Statements,* explicit reference was made to the problem which overdetermined the art of the sixties: the passage from the specific to the generic. This passage was always interpreted in terms of a shift from formal experimentation to conceptual inquiry. It was never understood for what it actually was. Up to the present, generic art—an appellation mostly suited to the recent trends exemplified by Allan McCollum, Haim Steinbach, or Jeff Koons, all of whom produce "generic objects"—has dragged in its wake an unresolved quarrel with Greenbergian formalism.

Although Kosuth can hardly be taken as a spokesman for all conceptual artists, his 1969 manifesto "Art after Philosophy" is exemplary of the state of this unresolved quarrel. Irksome and self-serving as it is, his reasoning is in some way flawless, carrying Judd's escape from formalism to its logical extreme. "The intensification, almost the exacerbation, of this self-critical tendency that began with the philosopher Kant," which Greenberg calls modernism, has come full circle in Kosuth's tautology. Of this absurd triumph of modernism over formalism, one might think that Kosuth's ultimate conclusion would be to posit the end of art. Not at all. Instead, it proclaims "the end of philosophy and the beginning of art."[67] This can only mean two things—that there is an absolute "separation between aesthetics and art,"[68] art now being identified with "art theory" while aesthetics is relegated to the realm of taste; and that there is an absolute historical beginning to this separation:

> The function of art, as a question, was first raised by Marcel Duchamp. In fact it is Marcel Duchamp whom we can credit with giving art its own identity. . . . With the unassisted Readymade, art changed its focus from the form of the language to what was being said. Which means that it changed the nature of art from a question of morphology to a question of function. . . . All art (after Duchamp) is conceptual (in nature) because art only exists conceptually.[69]

A Critical Reinterpretation

> There is a superficial similarity between modernist painting and Dada in one important respect: namely, that just as modernist painting has enabled one to see a blank canvas . . . as a picture, Dada and Neo-Dada have equipped one to treat virtually any object as a work of art—though it is far from clear exactly what this means.
>
> —*Michael Fried*

67. Ibid., p. 73.
68. Ibid., p. 75.
69. Ibid., p. 80.

Here, with the last of Kosuth's statements, we should pause, wonder and meditate. Duchamp's first unassisted readymade is the *Bottle Rack,* dated 1914. Out of what strange, fifty-five year long torpor has Kosuth's "discovery" awakened the artworld? If it is true that all art after Duchamp is conceptual in nature, why did this revelation come to the surface only "in artistic endeavor since Abstract expressionism, after which work began to appeal to the *logic of modernism* for art status rather than appealing to the tradition of Western painting for art status"?[70] Was it not precisely in an article entitled "After Abstract Expressionism" that Greenberg voiced his concern about work that could "appeal to the logic of modernism for art status rather than appealing to the tradition of Western painting for art" *quality*? And is it not the case that the thin line that separates logic and tradition, or status and quality, might be the one that Greenberg, confronted in October 1962 with the hypothetical case of the blank canvas, drew and refused to cross, the line between a picture and a successful one? Finally, is it not clear that this hypothetical case did not fall from the heaven of "art theory" but that its plausibility was prompted by the latest avatars of modernist painting, Stella's black and aluminum canvases in particular? Well, the blank canvas is a readymade. Marcel Duchamp's first unassisted readymade had to wait fifty-five years before it gave Kosuth the "revelation" that all art is conceptual in nature, because it is only after Abstract expressionism, and in the particular context that spawned the controversy between "Modernist Painting" and minimalism, that it reappeared from within the history of modernist painting under the guise of an unpainted canvas. Kosuth's contention that Duchamp's readymade "changed the nature of art from a question of morphology to a question of function" is ludicrous, as if a single artist could change the "nature of art." The readymade has of course demonstrated no such thing. But Kosuth's contention is a symptom, and one that is apt to give us a clue to the proper reinterpretation of the specific/generic problem which is overdetermining the art of the last thirty years.

70. Joseph Kosuth, "1975," *The Fox,* no. 2 (1975): 90.

Unlike Duchamp's bottlerack or urinal, the blank canvas is a *specific* readymade. It is a manufactured product, new and unused, as are all of Duchamp's unassisted readymades, but it is one that you can find at the artists' supply store, not at the Bazar de l'Hôtel de Ville where Duchamp bought the bottlerack. Even before it is touched by the painter's hand, it already belongs to the tradition of painting, or rather, to a particular tradition—that of Western painting since the Renaissance. While it is prepared to receive the traces of the painter's brush and is thus no more than a support, as part of the artist's materials, it has already incorporated, ready-made, the one convention established during the Renaissance—that one is to paint on a stretched canvas. To call it a picture, "though not necessarily a successful one," means to acknowledge the presence of that historical convention in an otherwise mundane commodity. But to call it a picture also means, of course, to recognize that this convention is the only one left from a five-hundred-year-old tradition. Greenberg, who knew this all too well, deemed this convention to be essential. As if in a mirror image to Kosuth's contention that Duchamp's readymades have changed the nature of art, there was already Greenberg's contention that the blank canvas had revealed the nature of painting. Since Duchamp avoided actualizing the blank canvas, Kosuth doesn't see its ready-made "nature," and Greenberg doesn't see the change in "nature" that the vantage point of the readymade imprints on it. The ready-made canvas is at once their common blind spot and the missing link between them.

But it needs to be reinterpreted. Greenberg sees flatness and its delimitation, as they are incorporated in the ready-made canvas, as an essential convention. While recognized as a mere convention, it is also deemed irreducible, irremovable, something you couldn't abandon without altering the very nature of the medium. Now, that one should paint on a piece of cloth braced to a wooden stretcher is a prescription with no ontological privilege. A convention it is, but it is no more of an essential convention than the one it gradually replaced, which prescribed painting on a wooden board. Not until the Renaissance did easel painting substitute for the retable and open a new category of *specific objects,* "limited in extension and different from a wall," as Greenberg said. Not until the Renaissance, when a painting began to be seen as an illusionistic window, did it detach itself from the wall, distinguish itself from the mural, gain mobility and autonomy from architecture and become "a plane one or two inches in front of another plane, the wall, and parallel to it," as Judd said. There is nothing essential to this plane's flatness, nothing essential either to its whiteness. The easel painting may share its rigid flatness with the retable and with the wall; it doesn't share it with the baroque cupola, the Greek vase, or the Chinese scroll. And the painter's virgin canvas shares its whiteness with the writer's blank page more than it does with other artifacts belonging to its own tradition, linen fabric included. The Venetians didn't gesso their canvases; they used a red undercoat. Not only are all conventions historical and not ontological, specific in the sense that they are embedded in a tradition rather than in the nature of the medium, but the one convention that modernism has not relinquished, the one that has heightened its purist sensibility for the surface so much, owes more to Mallarmé and the symbolist crossover of painting and poetry than it does to its own history since the Renaissance. After all, despite Lessing's Laocoon and Greenberg's "Newer Laocoon," modernism didn't succeed in doing away with the *ut pictura poesis:* kicked out of the illusionistic window, it crept back into the medium itself when painters began to take it for the subject matter of their practice.

Duchamp didn't actualize the blank canvas. Nor did he actualize the tube of paint, which is, as we have seen, the underground paradigm for all his readymades.[71] He abandoned painting in 1912 and switched to art. He abruptly jumped from the specific to the generic. Or so the story goes, both for all those—artists, critics, and art historians—who have applauded the invention of the readymade and seen in it new avenues and unprecedented freedom for art, and for those who have deplored it and read it as a symptom of a disastrous slackening in the standards of taste. Neither group has seriously asked what it meant to jump from the specific to the generic; neither has considered what

71. See chapter 3.

had made it possible; neither has devoted careful attention to its timing in history and its various repetitions. But the switch from the specific to the generic is not at all self-evident. That one could be an artist without being a painter (or a sculptor or a musician or a poet . . .) is indeed unprecedented and should be startling to everyone, even today. How did Duchamp get away with it? is one question. Why? is another. Did he deserve it? is still another. The fact is that he succeeded, and the presumption is that the conditions were ripe. Another fact is that his success is rooted in a failure, partly personal, partly general, but on both counts extremely significant and made significant by the acute intelligence and irony of his work. It sheds light, for example, on this: the passage from the specific to the generic is never one for which sheer "art theory" can account; it takes an investigation that probes the existential and the historical at the same time. You may become an artist without being a painter, but hardly without having been one. As we have seen, this holds true for all minimal and conceptual artists. Fifty years after the readymade, they had to reenact a certain rite of passage, which Duchamp was the first to accomplish. Similarly, something minimal or conceptual beyond the blank canvas can be art without being a picture, but not without the blank canvas having been one—which is why, ironically, the minimalists and the conceptualists sought their authority to do generic art from Greenberg's 1962 article, where he set out to posit the blank canvas as the embodiment of painting's ultimate specificity, as if warning not to transgress it.

The blank canvas is not a picture; it was one. It was a picture, a viable would-be picture, a potential picture, in the days when modernist painting had its tradition ahead of itself. For the modernist sensibility striving for purism and attuned to the "elements" of painting, the blank canvas's potential to become a painting had an extraordinary aesthetic appeal. From Malevich to Mondrian, there is not one pioneer of abstract painting who didn't respond to the appeal of the bare canvas. They were breaking with the past, relinquishing the strongest of all "expendable conventions," namely figuration; they also thought of themselves as laying down the basic alphabet of a future culture. Although none of them actualized the blank canvas, they sensed its promise. Kandinsky, for example, in 1913, praised "this pure canvas that is itself as beautiful as a picture."

This sensibility accompanied the history of modernist painting all along. When, as early as 1940, Greenberg spoke of "the pristine flatness of the stretched canvas," he was still surrendering to its magnetic appeal.[72] In fact it is the Mallarmean seduction of the virgin canvas that is the secret center of convergence of modernism as "self-critical tendency" with formalism as "tropism towards aesthetic value as such." And of course, it could keep this attractive power only as long as it was itself taboo. With each convention that proved "expendable," modernist painting came closer to actualizing the blank canvas. But the closer its actualization, the thinner its capacity to promise a future. By 1962 this actualization seemed imminent, and so did the end of modernist painting.[73] In

72. Greenberg, "Towards a Newer Laocoon," p. 36.

73. One wonders in retrospect whether, when writing "American-Type Painting" (1955–1958), Greenberg was not displaying an artificial overconfidence in the supply of "expendable conventions" that modernist painting had at its disposal. Perhaps it is the rather propagandistic overtone of this text, obviously written to sum up the achievements of American Abstract expressionism in the face of the then still dominant French art, that led him to silence the pessimism that is after all at the root of his conception of modernist painting. The "end of modernist painting" which he must have feared in 1962, when facing the imminent actualizing of the blank canvas, seems to me to have more to do with a return of this repressed pessimism than with a linear escalation in the actual history of modernist painting. To remind the reader that the appeal of the blank canvas was from the very outset haunted by the apocalyptic prospect of the end of painting, let me quote Barnettt Newman twice: "The artist must start, like God, with chaos, the void: with blank color, no forms, textures or details" (quoted in Thomas Hess, *Barnett Newman* [New York: The Museum of Modern Art, 1971], p. 56); and "Painting was dead a quarter of a century before God even realized it existed" (quoted in French by Barbara Rose, "Jackson Pollock et l'art américain," in *Jackson Pollock* [Paris: Centre Georges Pompidou, 1982], p. 18). As Yve-Alain Bois said in a very thorough article entitled "Painting: The Task of Mourning": "The pure beginning, the liberation of tradition, the 'zero degree' which was searched for by the first generation of abstract painters could not but function as an omen of the end" (in *Endgame, Reference and Simulation in Recent Painting and Sculpture* [Boston: The Institute of Contemporary Art, 1986], p. 30; this essay is reprinted in *Painting as Model*).

calling the blank canvas a picture, "though not necessarily a successful one," Greenberg anticipated its imminent realization. He didn't actualize it; he legitimized it instead and in so doing made its actualization futile. He would probably have been very surprised to learn that he was joining hands with Duchamp on this issue.

In Greenberg's retrospective account, reinterpreted via Duchamp, the history of modernist painting has, at the same time, both fulfilled and exhausted the promises of the blank canvas. In Kandinsky's eyes, it *was* a picture in 1914. It meant that on this tabula rasa a future abstract language called *Malerei* was going to be erected. In Greenberg's eyes, it *is* a picture in 1962. It means that modernist painting has finally surrendered to its essence, to its *being,* in the present participle. But seen through Duchamp's eyes, the blank canvas *will have been* a picture, for in 1914 it was and in 1962 still is a *readymade,* in the past participle—a picture to be made and yet already made. It will have been the picture that Kandinsky saw, potential and promising, and the one that Greenberg sees, finished even before it gets started. For it was ready-made as early as 1914, the year of the first readymade, and would become a finished picture only in 1962, when Greenberg legitimized it. One can apply to the theme of the virgin canvas (between *Vierge* and *Mariée,* there has to be *Le Passage de la vierge à la mariée*) the same, incredibly subtle treatment which Duchamp has applied to the theme of the tube of paint. One would then see in it the same "avant-garde melancholy"[74] with which, in 1914, again, speaking as if in retrospective anticipation of the "possibility of several tubes of paint becoming

74. I used this expression in an unpublished paper on Manet delivered at the 1984 College Art Association convention in Toronto in order to describe the dialectic of retrospective anticipation and anticipated retrospection in avant-garde art. I was speaking of the veil of melancholy in the eyes of Victorine—or Olympia: "It says: when you'll see me from where you are, there in 1984, I'll be dead for a long time. What you'll see in my eyes is the anticipation of my own death and the awareness that I have to look ahead into a future that I'll never inhabit, so that you'll be able to see me stare at you. And it also says: I still see in your eyes, your gaze only has meaning insofar as it is locked in mine and accepts the burden of looking

a Seurat," he posited the "has-been" as a "would-be" painter.[75] Seurat had been dead for more than twenty years and, in that time span, abstract painting had sprung out of his tubes, when Kupka and Delaunay "enlarged his pointilism in planes by color." In the same time span the abstract painters, and Duchamp himself in *Mariée* (his last canvas before the readymades), had raped the virgin canvas. Seurat's potential had been exploited and the blank canvas's promises were exhausted. How could you paint after that? While modernist painting followed its course, still inexorably attracted by the "pristine flatness of the stretched canvas," Duchamp quietly stopped painting, reserving the possibility of picking up his brushes again some day and of painting again, but *on glass*. And it is as though he told himself, in anticipated retrospection: "I shall have been a painter, therefore I am an artist." He did a few readymades and carefully refrained from doing any *specific* ones: neither tubes of paint nor blank canvases. Just as the tubes of paint had to remain sealed so as to retain their potential, just as the white canvas had to stay virgin so as to retain its promise, so the link between the specific and the generic had to be concealed in melancholy and humor, by way of a pun on *Peigne*, for example. Duchamp was simply waiting for 1962 to arrive, when a blank canvas not only could, but had to be called a picture, "though not necessarily a successful one."

Duchamp's extreme intelligence and acute sensitivity in not actualizing the blank canvas is echoed and, if properly interpreted, accounted for, in and by Greenberg's refusal to cross the thin line between a picture and a successful one. In order to call a blank canvas a picture, not an object or a piece of the artist's material, you need to "see" it as art. But only if your eye is trained and acquainted with the whole history of modernist painting down to Stella and Reinhardt to you "see" it as art.[76] This then means that you judge it to be art,

back upon the time-span that separates us, so that what you'll see in my eyes is my own future, still promising, yet accomplished. History undefeated, but disillusioned."

75. See chapter 3.

76. Of course there is another possibility. You can be a total philistine and still see the blank canvas as art provided you are informed of the latest trends. This is of course what Greenberg

involuntarily, in accordance with the strictest requirements of formalism. What you do is intuitively apprehend the blank canvas's generic *content,* the one that is, so to speak, perpendicular to its specific *form.* To call a ready-made canvas a picture thus requires, and indeed utters, an aesthetic judgment. It is only liminally a positive judgment, however, because it is virtually impossible to tell whether what you value is the thing you are supposedly beholding or the tradition that has made this thing a plausible candidate for aesthetic judgment. (The question is of course open as to whether this is not always the case with "advanced" modernist art at the very moment when its "advance" verges on the far-out and challenges aesthetic judgment.) To go beyond this liminal judgment and to call the ready-made canvas a successful picture would entail an interpretation in terms that Kandinsky or avant-gardistic art historians such as Herbert Read might have endorsed, but not Greenberg. You would have to sense either its liberating potential or its provocative "anti-art" value, or both. Yet to call it unsuccessful would entail a disavowal of the aesthetic pressure that the series of surrenders constituting the history of modernist painting had built up. It would have a retroactive effect on what appears, but only in retrospect, as the "logic" of modernism. (The confusion between retroactive and retrospective accounts for much of the hasty revisionism going on under the name of postmodernism.) It is thus essential to Greenberg's modernism and formalism that he should walk the thin line between a picture and a successful (or unsuccessful) one, and that he should suspend his judgment on the hypothetical case of the blank canvas, leaving it in its liminal, nominal state. Had the verdict fallen, whether positive or negative, it would have been final, if due only to the fact that when it is possible to aesthetically judge a hypothetical case—and it is perfectly feasible with the blank canvas; you don't need to see it (although, again, you would need to have seen one)—then a norm is set that is inescapable. The critic judging the blank canvas as successful would have been equivalent to an artist actualizing it.

---

dreaded, and rightly so. But it can hardly apply to his own acknowledgment of the blank canvas.

I find it extremely striking that, to my knowledge at least, there is not one minimal or conceptual artist who actualized the blank canvas per se. As if taking their clue from Stella's hollowed-out canvases, some stripped the wall of its "expendable conventions," either treating the painted canvas as a pointer or removing the canvas in the process: Robert Barry delimited an empty area on the wall with four tiny stretched and painted canvases, while one of Lawrence Weiner's *Statements* proposed "a 36″ × 36″ removal to the lathing or support wall of plaster or wall board from a wall." Some, perhaps carrying Rodchenko's red, yellow, and blue triptych to the point where color was drained from the monochrome, recorded their abandonment of painting in some object nominally referring to the medium: Jan Dibbets stacked a series of empty canvases and called the resulting assemblage *My Last Painting,* a gesture that Marcel Broodthaers (who had not been a painter but a poet) later parodied and referred to the nostalgia for the Mallarmean ideal. Some went from painting to concept via the painted word: under the title *Secret Painting,* Art & Language did a black square monochrome accompanied by a photostat stating: "The content of this painting is invisible; the character and dimension of the content are to be kept permanently secret, known only to the artist." John Baldessari, in a very Duchampian move, had a sign painter inscribe sentences such as "Everything is purged from this painting but art" on gessoed canvases, while Gene Beery did very similar *Word Paintings* bearing humorous phrases such as "Sorry this painting temporarily out of style." The closest someone ever got to the straight blank canvas was an early piece by Michael Asher, which was actually an unpainted square piece of canvas braced to a stretcher; but the stretcher was beveled, bringing the work closer to a "specific object" than to a painting. Besides, the artist never showed it, considering it as a student's attempt at dealing with the issues which were then very much in the air for those artists trying to move beyond the formalism/minimalism alternative. As far as I know, nobody did the ready-made canvas, and just that. Many of these artists made it a point of leaving painting behind and some of them wanted to show their scorn for formalism. Yet it is as if they dared not transgress this ultimate taboo. They went beyond the blank canvas, into real space or the linguistic realm; they acted out a variation on the theme of the ready-made canvas; but they avoided tackling the theme head on. They were probably aware that it would have been nothing but a bland repetition of Duchamp's gesture. Perhaps they even feared that such a move would have appeared less radical than Duchamp's. I suspect that the real reason was that they would have proffered an object that would have been vulnerable to a formalist judgment. Whether they wanted to or not, they would have claimed that an unpainted canvas is a successful picture, in other words a viable painting. They would have fulfilled their wish, no doubt, to turn the art of painting into a process of ideation aiming at generic art-status (or at specific art-status in Judd's sense, that is, art qualified as "minimal" or "conceptual"). Yet because the blank canvas remains specific in Greenberg's sense, they would also have invited the quality judgment that would call it art as a successful—or unsuccessful—painting. (In more psychological terms: they would have exposed their impotence as painters.) This is why the blank canvas had to remain hypothetical. These artists sought to pursue modernism—modernist art, not modernist painting—beyond the threshold of the blank canvas, while seeking to halt formalism—the requirement of aesthetic judgment—on that very threshold. They chose the left branch of the alternative set by Greenberg.

Of course, there was a lot of wishful thinking in this. It didn't succeed in intimidating Greenberg and other formalist critics or in preventing them from saying out loud that a lot of minimal and conceptual art is simply bad art. But in so doing the formalist critics, in the course of their everyday practice, have also jumped the threshold of the blank canvas, like the artists. And like the artists, they had very good reasons for doing so, for it is impossible to stay with the kind of judgment that led Greenberg to yield to the blank canvas and to admit that it be called a picture, at least not on the grounds of taste: such a judgment needs to stay poised on the *infra thin* line between a successful and an unsuccessful picture; at the same time it cannot avoid being "shaped" in the form of an inevitable either/or which would make its outcome fall on either side of the line. This might be a very Duchampian definition of aesthetic choice, but one for which formalism is definitely not prepared. Rosalind Krauss, who also contributed a discussion of the blank canvas as part of her interpretation of Olitski's residual illusionism, stated the problem the way a formalist critic would perceive it very clearly:

> Within the limits of its rectangular field, a blank canvas presents a viewer with two (mutually exclusive) inherent conditions or properties. The first involves its physical presence which the viewer acknowledges when he sees the literal flatness of its surface. The second is a perceptual property—equally a condition or aspect of the canvas—and that is the apparent opening up of an infinitely penetrable depth behind that surface. In looking at a blank canvas, one can *either* see its flatness (by identifying its flatness as the surface of an object, impenetrable and unyielding like the surface of any object), *or* one can see its nascent space. The blank canvas's either/or is like the either/or of a Gestalt puzzle: one sees it now as a rabbit or now as a duck; it is impossible to see it as both at the same time. In this situation the alternate and conflicting claims of apparent depth or literal flatness can neither be adjucated nor unified. The blank canvas cannot make one present through the coherence of the other. The fact that one sees this doubleness is merely a function of perception. These two irrevocable claims are given with eyesight itself.[77]

Krauss, who was still very much struggling with Greenbergian criticism when she wrote this piece, in 1968, failed to see the Duchampian implications of the impossible dilemma raised by the blank canvas. (She might, now.) Its implications for formalism, though, are in her text, if only implicitly: either you see the blank canvas's "nascent space," and then it might be a picture, or you don't, and then it's not art. The either/or is not an aesthetic choice but a mere perceptual mechanism that involves no aesthetic experience, no feeling, no verdict of

77. Krauss, "On Frontality," p. 42.

taste. However, it forces an aesthetic decision: either a picture, or non-art. A judgment has taken place, which I hesitate to call an experience because it is suspended between two experiences, posed on the infra thin line between either and or, and characterized by the impossibility of choosing. (Could it be that the rabbit/duck alternative inherent in the perception of a blank canvas provides us with yet another *allegorical appearance* of *l'impossibilité du fer?*) Anyway, the fact that Krauss discussed the blank canvas, the fact that Greenberg had to surrender to the blank canvas in order to call it a picture, the fact that he was able to write that "art turns out to be inescapable by now for anyone dealing with a flat surface, even if it is mostly bad art," are all obvious symptoms that "something" aesthetic has occurred. Despite Greenberg's conviction that "when no aesthetic value judgment, no verdict of taste, is there, then art isn't there either, it's as simple as that," his own suspended judgment on the blank canvas demonstrates that the matter is not simple at all. Just as actualizing the blank canvas seems to have been taboo for the artists, so drawing the consequences of the blank canvas's plausibility for aesthetics seems to have been taboo for Greenberg (and for Krauss). The modernist and antiformalist artists who went beyond the blank canvas but bypassed it chose the left branch of the alternative set by Greenberg. He himself chose the right branch when he allowed for a nonmodernist hybrid of painting and sculpture in order to save formalism; but he bypassed the blank canvas too. Thus, the consequences of the right branch of the alternative are worth considering, on a doctrinal level, when applied to the case of the blank canvas. These consequences are hypothetical, as is the blank canvas itself: what if formalism were allowed to pass the threshold of the ready-made canvas by calling it successful, while modernism would halt there? In a very interesting remark on Greenberg's paragraph on the bare canvas, Michael Fried has envisaged precisely these consequences, heretical as they may be for formalism:

> It is not quite enough to say that a bare canvas tacked to a wall is not "necessarily" a successful picture; it would, I think, be more accurate to say that it is not *conceivably* one. It may be countered

> that future circumstances might be such as to *make* it a successful painting; but I would argue that, for that to happen, the enterprise of painting would have to change so drastically that nothing more than the name would remain.[78]

Must we be grateful that, until now, no "future circumstance" has occurred that would make a bare canvas a successful painting? Are we so sure that such a circumstance cannot be anticipated at this point? Is it not what the likes of Peter Halley and Ross Bleckner and Philip Taaffe would like to see established, perhaps in spite of themselves? With an eye on her previous work, can we not extrapolate the "logic" of Sherrie Levine to the point where the unpainted painting is the predictable end of the line?[79] The blank canvas is once again in sight and, inasmuch as blind predictions are not foolish, there is nothing, this time, that upholds an a priori rejection of its putative success. Yes, a successful, even a convincing blank canvas is plausible, as a would-be painting that has come full circle, having recycled modernism, from Kandinsky to Greenberg and back, through Duchamp. Indeed, Fried's "future circumstance" has already

78. Fried, "Art and Objecthood," p. 123 n. 4. I have actually quoted a slightly modified version of this note, as it is taken up again in Michael Fried, "How Modernism Works," p. 223. I believe that the unstated and underlying reason why a successful blank canvas is inconceivable for Fried is that it is not meant to be beheld. It would be the ultimate in "absorption" and "theatricality" at once. If my surmise is correct, then I can anticipate a few strong objections on Fried's part to the last part of my essay, and I agree with him in advance that they would be tough. For Duchamp's readymades are not meant to be beheld either, especially in Fried's sense of "to behold." To engage in a discussion on this, I would have to draw in the issue of reproducibility and of the particular enunciative regime imposed on all works of art by the museum-without-walls. See chapter 7.

79. I am happy to say that I was wrong when I wrote this. Sherrie Levine's subsequent work did not grab for the predictable but, instead, turned toward Duchamp for references that the artist succeeded in making into works of art in their own right.

happened: it was the invention of the readymade. Toward the end of 1912 Duchamp abandoned painting and, in 1914, he put this abandonment on the record and gave it the shape of a ready-made bottlerack. That very same year, he scribbled on a piece of paper: *A kind of pictorial Nominalism (Control).* In 1916 he chose a small iron comb as a readymade. Its name (*Peigne*) put the name of painting, in turn, on the record, by way of a pun on the subjunctive of the verb *peindre,* a verbal mode which, in French, also acts as a weak, hypothetical, and melancholic imperative: *que je peigne!*[80]

Has pictorial nominalism seen to it that the "enterprise of painting" changed "so drastically that nothing more than the name" remains? Apparently, yes: there is nothing pictorial in a comb but the pun in its name. In fact, no: Duchamp did not actualize the blank canvas. It is still poised on the infra thin line between a picture and a successful one, as Greenberg wanted it to be. But there is nothing inconceivable about its being successful, even convincing: not in the sense that it would have potential, much less in that it would incarnate the "last painting," but inasmuch as a successful blank canvas would simulate. It would be a *replica* of a blank canvas, like most readymades, by the way, which have come down to us as replicas. There is much talk about simulation these days, and Baudrillard's writings have been put to frantic ideological use by more than one Neo-Geo painter.[81] Whether their work is hailed or dismissed, it is for the same reasons: they are insincere and rhetorical, they deny originality, they strip Newman of the sublime, Mondrian of his struggle against the tragic, Malevich of Ouspensky. They appropriate modernist painting and regurgitate it ready-made. I have seen too little of this painting to judge it with assurance, and I have yet to see the "ultimate" blank canvas. While I am not enthralled at the prospect, I am not ready, as is Michael Fried, to rule out a priori the eventu-

80. See chapter 3.

81. See Jean Baudrillard, *Simulations,* trans. Paul Foss, Paul Patton, and Philip Beitchman (New York; Semiotext(e) 1983), and Peter Halley, "The Crisis in Geometry," *Arts Magazine,* Summer 1984.

ality of its being a successful painting, but on terms that are, of course, no longer modernist, that is to say, utopian or apocalyptic.[82] Fried and Greenberg have taught me not to trust the "logic" of extrapolation but to let my eye decide. So I shall let my eye, not Fried, be the judge. In the meantime, and since the blank canvas is not yet a fact, I shall consider what simulation, when it does not foreclose emulation, teaches the retrospective eye of the historian. Was it not there all along in modernist painting? Have I not heard many times, even from Claude Lévi-Strauss, that the abstract painter paints what he would paint if, by any chance, he set out to paint a picture? Was it not Greenberg who said, in 1939, that avant-garde painting was "the imitation of imitating"?[83] Was it not Manet who let the simulation of the photographic simulacrum infect painting from within? Was it not Baudelaire who first understood that authentic aesthetic experience had to be sought in and regained from vicarious experience? Why would simulation, which is definitely not modernist in the Greenbergian sense (but then, was modern painting?) be more threatening for the future of painting now than it was throughout modernity? A successful ready-made canvas is no more—and no less—inconceivable now than impressionism was in David's time, cubism in Manet's time, or abstraction in Cézanne's time. Not only has successful painting always been inconceivable beforehand, but with each successive passage in modernism, the same anxiety about "future circumstances"—the one Fried expresses regarding the bare canvas—was felt, and the same risk was run regarding painting: "that nothing more than the name would remain."

82. Going over my text again, I realize that I have done exactly the same thing that Greenberg did in 1962, but in relation to today's dominant ideology. I just legitimized in writing a blank canvas that no one has actualized yet. I would be lying if I tried to hide that it is in the hope that it will never be.

83. Greenberg, "Avant-Garde and Kitsch," p. 7. And this, a propos of Picasso, trapped between *painting* and *object* and "committed to a notion of painting that leaves nothing further to explore": "The picture gets itself finished, in principle, before it gets started; and in its actual finishing, it becomes a replica of itself" ("Picasso at Seventy-five," in *Art and Culture,* p. 67).

A Reinterpreted Critique

> Something of the harmony of the original square of white canvas must be found in the finished painting.
>
> —*Clement Greenberg*

Since Fried's "future circumstance" is past, here is a string of past circumstances showing that the name of painting was at stake in its practice. In 1874, Manet submitted four canvases to the Salon; two of them were rejected (*Masquerade at the Opera* and *Swallows*) on the grounds that they were not finished enough. Mallarmé wrote an article in defense of Manet in which he asked, "What is an 'unfinished work,' if all its elements are in accord, and if it possesses a charm which could easily be broken by an additional touch?"[84] The times were far from ripe for a particularly unfinished painting—that is, the blank canvas—to be conceivable, but the "logic" (which is only retrospectively a logic, I insist) is the same. Mallarmé then went on to say:

> Entrusted with the nebulous vote of the painters with the responsibility of choosing, from among the framed pictures offered, those that are really paintings in order to show them to us, the jury has nothing else to say but: this is a painting, or that is not a painting.[85]

With this either/or verdict the jury's task ought to stop, contends Mallarmé. Enter the spectators, the public at large. Let them judge which paintings are good and which are bad. Now, what we have here, *mutatis mutandis,* is a situation identical to the one Greenberg found himself in when confronted with the

84. Quoted in George Heard Hamilton, *Manet and His Critics* (New York: Norton, 1969), p. 184.

85. Ibid., p. 185. I have modified the translation slightly to keep it closer to the French.

hypothetical case of the blank canvas. The jury ought to judge aesthetically, otherwise it is not a jury. Its task is not to recognize a certain family of objects that are called pictures in the way tables are called tables, but to choose, "from among the framed pictures offered, those that are really paintings." Really paintings, but not, for all that, successfully. Mallarmé wanted the jury to refrain from going beyond this nominal verdict, in order to let the public judge freely. Greenberg performed exactly this task. He gave the blank canvas the name "picture" and stopped short of calling it successful, leaving it instead in a nominal state and handing over the decision as to its quality to us, hypothetical or future spectators. This, Fried confirmed in his remark, when evoking "future circumstances" which "might be such as to make it a successful painting," without, however, seeing that an aesthetic judgment had already been expressed, albeit a liminal one:

> Moreover, seeing something as a painting in the sense that one sees the tacked-up canvas as a painting, and being convinced that a particular work can stand comparison with the painting of the past whose quality is not in doubt, are altogether different experiences: it is, I want to say, as though unless something compels conviction as to its quality it is no more than trivially or nominally a painting.[86]

There was certainly nothing trivial about the attribution of the name "painting" to Manet's *Masquerade at the Opera* in 1874; otherwise, it would not have been rejected. It is trivial now, but the fact that *Masquerade* has "compelled conviction as to its quality" has everything to do with this. I strongly doubt that to call the work a painting and to call it a convincing painting were "altogether different experiences." I say this in retrospect, of course, but that is precisely the point in avant-garde or modernist art. What was the nature of Manet's experience and judgment—the one Mallarmé calls "the nebulous vote of the painters"—when

86. Fried, "Art and Objecthood," p. 123 n. 4.

he declared the painting finished, although he knew that the jury would most probably find it too unfinished to even call it a painting? He had already gone through the Salon des Refusés, and we know of his anxieties and striving for public recognition. Was that experience, that aesthetic judgment, not in the nature of anticipated retrospection? Was it not a call for a consensus yet to come and retrospective by necessity, since the spectators always approach the work after the artist? Lee Krasner recalls this about Pollock: "He asked me: 'Is this a painting?' Not is this a good painting, or a bad one, but a painting! The degree of doubt was unbelievable at times."[87] Manet had more confidence in his own talent than Pollock and perhaps had only contempt for the jury, but even he could not guarantee posterity's verdict without a leap of faith. Was it not Fried who said, "Manet's problem, one might say, was not so much to know when a given picture was finished as to discover in himself the conviction that it was now a painting"?[88] Or, to put Fried's remark in its context, which is a discussion of Manet's relation to Courbet: that it was *un tableau,* and not merely *un morceau.*[89] I see no reason not to accept that the minimal, nominal judgment that was required of the jury in order to call *Masquerade* a painting is of the same nature as the one Manet asked of himself in order to call it *un tableau.* Both judgments are nominal and neither is trivial. And I see no more reason to suppose that seeing "the tacked-up canvas as a painting, and being convinced that it can stand comparison with the painting of the past whose quality is not in doubt, are altogether different experiences." Manet's work is now among the painting of the past whose quality is not in doubt, and it is the history of mod-

87. Lee Krasner Pollock, interview in B. H. Friedman, *Jackson Pollock* (New York: Marlborough-Gerson Gallery, 1964).

88. Michael Fried, "Manet's Sources, Aspects of his Art, 1859–1865," *Artforum,* March 1969, p. 73 n. 99.

89. "The ability to paint wonderfully—to paint wonderful *morceaux*—was something which even Courbet's detractors granted him without stint. What they refused to grant was that the final result amounted to a painting, *un tableau*" (ibid.).

ernist painting from Manet on, as told by Greenberg and Fried, which has allowed even a blank canvas to be compared with it. It takes far less conviction, I agree, for Greenberg to have called a blank canvas a picture in 1962 than it took for Manet to call *Masquerade at the Opera* a painting in 1874, but I am not accountable for the modernist narrative; Fried and Greenberg are. It may be that the bare canvas is nominally a picture only in comparison to a Stella, a Noland, or other immediate precedents, but Stella and Noland themselves (according to the modernist narrative) are painters only in comparison to their immediate predecessors, and so on. Fried, who reportedly once said that Stella painted stripes because he wanted above all to paint like Velasquez,[90] knows all too well that he could afford such bold ellipses only because the range of comparisons, although organized by the modernist narrative into a long chain extending far into the past, is explored by an eye that is shortsighted at each link.

Along with the Salon des Refusés and Mallarmé's protest against Manet's partial rejection from the 1874 Salon, the impressionist show at Nadar's that same year and other "alternative" events were among the responses which led those artists ostracized from the 1884 Salon to unite against the Société des Artistes Français, to set up their own Salon des Indépendants in April and finally, to found the Société des Artistes Indépendants in June. The Société's motto for its annual "anti-salon" was "Ni récompense ni jury." Thus, it went a significant step further than what Mallarmé had advocated for the jury ten years before: it granted the public at large—the crowd, the Baudelairian *foule*—not just the right to estimate the good and the bad in painting, but also the responsibility of tracing the nominal boundary between painting and non-painting. This means that from then on, in France (and why was the avant-garde launched in France?), all the moves by which the modernist painters tested the aesthetic validity of their conventions were at the mercy of public approval. What Greenberg calls a convention of the medium is an agreement, a pact, of which he never tells us between whom it is signed. It is as though only artists were

90. See Rosalind Krauss, "A View of Modernism," *Artforum*, September 1972.

involved. In a way this is true: artists are accountable only to their tradition and, of course, not to the average taste of the public. This is what "avant-garde" means. But there would be no avant-garde—we would simply call it the continuation of tradition—if the most intimate aesthetic decision made in the studio didn't have to take into account, in advance, the probable verdict of the crowd. So-called provocation and so-called non-art are only the inevitable byproducts of the relentless testing, deconstruction, or dismissal of painting's "expendable conventions." Conventions prove expendable in the eyes of the avant-garde painters because, once too easy a consensus is reached, satisfying the middlebrow taste of the public, this can only mean that tradition has been betrayed. Greenberg, who, in "Avant-Garde and Kitsch," has described this situation better than anyone, saw the momentary state of the social consensus as technical constraints immanent to the medium. Painters may indeed experience them that way. Fried saw them as more explicitly historical. Avant-garde artists indeed have that awareness. But neither Greenberg nor Fried considered critically that to call these technical and historical constraints "conventions" was misleading, since they are conventions only in retrospect, when they are abandoned and thus revealed as mere conventions, when the painter parts with the crowd and leaves a given state of the social consensus behind. It is not when the crowd says "this is a painting" that we have a true modernist or avant-garde painting, but rather when it says "that is not a painting."

The Society of Independent Artists was founded in New York at the end of 1916 by a group of artists who had belonged to or were closely associated with the only avant-garde movement in America at the time, the Ash Can School. As we remember, Marcel Duchamp, whose reputation as a provocative cubist painter had been established in New York by the presence of his *Nude Descending a Staircase No 2* at the Armory Show in 1913, was a founding member. It is he who suggested that the Society be modeled after the Parisian Société des Artistes Indépendants and that it adopt the same motto for its exhibitions: "No jury, no prizes." He had already been nominated chairman of the hanging committee when, under the pseudonym of R. Mutt, he submitted a readymade urinal rebaptized *Fountain*. It was a shrewd strategic move that put the members of the hanging committee in a nice quandary. If they abided by their democratic principles, they would make fools of themselves in the eyes of the crowd (and the press), and if they censored Mr. Mutt's entry, they would become a jury again, in the traditional sense, making Mr. Mutt the victim of a new Salon des Refusés. As we know, the urinal was not shown at the Independents and Duchamp, who had made a point of concealing Mr. Mutt's true identity, resigned from the hanging committee. He also made sure that the Richard Mutt case would be put on the record for posterity.[91] What interests me here is that the outcome of his strategic move is that, whether they wanted it or not, the members of the hanging committee were turned into a jury again, but a jury in Mallarmé's sense: they were forced to say "this is art," or "that is not art." Whatever the true story of the urinal's disappearance may be, all versions show what their predicament was: they could not decide. It seems that history has decided instead. Unless one is ready to erase from art history the innumerable works that have been authorized by Duchamp's readymades, it is impossible to deny that, whether good or bad, these are art.

The readymades are art, not painting, not sculpture and not something interspecific straddling both. They are not even specific in Donald Judd's sense, since they don't defend their identity through "holistic Gestalt" or "obdurate materials" against confusion with non-art. Quite the contrary: they are generic and nothing but generic. Thus, they are not even eligible for a formalist judgment, which is why they have been hailed by the antiformalist proponents of conceptual art. It is their context, not aesthetic judgment, that supposedly determined their "art-status." Greenberg and Kosuth agree on this. Kosuth says:

> A work of art is a kind of proposition presented within the context of art as a comment on art. . . . The "art idea" (or "work") and art

91. See chapter 2.

> are the same and can be appreciated as art without going outside the context of art for verification.[92]

Greenberg says:

> All art depends in one way or another on context, but there's a great difference between an aesthetic and a non-aesthetic context. The latter can range from the generally cultural through the social and the political to the merely sexual. From the start avant-gardist art resorted extensively to effects depending on an extra-aesthetic context. Duchamp's first Readymades, his bicycle wheel, his bottlerack, and later on his urinal, were not new at all in configuration; they startled when first seen only because they were presented in a fine art context, which is a purely cultural and social, not an aesthetic or artistic context.[93]

The issue of context is far too complex to be more than touched on here. But what Kosuth means by "context" is fairly clear: he means the *artworld.* Kosuth the artist identifies art with art theory, and his art theory is institutional; in fact, it is the same as that of the aesthetician George Dickie, developed around the same time.[94] Institutional theories always claim to be circular and beg the question of the institution's empowerment. A political critique of the patronage system could break that circle but would yield another danger, that of explaining away the aesthetic "power" to call something art by other power privileges such as money or social status. Unless very carefully handled, that kind of critique often leads to a blanket suspicion that the artists are compromised in advance

92. Kosuth, "Art after Philosophy," pp. 82–83, 85.

93. Greenberg, "Counter-Avant-Garde," p. 128. Notice the adjective "avant-gardist." In this text as elsewhere, "avant-garde" is opposed to "avant-gardism" in the same way "modernist art" is opposed to "concocted art."

94. Dickie, *Art and the Aesthetic.* See chapter 2.

by their patrons' aesthetic ideology (and sometimes leads to the conclusion that aesthetics is nothing but an ideology). As a result of combining such suspicion with a circular institutional theory, much of conceptual art—Kosuth's in the first place—was never able to get out of the entrapment in petty artworld politics which is designed for itself. Rather than taking Kosuth's and Greenberg's agreement on the issue of context at face value, we should examine a little more closely the kind of aesthetic context that Greenberg deemed relevant to art, not merely as status but as quality, and in which, according to him, Duchamp's urinal would not have been startling:

> Taste develops *as* a context of expectations based on experience of previously surprised expectations. The fuller the experience of this kind, the higher, the more truly sophisticated the taste. . . . Surprise demands a context. According to the record, new and surprising ways of satisfying in art have always been connected closely with immediately previous ways, no matter how much in opposition to these ways they may look or actually have been.[95]

I have shown—though not proven—that the Richard Mutt case belongs in such "a context of expectations based on experience of previously surprised expectations." For a number of reasons I would hesitate to call it taste, though, but I definitely call it aesthetic, in due faithfulness to formalism: it is a context made solely of aesthetic judgments (and when not, it is irrelevant). All appearances work against Duchamp, for it is true that the urinal was a strategic *coup* with regard to the institutional context, and that the institutional context doesn't seem aesthetic at all. But appearances are misleading, unless they lead us to their *apparitions:* the *coup* involving the urinal is not "political," it is aesthetic.[96] Duchamp had gained his institutional position as chairman of the hanging

95. Greenberg, "Counter-Avant-Garde," p. 131.

96. *Apparitions* in the same sense as encountered above (see chapter 2, n. 9), meaning the fact of appearing.

committee thanks to his reputation as a painter, and he had gained the latter (so far as New York is concerned) in the context of the Armory Show where, to say the least, the *Nude Descending a Staircase* was striking in its newness, but a newness "connected closely with immediately previous ways" of generating aesthetic surprise, cubism. There is no doubt that the other founding members of the Society had expectations vis-à-vis Duchamp: they wanted him to honor them with his presence in the show and what they expected from him was a painting, maybe a painting as surprising and scandalous as the *Nude* had been four years before, but a painting nonetheless, something they could call *un tableau* in the same liminal and nominal way that Mallarmé requested of the 1874 jury with regard to Manet's *Masquerade at the Opera.* Instead they got a urinal, which a perfect unknown by the name of Richard Mutt requested them to call a *work of art.*

In comparison with the Paris Indépendants in 1884, the New York Independents in 1917 went another significant step beyond Mallarmé's admonishing of the jury in 1874: the members of the public at large—already entrusted by the Independents' motto "Ni récompense ni jury" (or "No jury, no prizes") with the responsibility of tracing the nominal borderline between a *framed picture* and *un tableau,* successful or not—also received the duty of tracing the line between a mere thing, vulgar and tasteless and thus without any aesthetic context, and art in general. They were handed this duty by Richard Mutt. Why present them with a *specific object,* some flat thing hung on a wall and covered with colors assembled in a certain order, for example, since for such things, called paintings, they have no more specific competence than the layman? They are not professionals, after all. They know the conventions of painting, but have they experienced them aesthetically, have they judged them? Why then be more complacent than Manet when he refused to "finish" *Masquerade at the Opera* in order to please the jury? The New York public had already rushed to the Armory Show four years before. It had liked the *Nude Descending a Staircase* for the quantity of surprise it offered. Thanks to the publicity around the first Independents' show, the public was prepared—socially—for any surprise, but not for this one, not for the one that would compel the leap from the specific to the generic. Since the painters' tradition was no longer transmitted through the mediation of a jury of peers but through the crowd at large, there was the need to give the crowd something it could judge on its own scale: art at large. *Fountain* was conjured away before the crowd got a chance to judge. And the hanging committee had to betray its principles, in the name of specificity. It played the ostrich. In order not to become a jury again, in order not to judge aesthetically, it got away with saying, as Fried and Greenberg would say fifty years later, that what falls in between the arts is not art, rather some kind of theater, if not of circus. And so *Fountain* became non-art. And so *Fountain* became, like the blank canvas fifty years later, a candidate for aesthetic judgment of which it is impossible to know whether what you judge is the thing you don't even need to see (though you would need to have seen one of its kind), or the tradition that has made this thing plausible. And so *Fountain* became, *with all kinds of delays,* the outcome of an aesthetic judgment as well.

Duchamp's urinal is the outcome of an aesthetic judgment as surely as non-art is a "category" of art. There is no other way to account for its existence as art, unless you are ready to erase from art history the tradition it founded, which is, I am afraid, what Greenberg and Fried more often than not seemed to wish to do. Or unless you are ready to erase from art history the whole of tradition before Duchamp, which is obviously what Kosuth wished to do. The formalist doctrine, which is on the whole just, maintains that anything that is judged aesthetically—and thus deserves to be called art (as art)—needs to stand up to a comparison with the art of the past, at least of its immediate past. Before something can withstand comparison to something else, a comparison must be made. The modernist doctrine, which is incorrect or only partially correct, maintains that two things cannot be compared unless they share the conventions of a given medium. How could one compare a urinal to a painting! There were two ways of demonstrating that this was feasible, and I explored them both.[97]

97. In fact, there were three. The third one, which substitutes Duchamp's *algebraic comparison* for the formal comparison called taste—the only kind of comparison Greenbergian formalism recognizes—is the one I explored in chapters 1 and 2.

The first was to cling as faithfully as possible (too faithfully, as I did) to the modernist narrative of the history of modern art and to seek the missing link between the urinal and painting, between the generic and the specific. The second was (or would be, since I hardly scratched its surface) to replace the modernist narrative with another way of writing the history of modern art, a way that would reintegrate its political and institutional context into its aesthetic context.[98] The first way quite naturally led me to investigate an episode in history to whose shaping the modernist narrative literally contributed, and to notice—quite naturally—that it provided the missing link between the urinal and

98. One should remember, here, that Greenberg's early modernism, toward the end of the thirties, is the thinking of a Marxist, more exactly, of a Trotskyite. The fact that in time his formalism took a more and more fiercely apolitical stance has much less to do, as is often thought, with the fact that the man became conservative as he grew older, than with his early interpretation—in fact typical of a leftist intellectual who keeps in mind the recent encounter between Breton and Trotsky in Mexico—of the phenomenon of the avant-garde as a pocket of resistance where the progressive cultural forces came to nest in order to maintain aesthetic standards at their highest level of expectation and defend them against the philistinism of the industrial bourgeoisie. According to this interpretation, the avant-garde signed a sort of tacit and probably unconscious contract with the enlightened faction of the bourgeoisie, the only one that didn't seem to renounce cultural ambition, in order to autonomize the artistic sphere and eliminate all political and institutional considerations from aesthetic experience and judgment. With this rationale the young Greenberg believed he could clearly separate the aesthetic and the social context: the former's autonomy is the effect of the latter. Growing older, Greenberg has indeed abandoned his Marxism, but he has never relinquished this conviction that the avant-garde's apolitical stance was the necessary and paradoxical fruit of the political contradictions of modernity. The critics who reproach Greenberg for having abandoned Marxism, in order to condemn the way formalism silences the political and institutional dimensions of aesthetic experience (and who sometimes deduce from this that all aesthetics is but ideology), have chosen the wrong target. To the contrary, and paradoxically, it is the traces of Marxism in Greenberg's conception of the avant-garde which are in need of a critique, if one wants to reintroduce those dimensions into aesthetics.

painting. Indeed, the blank canvas can be compared to both: it is a picture, "though not necessarily a successful one," and it is a readymade, though, if I may add, not as successful a readymade as Duchamp's. As to the second way, and just as naturally, it led me to investigate the chain of "contexts." Kosuth had brought me back to Duchamp's first unassisted readymade by claiming that it had "given art its own identity," its generic identity. The readymades' public career begins with the Richard Mutt case. Thus I sketched a narrative which, run backwards, goes from the Independents' Show in 1917 to the Salon des Indépendants in 1884 to Mallarmé's admonition to the jury and Manet's partial exclusion from the Salon in 1874. It extends further back to the Salon des Refusés in 1863, to Courbet's strategies vis-à-vis the Exposition Universelle of 1855, and to his quarrels with the Salon of 1851, when, I would venture to say, something called the avant-garde began. This narrative is institutional but it is also aesthetic throughout. If worked out in details it would show itself not just as artworld politics, although it is that too, but also as the history of institutionalized aesthetic judgment.[99] Such a narrative presumes that conventions in art—and there are no conventions without a certain degree of institutionalization—do not mean properties of the medium (as if the medium could, of itself, stake such ontological claims) but rather a given momentary state of the social consensus, which is the context of aesthetic expectations that the amateur with a "truly sophisticated taste" precisely expects to see breached or surprised by

99. The Salon des Refusés is of course paradigmatic because it is there that the aesthetic judgment was structurally cast into the binary form of an either/or, substituting for the continuous scale of "taste." I believe the ubiquity of the paradigm of refusal (together with the very existence of public Salons) to be largely responsible for the fact that the phenomenon of the avant-garde was born in France. There is, however, another modern paradigm that appeared later and is relevant for Central Europe, that of Secession. I tried to posit Duchamp in relation to both refusal and secession in my book, *Pictorial Nominalism: On Marcel Duchamp's Passage from Painting to the Readymade,* trans. Dana Polan (Minneapolis: University of Minnesota Press, 1991). See the chapter "Resonances of Duchamp's Visit to Munich," also published in *Dada/Surrealism,* no. 16 (1987).

the avant-garde artist.[100] Now, didn't Duchamp fulfill these expectations admirably? He invited the jury or non-jury of the Independents to compare a urinal to the remake of the *Nude Descending a Staircase* they expected, and then to call it art. The jury proved that it was indeed a non-jury by not deciding: it had no grounds for comparison. And the non-jury proved that it was a jury by deciding in spite of itself: what had no grounds for comparison fell into non-art. There the urinal stayed for quite a while. Meanwhile, the non-art limbo became a category in itself, generic through negation, a strange "multimedia" medium progressively filled in with myriads of things, not always mediocre, to which Duchamp's urinal can be compared and, if I may add, to its advantage. We are the jury that the 1917 hanging committee didn't want to be. We have a whole tradition of things behind us that are neither painting nor sculpture, from dada-

100. How to disentangle the social and the aesthetic contexts is ultimately a matter of ethics. We would have to discuss them case by case. Here is an instance in which an artist, in a facsimile of Duchamp's "strategic" gesture, anticipated the advent of the blank canvas long before 1962. In 1949 Clyfford Still, who was teaching at the California School of Fine Arts in San Francisco, was invited to take part in a drawing show at the California Palace of the Legion of Honor, which was going to be a big social event for most faculty members. He declined, and when insistently begged, he replied in exasperation: "O.K. I'll give you a picture. After all, this show to an artist of integrity can only be a gesture. Since it is made for a museum program, I will give you my gesture, my respect for the public and gallery working in these terms. I will give you my contempt for the whole business: a six-by-ten-foot canvas blank as the fabric comes from the factory." The matter was not mentioned again, but there is a coda to the story: "I told the story years later to Ed [Holger] Cahill in New York. He said, 'I would have taken you up on that and hung your canvas.' I replied, 'I know you would have, Ed. That is why I wouldn't have made even that offer to you'" (John P. O'Neill, *Clyfford Still* [New York: Abrams, 1979], pp. 27–29). Still's response to Cahill seems particularly pointed, when we remember that, some time in the mid-1920's, Cahill, who would later become the director of the Federal Arts Project, had contrived a rather dadaist hoax with which he addressed the Independents: he submitted a scuffed and burned wooden board, supposedly as a piece of South American art from the *Inje Inje* tribe. (Marlor, *Society of the Independent Artists,* p. 22.)

ism and constructivism to minimal and conceptual art and beyond, in which to inscribe the readymade and verify its historical resonance. And we have the missing link—the blank canvas. Thus, we also have the tradition of modernist painting and the whole tradition of premodern painting as well, to which we can and must refer the readymade, so as to judge whether or not it withstands comparison.

It does. Who am I to say this? Nobody in particular. I judge like any member of the Baudelairian *foule* having access to today's generic art salons. Or maybe not. I judge like someone who has enough aesthetic acquaintance with modern art, especially with the sequence of works Greenberg called modernist painting. I agree with Greenberg that painting has a privileged position in the history of modern art, but not for the same reasons: the passage from the specific to the generic was acted out in painting and nowhere else. Modern music remained music, literature sought generalization under the name "text" or "textuality," but the "spatial arts," as they have been called since Lessing, became art *tout court* with the passage from painting—not sculpture or architecture—to art.[101] It was a switch of names, but it didn't erase history. I don't share Fried's fear that if a blank canvas deserved to be judged a successful painting, nothing more than the name would remain. I believe that in modernist painting, the essential thing was that the name remain and be transmitted. It has been, until now, and with Duchamp providing us with the link with the past of painting, I can be more optimistic as to its future: two of the greatest living painters, Robert Ryman and Gehrard Richter, are great precisely because they have acknowledged the readymade in their work while withstanding comparison with Manet. At the same time, I share Greenberg's conviction (not only for

101. Greenberg saw this in his own way when he said, "Back in the middle of last century a few poets, novelists and painters (not sculptors or architects) saw, in a surprisingly decided way, the need to maintain high expectations in and of art as they were no longer being maintained by cultivated art-lovers at large" ("Seminar Four," *Art International* 19 [January 1975]: 17).

American art but for art in general) that "to define the exact status of contemporary American art in relation to the history of art past and present demands a certain amount of mercilessness and pessimism."[102] Duchamp's urinal requires and deserves an aesthetic judgment. Perhaps it is only liminally and nominally positive; perhaps it is even undecidable, for us now as it was for the hanging committee in 1917. But then it would be with the same kind of undecidability that still puzzles me when I read Baudelaire's famous address to Manet: "You are only the first in the decrepitude of your art." Perhaps Duchamp was only the first in the decrepitude of art at large. In the light of Manet's achievement, it is not that trivial a compliment. Yet I am not ready to call the urinal great art. It is significant art, highly significant of the plight of our culture. We live in a century in which great art is simply not possible, and all the great artists of modernity have woven the stuff of their art out of that recognition. When Greenberg settles for Olitski after having understood Pollock so well, I find it sad. The fate of Kosuth and his colleagues in "theoretical" conceptual art is rather distressing too, and certainly I shall not vouch for them. But the saddest thing is to see Greenberg and Kosuth agree on Duchamp. If it were a matter of taste, I would leave it at that. No one can prove his or her aesthetic judgment. But they both claim that no aesthetic judgment is required in order to call a urinal by the name "art," and that Duchamp wanted it that way. In this case, the burden of proof is on them. It is not quite enough to say that I feel free to judge the urinal aesthetically; it would, I think, be more accurate to say that I feel obliged to, and all the more so because, in fact, Greenberg's surrender did not end with the blank canvas:

> If anything and everything can be intuited aesthetically, then anything and everything can be intuited and experienced artistically. What we agree to call art cannot be definitively or decisively sepa-

---

102. Clement Greenberg, "The Situation at the Moment," in *Collected Essays and Criticism,* 2: 192; first published in *Partisan Review,* January 1948.

> rated from aesthetic experience at large. (That this began to be seen only lately—thanks to Marcel Duchamp for the most part—doesn't make it any the less so.) . . . If this is so, then there turns out to be such a thing as art at large: art that is, or can be, realized anywhere and at any time and by anybody.[103]

103. Greenberg, "Seminar One," p. 44.

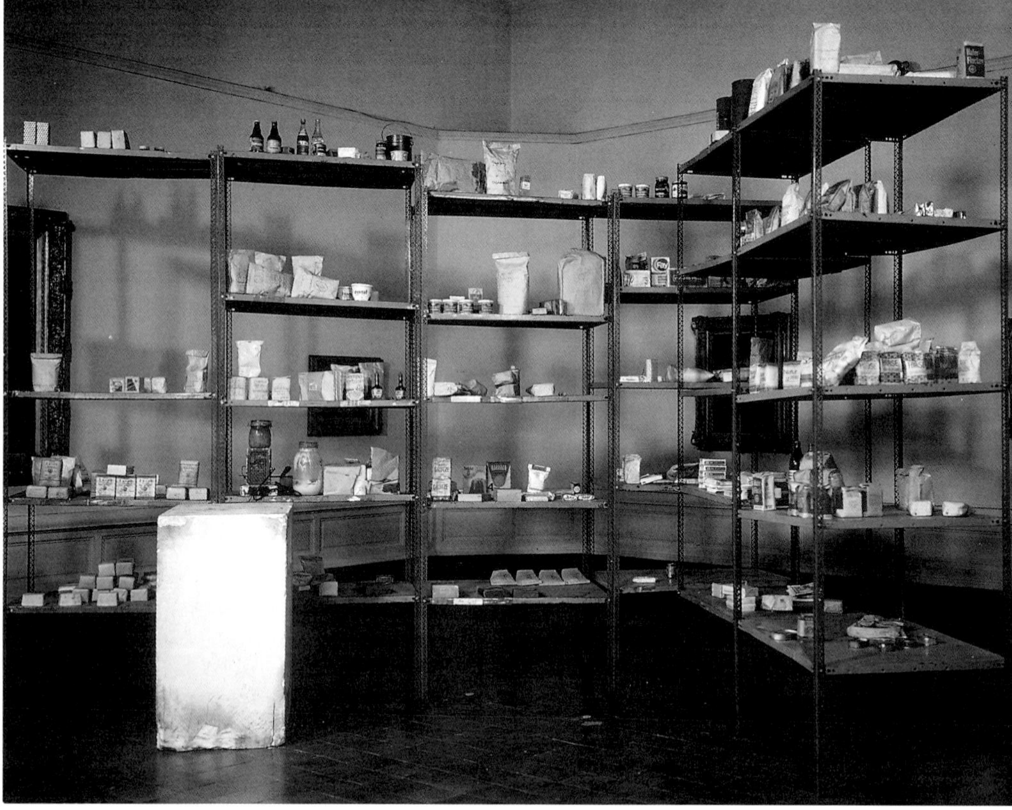

Joseph Beuys, *Wirtschaftswerte,* 1980, mixed media. Museum van Hedendaagse Kunst, Ghent (Photo Ronny Heirman).

Part III:

Anything and Everything

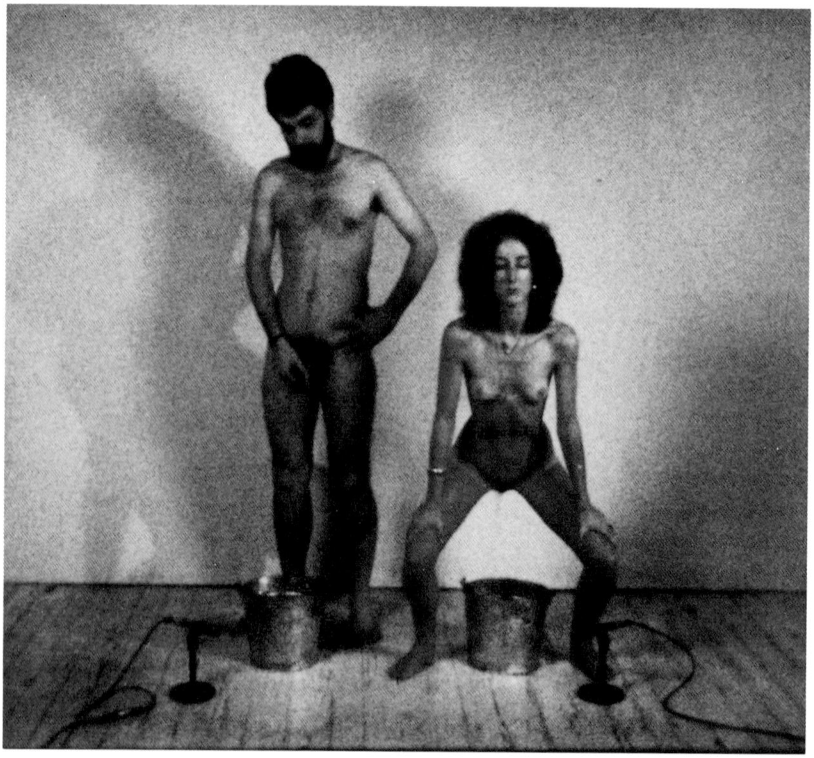

Michael Snow, *"Rameau's Nephew" by Diderot (Thanx to Dennis Young) by Wilma Schoen*, 1972–1974, 16mm film, 260 min., color, sound. Filmstill from the *Pissing Duet* sequence. Courtesy the artist.

5

Kant after Duchamp

The present investigation of taste, as a faculty of aesthetic judgment, is not being undertaken with a view to the formation or culture of taste, which will pursue its course in the future, as in the past, without the help of such inquiries.

—*Immanuel Kant,* Critique of Judgment

Those Were the Days My Friend

Imagine yourself a young artist or a young intellectual, a student perhaps, in the late sixties–early seventies. (If you belong to the same generation as I, it should be easy.) The Vietnam War was raging. If you hadn't burnt your draft card or your bra, you had at least thought of doing so. Even though, perhaps, you were living neither in San Francisco nor in Paris, Flower Power and May '68 were close. Whether your hero was McLuhan or Marcuse, the liberating promise of the global village and the multidimensional society seemed within reach. You were listening to Jimi Hendrix and Janis Joplin, and if you weren't busy building a Bucky Fuller dome in your backyard, probably you were leafing through the *Whole Earth Catalog* in search of some outlet for your creativity. "Do it" was your motto. Now, sit back and savor what in those days Jack Burnham had to say: "Obviously it is no longer important who is or is not a good artist; the only sensible question is—as is already grasped by some young people—why isn't everybody an artist?"[1] Those were the days my friend, and Jack Burnham was in tune.

Now, picture yourself in Germany at about the same time. George Brecht, Nam June Paik, George Maciunas, Dick Higgins were there more often than not. They had so gladly embraced Burnham's "sensible question" that everybody hanging around their happenings, actions, and performances was a Fluxus artist. But, while America had sent Fluxus to Germany, the German context yielded a Fluxus artist not quite like the others. Student upheaval, hard-line leftist politicization, extraparliamentary opposition, disgust with the consumer society and the German *Wirtschaftswunder,* and soon terrorism tinted the German cultural landscape of the hippie period with a pessimism, an anxiety, and an unbearable guilt-complex absent this side of the Atlantic. What was in the States a mild, Whitmanesque revival of the American Dream only subliminally spoiled by an unjust and not yet lost war expressed itself in Germany as the most contradictory need to heal a society traumatized by its own monstrous past. Such was the context in which Joseph Beuys—who was not exactly a young man when he founded the Organization for Direct Democracy the very year when Burnham asked, "Why isn't everybody an artist?"—had already answered, why indeed? Until his death, in 1986, he never strayed from his conviction. "The most important element, for someone looking at my objects, is my fundamental thesis: every human being is an artist. This is even my one contribution to 'Art history.'"[2] Those were the days my friend; Beuys had not yet set foot on American soil nor disdainfully proclaimed, "I like America, America

1. Jack Burnham, "Problems of Criticism," in Battcock, *Idea Art,* p. 69; first published in *Artforum* 9, no. 5 (1971).

2. Joseph Beuys, "Interview with Irmeline Lebeer," *Cahiers du Musée National d'Art Moderne* 4 (1980): 179; quoted in French, my translation.

likes me." The one European artist America liked best was Marcel Duchamp, whose silence Beuys judged overrated:

> I criticize him because at the very moment when he could have developed a theory on the basis of the work he had accomplished, he kept silent. And I am the one who, today, develops the theory he could have developed[3]
>
> He entered this object [the urinal] into the museum and noticed that its transportation from one place to another made it into art. But he failed to draw the clear and simple conclusion that every man is an artist.[4]

Jump the Atlantic again. Clement Greenberg—a disillusioned Jewish Marxist, a supporter of American involvement in Vietnam, the pessimistic defender of modernism, a genuine art lover, and perhaps the best art critic America had produced—was then seeing his star tarnish at the same pace as Duchamp's was rising with the young generation of artists, conceptual artists especially. He was impervious to the work of Joseph Beuys and couldn't have cared less about Fluxus. And certainly he wasn't smoking pot with Jack Burnham when he wrote, at about the same time: "If anything and everything can be intuited aesthetically, then anything and everything can be intuited and experienced artistically. . . . If this is so, then there turns out to be such a thing as art at large: art that is, or can be, realized anywhere and at any time and by anybody."[5]

Is it only my somewhat unfair collage of quotations that makes Greenberg appear to join hands both with Jack Burnham—the eco-sensitive enthusiast

---

3. Joseph Beuys, "Interview with Bernard Lamarche-Vadel," *Canal* 58–59 (Winter 1984–1985): 7; quoted in French, my translation.

4. Beuys, "Interview with Irmeline Lebeer," p. 176.

5. Greenberg, "Seminar One," p. 44.

of technology, the utopianist of art's dissolution into life—and with Joseph Beuys—the last grand and tragic incarnation of the German romantic tradition? Or is there some unacknowledged ground for the juxtaposition of those three statements, whose authors could not have been more opposed to each other? Greenberg's statement is one out of many that show him railing against the *Zeitgeist* Burnham's statement exemplifies. Not for a second does he share Burnham's "sensible question." To him the question is foolish and silly. A culture ready to erase the difference between art and life is what he dreads the most. And not for a second does he share Beuys's conviction that an artist should act on another artist's theory. Rather, he fears the consequences of Duchamp's gesture for practice. But like Beuys, what he grants Duchamp is a theoretical gain. The quotation cited above is extracted from a passage of "Seminar One" that shows him struggling very hard before finally surrendering to the awareness of how uncertain the difference between art and non-art, and thus between artist and non-artist, is.[6] And in that passage, he thanks Duchamp, though in paren-

---

6. To do Greenberg justice, I feel compelled to cite the passage in full, although I shall refrain from too pedagogical a comment myself. (I have given one elsewhere, in "Les tremblés de la réflexion. Remarques sur l'esthétique de Clement Greenberg," *Cahiers du Musée National d'Art Moderne* 45–46 [Fall–Winter 1993].) Since every word counts and is extraordinarily overdetermined, the only adequate commentary would have to be in the nature of a close reading verging on the psychoanalytic. Suffice it to say that all the threads that I have tried to follow in the previous chapter and will follow in this one, especially those dealing with the medium and its specificity, are interwoven here, and that Greenberg's constant oscillation between two notions of the medium, as a form on the one hand, as an agreement on the other, is highly indicative of the problems I am dealing with throughout this book:

> If anything and everything can be intuited aesthetically, then anything and everything can be intuited and experienced *artistically.* What we agree to call art cannot be definitively or decisively separated from aesthetic experience at large. (That this began to be seen only lately—thanks to Marcel Duchamp for the most part—doesn't make it any the less so.) The notion of art, put to the test

theses, as had he to ward off his lethal influence. As if poised between Burnham's "Why isn't everybody an artist?" and Beuys's "Every human being is an artist," Greenberg's admission that anybody could be an artist is, in his own

---

of experience, proves to depend in the showdown, not on skillful making (as the ancients held), but on the act of distancing to which I just called attention. Art, coinciding with aesthetic experience in general, means simply, and yet not so simply, a twist of attitude towards your own awareness and its objects. If this is so, then there turns out to be such a thing as art at large: art that is, or can be, realized anywhere and at any time and by anybody. In greatest part (to put it weakly), art at large is realized inadvertently and solipsistically, as art that cannot be communicated adequately by the person who realizes or "creates" it. The aesthetic intuition of a landscape when you don't convey it through a medium like language, drawing, music, dance, mime, painting, sculpture, or photography belongs to yourself alone; nevertheless, the fact that you don't communicate your intuition through a viable medium doesn't deprive it of its "status" as art. (Croce had a glimmering of this.) The difference between art at large and what the world has so far agreed to call art is between the uncommunicated and the communicated. But I don't find it a difference that holds. Everything that enters awareness can be communicated in one way or another, even if only partly. The crucial difference is not between the communicated and the uncommunicated, but between art that is fixed in forms that are conventionally recognized as artistic and art that is not fixed in such forms. On the one side there is unformalized, fleeting, "raw" art, and on the other there is art that is put on record, as it were, through a medium that is generally acknowledged as artistic. Yet even this difference is a tenuous one: a difference of degree, not of experienced essence or of demonstrable "status." You can't point to, much less define, the things or the place where formalized art stops and unformalized art begins. (Thus flower-arranging and landscape architecture can be said to belong to either, though I myself would claim that they both belong very definitely to formalized art. They are other such cases. It's the great theoretical service of the kind of art that strives to be advanced that it has made us begin to be aware of how uncertain these differences are: the difference

words, "the great theoretical service of the kind of art that strives to be advanced."

Whoever belongs—like me—to the generation that lived its youth in the heyday of Flower Power and May '68 must sense that to speak of that formidable liberation as a "theoretical service" is a total betrayal of the utopian impetus behind Beuys's conviction and Burnham's question. But whoever has eventually remained in the artworld since then must admit that the liberating utopias of the sixties have been more than shattered by subsequent events, even though "theory" survived. Some have locked the door on their youth and are content with the artworld as it is: business as usual. Others are bathing in nostalgia, without having grown any wiser. Still others have sought to solve the contradiction between the world and the artworld by conflating their political ideals and their theoretical endeavors into "critical theory." As for myself, I believe that *archaeology,* in Michel Foucault's sense, is what the times are calling for, and that the archaeologist's approach, which should aim at a postmodern rereading of modernity, is concerned with both acknowledging the "theoretical service" rendered by Duchamp's reception in the sixties and putting the "everyone-an-artist-utopia" into a broader perspective. The latter task is far beyond the scope of this book, yet I feel the need to at least indicate where it might take the archaeologist wishing to undertake it. The students of 1968, whether in the streets of Paris or gathered around Beuys in Düsseldorf, all shared a fundamentally emancipatory belief—Power to the imagination!—by no means dating from the sixties but as old as German romanticism, that is, as modernity itself. The Paris students may not have been very much aware of the romantic roots of their movement, but Beuys certainly was. It was Novalis who first conceived of imagination as "the mother of all reality" and who said for the first time: "Every man should be an artist."[7] Beuys has always claimed this legacy, as well

---

between art and non-art as well as that between formalized and unformalized art.) ("Seminar One," p. 44–45)

7. Novalis, *Werke* (Munich, 1969), pp. 310, 367. See Max Reithmann, *Joseph Beuys, La mort me tient en éveil* (Toulouse: ARPAP, 1944).

as that of Hölderlin, of Schelling, of Friedrich, or of Runge. Since their time, the main thrust of virtually every avant-garde or modern utopia has been that the practice of professional artists was to liberate a potential for art-making present in everyone individually and shared by humankind as a whole, a potential whose field was aesthetic but whose horizon was political. There have been spiritualistic and materialistic versions of that utopia, which in retrospect are far less incompatible than they appeared and sometimes claimed to be. In each case, past values had to be relinquished or destroyed and art had to be reconsidered on the basis of some faculty supposedly present in all men and women, yet independent of cultural heritage and social privileges. The new art was to rely on immediate feeling and emotion, and on some elementary visual alphabet and syntax. As aesthetic sensibility and artistic literacy would progress, the faculty to feel and to read would translate into the faculty to express and to articulate. *Creativity* is the name, the modern name of that conflation of faculties, the very name that Beuys made into the cornerstone of his doctrine. "Man/woman is *the* creative being," he used to say over and over.[8] The final horizon of the avant-garde utopia has been from the outset "Everyone an artist." In that respect, there is little difference between Kandinsky or Mondrian, who were spiritualists, and Tatlin or El Lissitzky, who were materialists. Whether they thought of themselves as spiritual or ideological trailblazers, they acted primarily as cultural pedagogues, with the same audience in mind: man/woman at large, "the layman." Whether the bourgeoisie had to be overthrown by a political revolution before humankind's creativity could be unleashed, or whether politics could be bypassed in favor of a spiritual revolution based on "inner necessity" and appealing to a common sense of humanity present in all men and women, even in "the bourgeois," accounts for differences that are crucial politically, but only politically. In retrospect, the choice was between two brands of humanism and universalism.[9] Both are ultimately the political heritage of the French

8. "Der Mensch ist das kreative Wesen."

9. There is, of course, a very strong tendency in today's art criticism to read the historical avant-gardes as radically antihumanistic. I don't think that this reading would have met with

Revolution—*Liberté, Egalité, Fraternité*—and the philosophical heritage of the Enlightenment. Both flared up one last time in the sixties. Both failed. Joseph Beuys was the last great tragic figure in that tradition, which goes as far back as Schiller's *Letters on the Aesthetic Education of Man,* published in 1795, or perhaps even to his poem, *The Artists,* written in 1788–1789. In his libertarian involvement in Fluxus, his militant teaching at the Free University, his founding of the German Student Party in his class at the Düsseldorf Academy in 1967, and his setting up of an office for the Organization for Direct Democracy at the 1972 *Documenta* in Kassel, Beuys made *human creativity* and the principle "Everyone an artist" the basis not only of his art but also of his relentless proselytism. With him, the spiritualistic and the materialistic versions of the modern utopia interweave with great charismatic power and ideological brilliance.

Duchamp, by contrast, was never a utopian. Nothing could be further removed from his way of thinking than the belief in universal creativity. His particular brand of art, the readymade, stemmed from neither the belief nor the hope that everyone can or should become an artist. Rather, it acknowledged—with more than a grain of salt, for sure—the "fact" that everyone had already become an artist. In front of a readymade, there is no longer any technical difference between making art and appreciating it. Once that difference is erased, the artist has relinquished every technical privilege over the layman. The profession of artist has been emptied of all *métier,* and if access to it is not restricted by some other padlock—institutional, social, financial—it follows that anybody can be an artist if he or she so wishes. As I have suggested in various ways throughout the previous chapters, this "fact" is not a consequence of the readymade, rather, it is its condition. The readymade only reveals it. If it were

---

the agreement of the artists involved, and I don't even think that—save a few ultra-Nietzscheans—it would meet with the agreement of the "poststructuralist" or "deconstructionist" authors (most often quoted are Jacques Derrida and Michel Foucault) whose specifically contextualized assessment of "the death of man" is rehearsed *ad nauseam* to uphold the anti-humanistic reading.

to be read as a utopian promise—as Beuys wanted to read it—it would immediately turn against itself. Art-making after Duchamp would simply be prone to absolute permissiveness, and art practice would be nothing but a social game whose codes and passwords would symptomatically indicate that some rules ought to replace the *métier* for the professional game of artist to be played at all. In this debased simulacrum of aristocratic etiquette, the modern utopia of "Everyone an artist" would translate into "Everyone a dandy."[10] But since the artworld, being comprised of a fraction of the middle class, does not embrace "the layman" in the universal sense, even that parody of a utopia would turn against itself, too. The only resistance to this state of affairs would then be an alternative coding, or recoding, of entry into the artworld. To remain faithful to the avant-garde utopia, one would have to, now as then, exclude "the bourgeois" from "the layman."[11] Impossible! Utopias have been gleefully or

---

10. This is what the art of Andy Warhol reveals, in which the early underground anonymity of the *Factory* and the very public marketing of the artist's name and fame resulted in pop-dandyism. It is highly symptomatic that, in the eyes of the young generation of artists, Warhol's superstar image is equal only to Beuys's charisma. Both have radically pushed their art and life (or in Warhol's case, *lifestyle*) to the point where they themselves became living symptoms revealing the truth of the crisis of modernity. But whereas Beuys thought he had a solution, Warhol knew he could only make the symptom exemplary.

11. What I elliptically refer to is the need to assign a social basis to alternative art practices, a need that does not have to be couched in terms of global class-struggle; it can appeal to various minority groups and to the recoding (see Hal Foster, *Recodings* [Port Townsend, Wash.: Bay Press, 1985]) of their specific ideological interests into viable cultural forms (feminism, the gay movement, antiracism, etc.). Although the naming of such groups and their subcultures certainly specifies "the layman," which otherwise would remain a blanket term, the problem of generalizing what links these groups together in a coherent sociocultural perspective cannot be avoided. When it is avoided (and I am afraid that Foucault's notion of the "specific intellectual," or Gramsci's notion of the "organic intellectual" are sometimes used to that effect), then the scarecrows of "the bourgeois," or of "capitalism," which are also blanket terms, are bound to reappear to fill in the void. Hence, the symbolic exclusion of "the bourgeois," once again,

regretfully abandoned, and while every graffiti-scribbler can claim the status of artist and ambitious artists retreat into a caste, is there anyone today who aspires to the Duchampian status of the *anartist?* Everyone should, for this status is simply the fact that when one and the same sentence, "this is art," serves to produce a work of art and to judge it as a work of art, it is as if such a sentence automatically turned anyone who utters it—whether professional or layman—into an "artist." In other words, it is simply the linguistic consequence of anyone's and everyone's right—and duty, but more about that in the next chapter—to judge art, as art. It entails neither belief nor hope that one will judge well; it entertains no illusion that aesthetic sensibility and artistic literacy can progress. Yet no social game, no coded password, restricts the possession of this "status" (which is, therefore, no status at all). And this is how it ought to be.

Back to America in the late sixties–early seventies, and to the "great theoretical service" that Greenberg said Duchamp's influence has rendered on "the kind of recent art that strives to be advanced." It is ironic to have to recognize, given Greenberg's resistance to precisely that kind of art, that he understood better than anyone that what he called *art at large,* and which he said is most of the time "realized inadvertently and solipsistically," is in fact nothing but the consequence of the fact that the modern aesthetic judgment is phrased, not as "this is beautiful" (or ugly), but as "this is art" (or not art). Greenberg's sad disgrace is somewhat a case of overkill to which, no doubt, he himself overreacted. From the late sixties on, hardly a single one of his articles has not contained a violent attack on Duchamp, blaming him for all the woes of the artworld. God knows he has been reproached for this. But what his detractors usually fail to notice is how, why, when and where, and with what scrupulous honesty he also acknowledged Duchamp, however reluctantly. In the early seventies, Greenberg the critic turned into a pedagogue and an aesthetician. In a somewhat pathetic effort to rally the young to what he considered the demands

---

and the revival of a nineteenth-century revolutionary myth in rather obvious contradiction to the actual possibilities of resisting the artworld as it is.

of high art, he began to lecture on aesthetics and, for the first time in his long career, ventured into philosophical matters. He went at them very empirically, occasionally citing Croce, Susanne Langer, or Kant, but most of the time relying on his own experience. This is what makes those lectures, later published as Seminars in various art magazines, extraordinary documents. For they don't have the academic dullness of a treatise; in them we hear the man's brain tick, we witness him thinking out loud and sharing his doubts and anxieties with his readers. In one of these Seminars, he said:

> Something has been demonstrated that was worth demonstrating. Art like Duchamp's has shown, as nothing before has, how wide open the category of even formalized aesthetic experience can be. This has been true all along, but it had to be demonstrated in order to be known as true. The discipline of aesthetics has received new light.[12]

What "new light," exactly?

> Since [Duchamp's readymades] it has become clearer too, that anything that can be experienced at all can be experienced aesthetically; and that anything that can be experienced aesthetically can also be experienced as art. In short, art and the aesthetic don't just overlap, they coincide.[13]

Art Without Aesthetics versus Aesthetics Without Art

The great obstacle to the proper understanding of Greenberg's insight is that in his doctrine, the overlapping of art and the aesthetic bears the name of taste: "It

12. Clement Greenberg, "Seminar Six," *Arts Magazine* 50 (June 1976): 93.

13. Greenberg, "Counter-Avant-Garde," p. 129.

remains: that when no aesthetic value judgment, no verdict of taste, is there, then art isn't there either, then aesthetic experience of any kind isn't there. It's as simple as that."[14] As we have seen in the previous chapter, matters are not as simple as that, especially not the minute Duchamp's readymade is recognized for having brought into the open not just the overlapping but the perfect coincidence of art and the aesthetic experience. Matters are all the less simple that Greenberg is more than ambiguous in his assessment of the kind of experience a readymade elicits: "But Duchamp's readymade already showed that the difference between art and non-art was a conventionalized, not a securely experienced difference."[15] And with regard to pop art, in his eyes the worst offspring of the readymades, he says that it "amounts to a new episode in the history of taste, but not to an authentically new episode in the evolution of contemporary art," while also stating that pop art afforded avant-garde sensibility "the chance to escape not just from strict taste, but from taste as such."[16] How an escape "from taste as such" might amount to no more than a "new episode in the history of taste" remains a little enigmatic. Matters are not simple, indeed. Perhaps we should consult Duchamp rather than Greenberg for clues.

Duchamp himself repeatedly dismissed the "category" of taste when applied to the choice of a readymade: "This choice was based on a reaction of visual indifference with at the same time a total absence of good or bad taste . . . in fact a complete anesthesia."[17] That would be simple if we could only believe him, but we can't. Absolute visual indifference is something impossible, and Duchamp left in his writings many clues showing that he was aware of that. Moreover, when the question of impossibility is read against the background of *l'impossibilité du fer,* the issue of indifferent taste, or of the "beauty of indiffer-

14. Clement Greenberg, "Seminar Seven," p. 97.

15. Greenberg, "Counter-Avant-Garde," p. 129.

16. Greenberg, "Post-Painterly Abstraction," p. 64.

17. "Apropos of Readymades," in *SS,* p. 141.

ence" (his words), far from getting simpler, becomes unfathomable.[18] Even if we accept at face value that his choice of a readymade was beyond taste, how are we to interpret a statement like "I took the thing out of the earth and onto the planet of aesthetics,"[19] when contrasted with: "When I discovered the readymades I thought to discourage aesthetics"?[20] Let us read on, for matters will perhaps get disentangled: "In Neo-Dada they have taken my readymades and found aesthetic beauty in them. I threw the bottle rack and the urinal in their faces as a challenge and now they admire them for their aesthetic beauty."

As long as the discipline of aesthetics has existed, the feeling of beauty has been the very substance of taste, and taste has been half of the domain over which aesthetics legislates (the other half being the realm of the sublime). Duchamp seems to agree with Greenberg that the neo-dadaists (i.e., the pop-artists), admiring the readymades for their "aesthetic beauty," have done no more than open a "new episode in the history of taste." And he seems to agree with Greenberg again when, claiming visual indifference for his choice of a readymade, he accepts the responsibility of having afforded avant-garde sensibility "the chance to escape not just from strict taste, but from taste as such." And yet the enigma is intact: "I took the thing out of the earth and onto the planet of aesthetics."

In the late sixties, this enigma was too dark and too subtle for many artists permeated with Duchamp's influence and rebellious against Greenberg's formalism. Here, as in the previous chapter, Joseph Kosuth's "Art after Philosophy" of 1969 is the canonical text. *Concept* was Kosuth's reply to *taste* and *beauty,* and

---

18. See chapter 3. For further investigation into the impossibility of the choosing, see my "Authorship Stripped Bare, Even," in *Res* 19–20 (1990–1991): 234–241.

19. Unpublished interview with Harriet and Sidney Janis, 1953.

20. Allegedly from a letter from Duchamp to Hans Richter, quoted in Hans Richter, *Dada Art and Anti-Art* (New York: McGraw Hill, 1965), p. 208. More recent studies have revealed that Richter made these comments, not Duchamp. (See William Camfield, "Marcel Duchamp's *Fountain:* Aesthetic Object, Icon, or Anti-Art," in de Duve, *Marcel Duchamp,* p. 179 n. 53.)

the *separation between aesthetics and art* was his alternative to Greenberg's total overlapping of art and the aesthetic: "So any branch of philosophy that dealt with 'beauty' and thus, taste, was inevitably duty bound to discuss art as well. Out of this 'habit' grew the notion that there was a conceptual connection between art and aesthetics, which is not true."[21] Kosuth and Greenberg thus read Duchamp's "theoretical service" in diametrically opposed terms. It seems, in retrospect, that Greenberg's reading allowed him to confine his own aesthetics to the realm of modernist painting and sculpture, while Kosuth's reading set the rules for several of the artistic practices appearing in the sixties that questioned the specific boundaries of the traditional media. For those practices, the alternative seems to have been the following: either we claim the name "art" for what we do, but then at the expense of the aesthetic; or we claim the aesthetic, but then under a name that is not "art." This alternative has been very humorously laid out by the Canadian couple, Ian and Elaine (or Ingrid) Baxter, who chose to call themselves by the very Duchampian name, *N. E. Thing Company.* They divided their practice into two categories: *ACT* and *ART. ACT* stood for *Aesthetically Claimed Things,* and *ART* for *Aesthetically Rejected Things.* (Notice that they were not as rigorously dogmatic as Kosuth: *ART* is not made of the rejection of aesthetics but of aesthetically rejected things. Nevertheless, they indicate the problem very symptomatically.)[22] So, let's adopt their nomenclature to categorize some well-known conceptual or protoconceptual works. On the side of *ART,* we find works whose issue is that they be called art, while all aesthetic quality is supposedly removed from them, works such as Robert Rauschenberg's *Erased de Kooning* (1953), Robert Morris's *Statement of Esthetic Withdrawal* (1963), Gene Beery's *Word Paintings* (1960–1963, one of which, for example, states: "Sorry this painting temporarily out of style. Closed for updating. Watch for aesthetic reopening"), or Bruce Naumann's *Burning Small Fires* (1969), a work which brings Rauschenberg's *Erased de Kooning* full circle, since

21. Kosuth, "Art after Philosophy I and II," p. 76.

22. See Lucy R. Lippard, *Six Years: The Dematerialization of the Art Object from 1966 to 1972* (New York: Praeger, 1973), pp. 66–67.

Various Small Fires, a little book by Ed Ruscha with a number of photographs depicting small fires (a match, a burning candle, etc.), was itself a work of conceptual art, which Naumann decided to burn, photographing the resulting "small fire." In each of the above cases, the removal of aesthetic quality was half of the issue. The parallel with the history of modernist painting down to the blank canvas—indeed its ironic rerunning—is obvious. Christine Kozlov, for example, did for the art of cinema what the blank canvas would have done for the art of painting: in 1967 she produced an untitled work consisting of a reel of clear 16 mm film. And while aesthetic quality was supposedly removed from such objects, their being called art was the other half of the issue. Claiming the lesson of Duchamp and his readymades, some conceptual artists made it clear that they considered that anything (N. E. thing) could be art if it was so called. See for example Don Judd's 1965 declaration: "If someone calls it art, it's art." Everything revolves around the issue of the name. Conceptual artist Ian Wilson, whose practice, called art, was to have conversations ("oral communication") with people about art, expressed this very clearly in a conversation with Robert Barry (himself a conceptual artist):

> IW: What struck me as important with oral communication was that when a person makes something that he is attached to, and he wants to call it art, he has to *call* it art. To call anything anything, you have to either speak it or print it or use sign language, if you're deaf and dumb. These are the three alternatives.
> RB: Well, you could put it in a certain place so it would be designated as art—an art gallery, an art museum, an art magazine.
> IW: But that place would have to be *called* too . . . [23]

On the side of *ACT,* we find works belonging most of the time to the less theoretical but most utopian branch of conceptual art, or to Fluxus, works that sought to produce or induce aesthetic experiences, but without claiming

23. Ibid., p. 181.

that they should be called art or that they should be placed in a context called artistic. Exemplary of this tendency are the so-called "command-pieces" or "instruction-pieces," which could be executed, but didn't necessarily have to be, by the artist or by someone else, in fact by anybody. For if the name "art" was to be removed from the piece, then the name "artist" should also be removed from its author. The vanishing of the difference between artist and non-artist was very much a part of the utopian content of this tendency, popular among Fluxus artists and typical of the "hippie pot-smoking" period (the experience is happening in the head of the person who executes the piece; the ideal work of "art" is an LSD tab; etc.). Needless to say, this utopia was bound to fail, for unless the experience in question is somehow recorded and communicated to the artworld, one would never know that some "art which doesn't want to be called art" had been made. Which is why it is appropriate to head a list of examples of such "command" or "instruction-pieces" with an artist who has indeed disappeared as artist and didn't want to "make it" in the artworld (but whom Lucy Lippard somehow managed to "rescue" for her book, *Six Years: The Dematerialization of the Art Object from 1966 to 1972*). I am talking about Lee Lozano, whose *Dialogue Piece* (1969) appears, in its form, quasi-identical to the practice of Ian Wilson (who was very much part of the artworld). The piece was directed at herself:

> Call, write or speak to people you might not otherwise see for the specific purpose of inviting them to your loft for a dialogue. . . . Note: The purpose of this piece is to have dialogues, not to make a piece. No recordings or notes are made during the dialogues, which exist solely for their own sake as joyous social occasions.[24]

Another piece by Lee Lozano, her *General Strike Piece* (1969), also directed at herself, extends the removal of the name "art" to the artworld, or rather, since

24. Ibid., p. 98.

it was not in her power to do this, instructs her to remove herself from this context:

> Gradually but determinedly avoid being present at official or public "uptown" functions or gatherings related to the "artworld" in order to pursue investigation of total personal and public revolution. Exhibit in public only pieces which further the sharing of ideas and information related to total personal and public revolution.[25]

There were many other such pieces: Yoko Ono's *Tape Pieces* (1960–1963: "Listen to the sound of the earth turning. / Take the sound of the stone aging," etc.), for example, or George Brecht's *Two Exercises* (1961):

> Consider an object. Call what is not the object "other." Add to the object, from the "other," another object, to form a new object and a new "other." Repeat until there is no more "other." Take a part from the object and add it to the "other," to form a new object and a new "other." Repeat until there is no more object.[26]

The two problems facing conceptual art have been often underlined. Inasmuch as works of *ART* are objects, they cannot avoid having visual properties that offer themselves to an aesthetic appraisal. And if works of *ACT* are not put into an art context or communicated to the artworld, they run the risk, as Greenberg surmised, of being done solipsistically, if not inadvertently. Hence the ever-repeated endeavor to remove all visual materiality from the piece, to communicate this very removal to the artworld itself, and to consider the piece self-referentially (a very modernist attitude) as being something that the art institution cannot possess or even show but that nonetheless depends on

25. Ibid., p. 78.
26. Ibid., p. 11.

the institution for its existence. Robert Barry, for example, is typical in having consistently followed a quasi-schizophrenic strategy, splitting his art into, on the one hand, a mental, purely solipsistic part that doesn't call for the name "art" at all, as in this piece from 1969: "All the things I know but of which I am not at the moment thinking—1:36 P.M.; 15 June 1969, New York," and, on the other hand, a relationship with the art-institutional context, which seeks to deprive it of its power to call what it is showing by the name "art," as in his piece at Art and Project in Amsterdam, also in 1969: "During the exhibition the gallery will be closed."

Those were the days my friend. Fascinating days, enthralling days, liberating days, and yet, in the long run, sterile. All symptoms point to one and the same contradiction, belonging to the reception history of the readymade in the sixties, and variously formulated as: either *ACT* or *ART;* either aesthetics, in Greenberg's sense, or art, in Kosuth's sense; either taste or concept. Unless this contradiction, or antinomy, is resolved, we are forever caught in the following double bind: either we believe, together with Kosuth, that Duchamp's readymades "changed the nature of art from a question of morphology to a question of function," and that "all art (after Duchamp) is conceptual (in nature) because art only exists conceptually."[27] Or, we don't believe that the nature of art has been changed in any way or that the judgment of taste, as it applies to works of modernist painting and sculpture as well as to the whole of ancient art, has lost its rights. But, having in the first instance drawn the line with Duchamp, we might be tempted to retroactively project this new conceptual nature of art onto its past, to the point of erasing all art before Duchamp, which is certainly what Kosuth wants to do when he says: "As far as art is concerned, Van Gogh's paintings aren't worth any more than his palette is."[28] And in the second instance, we might be tempted to declare the readymade a fraud, to refuse to draw a line with Duchamp or to acknowledge a rift in the fabric of art history

27. Kosuth, "Art after Philosophy I and II," p. 80.

28. Ibid., p. 82.

and, retroactively projecting our preference for continuity, to reject all anti-art, or rather, anti-taste movements from dadaism on. Only the "mainstream" would stake a legitimate claim on art, and many movements such as English vorticism, Russian productivism, German functionalism, and other movements embracing the machine aesthetics, industrial design, "total" architecture, photography and photomontage, or the forms of advertising and propaganda—movements which, though not directly rooted in the idea of the readymade, form a stream which, in the reception history of modern art, runs together with that issuing from the readymade—would be rejected as well. Such an alternative is intolerable, not only because either solution erases half of the facts from the record, but also because both take individual works of art hostage to an ideology and forsake the right and the duty to appraise them on their own merit. The double bind needs to be broken and the antinomy needs to be resolved. There is no other way of doing it—and no other way of accounting for the readymades' existence as art in continuity with both its past and its future—than to suppose that "this is art," the sentence through which the readymades were produced, expresses an aesthetic judgment, in the Kantian sense, and that the antinomy in question is none other than Kant's antinomy of taste, rephrased as the antinomy of art. This is what the title of this chapter—and of this book—concerns.

Critique of the Modern Aesthetic Judgment

In its eighteenth-century version, the antinomy of taste is at the core of the *Dialectic of Aesthetic Judgment,* itself the centerpiece of Kant's *Critique of Aesthetic Judgment,* which is the first part of the *Critique of Judgment.* Here is how Kant stated it:

> Thesis. The judgment of taste is not based upon concepts; for, if it were, it would be open to dispute (decision by means of proofs). Antithesis. The judgment of taste is based upon concepts; for otherwise, despite diversity of judgment, there could be no room even

> for contention in the matter (a claim to the necessary agreement of others with this judgment).[29]

Kant's definition of taste is that it is "the faculty of judging of the beautiful," and his main concern is with beauty in nature. (Although he has interesting things to say about art, they will not come under review here.) A judgment of taste is essentially sentimental, not cognitive:

> In order to distinguish whether anything is beautiful or not, we refer the representation, not . . . to the object for cognition, but . . . to the subject and its feeling of pleasure or pain. The judgment of taste is therefore not a judgment of cognition, and is consequently not logical but aesthetical, by which we understand that whose determining ground can be *no other than subjective.*[30]

Such a judgment naturally expresses itself (if it expresses itself out loud, which is of course not necessary) through a sentence such as "this is beautiful." Let's call it the classical aesthetic judgment. Other formulas, even the most contemporary and colloquial ones, such as "this is super," as well as the ones that are usual in regard to works of art, such as "this (painting) is good," may replace it without its ceasing to be a classical aesthetic judgment. With the readymade, however, the shift from the classical to the modern aesthetic judgment is brought into the open, as the substitution of the sentence "this is art" for the sentence "this is beautiful." To say of a snow shovel that it is beautiful (or ugly) doesn't turn it into art. That judgment remains a classical judgment of taste

29. Immanuel Kant, *Critique of Judgment,* trans. J. C. Meredith (Oxford: Clarendon Press, 1952), p. 206.

30. Immanuel Kant, *Critique of Judgment,* trans. J. H. Bernard (New York: Hafner, 1951), p. 37. I have sometimes used the Bernard and sometimes the Meredith translation. References will hereafter be indicated by the translator's name.

pertaining to the design of the snow shovel. The paradigmatic formula for the modern aesthetic judgment is the sentence by way of which the snowshovel has been baptized as a work of art.[31] Whether or not "this is art" still *means* "this is beautiful" or something similar is irrelevant. As I have tried to show in the previous chapters, a lot depends on whether one situates one's judgment within the accepted conventions of art, or whether those conventions are themselves at issue. The history of modernism and of avant-garde art tilts the balance toward the latter but settles the question of meaning only in those extreme but highly significant cases where disgust has prompted first the rejection then the acceptance of the work. Indeed, every masterpiece of modern art—from Courbet's *Stonebreakers,* Flaubert's *Madame Bovary,* and Baudelaire's *Fleurs du mal* to Manet's *Olympia,* Picasso's *Demoiselles d'Avignon,* Stravinsky's *Rites of Spring,* Joyce's *Ulysses,* and Duchamp's readymades—was first met with an outcry of indignation: "this is not art!" In all these cases, "this is not art" expresses a refusal to judge aesthetically; it means, "this doesn't even deserve a judgment of taste." Reasons invoked boil down to either disgust or ridicule, the two feelings that Kant deemed incompatible with the judgments regarding, respectively, the beautiful and the sublime. In the third *Critique,* Kant wrote: "One kind of ugliness alone is incapable of being represented conformably to nature without destroying all aesthetic delight, and consequently artistic beauty, namely, that which excites disgust."[32] And in the *Observations,* he had already noted: "Nothing is so much set against the beautiful as disgust, just as nothing sinks deeper beneath the sublime than the ridiculous."[33] Yet all the works just listed—and there are many more—have subsequently been judged as masterpieces of avant-garde art, and of art *tout court,* and it is safe to assume that, even for us now, they retain some of their ability to arouse an uncanny feeling of disgust or of ridicule

31. See chapter 1.

32. Meredith, pp. 173–174.

33. Immanuel Kant, *Observations on the Feeling of the Beautiful and Sublime,* trans. J. T. Goldthwait (Berkeley: University of California Press, 1965), p. 83.

that disturbs the enjoyment of beauty or of sublimity. In the face of the historical record concerning these crucial cases, we must part with Kant, and this is important in helping us to understand why the historical record strongly supports (though does not prove) the thesis that "this is art," as applied to a readymade—or to a Courbet, or to a Matisse, or to anything for that matter—is an aesthetic judgment, while not necessarily a judgment of taste. Although Kant wanted taste to rest on the feeling of pleasure or displeasure, he never excluded other feelings, except these two: in case a work arouses disgust or ridicule, "this is art" cannot *mean* "this is beautiful." In all other cases it may retain that meaning, but the important thing is that here too, "art," whatever it means, *substitutes* for "beauty."

The rereading of Kant, which will now be attempted, rests on only one hypothesis: that the sentence "this is art," though not necessarily any longer a judgment of taste, remains an aesthetic judgment, even though no particular meaning is attached to the word "aesthetic" until the rereading is completed. The logical thing is to replace the word "beautiful" by the word "art" wherever it occurs in the third *Critique,* starting with the antinomy itself, which then becomes:

> Thesis. The sentence "this is art" is not based upon concepts.
> Antithesis. The sentence "this is art" is based upon concepts.

Or, in a more condensed and more general phrasing:

> Thesis. Art is not a concept.
> Antithesis. Art is a concept.[34]

34. This second phrasing derives directly or indirectly from the first one: directly when the concept upon which the sentence "this is art" is based (or not based) is the concept of art itself, and indirectly when it is some other concept. In the latter case, art is instrumental with regard to its grounding concept and must therefore be a concept too.

The mutual excommunication of Greenberg's formalism and Kosuth's conceptualism exemplifies the antinomy clearly when couched in such terms. Although, as hopefully I have established, this antinomy summarizes the whole *ACT* versus *ART* dilemma that overdetermines the sixties, it is easier to unfold it in their respective texts. It is clear that formalism upholds the thesis while conceptualism upholds the antithesis. As Greenberg said in one of the Seminars in which he struggled with the "theoretical service" rendered by Duchamp and his conceptualist epigones:

> I don't think it is appreciated enough that aesthetic judgments, verdicts of taste, can't be proven in the way it can be that two plus two equals four, that water is composed of what is called oxygen and what is called hydrogen, that the earth is round, that a person named George Washington was our first president, and so on. In other words, that aesthetic judgments fall outside the scope of what is ordinarily considered to be objective evidence. Kant was the first one I know of to state (in his *Critique of Aesthetic Judgment*) that judgments of aesthetic value are not susceptible of proof or demonstration, and no one has been able to refute this, either in practice or in argument.[35]

For Kosuth, on the other hand, "One begins to realize that art's 'art condition' is a conceptual state."[36]

Now, both formalists and conceptualists must have felt that upholding only one side of the antinomy is not enough. Greenberg was, of course, aware that judgments of taste claim a universality of agreement that makes quality in art a seemingly objective fact. He was also aware that taste has a history intimately intertwined with that of the medium and its conventions. In a puzzling article

35. Greenberg, "Seminar II," p. 72.

36. Kosuth, "Art after Philosophy I and II," p. 83.

contemporary with the Seminars, "Can Taste Be Objective?" he suddenly broke with his hitherto often-asserted Kantianism and upheld a historical version of the antithesis:

> The objectivity of taste is probatively demonstrated in and through the presence of a consensus over time. . . . And there's no explaining this durability—the durability which creates a consensus—except by the fact that taste is ultimately objective. The best taste, that is; that taste which makes itself known by the durability of its verdicts; and in this durability lies the proof of its objectivity. (My reasoning here is no more circular than experience itself.)[37]

I have discussed this passage and its implications elsewhere.[38] Suffice it to say that there is some truth in Greenberg's claim that his argument is "no more circular than experience itself," and this is due to the fact that consensus over time can only be "verified" by the aesthetic judgment that approves of it, making this "verification" reflexive rather than circular, but also, suppressing its actual objectivity and leaving only the *claim* to objective consensus valid.[39] This would be the Kantian approach to the antinomy, but Greenberg does not work it out. On the contrary, he boldly states: "I realize that I take my life in my hands when I dare to say that I've seen something better than Kant did."[40] Alas, he hasn't, and in the end, his argument is circular: "It's the record, the history of taste that confirms its objectivity and it's this objectivity that in turn explains its history."[41] Whereas circularity is a problem for Greenberg's formalism, it is the solution for Kosuth's conceptualism:

---

37. Clement Greenberg, "Can Taste Be Objective?" *Artnews,* February 1973, p. 23.

38. See my "Les tremblés de la réflexion."

39. The concept of jurisprudence, with which I defined the "consensus over time" in chapter 1, accounts for this.

40. Greenberg, "Can Taste Be Objective?," p. 92.

41. Ibid., p. 23.

> A work of art is a tautology in that it is a presentation of the artist's intention, that is, he is saying that that particular work of art is art, which means, is a definition of art. Thus, that it is art is true a priori.[42]

> To repeat, what art has in common with logic and mathematics is that it is a tautology; i.e., the "art idea" (or "work") and art are the same and can be appreciated as art without going outside the context of art for verification.[43]

It is of course easy to dismiss a theory that stakes a claim to a tautological definition, since it is no theory at all but rather a *petitio principii.* Philosophically speaking, "Art after Philosophy" is in any case full of loopholes: neither its inverted Hegelianism nor its borrowed Wittgensteinianism resist close examination.[44] Suffice it to say that Kosuth's most blatant confusion is between the logical genre of discourse, which does not need a referent to assign truth value to a proposition, and the cognitive genre, which requires the designation of a referent for its verification. In short, conceptualism simply ignores the thesis in the modern version of the Kantian antinomy, by making the sentence "this is art" run in circles. Both formalism and conceptualism remain unsatisfactory.

How does Kant solve the antinomy of taste?

> In the thesis we mean that the judgment of taste is not based upon *determinate* concepts, and in the antithesis that the judgment of taste is based upon a concept, but an *indeterminate* one (viz. of the

42. Kosuth, "Art after Philosophy I and II," p. 83.

43. Ibid., p. 85.

44. See Richard Sclafani, "What Kind of Nonsense is This?" *Journal of Aesthetics and Art Criticism* 33 (1975): 455–458.

> supersensible substrate of phenomena). Between these two there is no contradiction.[45]

Before we ask ourselves what this indeterminate concept of "the supersensible substrate of phenomena" might be, let us recall how Kant arrives at the antinomy's solution:

> The judgment of taste must refer to some concept; otherwise it could make absolutely no claim to be necessarily valid to everyone. . . . Now the judgment of taste is applied to objects of sense, but not with a view of determining a *concept* of them for the understanding; for it is not a cognitive judgment. It is thus only a private judgment, in which a singular representation intuitively perceived is referred to the feeling of pleasure, and so far would be limited as regards its validity to the individual judging. The object is *for me* an object of satisfaction; by others it may be regarded quite differently—everyone has his own taste.[46]

In the passage above, Kant first states the antithesis and then the thesis. Then in the following paragraph, he goes back to the antithesis, and in the last sentence states the thesis once again:

> Nevertheless there is indoubtedly contained in the judgment of taste a wider reference of the representation of the object (as well as of the subject), whereon we base an extension of judgments of this kind as necessary for everyone. At the basis of this there must necessarily be a concept somewhere, though a concept which cannot be determined through intuition. But through a concept of this

45. Bernard, p. 186.

46. Ibid., pp. 184–185.

> sort we know nothing, and consequently it can *supply no proof* for the judgment of taste.[47]

Further along he presents his solution:

> But all contradiction disappears if I say: the judgment of taste is based on a concept . . . ; from which, however, nothing can be known and proved in respect of the object, because it is in itself undeterminable and useless for knowledge. Yet at the same time and on that very account the judgment has validity for everyone . . . , because its determining ground lies perhaps in the concept of that which may be regarded as the supersensible substrate of humanity.[48]

The solution to the antinomy lies in the indeterminate concept of the *supersensible,* referred to in the above two phrasings of the solution as "the supersensible substrate of phenomena" on the side of the judged objects, and as "the supersensible substrate of humanity" on the side of the judging subjects. It is well known to readers of the first and the second *Critiques* that the supersensible is not a concept of understanding but an Idea of reason. It is beyond the sensible, because nothing can be shown or otherwise presented and communicated through sensible, empirical experience that could be subsumed under its idea. And it is not provable or demonstrable as are mathematical equations, which are also beyond intuitive perception, but which rely on the categories and the schematism of pure understanding. The supersensible is a realm, or rather a field, "an unbounded but also inaccessible field" beyond the sensible, whose reality cannot be asserted and should certainly not be believed in, but whose necessity ought to be postulated and which "we must indeed occupy with

47. Ibid., p. 185.

48. Ibid.

ideas."[49] It is therefore a transcendental Idea, which means that it is known and recognized to be merely an idea, but a necessary one.[50] It is a requirement of reason, without which it is impossible to think that nature is intelligible (first *Critique*) or that ethical freedom exists (second *Critique*), or that the judgment of taste is entitled to claim universal validity, although it is the outcome of a merely subjective, personal, feeling. What the supersensible thus postulates, from the vantage point of the third *Critique,* is a subjective principle which, although subjective, is not merely personal but shared by all human beings.

This "subjective principle, which determines what pleases or displeases only by feeling and not by concepts, but yet with universal validity"[51] is what Kant called *sensus communis.* This common sense, or better, common sentiment, is not a certainty but ought to be presupposed, that is, posited *as if* we were certain that it is a common substrate of humanity. Whether it is constitutive or simply regulative cannot be determined, *so that* the claim to universal aesthetic judgments merely testifies to the necessary presupposition of a *sensus communis.* This, in turn, is nothing but the faculty of judging itself:

> This indeterminate norm of a common sense is actually presupposed by us, as is shown by our claim to lay down judgments of taste. Whether there is in fact such a common sense, as a constitutive principle of the possibility of experience, or whether a higher principle of reason makes it only into a regulative principle for producing in us a common sense for higher purposes; whether, therefore, taste is an original and natural faculty or only the idea of an artificial one yet to be acquired, so that a judgment of taste with its assumption of a universal assent in fact is only a requirement of

---

49. Ibid., p. 11.

50. I shall from now on capitalize the word "Idea" (including in the quotations from Kant) each time I mean it as a transcendental Idea in the sense just defined.

51. Bernard, p. 75.

> reason for producing such harmony of sentiment; whether the ought, i.e. the objective necessity of the confluence of the feeling of any one man with that of every other, only signifies the possibility of arriving at this accord, and the judgment of taste only affords an example of the application of this principle—these questions we have neither the wish nor the power to investigate as yet.[52]

The extraordinary ascending movement of thought in this passage does not lead us into some Platonic heaven whence we could then descend to earth and dogmatically affirm the existence of a universal faculty of taste in conformity with its Idea. On the contrary, this movement is sceptical throughout, and when it finally comes down to earth and Kant takes up the task of investigating the previously postponed questions, his *deduction* of the judgments of taste is not of the same kind as, say, the transcendental deduction of the categories in the first *Critique;* it is itself a reflexive and regulative usage of the faculty of judgment, which is why Kant, apparently to his own surprise, finds it easy:

> This deduction is thus easy, because it has no need to justify the objective reality of any concept, for beauty is not a concept of the object and the judgment of taste is not cognitive. It only maintains that we are justified in presupposing universally in every man those subjective conditions of the judgment which we find in ourselves.[53]

It is thus for Kant one and the same thing to call these subjective conditions the supersensible substrate of humanity, a *sensus communis,* or more simply the faculty of taste (which shows, by the way, that even if we were not going to replace "taste" by "art," taste in the Kantian sense is of a much broader scope than mere preferences and cultural habits). Taste, not this or that taste, but the faculty of

52. Ibid., p. 77.

53. Ibid., p. 133.

taste, which ought to be supposed or postulated as the endowment of every human being, is what justifies not the universality itself (my taste being no more universal than yours), but the claim to universality of every singular aesthetic judgment. And the solution to the antinomy may be restated:

> The subjective principle—that is to say, the indeterminate Idea of the supersensible within us—can only be indicated as the unique key to the riddle of this faculty, itself concealed from us in its sources; and there is no means of making it any more intelligible. The antinomy here exhibited and resolved rests upon the proper concept of taste as a merely reflective aesthetic judgment, and the two seemingly conflicting principles are reconciled on the ground that they *may both be true,* and this is sufficient.[54]

The faculty of taste is the faculty of judging the beautiful, whether in nature or in art. This faculty is a *sensus communis,* that is, a feeling necessarily assumed to be common to all men and women. Now, what if, as suggested, we read "art" wherever Kant wrote "the beautiful," and simply draw the consequences of this substitution, refraining from all interpretation? The presumed *sensus communis* then becomes a *faculty of judging art by dint of feeling* common to all men and women. The readymade, which has led to this reading, also erases every difference between making art and judging it, so that we must suppose that, by the same token, this faculty also becomes a *faculty of making art by dint of feeling.* The artist chooses an object and calls it art, or, what amounts to the same, places it in such a context that the object itself demands to be called art (which means that, if only privately and solipsistically, the artist has already called it art). The spectator simply repeats the artist's judgment. Anyone can do it; the required skill, the know-how, is nil; it is accessible to the layman. Kant, of course, could not foresee such a perfect coincidence of art with the aesthetic.

54. Meredith, pp. 208–209.

In his time, art-making evidently involved the apprenticeship and mastery of a skill and had to obey all sorts of rules and conventions, within which room was left for judgments about beauty. But Kant was also aware that if the artist's talent merely consisted in mastering skill and applying rules, the judgment of beauty (his or her's as well as the spectator's) would not be free (*pulchritudo vaga*) but dependent (*pulchritudo adhaerens*) on those very rules and conventions, that is, on a concept determining what an artwork should be. In order to allow for the free judgment of taste in the making of art, talent had to involve something else, something unconscious even in the artist, a gift of nature rather than an acquisition of culture, through which the artist could transcend or bypass the rules and conventions of his or her trade. This "innate mental disposition (*ingenium*) through which nature gives the rule to art" was *genius*.[55]

> For estimating beautiful objects, as such, what is required is *taste;* but for fine art, i.e., the production of such objects, one needs *genius*.[56]

Since, with the readymade, estimating and producing art are condensed into one and the same act, we are led to suppose that "taste" and "genius" also merge into one and the same faculty. (I put these words in quotation marks so as to insist, again, that we are dealing here with the formal consequences of a mere substitution of words, not with their content.) And since Kant defines genius as "the faculty of *aesthetic Ideas*,"[57] we are led to project this definition onto that of taste, that is, the faculty of "merely reflective aesthetic judgments." But what is an "aesthetic Idea"?

> Ideas, in the most comprehensive sense of the word, are representations referred to an object according to a certain principle

55. Bernard, p. 150.

56. Meredith, p. 172.

57. Ibid., p. 212.

> (subjective or objective), in so far as they can still never become a cognition of it. They are either referred to an intuition, in accordance with a merely subjective principle of the harmony of the cognitive faculties (imagination and understanding), and are then called *aesthetic;* or else they are referred to a concept according to an objective principle and yet are incapable of ever furnishing a cognition of the object, and are called *rational Ideas*. . . . An *aesthetic Idea* cannot become a cognition, because it is an intuition (of the imagination) for which an adequate concept can never be found. A *rational Idea* can never become a cognition, because it involves a concept (of the supersensible), for which a commensurate intuition can never be given. Now the aesthetic Idea might, I think, be called an *inexponible* representation of the imagination, the rational Idea, on the other hand, an *indemonstrable* concept of reason.[58]

Thus, to reread Kant after Duchamp, replacing the judgment "this is beautiful" by the judgment "this is art," is to consider that the word "art" conflates genius and taste and refers both to an "inexponible" aesthetic Idea and to an "indemonstrable" rational Idea. (In the Kantian vocabulary, *exponible* means "what can be established theoretically"; *demonstrable* means—in this context—"what can be shown to the senses."[59] And "intuition" means perception, a presentation precisely offered to the senses in the perceptual world.) This rereading, by the way, sheds light on the aporias of formalism and conceptualism. When Greenberg acknowledges the coincidence of the aesthetic with the artistic experience as "the great theoretical service of the kind of recent art that

58. Ibid., pp. 209–210.

59. "To reduce a representation to concepts is the same thing as to *expound* it [*exponieren*]" (Bernard, p. 189). "*To demonstrate* [*demonstrieren,* as opposed to *beweisen*] (*ostendere, exhibere*), is equivalent to presenting a concept in intuition. . . . If the intuition . . . is empirical, then the object is displayed by means of which objective reality is assured to the concept" (Bernard, p. 188).

strives to be advanced," he believes the aesthetic Idea whose name is art to be "exponible," if only as a *conceptual* uncertainty in distinguishing art from non-art. And when Kosuth identifies the work of art with its "art idea" and this, in turn, with art in general, he believes the rational Idea whose name is art to be "demonstrable," if only as an impossibility of escaping the *formal* presentation of the work. Both succumb to the same transcendental illusion, which is to believe, as Kant would say, in the possibility of *intellectual intuition*. As for Beuys, he is the direct heir to a tradition which, beginning with Fichte perhaps, with Hölderlin and the young Schelling certainly, broke with Kant to claim the reality of the intellectual intuition. He may be seen as the belated executor of *The Oldest Systematic Program of German Idealism,* which converted the Kantian merely regulative Idea into the speculative Idea, founded both the world (nature) and human work on the free self-conscious subject's *creation from nothing,* and called for a new rational mythology to educate humanity.[60] Hence Beuys's systematic recourse to human creativity; hence his mythopoetic conception of sculpture as *Soziale Plastik;* hence his assertion: "form = supersensible."[61]

Kant's supersensible, of course, never assumes a plastic form. As a postulate of pure understanding, it is beyond the sensible and stays there. As a postulate of pure practical reason, it requires freedom transcendentally, but it does not ground ethics, let alone the world, in the free self-conscious subject, as it did

60. *The Oldest Systematic Program of German Idealism* is a short incomplete manuscript in Hegel's handwriting found in 1917 in Hegel's papers by Rosenzweig, who gave it this title. The date of Hegel's transcript is probably 1796, but the author of the *Program* is uncertain: possibly Hegel himself, most probably Schelling, possibly Hölderlin too. For a very good analysis of *The Oldest Systematic Program of German Idealism* as the philosophical crossroad wherein Kant's legacy opens up the possibility of romanticism, on the one hand, and of speculative idealism, on the other, see Philippe Lacoue-Labarthe and Jean-Luc Nancy, *L'absolu littéraire* (Paris: Editions du Seuil, 1978), pp. 39–54. For a convincing interpretation of Beuys's sources in this text, see Reithmann, *Joseph Beuys,* pp. 235 ff.

61. Joseph Beuys, *Unveröffentlichtes Manuskript,* partly reproduced in Heiner Stachelhaus, *Joseph Beuys* (Düsseldorf, 1987), pp. 80–81. See also Reithmann, *Joseph Beuys,* p. 278.

for the author of the *Oldest Systematic Program*. Which is why, as we shall see, a "Kantian-after-Duchamp" reading of Beuys's notion of creativity inevitably betrays Beuys. Yet it offers another, radically nonutopian interpretation, of his "Everyone an artist." Concretely, Kant's *sensus communis* may be restated after Duchamp as follows: every woman, every man, cultivated or not, whatever her or his culture, language, race, social class, has aesthetic Ideas which are or can be, by the same token, artistic Ideas. This cannot be proven but has to be supposed. Neither the "good taste" of the ruling class nor the "bad taste" of the oppressed classes nor, for that matter, the numerous insurrections aimed at overthrowing this hierarchy, prove that there exists a faculty of aesthetic/artistic Ideas shared by humankind as a whole. Neither do they prove the opposite. That all women and men have "taste" and even "genius" is merely a requirement of reason. It can be empirically denied on elitist or on populist grounds, denounced or deconstructed as an ideology reflecting particular class interests, or idealized and fostered as a goal to be attained in a future liberated or emancipated state of humankind. But there is no empirical, sociological, or historical settling of the question of whether there exists such a thing as a universal faculty of judging/making art by dint of feeling and not of concepts.

There is, however, a historical correlate to the mere thought of such a thing, as it was prompted by the rereading of Kant after Duchamp: this woman and this man, who ought to be granted the faculty of aesthetic/artistic Ideas, are the modern woman and the modern man. They belong to the historical era that starts with the Enlightenment (or shorly before) and that ends (but is it ended?) with the readymade or shortly after, with its repeated reception by the postwar neo-avant-gardes. The ground for Kant's third *Critique* had been prepared by the writings of Roger de Piles and the Abbé Dubos, who had claimed for the mere *amateur* the right and the ability to judge art aesthetically, that is, by dint of feeling. This right had been implemented, in France at least, from the end of the seventeenth century, by the Salons where, though juried as art, the practice of living painters and sculptors was annually opened to public appraisal and subjected to the layman's judgment of taste. Toward the middle of the nineteenth century, with the quarrel of Courbet's Realism and then with the Salon des Refusés, the jury's refusal to judge aesthetically, and thus to call art, what it found disgusting or ridiculous, was countered by the institutional decision to appeal to the layman's verdict. There had been sharp controversy among the jury members as to the fate of the nine paintings Courbet had sent in for the 1851 Salon. All but one, the *Burial at Ornans,* were taken upstairs and refused in the *Salon Carré*. As to the Salon des Refusés (1863), despite its anti-institutional character, it was placed under the auspices of *Sa Majesté l'Empereur.* There is no doubt that demagogy, not cultural egalitarianism and not aesthetic insight, is what motivated Napoleon III. But the result is the same: the padlock of the jury was broken, and for the first time in history, the crowd was invited to decide not merely whether the refused paintings were beautiful, but whether they were art. From this moment on, it was art that was at stake rather than beauty within art. The last link in that chain, which in the previous chapter I called the history of institutionalized aesthetic judgment, was Duchamp's "Richard Mutt Case": it symbolically granted the layman the right to produce art aesthetically, that is, by dint of a feeling whose source—to be taken with a grain of salt, for sure—was not merely "taste" but also "genius," in the provocative guise of a disgustingly plebeian taste and a ridiculously sick genius.

Of course, this conflation of taste with genius did not happen overnight and was never theorized in the way suggested here, as the requirement of an archaeological method that seeks to make sense of Kantian aesthetics, in the light of subsequent art history. It was in fact theorized by at least one modern aesthetician, namely by Croce, as a corollary of his "theorem" that to judge a work of art aesthetically is "to reproduce it in oneself," itself a consequence of his conviction that intuition and expression are one and the same thing:

> It is clear from the preceding theorem that the activity of judgment which criticizes and recognizes the beautiful is identical with what produces it. The only difference lies in the diversity of circumstances, since in the one case it is a question of aesthetic production, in the other of reproduction. The activity which judges is called

> *taste;* the productive activity is called *genius:* genius and taste are therefore substantially identical.[62]

I don't find it too surprising that it should be Croce, who was perhaps the philosopher of his generation the most thoroughly informed in the history of aesthetics, who arrived at this solution. I don't see his aesthetic theory applying to Duchamp's readymades, however. It is mostly interesting as an indicator of how the conflation of taste and genius was a latent ingredient of the romantic culture and has indeed accompanied the shift from romanticism to modernism. What is striking to the retrospective eye of the "archaeologist" is how almost every road leads to Freud, as if psychoanalysis had established nothing but the theory of the romantic self, the "components" of which were, from the very outset, the unconscious and the *Witz,* both variations on the theme of genius as something with which, ultimately, everyone is endowed. From the moment Schelling had systematized Kant's notion of genius as a gift of nature into the notion of an unconscious creative power unknown to the artist, genius began to be seen as the dark, unconscious side of human nature, verging on insanity. Time and again, in Schopenhauer, in Hartmann, in Nietzsche, in Dostoyevsky, in the poetry of the symbolists and the Décadents, the association was made between madness and genius, until it became, with Lombroso and Max Nordau, the most hackneyed pseudoscientific cliché of late-nineteenth-century thought. That the romantic notion of genius, which had started as natural innocence in the poetry of Hölderlin, could by the end of the century have been turned into natural degeneration in the criminology of Lombroso, is an indication that a claim of universality was built into the notion from the start. Certainly, genius had to be the exception for the romantics—Schelling said that it was a power that isolated the man of genius from other men—but an exception resulting from nature's random and uneven distribution of gifts rather than one

62. Benedetto Croce, *Aesthetic as Science of Expression and General Linguistic* (Boston: Nonpareil Books, 1978), p. 120.

rooted in social order. As the century went on and the various artistic/political utopias already implied, for example, in Schiller's *Letters on the Aesthetic Education of Man* merged with the climate of bohemianism of later romanticism, both madness and genius began to be conceived as forms of alienation that could be brandished as signs of the artist's exclusion from bourgeois society. Herein lies one of the romantic roots of anti-art: this alienation stood and accounted for a paradoxical *sensus communis,* which ran against the bourgeois common sense and was rather a taste for the marginal, the bohemian, the *Lumpen,* the socially deviant. Combined with this taste, the irrational power of the unconscious was to be the liberating potential of everyone except the "bourgeois," whose revenge, not surprisingly, came in the form of criminology. It is unfair to Freud to lump him together with Lombroso, but the fact remains that most heuristic ideas of psychoanalysis stem from a *Zeitgeist* conviction that the secret of the most exceptional creative talent had to be sought in neurosis, the most common fate of common man. And the fact that, for Freud, talent and neurosis alike betray themselves in slips of the tongue, puns and spoonerisms—in other words, in *Witze*—is also an indirect heritage of romanticism, more precisely, of the most philosophical branch of early romanticism, that of Iena and the *Athenaeum.*[63] It took a century or so for the *Witz,* defined by Friedrich Schlegel as "fragmentary geniality," to become a matter of common sense (or nonsense) pried open by the *Psychopathology of Everyday Life.* But then the times were ripe for a Duchamp, the times were ripe for the layman's wit to be called art, and the times were ripe for Duchamp's Freudian (even Lacanian) witty and ironic redefinition of the romantic self: "The personal 'art coefficient' is like an arithmetical relation between the unexpressed but intended and the unintentionally expressed."[64]

Such is the "personal art coefficient" that individualizes the creative act according to Duchamp. It is presented as if it were the measurable ratio between

63. See Lacoue-Labarthe and Nancy, *L'absolu littéraire.*

64. Marcel Duchamp, "The Creative Act," in *SS,* p. 139.

repressed or failed intentions, idiosyncrasies and preferences on the one hand, and the return of the repressed, Freudian slips and failed acts on the other—in other words, the ratio between (disgusted) "taste" and (ridiculous) "genius." If the ratio itself is measurable, the two quantities involved must be measurable too, like samples of two faculties present in anyone. The "personal art coefficient" measures the individual creative act, but *creativity* is the universal faculty of making art that is thereby presupposed. Now, creativity is precisely the name, the modern name, that has been given to the conflation of taste and genius and their various "arithmetical" relations. That it is quantifiable and that it can thus be increased through cultural progress is the fundamental belief of every modernist and avant-garde utopia. But for Duchamp it was only an analogy, an "as if–belief": "the personal art coefficient is *like* . . ." However, this analogy is a necessary one, not because it is a fact that all men and women on earth have taste and genius, if only that little, and not because it is the noble purpose of culture to allow anyone, if only potentially, to become an artist; rather, the analogy is necessary because everyone is assumed to be an artist already. This assumption is, after all, nothing but a requirement of the sentence with which the readymades have been called art. Unless the antinomy between formalism and conceptualism, between *ACT* and *ART,* between modernism and avant-gardism, between the mainstream and the "tradition of the new," or between the Picasso- and the Dada-lineage in modern art, is to remain forever unsolved and the ensuing historical double bind never allowed to loosen its grip on today's artworld, the sentence "this is art," by which a readymade is both produced as a work of art and judged to be one, ought to be read as an aesthetic reflexive judgment with a claim to universality in the strictest Kantian sense.

Modern or Postmodern?

The antinomy of the modern aesthetic judgment is thus resolved. Its solution can be phrased as follows:

> Thesis. The sentence "this is art" is not based on the concept of art; it is based on the aesthetic/artistic feeling.
> Antithesis. The sentence "this is art" assumes the concept of art; it assumes the aesthetic/artistic Idea.

In the thesis, the word "concept" refers to a determined one that should be asserted theoretically, and the word "feeling" refers to all feelings entering the love of art, including disgust and ridicule. In the antithesis, the word "concept" refers not to a determined concept of understanding but rather to an undetermined Idea of reason. It cannot be theoretically proven since it is "inexponible," and it cannot be empirically shown since it is "indemonstrable." But it can be exemplified analogically at the hand of any object designated by the word "this" in the sentence "this is art." For "this," you may substitute your favorite artwork and endorse any doctrine, any Idea of art that you fancy. If your doctrine is rigid and you think that you possess a concept of art, then your idea of art is determinate but is bound to be countered by somebody else's. If your doctrine is one of taste, then your idea of art is indeterminate and appeals to singular examples, but it can still be countered both by those people who do not share your taste and by those who think that art is not a matter of taste. As for myself, there are many examples of artworks that I might want to substitute for "this," but Duchamp's urinal is the one I find most exemplary. By calling it art, I endorse a certain Idea of modern or avant-garde art that is not only indeterminate but stands for its own indeterminacy.

Thesis and antithesis are compatible, in conformity with Kant and with Duchamp, and in congruence with the modern cultural space framed by the names of Kant and Duchamp. But, if you remember, there was a more condensed and more general phrasing to the antinomy. It also has a solution, but one that shows that it is no longer perfectly congruent with modernity:

> Thesis. Art is not a concept; it is a proper name.
> Antithesis. Art is a concept; it is the Idea of art as proper name.

I have explained this solution in the first chapter. Now I want to underline the slight shift that the solved antinomy receives from this second phrasing and its date. Whereas it was Duchamp's readymade that led me to the replacement of the word "beautiful" in the third *Critique* by the word "art," it was the opposition of formalism and conceptualism, or of *ACT* and *ART,* in the late sixties–early seventies, that led to the reading of this opposition as a new version of Kant's antinomy of taste. It has long been evident to me that there were two, and only two, major bones of contention between Greenberg and his conceptualist (and minimalist) opponents, Kosuth in particular. One was Duchamp's place, or rather, rank, in art history; the other was Kantian aesthetics. Greenberg has never disavowed his Kantianism,[65] but he never understood Kant either. He was too much of an empiricist to see that art opens up a transcendental field which "we must indeed occupy with Ideas." He was an extremely fine phenomenologist, but for that very reason, his aesthetics is *empiriocriticist* and not Kantian at all. As far as I know, most critics of Greenberg, from the conceptualists on, have taken his reading of Kant for granted and have rejected the Kantian aesthetics along with its Greenbergian misreading. This is the first element in a huge misunderstanding. The other is that Greenberg began to lose his prestige as an art critic exactly when Duchamp's star began to rise with the young generation of artists. Symptomatic of this is the quantity of articles, from the mid-sixties on, where he waged war against Duchamp, blaming him for the disastrous slackening in standards of taste that he deemed the result of pop art, minimalism, and conceptualism.[66] But this only shows that Greenberg shared the same reception conditions for Duchamp's work as the artists he opposed,

65. Not even in "Can Taste Be Objective?" In fact, Greenberg thought that he could make an empirical case for Kant's *sensus communis* as the founding ground for the objectivity of taste.

66. "Seminar One" and "Seminar Six" contain an *ad hominem* attack on Duchamp, and all the other Seminars (there are eight of them) make an indirect one. Most typical of Greenberg's trial against Duchamp are the already quoted "Counter-Avant-Garde" and his John Power lecture in Sydney in 1968 entitled "Avant-Garde Attitudes."

and that he took their reading of the readymade as much for granted as they did his reading of Kant. Greenberg's personal taste notwithstanding, his unwillingness to judge beyond taste was only matched by his opponents' unwillingness to see that the judgment which has brought "art-status" to the readymade is an aesthetic judgment, albeit not one of taste. In retrospect, the pop interpretation of the readymade in terms of appropriation, its minimalist interpretation as an art of the real or the literal, and its conceptualist interpretation as concept and institutional status appear as much fraught with naïveté as Greenberg's rejection of the works legitimated by those interpretations appears fraught with bad faith. Perhaps the reception conditions of the readymade were such that they did not allow another reading. But this was thirty years ago, and the double bind that results from the aporias of the sixties has not yet released its grip on the artworld, which is why the date of the antinomy's resolution is important. To interpret Kant after Duchamp is not exactly the same thing as to reinterpret Duchamp after Kant. There are thus, as we have seen, two phrasings to the antinomy's solution; the first is modern, the second, postmodern.

Here is what the modern phrasing entails. Considered after Duchamp, the Kantian Idea of the supersensible, or his *sensus communis,* states that it is a requirement of reason that anyone be endowed, *de jure* if not *de facto,* with the faculty of making art. Not only taste but also genius, or better, to use the modern term that conflated them, *creativity,* ought to be assumed as an ability shared by humanity—itself an Idea of reason, by the way—so that the claim to conceptual objectivity laid down by the judgment "this is art," which is however merely aesthetic and subjective, be grounded and justified; so that the modernist quest for an ontological definition of art, its striving for theory, its self-referential reduction to essential conventions, be meaningful; so that neither the enthusiasm with which so many modern artists prophesied the advent of a universal language, nor their pedagogical efforts in that direction be in vain; so that the propensity of so many art and anti-art movements alike to link their fate with that of a revolution, material, spiritual, or cultural, retain its emancipatory value; in short, so that the Idea of the avant-garde be kept—or guarded, I should say—and not drained from the works of the avant-gardes, now that they have become "historical." Whether creativity is, as Kant said of taste, "an original and natural faculty or only the Idea of an artificial one yet to be acquired," it is an ethical obligation to suppose that it is everyone's endowment.

Here is now what the postmodern phrasing entails. Considered after Kant (himself considered after Duchamp), the Duchampian Idea of art as a proper name, or his *pictorial nominalism,* states that it is a requirement of reason, today, that we should have supposed, yesterday, that there exists a faculty called creativity shared by humanity as a whole. Otherwise, the essentialist and universalist utopias of modernity would have been nothing but *Schwärmereien;* otherwise, the destructive impulses and the revolutionary hopes of the avant-gardes—some of which have bred unforeseen monsters—would have been dangerous vanity and irresponsible optimism; otherwise, the name of art, which was at stake in modern practice, would have meant nothing but a social status cynically acquired. Whether creativity exists, as inscribed in the genetic code of the human species, for example, or whether it is an illusion, merely useful as a guide for cultural pedagogy or policy, it is an intellectual obligation to suppose that it was a fruitful regulative Idea for modernity.

Is it still fruitful? Do we have to choose between the modern and the postmodern phrasings of the antinomy's resolution, between the Habermasian hope that modernity is an unfinished project and the disenchanted detachment of the historian who looks back and pretends to understand what went astray? That choice is not a matter of taste; it is a matter of conviction. However, conviction is tantamount to faith, and the belief system that sustained modernity has been shattered. Lack of conviction, on the other hand, is tantamount to cynicism or nihilism, and the postmodern eclecticism too closely resembles the melancholic detachment of Nero, watching Rome burn, to be trusted. Moral paralysis seems to be unavoidable. Well, perhaps that choice is a false one. The modern obligation, as drawn from Kant's encounter with Duchamp, is ethical; the postmodern is intellectual. They are thus heterogeneous, and it is the great lesson of Kantian *criticism* that we should not confuse the ethical with the intellectual, practical reason with theoretical understanding, the realm of the second *Critique* with that of the first. But was it not the achievement of the third *Critique* to throw a bridge over the gap between the first two? And is it not the function of judgment, of the merely reflexive aesthetic judgment, to symbolically testify to the necessity of that bridge? It is part of the postmodern heritage of modernity that this judgment should be anyone's, so that my judgment is no better than yours. What to do with our modern past cannot and should not be decided by collective agreement. The sentence "this is art" is uttered individually and applies to individual works. Depending on one's convictions, the modern heritage will include the Dada- or the Picasso-tradition, or an eclectic sampling of both, or a personal collection of works selected not on the basis of a stylistic label or an ideological affiliation, but judged to be convincing in their own right. Conviction is not a ground for judging but a reflexive outcome of judgment itself. It used to be that "taste," then "art," stood for that kind of conviction. What its name will be in the future, I do not know. And I cannot list here all the works of modernity that I personally find convincing. But certainly Duchamp's urinal is among them. Its exemplary value is more than aesthetic; it is symbolically ethical, as it should be. It is also theoretical, which brings me to state my last conviction, one that I cannot prove but that is as close to Kant as it is to contemporary science. Whether creativity exists and will be fruitful to postmodern culture, or whether it is merely a regulative Idea that once was fruitful to modern culture, I cannot say, but I am convinced that if it exists, it is a faculty both innate and acquired, or rather, already encoded in our genes and still to be acquired through history, because it is inseparable from the fact that humans are "programmed" to be born prematurely, inseparable from the incompleteness of their central nervous system, and from the ensuing fragile selective advantage which, for better and for worse, forces all men and women to link their personal growth to the cultural progress of the species. From this angle, the choice between the modern and the postmodern is a false one. Both are, and will always be, premature.

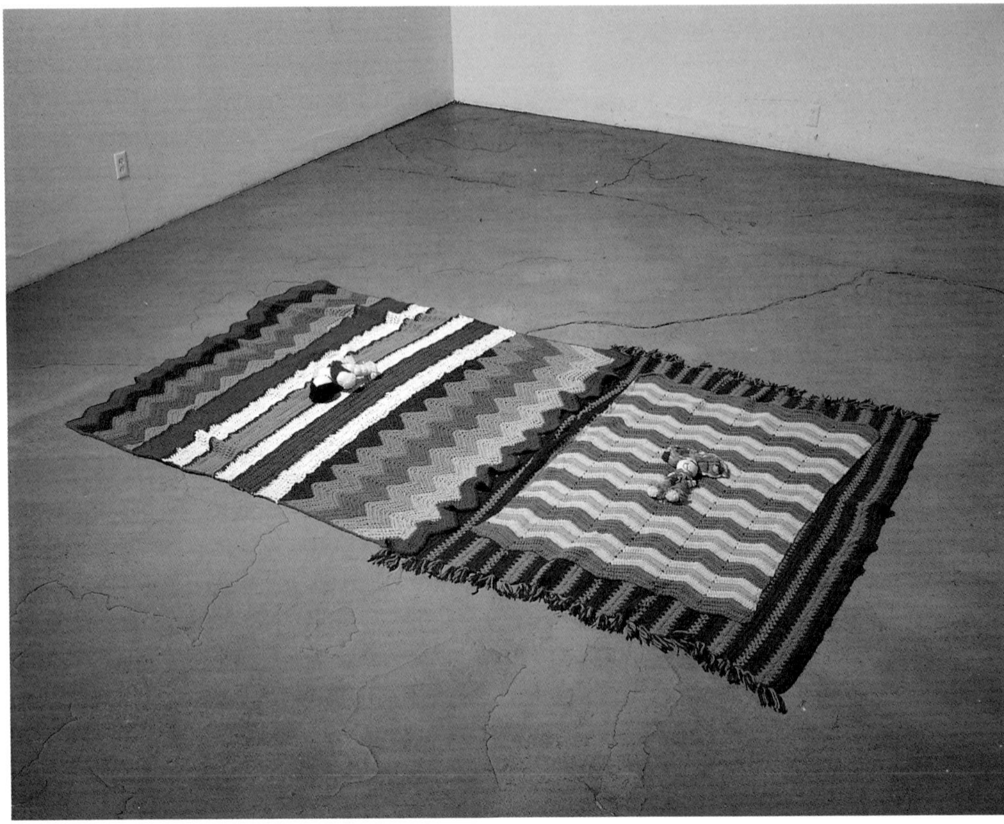

Mike Kelley, *Untitled,* 1990, afghans and stuffed animals, 163 × 257 cm. Courtesy Galerie Ghislaine Hussenot, Paris.

6

Do Whatever

To be Modern Art a work need not to be either modern nor art; it need not even be a work. A three-thousand year-old mask from the South Pacific qualifies as Modern and a piece of wood found on a beach becomes Art.

—*Harold Rosenberg*

Dada, the Pivot

There is more than just one man-on-the-street who thinks that contemporary art is the reign of the anything-whatever.[1] This situation is far from new. If, with the *Stone Breakers,* Courbet brought just anyone onto the stage, Manet's *Bunch of Asparagus* made room for anything whatever to be represented in painting. After all, the history that goes from the *Stone Breakers* to the readymade,

1. This chapter was written in French ("Fais n'importe quoi"), and very much prompted by the extreme commonness in art parlance of the exclamation "N'importe quoi!" It is always used disparagingly, though not necessarily in anger, to refer to something that claims to be art but that, in the eye of the beholder, lacks that minimum of form, content, beauty, or

from Courbet to Duchamp, from the represented anything-whatever to the anything-whatever plain and simple, is brief and well known. It is inseparable from the devaluation of the precious, the finished, the noble, of all the values that gave art a precise function in the system of aristocratic power, and from the correlative rise of new egalitarian values—or anti-values—themselves in bourgeois consciousness often bearing the mark of the vulgar, of the unfinished, of the ignoble. All this, which is well known, means that the whatever still carries the stamp of its plebeian origins, pointing, depending on one's viewpoint, to the specter or to the utopia of an art made by the passer-by.

This being said, the whatever poses a philosophical question that is first of all the enigma or the paradox of there having been a history of it, in spite of its seemingly implying a radical or final ahistoricity. "This is anything whatever!" seems to say: this is the most definitive chaos; nothing uglier, more disorganized, more vulgar could possibly be made; it's the end of painting; it's the end of art. Such things have been said all too often. The whatever was thus repeated again and again, and its history is inhabited by a philosophical paradox that I

---

structure that might sustain its claim. Translating "N'importe quoi!" by "Gibberish!" or "Rubbish!" might convey the intent of the exclamation more adequately than the literal translation that has been retained here, but would miss the crucial connotation of a generalization beyond all boundaries conveyed by the French, and especially, by the conversion of the exclamation "N'importe quoi!" into a noun, "le n'importe quoi." Since the whole argument of this chapter hinges around this generalization (to which the reader who went through the second part of this book, "The Specific and the Generic," should be alerted), it has been necessary to keep to the most literal translation: hence "whatever" and "the anything-whatever." As to "the man-on-the-street" encountered in the first sentence, the French read: "le profane." It is also an important word, for its meaning can slip from the religious connotation of profanation attached to it to its (still remotely religious but more general and contextualized, in contrast to "professional") meaning as "the layman," to a more specifically artistic usage of the word when it is translated as "the uninitiated." All three translations will be alternated here, but at the very end of the chapter, we will have to resort to "the profane," as a specific play on words will be needed there that allows no translation.

shall ask you to keep in mind while, first things first, I will try to describe its unfolding over time.

I have just framed the whatever's opening phase with two artists' names, Courbet and Duchamp, and with one crucial reservation, I could do this with the names of two schools: realism and dadaism. In this first phase, the whatever belonged to the reception history of art more than to its production history. It wasn't the artists who made or claimed to be making just anything whatever, nor even the public in general that accused them of doing so; it was the public's professional spokesmen, the art critics, along with members of the juries, and the academic authorities, in short, the art establishment mobilized for the defense of tradition. Before the dadaists no artist had the feeling of abandoning in one stroke all the rules of his or her art, and no artist claimed the right to make anything whatever. As for the public at large—this crowd whose historical rising Baudelaire so clearly foresaw—recently encouraged to mix into the affairs of art, it stampeded the Salon, particularly the Salon des Refusés, and its interest clearly showed that the feeling of the whatever was not what impelled it. In the *Stone Breakers* or the *Bunch of Asparagus* the people could recognize themselves to a certain extent and could perceive issues in which they had an interest. That the farmers from Flagey or the workers from Ornans could become subjects of painting, that a simple bunch of asparagus could display its triviality without any of the artifices that, even for Chardin, still gave it class and distinction, is certainly something that didn't dissolve meaning into the whatever for everyone. It was the art establishment that got upset by realism and its excesses of ugliness and vulgarity, by the flatness of Manet's images, by the absence of drawing in Cézanne's, by the chaos of cubism. And it was the critics and the juries who did their all to imbue the public with the fear of the whatever and to foment a scandal nourished by their indignation alone. Now, the critics' and juries' outrage was argued on professional grounds all leading back to a single call to order: respect for the rules of the trade. It was on the strength of their expertise and in their capacity as guardians of the law—aesthetic as well as technical—that the traditionalists fired vollies of anathemas at the avant-garde painters in order to exclude them from artistic legitimacy. The formula "this is not art!" which returns with ritualistic insistance in the judgment passed by experts throughout this first phase of modern art, translates the feeling of the whatever and soon crosses it with a prohibition. It means, "this can't be art," or again, "it's forbidden to make whatever."

With dadaism, this formula is taken over by the avant-garde artists and turned against itself out of provocation. These artists counter the prohibition of the whatever with its claimed authorization. "It is permitted to make whatever," expresses the gist of the slogan of the Dada liberation, with the consequence that their aesthetic judgment assumes a negative formulation: "this is non-art." Thus the Dada artist adopts the posture of the jury in the nineteenth-century painting salons and derisively inverts it. He pretends to be a technician of the absence of technique, a warrantor of the destruction of the trade, a traditionalist of the anti-tradition. He depends on the exclusion of the avant-garde to call himself avant-garde; he relies on the judgment "this is not art" to annoint his art with the negative ontology of non-art.

Dadaism marks a turning point in the history of the anything-whatever and opens its second phase, which, I think, is coming to a close right before our very eyes. I would be speaking too hastily if I said that the dadaist liberation succeeded or that history has validated its claim. Besides being inexact, this would only render the establishment of the causes for this success more obscure. We would then have to ask what the aesthetic, artistic, or historical criterion was that might have made the dadaist whatever acceptable. And if the whatever had a criterion at hand, this means that it wasn't just anything whatever. But for all practical purposes, Dada seems to have succeeded in its exploit. One of the consequences of its acceptance was to have profoundly changed the feeling of the whatever and to have performed a quasi-inversion of its social distribution. Today, and this largely since the apparent success of the dadaist liberation, that is, since Dada's reception, since Dada has been "recuperated" by and in the history of modern art, the public at large has lost all interest in contemporary art, in which it sees nothing but the reign of the whatever, while the art establishment works hard to prove to the public, or to itself, that this whatever is not just anything whatever. As for the feeling of the whatever, it is now rarely composed of fear and indignation; most often it is made up of indifference. As far as the visual arts are concerned (but the dates coincide for literature and music: Joyce is contemporary with Dada, Russolo and Varèse frame the Dada period almost exactly), the history of the whatever is roughly articulated around dadaism. Before Dada it was a judgment pronounced by the establishment in the name of a feeling of fear and outrage; after Dada it became a judgment pronounced by the public at large in the name of a feeling of indifference.

This historical description is crude, I admit. Perhaps one ought to look more closely at the successive receptions of Dada; to describe the role played by surrealism and by Breton in particular in the effacement of the dadaist whatever; to ask to what degree the surrealist sanitizing of the whatever laid the ground for official art history's incorporation of Dada and travesty of its historical meaning; to reconstitute the channels through which the Dada impact crossed the Atlantic, paying particular attention to the exile of the surrealists to New York during World War II; and finally, to ask what the respective roles of Motherwell and Duchamp were in the belated and contradictory reception of dadaism in New York in the early fifties.[2] But these are the historian's questions, which scruple forces me to raise; they are not philosophical questions, and it's the philosophical issue of the whatever to which I would rather turn here.

Yet, if you bear in mind the paradox of this philosophical question, you will admit that even as simplified as its summary is here, the historical requirement is not yet wholly ready to yield to philosophy, if only because the question of the whatever begs a philosophy of history. The fact that there is a history of the whatever voids the concept, it would seem. The fact that the whatever evolves

2. The essays and eyewitness accounts assembled by Robert Motherwell in his book, *The Dada Painters and Poets* (New York: Wittenborn-Schultz, 1951), give more importance than it deserves to a dadaism filtered by French surrealism, within which they locate Duchamp, apparently with his approval, since he advised Motherwell in his editorial work. However, during the same period, another interpretation of Duchamp, centered on the readymade, and through this another reception of dadaism, began to surface in the works of John Cage, Merce Cunningham, Robert Rauschenberg, and Jasper Johns.

over time and is transformed, referring in 1880 for example to the insignificance of the *Bunch of Asparagus* or to the absence of perspective in the painting, in 1913 to the unrecognizable disorder of Kandinsky's first abstract watercolors, or in 1960 to the blunt provocation of Manzoni's cans of *Artist's Shit,* the fact therefore that the whatever doesn't refer to chaos, arbitrariness, chance, or destruction as established once and for all, obviously invalidates the scope and pertinence of such a judgment. Conversely, the fact that at each of these historical stages the judgment of the whatever was revealed to be excessive or blind in retrospect, the fact that new aesthetic criteria emerged after the fact from a destruction that seemed in its own time like the negation of all criteria, the fact that the history of the avant-gardes doesn't present itself solely as an irreversible process of increasing entropy but also as the chronology of a series of redemptions, of *Aufhebungen* of the whatever, makes the concept yet more fragile, even silly. It would be enough for art historians to be aware of this dialectical history of the whatever—and who isn't precisely since the reception of dadaism?—for them to consider the judgment of the whatever to be philistine even though, before Dada, it was uttered by the experts. They will even consider the dadaist claim of the whatever as so much childish provocation, which might have been explosive in its own days, but which they are duty-bound to invest with meaning and value. It is enough, further, that historians reflect or theorize the conception of history that the events seem to impose, for them not to fail to notice its Hegelian appearance nor to see the famous prediction of the death of art and the end of history confirmed or at least illustrated. If moreover they have some philosophical awareness, they will also have understood that for Hegel or for the artists who seemed to live out the Hegelian destiny, it was never a question of an actual stoppage of the historical process nor of an actual cessation of artistic activity, but rather of the appearance of a history that survives its end because it always lived off its end, of the phenomenology of an art that the threat of its own death, far from stopping, maintains as the always repeated and always *aufgehoben* recasting of its own death sentence.

This philosophical vision of the history of modern art has such currency today that it would be heavy-handed to insist upon it. It is as if the history of the avant-gardes were a dialectical history cast off by the contradiction of art and non-art, the history of a prohibition and of its transgression. A slogan could sum it up: it is forbidden to do whatever, let's do it. The Dada moment would be that of an *Aufhebung,* the moment when the prohibition and its transgression flow together into their contrary: it is permitted to do whatever, let's do it. From this moment on, the end of history and the death of art are the order of the day, so to speak, and make up the regular diet of a history of art that is self-conscious, at last, but pays for this by being forever forced into unhappy consciousness. The absolute whatever is the target at which history forever aims, abandoned to its own perpetual retelling, with its motor strength exhausted, always already denied, always already reaffirmed, accomplished in advance and therefore prevented from any real possibility of happening.

Now I want to insist that as far as art goes, the absolute whatever has taken place. It has already happened and this, far from confirming the Hegelian vision, renders it suspect. Happened when, where, through whom? One doesn't go too far wrong in answering once again: with Dada. But the reference to Dada is much too loose. Which Dada? Zurich, Berlin, Hanover, New York, Paris? Dada never consisted of a group marching in step to the same ideology. I have to say through what particular work the absolute whatever happened to the history of art. The answer, not surprisingly, lies in Marcel Duchamp's readymade—in the singular, even though several works by Duchamp carry this name. I shall not justify the use of this singular here. Both a factual and a theoretical question of great importance, it seems to me resolved by defining *the readymade* as neither an object or a set of objects nor a gesture nor an artistic intention, but rather, as a statement. It is the sentence, "this is art," such as it is pinned to absolutely any object whatsoever, *given* (I say "given," and not "provided") that it was recognized—that is, judged—as art.[3]

Of course, one might object here that in short-circuiting the object and the artist's intention I have failed to justify the readymades' (in the plural)

3. The question of the singular of "*the readymade*" will be taken up in the next chapter, where the status of "this is art" as *statement* will also be explained.

existence as art, and that I have neglected other people's justifications for their art-status as well. True, and I did it on purpose, being convinced that you cannot justify an aesthetic judgment, or, what amounts to the same thing, that in order to justify a judgment, another one is needed. One might also object that in adopting the Duchampian point of view of the *given,* I have confused the given fact that Duchamp's readymades are on the record with the possibility of pinning the sentence "this is art" to any object whatever, and that, since the former is a given and the latter a mere possibility, I am basing my thesis of the absolute whatever on a *petitio principii.* By what right indeed can I hold the morphology and the symbolism of the bicycle wheel, the bottle rack, the snow shovel, or the urinal as null and void? By what right can I call these objects indifferent and see in them a manifestation of the whatever, *a fortiori* of the absolute whatever, when, as interpreters have never failed to show, they lend themselves quite complacently to a variety of readings as well as to considerations of taste? I could give a series of answers to this objection but, since it is the issue of right that is raised, my preferred answer, the most ironic one, is this: by my right of judgment. Despite their beauty, their meaning, their originality, but also despite their ugliness, their meaninglessness, their banality, I judge that all the objects Duchamp baptized readymades are indifferent. In other words they are anything whatever. And I don't have to account for my judgment, any more than anyone would. I don't claim the privilege of the expert, quite the contrary: I judge after all as the man-on-the-street who finds that from dadaism on, contemporary art is the reign of the whatever. And like him, I judge with indifference, which is to say, I don't accompany my judgment, "this is whatever," with an outraged judgment, "this is not art!" That's of course where I stop being the man-on-the-street. I know all too well the absurdity of denying that today, those objects that Duchamp chose as readymades are art. Insofar as it constituted *the readymade* in affixing itself to a series of objects absolutely unprepared to be art, the sentence "this is art" was also a judgment, an aesthetic judgment that history has already pronounced and registered, setting a precedent in the jurisprudence of art. I would even add, without the slightest derogatory innuendo, that once on the record this sentence has become the prejudice *par excellence* of contemporary art.[4]

As an "expert" taking sides with the man-on-the-street, I also discreetly take a stand against the discourse of the art-historian-interpreter who "recuperates" Dada by justifying it and justifies it in denying it; this discourse would argue: in the end it was okay to make whatever because, you know, it wasn't just whatever. This discourse is not false, it even has a good chance of being automatically true. Once *something* is extracted from the whatever, chosen and individuated, it will always be *this* thing, with *this* form, and the possibility of giving it *this* meaning. That's inevitable. It's obvious in retrospect that the dadaists didn't do anything whatever, Duchamp any more than the others. What they did is what they did. The discourse of the art historian-interpreter is thus true, or veracious, by virtue of fate. But it isn't serious. Refusing—and this really is the last straw for a historical discourse—to register the Dada claim ("let's do whatever") as a historical fact by reading it as mere provocation extrinsic to the works, it disallows the possibility of inheriting the question the Dada claim raised, as if it were no longer something to interpret, even less to judge. In this way this discourse blunts the cutting edge of the question of the whatever, and prevents one from perceiving the enormous difference separating Duchamp from the dadaists as they have been "recuperated" (including Duchamp).

Duchamp wasn't a dadaist. Insofar as questions of antecedence are not futile, mightn't we recall that the readymades predate the Dada movement? The date itself is problematic: 1913, if we consider the *Bicycle Wheel* to be the first readymade; 1914, if we opt for the *Bottle Rack,* the first object to have been

4. I mean "prejudice" literally, as pre-judgment. To speak of art *after* Duchamp is to speak of a situation in which the "experts" are ready to grant *beforehand* art *status* to anything whatever, regardless of medium or skill: in the sentence "this is art," anything can come to occupy the position of referent pointed at by the word "this." Not so, of course, when art *quality* is at stake: then "this" has a precise referent and the prejudice needs to be re-judged. More about this in the next chapter.

chosen as is; 1915, if we date *the readymade* from the invention of the name—which is my preference; and 1917, if we date it from the Richard Mutt case, the first public appearance of a readymade. Even if we opt for this last choice, the place and the circumstances surrounding the establishment of the famous *Fountain* show well enough that *the readymade* owes nothing, absolutely nothing, to the *Zeitgeist* of the *Cabaret Voltaire* (1916). Duchamp is not dadaist, then, for this first reason. Besides, he always kept aloof, not just from the Dada group—since beyond tactical alliances among extremely diverse individuals, Dada didn't even form a group—but also from everyone claiming ownership of the name Dada. In this he showed a prudence well in line with his own *pictorial nominalism*. The name "readymade," being specific, must have seemed to him a much preferable heading under which to bring his own whatever than a generic name like Dada, charged as it was with establishing a new artistic genre: the authorized whatever. Duchamp is not a dadaist for this second reason.

But that's not all. Let's go back to the (admittedly crude) outline of the history of the whatever that I sketched out earlier. Before Dada it was the experts—art critics, painting juries, academic big-wigs—who decried the anathema of the whatever in modern art and judged in outrage that it didn't deserve to be called art. The public at large—the crowd of the laymen—for the most part abstained from such legislating judgment (for which it didn't have the political means anyway), but it showed through its interest that it perceived some of the social issues at stake in modern art, and thus, that it by no means held modern art as just anything whatever. After Dada (or after its reception, its "recuperation"), things were reversed. Since then, the experts—at least those who legislate over current artistic practices—proselytize ceaselessly their interest in contemporary art, whose name "art" they seek to justify on the basis of all the qualities that make it anything but whatever. And the public at large has lost all interest in art. Deaf to the explanations of the experts, it persists in seeing in contemporary art a huge whatever to which it remains indifferent. Between these two historical "blocks," Dada marks a turning point, involving the derisive posture adopted by the Dada artist: he mimicks the traditional expert's behavior. Like the expert, he exclaims: "This (the work I've just made) is whatever, it's not art." But he turns the expert's feeling inside out, so to speak, and whereas the former experienced outrage, he experiences enthusiasm. And so, in his relation to tradition, he claims the contradictory positiveness of a negative judgment: non-art—the new name of what is judged not to be art—is the dialectical negation of art, and the art named Dada, which must sound the death-knell of art and end tradition, is the negation of this negation.

Nothing could be more foreign to Duchamp than this behavior. Even derisively, Duchamp didn't assume the posture of the conservative expert. Rather, he anticipatively assumed the posture of the layman of the future. He placed the artist, the author, in the enunciative position of the spectator, of today's spectator who no longer belongs to the crowd in Baudelaire's sense but to the mass in the sense this word takes in the expression "mass media," to the "mediatized" mass.[5] He had the author say "this is whatever," but in his state of

5. Walter Benjamin described the Baudelairian crowd thus: "They do not stand for classes or any sort of collective; rather, they are nothing but the amorphous crowd of passers-by, the people in the street" (*Charles Baudelaire: A Lyric Poet in the Era of High Capitalism,* trans. Harry Zohn [London: New Left Books, 1973], pp. 119–120). Now, the mass as we might understand it today is not amorphous. It is, on the contrary, ceaselessly "mediatized" by the mass-media, whose main function precisely is that of gridding the amorphous crowd and differentiating it according to a variety of finely meshed semiotic grids that are so many networks of imposition and circulation of power: social class, age-class, professional category, level and type of education, political affiliation, leisure-class (in Veblen's sense), mode of consumption, cultural behavior. At the nineteenth-century painting Salon, the spectator/man-on-the-street belonging to the crowd found himself at once solicited and excluded: his judgment, pre-judged as vulgar and philistine, was precisely to make the difference between the experts and himself. In today's art institutions, of which the Pompidou Center in Paris offers the "mass-mediatized" paradigm, the man-on-the-street belonging to the masses finds himself included and so to speak cloaked in a cultural behavior that classes and channels him, but he is no longer solicited. His very indifference leaves the institution indifferent. Whatever the pedagogical intentions and goodwill displayed by a cultural apparatus like the Pompidou Center, its real function is to produce spectatorship, in other words, to turn "visitors" into

indifference, he abstained from having him judge on the matter of art or non-art. "It's the viewers who make the pictures," and they make them with that distracted look Walter Benjamin attributed to movie-goers and which turns them into "experts" of profane, de-cultualized, art. Unlike the Dada artist, the Duchampian author—say, Rrose Sélavy—is not the priest of the anti-cult, the professional of the anti-profession, the traditionalist of the anti-tradition, or the mocking keeper of the anti-law. She doesn't authorize herself to do whatever, she projects herself in anticipation as a subject of the law among other subjects, submitted like no matter whom to the anti-law of no matter what. It is as if Duchamp had grasped the historical reasons behind dadaism and had dispossessed the Dada artists of their illusion of being the authors of their own liberation. It was ludicrous to believe that one could authorize oneself to do whatever when the whatever was already the law, that one could liberate oneself by profaning when profanation had already happened, that it was appropriate to parody the guardian of the old law—namely academicism, i.e., the little that was left of the aristocratic and religious orders—when the artistic imperative already was—and this is the gist of the modern utopia to which Duchamp never naïvely subscribed but which he exposed—the production of a mass art for a society of laymen that had already undertaken the mass-mediatization of the Baudelairian crowd.

Duchamp wasn't a dadaist for this third reason: he profaned nothing. Whatever profanation there is in his work is on the order of the *étant donné;* it is a

"spectators" by mapping a semiotic grid, which is only nominally summed up by the word "art," onto the flow of people passing through the institution. This production of spectatorship, however, has not yet reached the level of reification that is found elsewhere in the production of commodities. It includes a ritual moment of authentification which, in the case of the Pompidou Center, was *massively* achieved at the time of its inauguration, as chance would have it, through a Duchamp retrospective. (See my "La condition Beaubourg," *Critique,* no. 426 [November 1982].) The posture of the future man of the street that Duchamp anticipatively assumed is that of the occasional visitor to the Pompidou Center, who proves that he or she is an art lover by producing his or her entry ticket.

given. It wasn't even the achievement of those artists who, from Courbet to the dadaists, translated and betrayed tradition, and transmitted their betrayal; it was the work of those who thought that they were the exclusive guardians of tradition and whose posture the dadaists derisively assumed. Blinding themselves to the social upheavals of the nineteenth century and deaf to their calls for legislative redress (it is not by chance that the avant-garde began with Courbet—Proudhon is not far away), those who were by profession guardians of the aesthetic law let tradition become ossified by going to any lengths to prevent it from falling into the hands of the uninitiated. Once the Salon and a public market for painting existed, the crowd could no longer be held at bay, but academicism thought it could still show the crowd its place. This wrong needed to be righted as the crowd—or the masses—waited for their right to legislate to be rendered. This had to be done so that art, whatever it may become, might live and not be suspended in the forever *aufgehoben* reiteration of its own death sentence, and so that it might live as it always has done, as a ceaseless production of differences, even in the henceforth fatal conditions of standardization, of mass culture, of what we a bit too quickly call indifference. It is this transfer of legislative power that the readymade symbolically accomplished, as its author anticipatively assumed the position of the viewer, of the uninitiated, and handed him or her the right to judge about art, to judge anything whatever as art. With Duchamp, "it is permitted to make whatever" is not the formula of authorization; it doesn't free authors. It is indeed the formula of profanation, but then only thanks to a pun on the word "profane": it frees the layman, the uninitiated, the man or woman-on-the-street, authorizing him or her to judge. It is this very authorization I availed myself of in order to judge that the readymades were indifferent and, as such, an exemplary manifestation of the anything whatever. It seems to me that I have not been unfaithful to Duchamp; I have judged along with him and not against him.

And I repeat my judgment, or rather his, the uninitiated's judgment: the readymade is whatever. Or still: the readymade is absolutely indifferent. It is my democratic right to judge as the man-on-the-street that authorizes me to say that despite their formal qualities—or lack of formal qualities—the bottle rack, the urinal, or the snow shovel, are indifferent objects. But, you might say, nothing authorizes me to say that they are *absolutely* indifferent. Indeed, nothing does authorize me to do so. But everything obliges me to. Having anticipatively projected the author of the readymade into the position of the uninitiated spectator who judges that modern art, at least since dadaism, is whatever, Duchamp obliges this spectator in return—especially if he or she is an "expert"—to project him- or herself retrospectively into the very position of this author and to submit to the same law that he did. It is the law of modernity and it says nothing but: do whatever.

The law doesn't merely proscribe, it prescribes. I thus call that artist modern whose duty is (was, has been?) to do whatever. This is a duty and not a right. It is a commandment the modern artist receives and not an authorization he or she gives him- or herself. As such, it is not even a law in the ordinary or juridical sense. The phrase "do whatever" doesn't state a rule to which a case may be submitted; rather, it prescribes action in the absence of rules. It is injunction as such: act; you ought to make. But what should I make to obey the injunction if the injunction doesn't say? Well, do what you want. Act according to your free will. If this was an order, it was easy enough to obey it, and on the contrary impossible to disobey it. Whatever I do, I comply. But if it wasn't an order, if it was instead a permission as the dadaists believed, then my will is useless and that it be free is useless too. Whatever authorization I give myself, I am never the author of what I make. Anyone whoever can make anything whatever if anything goes. What can I make, then, so as to be an artist? What could I possibly do with an imposed freedom or with an order there is no way of infringing? What could anyone do once it is mandatory that everything be permitted or, as the rebelling students said in May '68, once it is forbidden to forbid? Do I need to insist? Between a Leninist question (What to do?) and its anarchistic reply (Anything goes), everybody will have perceived the resonance of the political issues brought to mind by the imperative—which is nonetheless merely aesthetic—to do whatever. And it would be insulting to those many artists who, in Duchamp's wake, felt summoned by the injunction to do whatever, to insinuate that they were not aware of these issues.

Up to now little has been done, however, to interpret the modern whatever as an imperative. Considerable resistances, supported in part by the already noted paradox which holds that the whatever has a history, oppose such a reading. No one would deny that in art there are prescriptions—norms, canons, criteria—destined perhaps to be transgressed and displaced, but remaining criteria all the same. Neither would anyone deny the massive dismantling of criteria that modern and contemporary art clearly accomplished. But the mind resists linking the two: logic is opposed to making a criterion out of the absence of criteria; psychology is opposed to recognizing any principle of liberty in the double bind of an order impossible to transgress; and ethics, although ready to admit that people should be free, doesn't easily grant freedom without conditions. In short, interpretation resists the modern law, unless it is the law that resists interpretation. Only reluctantly do we admit to a commandment as unbridled as *do whatever,* and the first temptation is to add on a clause that gives it purpose: do whatever in order to . . .

Do Whatever in Order to . . .

Here is a first interpretation, a first misinterpretation, actually, of the modern imperative: do whatever in order to . . . According to this interpretation, of which there are many historical variants, art-making should be subordinated to a goal. Art, or at least the making part of it, is concerned with means, not with ends. As for the ends, they are either immanent or transcendent. In the first instance, the making—skill, technique—serves an end that is art itself. Such is the case with the doctrine of art-for-art's-sake, for example: do whatever, you are free, but do it in order that it be art, do it for the sake of art, do it for the purpose of making art's autonomy manifest. In the second instance, technique is in the service of an end that transcends art itself. Such is the case with nineteenth-century academicism when it justifies itself through classical aesthetics: represent what you want (we haven't reached the "do whatever" yet), but do it in order to please, do it for the sake of beauty or for the purpose of serving the values of harmony and continuity, or perhaps to honor nature.

Closer to the present, formalism represents the most widespread variant of an art doctrine given its purpose through immanence. Here the end folds back onto the means. Art-making—which is *poiesis*—constitutes the subject matter of art, which in turn displays the critique, the deconstruction, or the self-analysis of its technical means, while the whole process tends towards establishing art's ultimate identity through a succession of reductions. Clement Greenberg has summed up this doctrine perfectly in saying, "The essence of Modernism lies, as I see it, in the use of the characteristic methods of a discipline to criticize the discipline itself—not in order to subvert it, but to entrench it more firmly in its area of competence."[6] At the opposite pole, that of an art doctrine given its purpose through transcendence, we find the applied arts, commercial art, pedagogical and didactic art, erotic and pornographic art, and of course, political art. Only this last form is really significant, for it is the only one to fully claim the title of art while making it subservient to a higher cause. Here, but not without pain, the end justifies the means, and art-making—which is *praxis*—is a strategy operating within the superstructure. Construction of heroic figures, denunciatory pamphlet, or patient critique of the dominant ideology, political art aims at social transformations trespassing the boundaries of art. In order to achieve them, it can and must make use of whatever. In the wake of Dada, such were the doctrines of the Berlin Spartakists and of Agit-Prop, or closer to the present, that of Situationism.

---

6. Greenberg, "Modernist Painting," p. 67. On the disentanglement of Greenberg's notions of formalism and modernism, see chapter 4. Keeping this disentanglement in mind, it should be noted that although Greenberg's particular brand of modernism does fold back the technical means of art upon its end (i.e., treats the medium as art's subject matter), his formalism considers the end (art as art) as the involuntary result of a "tropism toward aesthetic value as such." Thus the Greenbergian doctrine is far less a misinterpretation of the modern imperative than art-for-art's-sake, inasmuch as it is never an act of will that carries out the injunction "do whatever, in order to . . . ," but rather, a feeling. See below, the third interpretation of the modern imperative.

The doctrines and ideologies of modern art never ceased being torn between these two purposivenesses, one immanent and the other transcendent, while art itself—theory and practice—never stopped wanting to reinscribe both these ends into one another. Evidently the immanence of formalist art entails the requirement of a vertical transcendence. It was given names like the sublime, the spiritual, utopia, the future. And the horizontal transcendence of political art requires a so to speak vertical immanence. It has been called consciousness-raising, discourse of truth, call for freedom, critical dimension, or once again, utopia. Finally, the tugs-of-war and the boxes within boxes of immanence and transcendence which, for this first interpretation of the modern imperative, must endow the whatever with purpose, are well suited to remind us that, despite all bestowal of purpose, *do whatever* is first and foremost a command, one whose end as well as its origin remain unknown. When we focus in hindsight on the internal contradictions of Italian futurism, the personal conflicts between Walter Gropius and Hannes Meyer at the Bauhaus, the warring propensities at the Vhutemas of the suprematists and the productivists, to say nothing of the reciprocal excommunications of the surrealists or of Aragon's moral torments, we come to think that we have no way of interpreting all this suffering in modernism. Between the two conflicting purposes of modern art, we see no dialectical resolution, especially if we look at what their practical destiny has been on the stage of history. Formalism, with its demands and its ideals, has degenerated into mere formalism, in the pejorative sense this word has taken on: an academic and stupid art which repeats empty, contentless forms. Newman and the sublime are dead, and a doctrine of artistic immanence, once it forgets about transcendence, leads nowhere but to a cynical or desperate practice of quotation. As for the destiny of political art, it is even more painful. Where art practice was offered a historical opportunity to realize its political ends, it soon ran up against the reality of the power enslaving it. From Plekhanov to the latter Lunacharsky and from Lunacharsky to Zhdanov, the road was very short. And where this opportunity wasn't offered, the social transcendence of art practices that felt compelled to make use of any means whatever—pamphlets, photomontage, cinéma-vérité, street theater, cultural guerilla—to incite disalienation and liberation, this transcendence is now totally reabsorbed in the affirmative immanence—as Marcuse would say—of a market that is in fact ready to accommodate and commodify whatever. On all sides, on theoretical as well as historical grounds, in the register of *poiesis* as in that of *praxis,* the injunction "do whatever in order to . . ." sadly rings out its own failure.

Now, this injunction was an interpretation, a purposive interpretation of the naked injunction "do whatever." It took place, it is even widespread, it isn't a mirage that can be dissipated with another interpretation. But it failed. It is thus false and it isn't just. By which I mean that it simply isn't true, and not that it would be possible to substitute a true interpretation for it. At most one could give an accurate historical account of it. By which I mean above all that it is unjust, which is to say that it doesn't do justice to the history of modern art as it happened. It is even all the more unjust that it is false but that its account is correct. It thus demands that we redress a wrong; that we do justice to modern art, that we judge. And a judgment is not an interpretation. This judgment, which is required and all the more final that it cannot subject means to an end, has already been rendered. It was handed down to us with Duchamp's readymade. Modern art is whatever. Period. Such is its law, its imperative. It knows of no purpose. In the midst of the dadaist confusion, as soon as the readymade began to produce its historical effects, it found some artists—very few, but it found them—whom the imperative of the whatever summoned violently enough. Breton was surely among these. But he gave this imperative a name that interpreted it, raising it above reality: surrealism. He also gave it an end, and twice over, in terms of formal immanence and of political transcendence. On the one hand, it's *La révolution surréaliste,* and on the other, *Le surréalisme au service de la révolution.* What remains of surrealism, once these two ends, false and unjust, are stripped bare? Nothing but the violent and incomprehensible imperative: do whatever, make the revolution!

Do Whatever Provided . . .

Here, now, is a second interpretation, a second misinterpretation, actually, of the modern imperative: do whatever provided . . . Instead of purposes, here are conditions. Instead of a prescribed violence, whether it be that of ends or means, here is the order to restrain and contain violence. Instead of a founding barbarism (as Nietzsche understood, whether it founds language or the State, it's always the same thing, and it's always the act of an artist), here are police regulations. Instead of the formally or politically revolutionary avant-garde, here comes the avant-garde academy, or the avant-garde as academy. Here again, "do whatever provided . . ." can be interpreted immanently or transcendently. If the condition of the artistic whatever is immanent to art, the precept is translated thus: do whatever as long as it remains art. There are no limits to your freedom short of the very limits of art, and these are unsurpassable because they bear on its very essence. They aren't a restriction nor, consequently, the fruit of a prescription, unless we call prescriptions the limits assigned by a natural order of things. Do whatever in art, but do it in art only. As an exemplary profession of this doctrine, here we encounter formalism once again, but it is not alone. In the end, it is all of modernism—striking one as an "ism," that is, as an irrepressible desire to legislate—that sees itself obliged to require that art's condition be art itself. Only with late modernism, that of the conceptual art of a Joseph Kosuth, for example, was this requirement led to avow flatly its tautological character of re-quiring. Literally, it's begging the question. Interpreted conditionally and immanently, the modern imperative of the whatever has thus taken the endlessly revived form of an inquiry into the presuppositions of its requirement. Indeed, the quest or the question has been there since the beginnings of modernism, which is to say, since Courbet, and since that beginning it has swallowed its own tail. Do whatever provided it is art. But what is art? To act under these conditions a definition is needed. And how to find it if not in asking the very question of art's conditions? Ask the question, then, and to know if something is art, anything whatever, do whatever then. In order to see.

To see and to know. The prescription of the whatever announces and promises the coming of knowledge, of a description, which in turn prescribes the whatever, until it can be known under what necessary and sufficient conditions anything whatever can be said to be art.

There is a whole program in this, and as everyone knows this program was carried out. The prescription was followed and, furthermore, followed by a description. That is, for example, what formalism gives when Greenberg describes the history of modernist painting as the progressive reduction of the conventions of pictorial art to flatness. Modernism was, thus, an experimental laboratory where for almost a century the essence of art was tested. I'm hardly joking, so widespread is this conception of modern art in which positivism holds hands with metaphysics. Greenberg deserves more than a joke, that's for sure. Besides, he was not just a positivist. But his obstinate refusal to incorporate Duchamp's readymade into modernism is a clear symptom of formalism's blindness vis-à-vis, precisely, the object of its quest and requirement. For isn't this object right there, before our blinded eyes? Whether urinal or snow shovel, it is a thing, any thing perhaps, in any case something, which is always already required so that we might know where to turn our eyes and about what to ask the question. Wasn't this question one of knowing—and seeing—what the necessary and sufficient conditions were for something to be art? Apparently. But Duchamp—as he said himself—was only interested in appearances in order to track down the *apparition*.[7] The condition allowing for the readymade to appear was that the question of the whatever and of its conditions had appeared. And it has been apparent since Courbet. Like the thing, the question itself was a prerequisite; but it was a given, too. For all of us to ask the question, it was required that someone, anyone whoever but not everyone, produce this something, whatever, and put it under our nose. But it was also required that someone, anyone whoever and perhaps everyone, had already asked the

7. The *apparition* in the same sense as encountered above (see chapter 2, n. 9 and chapter 4, n. 96), meaning the fact of appearing.

question for us all to have our noses set before this thing, all of a sudden, as before a *fait accompli.*

Here we are, before the modern imperative as a *fait accompli.* But it is not because the readymade has answered the question of the necessary and sufficient conditions—or conventions—of art that the modern imperative appears accomplished. This was Greenberg's fear, and it explains his resistance. If it were justified, we would have to share it. In this case, we would know that anything whatever is art provided it is whatever. And Duchamp's gesture, repeated somehow by Ad Reinhardt and Kosuth, would only have the arid splendor of a definitively sterile inquiry and requirement. It would have answered the great question of modernism in the terms that modernism set for itself, in ontological terms. It would have shown—made known and seen—in a sort of (anticipated) *reductio ad absurdum* of a generalized Greenbergian formalism, that the essence of art is whatever. But *a* readymade shows nothing; it doesn't even show itself, since it still requires to be shown, designated: this is art. Without the deictic "this," art has no being. And *the* readymade doesn't show anything either, since it is nothing but the statement "this is art," as it is affixed to any "this" whatsoever. Finally, *this* readymade, *Fountain,* for example, doesn't make anything known or seen about art either beyond itself; today as in 1917, it leaves us blind before it. We, the viewers who make the pictures, we are and remain *The Blind Man.* The readymade doesn't tell us what the essence of art is, but for that matter it doesn't tell us that art has no essence. It abandons us to our own ignorance. It doesn't tell us what the necessary and sufficient conditions are for any object, absolutely any object, to be art.[8] But for that matter it doesn't tell us that art is without conditions. It abandons us to our ignorance and our responsibility. If it tells us anything, and it does, it is that art is not of the order of seeing and knowing but rather of that of judging, not of the order of the descriptive but of the prescriptive. Misinterpreted conditionally and immanently, the modern imperative prescribed: do whatever in art, but do it in art only. Well, in art

8. More about this in the next chapter.

there is precisely nothing but judgment. To make is to judge, and this judgment carries an obligation with it. To make art is to judge—not what is art but what ought to be art, not what art is but what art ought to be. The best judgment is, as always, that of the uninitiated who, faced with the readymade, exclaims: I could have done this! Too late, it's been done. The readymade exists, already made, chosen, judged. *Mene, Tekel, Epharsim.* What's left to do, now that we are faced with its *fait accompli*? What's left to make, given the fact that judgment has been rendered? The unconditional imperative remains: you ought to!

The precept "do whatever provided . . . ," the second misinterpretation of the modern imperative, can also be interpreted transcendently. Here, art's condition is external to art. Depending on the nature and structure of this condition, depending on the domain of reality over which it legislates, the precept cuts the field of modern art into local areas, demarcated styles, or particular theories. Do whatever as long as it is beautiful, as long as it is well made, as long as it makes sense, as long as you express yourself or express your times. Weak and conservative versions of the modern imperative. Or on the contrary: do whatever as long as it is shocking, as long as it is disappointing, as long as it produces nonsense, as long as your unconscious or that of your times expresses itself, as long as it is difficult or hermetic, as long as it is new. Strong and avant-gardistic versions of the modern imperative. Each of these versions had its hour in the sun, each still has its partisans, but there is not one of them that hasn't entered a crisis today, as though they had all reached their critical moment together. They offer themselves to the artist as an array of styles none of which any longer carries enough conviction to impose itself; they offer themselves to the art critic as a collection of theories none of which any longer has power enough to carry the day for its side. Do whatever provided that, under the condition that . . . Are there still conditions for art, now that it is provided with a choice of norms all equally available and interchangeable, now that all the moments of modernity have begun to implode before our very eyes? The modern imperative had its day, here comes the reign of eclecticism and of historicism, here again the reign of the whatever. Those who call it postmodern don't even know what they're saying. Whereas hard-and-fast modernism,

Greenberg's formalism, for example, was both conventionalist and essentialist as a philosophy of art, what runs around these days under the name postmodernism is nothing but a doctrineless pseudophilosophy, at once opportunist and functionalist. If all the conditions of the whatever are available and interchangeable, this only means that it depends on any conditions whatever, that is, on no one. Anything goes is postmodernism's answer to the question of modernism. Of course, it swallows its own tail as much as modernism's question did. But it is an answer, it gets realized in the social field, whereas the modern question had to retreat from the world. It's not surprising that once the reduction of art to its "essential conventions" had purportedly reached them, the question of art's essence, in order to be asked one last time, had to beat a strategic retreat into the etherial spheres of conceptual art or into the deserts of land art. It's not surprising either that this retreat, pathetic in hindsight, has been a last-ditch defense against the fall of art into commodity status, a last try for the possibility of the sublime, a last attempt to redeem the horizontal immanence of the modernist inquiry with vertical transcendence. And it's perhaps no more surprising but highly significant that minimal art, Arte Povera, conceptual art, and land art appeared at the height of a period of economic growth, at a historical moment when the West could not imagine that there would be an end to the welfare society. Conversely, it's all too significant, perhaps, and no more surprising, that it was in the very depths of the economic crisis of the eighties that the art market boomed anew for a reified art. It's not just the return of the repressed, as some have said of the symptomatic resurgence of figuration and expressionism. It's not just the equally symptomatic return of the sublime as effect and theater, as quotation, as reproduction, as aura of the consumable commodity. It's not just the artists' return from exile or from their wandering in the desert, not just their dealing again in worldly matters. Even if it's also all that, what comes in the guise of postmodern eclecticism and historicism is in fact the return of the law.

The law returns with a vengeance as the law of the market, the law of exchange, the only law in the capitalist regime to be both real and universal. It strikes everything and everyone beneath its fist: all the objects it reifies, all the subjects who serve it. Not a single artist escapes it if he or she wants to survive. All draw pain or pleasure from their servitude, but it is always the pain or pleasure of the slave, without dialecticization. For there is no longer any Master; there is the System and the System is not the Subject, nor is it the Signifier. It is the law sure enough, but perverted, pure pragmatic and operational immanence reabsorbed into its own behaviorism. What this law tells artists to do can only go in the direction of its own enforcement. It enriches some, it crushes many, it frees no one. Yes, artists are free: they are free to exchange and exchange whatever, but only there where exchange takes place, in the market. They are also free to do whatever, but the violence of this freedom is no longer that of revolution, it is merely that of economic competition. All the styles, manners, forms, and media are exchangeable and interchangeable. They all compete without contradicting each other, much less as ideologies than as commodities. Painting, which sells best these days if it is figurative, has never been so abstract; it has the abstract quality of money.

The law of the market is not new. It has been there ever since an art market came into being. Even before Courbet it set the economic conditions of modernism and fixed the social condition of the modern artist as a "free worker" or small entrepreneur. It is only with late modernism, that of Warhol for instance, that the economic conditions of art practice, understood until then to be contingent and external to art properly speaking, became its subject, its substance, and its form. Only when the modern imperative, conditioned by the horizontal transcendence of its economic determinants, began to interpret itself as if it were nothing but the expression of the law of the market, was it also able to be received—all transcendence dispensed with—as a cynical encouragement to radical opportunism: do whatever provided it sells. Warhol deserves better than a trial based on assumptions, that's for sure. Besides, he wasn't an opportunist. But the shadow of his success hovers today over a whole generation of artists who suffer neither from his feigned schizophrenia, nor from the hypersensitivity of his insensitivity, and who alternately feel pain and pleasure with the purely functional role that the market makes them play in enforcing its own law. What was cool desire for Warhol ("I want to be a machine") has become pathetic reality. This reality is easily interpreted. It even interprets itself, self-referentially and to the point of being sickening, in the glossy reproductions spreading the glamor of the artworld all over the pages of art magazines. Artists no longer offer spectacles to art collectors. It is the art market as a whole that turns itself into a spectacle for the masses. But what doesn't interpret itself is the pathos of this reality. It expresses itself, that's all. It allows one perhaps to find a symptomatic meaning in the return of expressionism in the eighties and to explain its coercive quality, but it itself has no meaning. Insofar as it expresses itself, this pathos is the feeling of the law, the feeling of someone who finds him or herself under the law of the market, under the universal law of exchange, and under its vengeance. But insofar as it is an imperative, it is also the feeling or the foreboding of another law, the necessary call for another universality, and a reminder that, despite all wishes for postmodernism, the modern imperative still holds us under its necessity: do whatever. Period. Unconditionally. Do absolutely whatever. It was the imperative of the readymade, and the readymade isn't the *Brillo Box*. From pop art and minimal art date the last of the successive receptions of Dada, that from which conceptual art arose and to which it owes having painted itself into a corner, that which makes an avenging return today as the law of the commodity, overdetermined on the one hand by the figure of Warhol and on the other by the resurrection of expressionism, this near-contemporary of Dada. What is left of it today? There is a weak and liberal version of the "do whatever provided . . ." left over, a ghost of utopia to which some naïvely attach their last hopes and which they call pluralism. There is also a strong and almost fascist version of the "do whatever provided . . ." left over, to which some subscribe—others, but not necessarily—which we could call simulation but whose real name is cynicism, desperation, and irresponsibility. There is thus a lot left, since these two versions—the strong and the weak—hold almost the totality of the artworld between them. But there is nothing left since they are false and unjust. Cynicism is unjust because it always sides with power. It is not false, it simply states that the reason of the strongest is always best. Irresponsibility is unjust because it refuses to judge. And despair is true. But it is unjust that all hope should disappear. Pluralism is not unjust but it is false. It is generous and still hopes. It defends freedom, or rather, liberties, in the plural; but these are the illusory liberties we grant ourselves when we believe that anything is permitted. This would be just, perhaps, but it is not true. The truth is that everything should be permitted. Liberties are relative but freedom ought to be absolute. The readymade is pluralist—a plurality of them exists—but it must speak universally. An indifferent object is never really indifferent but it must claim to be so, absolutely. And the "do whatever" is never unconditional but it ought to be. To the universality of exchange—the law of reality—one must oppose the silent and incomprehensible law of necessity, which is also the necessity of the law. The imperative "do whatever" is a categorical imperative.

The Categorical Imperative of Modern Art

Here, against the wall of the categorical imperative, the interpretation of the whatever stops for the time being. From the readymade's "profanation," I have drawn the permission to judge it indifferent. But nothing authorized me to judge it absolutely indifferent. Nothing authorized me to, but everything obliged me, and everything still obliges us to do so. I would even add that this obligation is the requirement of "the everything," of totality, but of a totality that is not Hegelian. What is at stake, of course, is the law's universality, and, since we are talking about art, it is art's universality. In the *Foundations of the Metaphysics of Morals,* Kant gives several formulations of the categorical imperative. The first is:

> For since the imperative contains besides the law only the necessity that the maxim should accord with this law, while the law contains no condition to which it is restricted, there is nothing remaining in it except the universality of law as such to which the maxim of the action should conform; and in effect this conformity alone is represented as necessary by the imperative. There is, therefore, only one categorical imperative. It is: Act only according to that maxim

> by which you can at the same time will that it should become a universal law.[9]

To the extent that artists abide by the compelling injunction to do whatever, received from no one knows whom, perhaps from what Kandinsky called inner necessity, they also avail themselves of the authorization to it. They relay the command, "you must," with "I want." In Kantian terms: to do whatever is the maxim of their will. Earlier, we asked the following question: how obey the injunction if the injunction doesn't say? Well, I do what I want, the maxim answers, I do whatever. Delivered over to its sole authorization, the maxim is merely liberal or anarchist. It fails to be necessary, lacking the inner or outer, immanent or transcendent (no one knows) necessity that obliges artists, and through which they can will the universality of their art. Do what you want, yes, do whatever freely, but do it so as to convey, through the maxim that you give yourself, the feeling that you obey an injunction which you have received, and that it is this injunction which compels you to will that your maxim should become a universal law. The maxim of the whatever is legal only if it is willed for whomever. This is the first side of the modern imperative, its generous and utopian side, that which admonished Kandinsky, for example, to anchor to the maxim of abstraction the foundation of a universal pictorial language speakable by anyone. I could multiply examples; they are all instances of a democratic, universalist ideal inherited from the Enlightenment: the functionalist ideal, from the Werkbund to the Athens Charter; the Dada ideal of liberation; the revolutionary ideal of surrealism; the ideal of the Whitmanesque ego of the American Abstract expressionists; the ideal of spectator participation in the sixties, from Fluxus to kinetic art; and finally, as one would expect, in May '68, the ideal of power to the imagination. That is the side of hope, but it is also that of disappointed hopes. None of these ideals has kept its promises; on this side only

9. Immanuel Kant, *Foundations of the Metaphysics of Morals,* trans. Lewis White Beck (New York: Bobbs-Merrill, 1969), p. 44.

disenchantment is left. The other side of the modern imperative never promised enchantment. It only proclaimed terror. How obey the injunction if the injunction doesn't say? Well, I do what I want, the maxim answers, and whatever I do, whatever I want, I obey. My violence is legitimate and my will is pure. But the more violent I am in my will for freedom, the more I am hostage to my violence. Is there a free individual who can freely give himself such a maxim without soon feeling terrorized by the injunction of terrorism with which his maxim invests him? Delivered over to its sole radicality, the maxim is merely necessary, but of that blind and irresponsible necessity that produces happenstance crimes to which all are hostage, their authors as well as their victims. It lacks freedom, the freedom, that is, to disobey. And that is what the whatever, as maxim that obliges and authorizes all at once, prohibits. But it is also what the whatever, as categorical imperative, prohibits being prohibited.

Once I receive the order to do whatever, I receive it as a "you must," which addresses me—that's beyond doubt—but which does not address itself to me, or to a *me.* It falls on me. As long as I haven't made it the maxim of my will, I remain a *you,* I am not yet authorized to say "me," or "I will." (In other words, I shall never be the author of the law, only of my maxim.) It is at the most intimate point of this *you* who is not me that the duty of freedom is lodged: I ought to have the possibility of not endorsing the imperative of the whatever and of not making it my maxim. And it is at that same intimate point—between the *you* who is the recipient of the law and the voluntary *I* of my maxim—that the order of disobeying is conveyed to me: don't do whatever. Needless to say, between this *you* and this *I* there is nothing like space, not even the space of a speech act; between the "moment" when I receive the categorical imperative and the "moment" when I make it my maxim there is no time that passes, not even the time of making a decision. For it is as much through the maxim I give myself that I receive the imperative and *at the same time*—Kant says—that I can will that my maxim become a universal law. We have there, quasi outside space and time, a philosopheme that is the exact equivalent of the above paradox which, within time and space, held that there was a history of the whatever. On the one hand, it is indeed impossible to disobey the modern imperative.

Whatever the modern artist does—the one, I remind you, who feels summoned by the duty of doing whatever—he or she authorizes him- or herself as well and always obeys his or her maxim. The dadaists limited themselves to this authorization, and it is obviously in large part from the feeling that that was too easy that the escalation of the artistic whatever began. But on the other hand, it is just as impossible to obey the modern imperative without resistance. Whatever artists want to do, including the anything whatever—a work made by chance, say—they have do to *something*. In other words, they can't do everything; their finitude prohibits this. The art historians-interpreters of Dada limited themselves to this resistance, and it is largely because it is so obvious that they didn't take the whatever seriously. Blinded by so much obviousness, neither the dadaists nor their interpreters perceived the necessity of the whatever insofar as it is simultaneously impossible to obey it without getting caught up in terror and escalation and to disobey it without taking the initiative of what must be called, after the fact, a tradition. Or, more radically: neither perceived that is impossible to obey and disobey the imperative of the whatever freely without having to say, categorically, that to do anything whatever is impossible.

As I said, what is at stake is the universality of the law, the universality of art, the universality of the categorical imperative *do whatever.* It is understood that the Kantian categorical imperative is not the law of someone and that it gives no one the right to institute his or her personal maxim as a universal rule. To the contrary, that's the only thing it proscribes. It is understood as well that the Kantian categorical imperative states no content of the law but that it prescribes the conformity of the maxim to the universality of a law in general. As Jean-Luc Nancy says, "The law prescribes legislating according to the form of the law, that is, according to the universal form. But," he adds, "universality is not given."[10] If, as I hold, *do whatever* is rightly a categorical imperative, then we must go further and say that the universal is impossible, or that impossibility is, today, the modality of the universal.

10. Jean-Luc Nancy, *L'impératif catégorique* (Paris: Flammarion, 1983), p. 24.

The phrase *do whatever* doesn't give the content of the law, only the content of the maxim. Moreover, this content is any content whatever and becomes determined only by the action that puts the maxim into practice. *Do whatever* prescribes nothing determined. It only prescribes a form conformant to the universal, in the radical and final condition of finitude. And that means: conformant to the impossible. Do whatever; but you can't do everything; then do something that will conform to anything whatever, to *a* thing in general, better still, to *the* thing, extended to its infinite and indefinite universality; do something impossible. Duchamp chose things, whatever, a urinal for example. Once chosen, this thing is forever fatally and excessively overdetermined. It is impossible to choose anything whatever while avoiding that it be *this* thing by the same token. It is impossible to judge whatever, or the whatever, while judging. It is impossible to make, universally. Thus Duchamp, with a pun, defined genius: as the impossibility of the making.[11] And indeed this is the genius of modern art, its *Witz* but also its law. It is impossible that something, this or that, should conform to the thing-in-general.

I said earlier on that with Duchamp's readymade, the absolute whatever happened to the history of art. Now, it is not as a result of the things chosen by Duchamp that we have to say that *the readymade* amounts to absolutely anything whatever, or that it is absolutely indifferent. The readymades are not indifferent at all, and the urinal, for example, is not at all just *any* thing. Its choice was decisive of the thing and determined it. But Duchamp's maxim of choice was decisive of the choice and it undetermined it: "A point which I want very much to establish is that the choice of these 'readymades' was never dictated by esthetic delectation. This choice was based on a reaction of visual indifference with at the same time a total absence of good or bad taste . . . in fact a complete anesthesia."[12] Anesthesia, visual indifference, better, the *freedom of indifference,*

11. "'What is genius?' Marcel reads his reply: 'The impossibility of the iron [l'impossibilité du fer].' And he adds: 'Another pun, of course.'" Denis de Rougemont, "Marcel Duchamp, mine de rien," p. 45. See chapter 3.
12. *SS,* p. 141.

specify the maxim of the choice of a readymade.[13] However, it is not yet by virtue of the maxim, of indifference as a subjective attitude, that we must say that the readymade amounts to absolutely anything whatever. The maxim of choice presents the chosen thing as a specimen drawn from a totality unpresentable as such due to the fact of finitude. It presents it as an example chosen so as to be exemplary of a choice that would convey the whatever as such. Insofar as it is exemplary, the urinal Duchamp chose stands for any urinal whatever, but only relatively: he could have chosen another one drawn from a series that is only virtually infinite. Insofar as it also stands for any industrially produced good, this urinal also reads as a symbol of any thing whatever, but it would still be relatively. What forces us to say that *the readymade* (not the urinal) amounts to the absolute whatever is that through the maxim according to which Duchamp chose the urinal, according to which he judged, he was able—and with him the uninitiated spectator whose judgment he anticipated—to will that the whatever become at once a universal law: art, what one universally calls art, must be whatever and be named as art by whomever. This is the modern imperative stripped bare, the one all those artists obeyed—yet without interpreting it correctly—who gave their art an ultimate purpose set against the universalist horizon of the modern utopia par excellence: we will all be artists some day. And it's the same imperative followed by all those artists who—without interpreting it any better—conditioned their practice according to the universalist

13. The expression *freedom of indifference* is put forth in a note on the "poids à trous" in the *Large Glass* (*SS,* p. 62), but the context allows it to be interpreted in the framework of the problematic of choice, whose Duchampian formula is: "Free will = Buridan's ass." Paul Janet's *Traité élémentaire de philosophie,* which was current in French high schools during Duchamp's youth, contained a discussion of the dilemma of Buridan's ass under the heading "Liberté d'indifférence." This indicates that when Duchamp makes free will, which is no more than the condition for moral freedom, into the maxim "freedom of indifference"—a move that indicates that he is making a reflexive use of it—he understands that it is no more than the formula for authorization (for the author, the "me"), and not yet the summoning by the categorical imperative which, according to Kant, both proves and requires moral freedom.

postulate of the modern myth par excellence: we are all artists already. No wonder Joseph Beuys incarnates the end of modernity: both roads—"do whatever, in order to" and "do whatever, provided," lead to him, to both the myth and the utopia of creativity. Creativity *was* this faculty of making art supposedly shared by all human beings, and which education, social, economic, or cultural progress would some day unleash as the perfect conflation of taste and genius.[14] But Duchamp outstripped the moderns. He didn't believe in creativity; and he didn't aim for it either. That the passer-by has "taste" and even "genius" is nothing but a formal requirement of the categorical imperative of the whatever. In the matter of taste: the freedom of indifference. So much for the maxim. In the matter of genius: the impossibility of the making. So much for the law. A priori, art ought to be whatever and be called art by whomever, but the modality of this *ought,* of this subjective necessity, which remains exemplary like that which Kant required for the judgment of taste, takes the route of a negative necessity, of an impossibility.[15] So, creativity is no longer a utopian program in the form of a maxim, or a mythic belief in the form of a presupposition, it is an impossible imperative in the form of a conformity to itself, and such is the supremely ironic law of the readymade. It not only boxes the thing into the overdetermined double bind of having to be at once something and anything whatever (which is nonetheless empirically the case), it not only opens the thing to its undetermined virtuality, only exemplary—or symbolic, as Kant would have said—of standing for whatever (which remains transcendentally required), it also abandons the thing to its absolute impossibility of being determined as undetermined, that is, to its impossibility of conforming to the law or the neces-

14. See chapter 5.

15. In chapter 3, I have interpreted the "impossibility of the iron/of the making" as a mere feeling, but also, as a mandatory one, as the quasi-moral feeling that any painter sensitive to the historical conditions that have made painting useless must feel. It is obviously with the passage from the specific to the generic, from painting to art, that this subjective sense of moral obligation entails as its objective counterpart the logical, even technical, impossibility of making something—anything—that would not be *this* thing.

sity of a universal whatever. And it's precisely thanks to this abandonment that *the readymade*—and not the readymades—conforms to the universal of this impossibility. In other terms, that the phrase "this is art," as it can be applied to anything, ought to be applied to a "this" that is absolutely, or better, categorically, anything whatever.

Do Whatever So That . . .

Here, finally, is a third interpretation of the modern imperative: do whatever, so that . . . To go right to the essentials of a philosophy of art having categorically given up naming the essential, I would say, with a rather poor pun: once there is no more ontology you need a deontology. Or better, since under different light all of the following amounts to the same thing: when we no longer dare, or can, or know how to postulate or to will the universal, when the names Kant gave it, names like the Supreme Being, the Sovereign Good, the Supersensible, the *sensus communis* or even the Idea of humanity, are, for many philosophers today, in danger of being so many *Schwärmereien* for which we are in a state of mourning, then universality itself is what we must decide about in each singular instance. A superhuman philosophical and political task that possibly drove Nietzsche mad, it is also happily a human, all too human, task to which what we persist in calling art offers the basis for a practice having the symbolic value of warning. When, from inside this empirical domain—which as such doesn't need to stake a claim to universality, only to culture—the universality of art has become its impossibility and its impossibility nonetheless remains prescribed as a duty vis-à-vis universality, then art as a whole must be judged case by case. When it is more than doubtful that there exists in every man and woman on earth a universal faculty of taste and—even more doubtful—a universal conflation of taste with genius, then we must hold on to the built-in claim to universality of the sentence "this is art" in full consciousness of its impossibility to realize itself in society and in history. When the postmodern is also the posthistorical, when the presupposition or the postulate of history's direction is categorically abandoned for having been all too materialized as systemic or totalitarian menace, then history's direction must be decided here and now, locally and in what Walter Benjamin called "the instant of peril." *Hic et nunc,* but also *ad hoc:* judiciously and with "there" in view.[16]

The angel of history marches into the historical wind facing backwards. Its gaze is retrospective in a way that is not dialectical; it is not turned toward the past so as to predict the future. It judges the past in the imperative urgency of the present moment and without knowing what awaits it. Whence the infinite melancholy of the one who lives with the feeling of permanent catastrophe. The angel of history judges the past and communicates the duty to reinterpret it to the historian or the "archaeologist." It is this duty, and it alone, that I would like to call postmodern. It is modern at the same time, not because modernity is an unfinished project, as Habermas thinks—it is perhaps not finished but it is no longer a project—but because modernity must be guarded; not even safeguarded—in order to be reinterpreted, it will have to be violated—but guarded. We are the guardians of the modern tradition, a tradition to be at once translated and betrayed, as the proverb, *traduttore traditore,* says. Here are some of this reinterpretation's outlines.

(1) Modern art, at least those works that have made the modernity of modern art and of which Duchamp's readymade is exemplary in every way, has not been an autotelic activity folding its end upon its means. Neither art-for-art's-sake, nor art as art, nor art about art, does justice to what has happened. The purism and "formalism" of a large part of modern art have been the manifestations of a purely formal conformity to purposiveness, the very one that Kant called the "purposiveness without purpose" of aesthetic judgment. (2) The best works of modern art have not for that matter been subjected to external purposes, be they revolutionary in the sense of a redemptive social violence. They have not been the means or the mediums of a revolutionary program or ideology that would have justified them. They have been the manifesto of a revolu-

16. Walter Benjamin, "Theses on the Philosophy of History," in *Illuminations,* trans. Harry Zohn (New York: Schocken Books, 1968), p. 263.

tion—that, granted—the pure manifestation of this "sovereign" violence, neither means nor end, of which Benjamin had begun the conceptual elaboration.[17] (3) Modernism has not been the laboratory in which the necessary and sufficient conditions of art were tested by progressive elimination. It has not been a reductionist practice and it has not issued into essential conventions. It has been a tradition—that, granted—often inspired by the idea of an essence of art, but a tradition that never ceased judging this idea, here and there, in contingent historical circumstances, without determining criteria. (4) The era in which we live has not leveled all styles or made all avant-gardes interchangeable with each other under the universal law of the commodity. The marketing of the transavant-garde will not last. The rampant pluralism of the artworld is only the fear of judgment and its opportunism a lack of integrity. But ours is a time of peril in which, not by accident, practices are summoned up from the past, some to maintain repression, others to testify as symptoms, others still to re-judge.

The categorical imperative is the imperative of judgment. To make art is to judge art, to decide, to choose. "Making something," said Duchamp, "is choosing a tube of blue, a tube of red, putting some of it on the palette, and always choosing the quality of the blue, the quality of the red, and always choosing the place to put it on the canvas, it's always choosing. . . . Choice is the main thing, even in normal painting."[18] The categorical imperative enjoins the modern artist to choose in the absence of criteria not because artistic criteria no longer exist and because in our era of "moral dissipation" art has foundered in the laxity of the whatever, but because the criteria, norms, and conventions

17. In "Critique of Violence" (Walter Benjamin, *Reflections,* trans. Edmund Jephcott [New York: Schocken Books, 1986], 277–300), an extraordinary rich and dense text that remains enigmatic in many ways. This text today asks to be reread and projected into its own intertextual network, where Kant is discreetly played off against Hegel or Marx, and also where Sorel is played off against Kant and Nietzsche against himself.

18. Marcel Duchamp, interview by Georges Charbonnier, radio interviews, RTF, 1961 (my translation).

that structure the practice of one artist are for another artist but someone else's maxim. And no maxim can be instituted as a universal law. However, this doesn't prevent maxims—norms, criteria, styles, if you prefer—from being transmitted from one artist to another, from one group to another, or from one era to another. It's what is called influence on the individual level and tradition on the collective one. But influence is a causal concept that is incapable of explaining the evolution of art without postulating ruptures of influence that are always very visible at the moment but fade with distance. And since it is solely interpretive whereas it should be evaluative, what this concept fails to take into account is that when a maxim is transmitted it is also rejudged. The concept of influence should be banished from the vocabulary of art history. As for that of tradition, it should on the contrary be kept, in both senses of the term: it should be preserved and it should be guarded, as should the modern tradition itself. For there is a tradition of the whatever, and it's neither the tradition of the anti-tradition nor the tradition of the new. We have been long warned about the massive failure of the first, since futurism, to be precise. When artists receive the imperative of the whatever as given ultimate purpose by the future, they also receive it as a command to make a tabula rasa of the past. This started with the slogan about burning the museums and ended in an apology for total war. Perhaps Fascism and Nazism were the *Gesamtkunstwerk* of a Hegelian vision of history where the whatever replaced the Absolute Spirit. The paradoxical lesson of this tragic history, if one can draw a lesson from it, is that the politicization of art is not the response to the aestheticization of politics. When Benjamin wrote that, Auschwitz was still a futurist prognosis and his own melancholy had not yet driven him to suicide.[19] This lesson, if there is one,

19. I certainly don't want to overlook the dramatic circumstances that provoked Benjamin's suicide at the Franco-Spanish border in September of 1940. But it in no way detracts from the exemplary historical character of this suicide to remark—as Gershom Scholem has moreover (*Walter Benjamin: The History of a Friendship* [Philadelphia: Jewish Publication Society of America, 1981])—that Benjamin was tempted by suicide well before. To the contrary, we

is that like the word *tradition* the word *art* as well must be kept—no doubt less for its impossible universality than for its specific finitude of being only one social practice among others—if one wants to avoid coming, or returning, to total war considered as one of the fine arts.

No more than an anti-tradition, that of the whatever was not a tradition of the new. From Baudelaire to Rosenberg the new was just one of the maxims of modernism, conforming to only one of the two aspects of its imperative, which also prescribed that it be disobeyed: be new, but be classical too, be classical in being new. It has been some time now since we became aware that the tradition of the new is running in a circle. It's running so much in a circle that, for today's historicism, the latest novelty is to revive old styles. The paradoxical lesson of this farce, pathetic perhaps but at least harmless, for once, is that the word *art,* which must be kept, must also be forsaken, abandoned to its insignificance and to the indifference with which the uninitiated, who knows best, judges it. Put otherwise, the socialization of art, which has to blur the contours of the word in order to put it on equal footing with all other kinds of signifying practices, is the response to the sickening circular cooptation of its institutionalization.

What's left to be said is the lesson of these two lessons. There is a tradition of the whatever, there is a history of the whatever, with regard to which it is now possible to unravel the historical paradox encountered at the outset of this chapter. It aligns judgments, since each work that is part of this history is made up of nothing but judgments, of choices. But this alignment is neither linear nor circular: neither progress nor status quo; neither escalation nor tautology. This history or this tradition is transmitted from one artist to another, from one art movement to another, from one historical moment to another, and from

might wonder if Benjamin, who for example wrote, "Modernism must be under the sign of suicide. . . . It is *the* achievement of modernism in the realm of passions" (*Charles Baudelaire,* p. 75), would have had so clearsighted a conception of melancholy as a historical feeling if it had not been for his own melancholic tendencies.

one work to another as judgments are transmitted, that is, through judgment: as rejudged prejudices retrospectively constituting a jurisprudential record. The history of the modern avant-gardes, now that their violence is "recuperated" by and in the discourse of historians and now that the conflicts having propelled it have become historical objects, reveals itself to have been much less war-like than juridical. That's why the word *avant-garde* disturbs so many people today; it can't be bypassed by substituting the transavant-garde for it, especially when despite all its denials the latter pretends to be the latest avant-garde.

The judgment through which the tradition of the whatever is transmitted—that is, must I repeat? translated and betrayed—is aesthetic judgment. Today as in the time of Kant, who was the first to establish its form and this once and for all, aesthetic judgment is a reflexive judgment. Its form, "form of purposiveness" reflected by the "purposiveness of form," is neither linear nor circular; if it could be represented it would sooner be—right, Marcel?—spiraled, like the idea of a circle that doesn't know what a circle is, so that it escapes it. It doesn't lead from conditions to consequences; neither does it lead from a projected goal to the means of obtaining it, and from the means to the achieved goal. Art is not the condition, norm, or citerion of what artists do, any more than it is its consequence, result, or effect. Neither is art the project, goal, objective of what artists do, any more than it is its means, medium, or technique. This is not to say that art is not to be found in the outcome of what artists make as well as in the making itself, or that it is to be sought in the idea of art and in its name, in the regulative idea by which one judges art so as to name it as such. Here for the last time is the law of the readymade, the law of the modern: do whatever so that it be called art. But make it such that, through what you will have made—the thing resulting from your maxim—you make it felt that this something was imposed on you by an idea of the anything whatever that is its rule. This regulative idea can be an idea of the beautiful or of the sublime, an idea of painting or of any other medium, an idea of revolution, an idea of real or utopian society, an idea of the artist or an idea of art or of the non-artist and non-art. This regulative idea that truly imposes itself can be whatever idea, so that you can act as if all such ideas were simultaneously valid, and imperatively valid. Act as if you had to take them all together for maxim, so that what you will do will conform to any idea whatever, to the universal, i.e., impossible, Idea of the whatever, this very Idea that modernity precisely called art.

The modern tradition was the network of transmission of two names, of two proper names.[20] Up until Dada the name of art was at stake in every art practice. Fights around it and for it were engaged in. The establishment and the avant-garde, but also the various avant-gardes among themselves, disputed over it, often by way of refusal, as was the case in France, sometimes by way of secession, as was the case in Central Europe. With the readymade, with Duchamp, it is as if the name of art, devoid of meaning—for proper names have no meaning, they only have referents–had tumbled into the condition of the proper name in general, of any proper name, a name whose referents, without ceasing to be singular objects, could just as well take on any name whatever, whether they would be baptized anew, like *Fountain,* or left with their common noun, like *Hat Rack.* So that the name of art became synonymous with anything-whatever. Such is the judgment of the uninitiated today, after Dada and its "recuperation." Such is also that of the "expert" (although, as you see, it's obviously not a matter of expertise) who, along with Duchamp but with some delay, judges the judgment of the uninitiated convincing and reflects on it: modern art is the reign of the anything-whatever. That's what's said in the streets. What's said here is the same but ought to be a little more precise: the regulative Idea of modern art, after Dada, was the whatever.

I just named this Idea, and throughout this chapter I have named it often, making it into a substantive by saying *the* whatever. Now, things can be named only when they are nameable, that is, somehow finished, shaped, defined. Only then are we allowed to name on solid grounds and in order to describe. It's for the purpose of description, of historical truth if you will, that I availed myself of the uninitiated's judgment and of its anticipation on the part of Rrose Sélavy: I named the whatever; it is the postmodern name of modern art. But I can't

20. See chapter 1.

side-step my responsibility. I had to name and I couldn't wait for whether things were at all nameable. There was an urgency prompting me to call modern art by that particular name; like Benjamin, I could not escape the somewhat melancholic feeling of the one who senses permanent catastrophe, his back turned into the wind of history. It blows hard and I don't know what it blows. In any event there is little if no pleasure in having to say that modern art was the reign of the whatever, even keeping in mind its contradictory richness. And this is no longer a description, it's a judgment; it's no longer a name, it's a tone of voice.

Is it a pessimistic tone? No. The pessimist expects something from the future, he expects the worst. Is it a realist tone? No. The realist is resigned. Is it a disenchanted tone? Yes. Modernity hasn't kept its promises. Is it a despairing tone? Yes and no. If hope is always turned towards the future, then this tone should be that of the hopeless ones, of all the hopeless ones of this world. But it should also be that of hope—once a theological virtue and, since Ernst Bloch, a principle—this hope about which Benjamin said that it is only problematically given to those whom all hope has first abandoned. But he who signs these lines doesn't feel he has the right to speak with this tone. He is much too privileged to be able to speak with the intonation of the hopeless ones. He is also too modern, still, too full of false hopes, arrogance, and immaturity, too depending, in his historical and private being, on the Promethean pride of modernism, to have reached the depths of despair. In writing this text he felt painfully run through by an injunction beyond his will and summoned by its imperative tone, which he had indeed to take on. But he is suspicious. Too much pathos, still, and not enough ethos. After all he is but a child of his times, and the imperatives of the time are perhaps only circumstantial and not as categorical as he might think. But that's precisely what he wanted to say! One must judge *hic et nunc;* when the universal is impossible, there are only circumstances! So, now that he has spoken and judged, he has nothing to verify his judgment with except his feelings. And these tell him that it is very hard, and perhaps impossible, to judge whether the tone that grips his voice is that of the categorical imperative or that

of the double bind. For there was more than just pain and fear entering the writing of this text. There was also enthusiasm and much joy. But even the joy is ambivalent. It was that of discovery, of words that come easily to the pen, of ideas that arrange themselves on their own. It was the joy of seeing the description of an archaeological site compose itself without engaging the responsibility of its scribe, for he wasn't its author. The circumstances of modernity, in being ordered, ordered him to describe it thus. That stands, that doesn't belong to him, the ground is cleared, one can look ahead anew. But precisely here the scribe falls prey to suspicion, again. Isn't this joy impure and interested? What if it were once again the vengeful joy of mastery? Hasn't the scribe once more been the plaything of a ruse of history? Hasn't he given in to a seductive maneuver, his own, as if despite himself he wanted to extort from history a supply of future? Is he really free of Hegel, of the Hegel who lies dormant in every theoretician? He wants to cry out as a way of concluding without concluding: yes, stop accusing me! Anticipation is not just the desire for prediction and mastery, it is the biological duty of humankind! Humans themselves are premature; and so was modernity! But this would still be a judgment. Who is he to dare? Isn't he premature too? Shouldn't decency force him to retract his judgment on the spot? He will cry, still more indecently yet: premature? Yes, I have come too early. But if he cries that, especially if it's not in the wilderness, then the tone of his voice will sound too much, infinitely too much not to be ridiculous, like the sublime tone of the prophet. And the vice will retighten, Hegel will be avenged again, this time as a farce. Does the one who recites these lines in a tone that never has the ring of truth want to finish up with the prophets of doom and those of liberation, with the two prophetic faces of modernity, that of the Cité radieuse and that of Metropolis? But who does he think he is? He's now playing the prophet himself! And yet, since ending is a must and avoiding conclusion another, sanity perhaps requires that one ends with the irony of the farce. Or with its *ironism of affirmation,* as Duchamp said, who, as you well know, never spoke in the tones of a prophet, something that didn't prevent his posterity from reserving him a choice place among the prophets of contemporary art. A spurious etymology, which amuses me all the more that it is incorrect but has been made—so it seems—by the people, wants *prophet* to be related to *profane*.[21] In the Hebrew tradition the prophet receives the command to speak the law, he doesn't predict the future. And the profane, the uninitiated, stands before the temple, before the law. In short he keeps it. If the prophet speaks with the tone of the profane, then I am set free: he who just spoke of the anything-whatever could have been anyone whoever.

---

21. Profane comes from the Latin *pro-fanum,* "before the temple," and prophet from the Greek, *pro-phèmi,* "to speak ahead." In order that the first derive from the second, one would have to establish that *fanum* derives from *fari,* "to speak." The *Lateinisches etymologisches Wörterbuch* by A. Walde says in the article *fanum:* "Die Ableitung der Alten von *fari* (Paul. Fest. 88.93) ist trotz Vanicek 180, Prellwitz BB. 22, 79 (als "Bann" oder "Zugesprochenes Geweihtes") nur Volksetymologie."

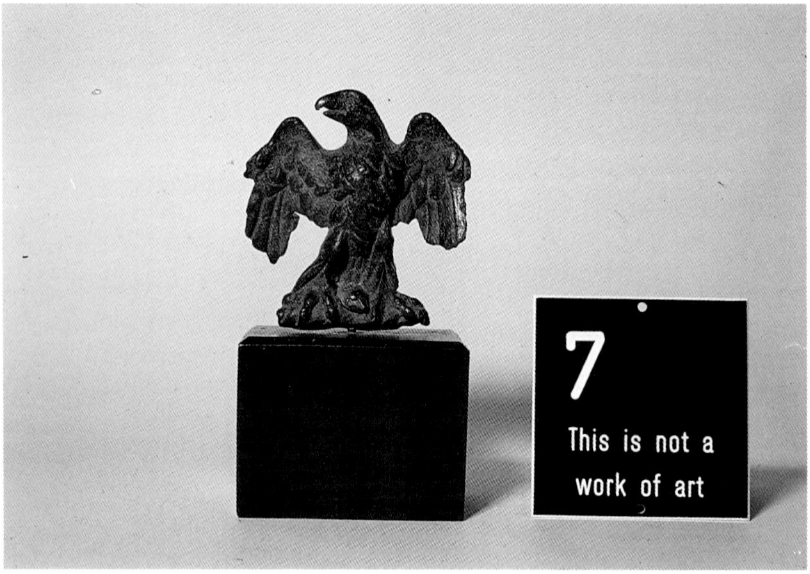

Marcel Broodthaers, Object from the exhibition "Der Adler vom Oligozän bis heute," Städtische Kunsthalle Düsseldorf, 1972 (eagle with spread wings, Roman, bronze, 5.6 × 5.3 cm, Staatliche Museen Stiftung Preussischer Kulturbesitz, Antikenabteilung, Berlin). Courtesy Maria Gilissen-Broodthaers.

Part IV:

After and Before

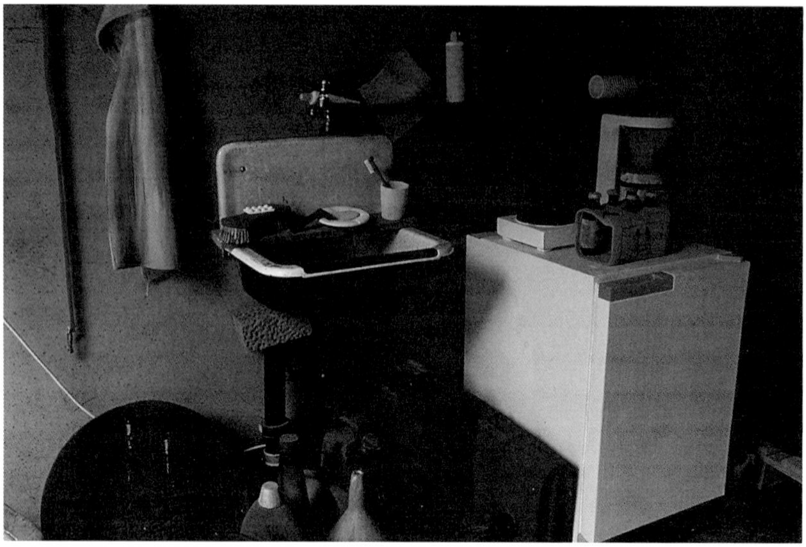

Peter Fischli/David Weiss, *Untitled*, 1991, hand-carved and painted polyurethane objects, installation in the exhibition "Chamer Raüme," Cham, Switzerland. Courtesy the artists.

7

Archaeology of Pure Modernism

> I identify Modernism with the intensification, almost the exacerbation, of this self-critical tendency that began with the philosopher Kant. Because he was the first to criticize the means itself of criticism, I conceive of Kant as the first real Modernist. The essence of Modernism lies, as I see it, in the use of the characteristic methods of a discipline to criticize the discipline itself—not in order to subvert it, but to entrench it more firmly in its area of competence. Kant used logic to establish the limits of logic, and while he withdrew much from its old jurisdiction, logic was left in all the more secure possession of what remained to it.
>
> —*Clement Greenberg*[1]

With a Grain of Salt

What about a modernist mayonnaise presenting itself to a formalist culinary critic's judgment of taste? He finds it awful but he doesn't stop with his own

1. Greenberg, "Modernist Painting," p. 66.

judgment. This mayonnaise is put together in such a manner, he says to himself while tasting it, that something of the pure ingredients that go into it are to be found in the final results.[2] It brings off the feat of displaying its composition to me, of taking the "conventions of mayonnaise" for its subject matter, of being a self-referential mayonnaise, a "mayonnaise about mayonnaise," in short, a critique of mayonnaise brought about by the means of mayonnaise itself, "not to subvert it, but to entrench it more firmly in its area of competence." Perhaps it isn't very successful, tasting something like Heinz. But it has "taken," and the emulsion is all the more mysterious in that the cook's handiwork is not apparent, even though it ends up telling me, if I examine it closely enough, that the necessary and sufficient conditions of mayonnaise-in-general are four in number: egg yolk, oil, vinegar, and mustard. The grain of salt is optional.

Or perhaps mandatory, given that the salt was of course sprinkled over the modernist mayonnaise by *Marchand du sel* himself. Please keep this in mind, for we are going to play Greenberg's game and ask ourselves if Duchamp was not, after all, a modernist; if he has not exacerbated "this self-critical tendency that began with the philosopher Kant"; if he has not used "the characteristic methods of a discipline . . . to entrench it more firmly in its area of competence." In the same way that modernist mayonnaises are an exception, not all modern art is modernist. To be modernist is to be a work that takes its own conditions of possibility for its subject matter, that tests a certain number of the conventions of the practice it belongs to by modifying, jettisoning, or destroying them, and that in so doing renders the conventions or conditions thus tested explicit or opaque, revealing them to be nothing but conventions. At the end of this process we should find isolated—stripped bare—the "essential conventions," otherwise called the necessary and sufficient conditions of the given practice, visible

2. "Something of the harmony of the original white square of canvas should be restored in the finished painting." Clement Greenberg, "Review of Mondrian's *New York Boogie Woogie* and Other New Acquisitions at the Museum of Modern Art," in *Collected Essays and Criticism* 1:153.

or legible in the work itself. Fine. Does Duchamp's work do that? I wish I could offer a straightforward answer, but unfortunately I can't, at least not on Greenberg's terms. Clearly, Duchamp's work performs something of that kind; it invites a self-critical or self-referential reading that makes it appear as art about art, that is, as works of art testing their own conditions of possibility. But just as clearly, Greenberg's definition of modernism doesn't quite fit the Duchampian mayonnaise . . . too much salt; too *uncharacteristic*. There are in fact three problematic terms in Greenberg's conception, the first two in need of clarification, the third in need of total displacement, before the topic of Duchamp's modernism can be broached: (1) discipline; (2) convention; (3) critique. Let's review the evidence gathered in the previous chapters.

Of Disciplines: Restricted and Generalized Modernism

Something unprecedented in the whole history of art surfaced in the sixties: it had become legitimate to be an artist without being either a painter, or a poet, or a musician, or a sculptor, novelist, architect, photographer, choreographer, filmmaker, etc. A new "category" of art appeared—art in general, or art at large—that was no longer absorbed in the traditional disciplines. With conceptual art, the possibility of making art in general came to be interpreted as if it were a new artistic discipline in it own right, and the paternity for this was attributed to Duchamp. Kosuth says this plainly: "In fact it is Marcel Duchamp whom we can credit with giving art its own identity. . . . All art (after Duchamp) is conceptual (in nature) because art only exists conceptually."[3] As I have shown in chapter 4, it is from a struggle with, and to a large extent within the Greenbergian doctrine of modernism that this interpretation—misinterpretation, actually—at the root of a large part of conceptual art arose. If Kosuth took the expression "conceptual art" from Sol LeWitt, it is from Donald Judd

3. Kosuth, "Art after Philosophy I and II," p. 80.

that he borrowed his argument in favor of an art that pushes the "logic" of modernism beyond the limits that Greenberg's doctrine seemed to impose on it. But while Judd used the term *specific objects* for the minimalist hybrids of painting and sculpture that he interpreted as being neither the one nor the other, Kosuth envisaged a practice that would not be painting or sculpture, or anything else related to a specific medium or discipline, and which would isolate, as such, the nature of art in general: "Being an artist now means to question the nature of art. If one is questioning the nature of painting, one cannot be questioning the nature of art. . . . That's because the word *art* is general and the word *painting* is specific."[4]

To question the nature of art through the means of art is of course a strategy that corresponds perfectly to the definition of modernism given by Greenberg in "Modernist Painting." However, while Greenberg could not conceive of any areas of artistic competence that weren't specific, discipline by discipline, medium by medium, Kosuth meant to submit modernist art pure and simple to analysis. He harnessed conceptual art to the program of accomplishing the passage from a restricted modernism to a general one. In this he seized on something very sound, but since he didn't admit that, according to Greenberg, modernism was never a program but an involuntary tendency that one can only attest to retrospectively, neither did he admit that art pure and simple cannot possibly be a discipline. Followed by most commentators of conceptual art (even some of those who strongly criticized him), he thus committed several theoretical mistakes and one ethical fault: he had the activity of the artist rest not on formal appreciation and practice but rather on declarative intentions and on conceptual knowledge of the "logic" of modernism. He took the word "art" to be a concept instead of a proper name. He claimed to break with all the art of the past and to substitute a linguistic model for an aesthetic one. He saw art after Duchamp as radically cut off from the technical and aesthetic conventions of any specific art form. He wanted to grant art a new status as a discipline in a quasi-scientific sense, whose task was to investigate the linguistic nature and the

4. Ibid., p. 79.

conceptual content of the word "art." Finally, he made of art a professional activity that addresses other professionals and excludes practically everybody else. Each of these comes very close to the truth but each is nonetheless wrong, the irony being that when Kosuth set up the goal of widening the modernist procedure to art at large, it was way too late. Tongue-in-cheek, Marcel Duchamp lay in wait for him.

His first unassisted readymade—the bottle rack—dates from 1914. A bottle rack is neither a painting nor a poem nor a piece of music nor even a sculpture; it's art, or else it's nothing. And so is a mustachioed reproduction of the Mona Lisa; and so is the ball of twine called *A bruit secret;* and so are the rotoreliefs; and so is the door, 11 rue Larrey, which is never open or closed; and so is the *Large Glass,* although it is painted; and so are the notes in the *Green Box,* although they are poetic; and so is *Etant donnés,* for which the word "installation" had not yet been coined; and so on. It is tempting to say that not just the readymades but the whole of Duchamp's oeuvre has already achieved the reduction of art in general to its necessary and sufficient conditions. (Indeed, I shall say so, but not before Greenberg's notion of modernism as a *critique* that began "with the philosopher Kant" has been totally displaced.) Kosuth, I'm sure, must have felt this very strongly when he tried to come to terms with both the tasks of doing art after Duchamp and of carrying Greenberg's modernism beyond the boundaries where all disciplines have melted down and all conventions have dissolved. It is therefore not surprising at all—though it is the height of irony—that it is precisely when all a priori knowledge had withdrawn from the word "art" that conceptual art set out to investigate its cognitive content. Precisely when it surfaced that "art" could only be a proper name emptied of all knowable meaning was this unacknowledged revelation strongly felt as the urge to seek out its meaning and to determine what the necessary and sufficient conditions of art as concept might be.

Of Conventions: Test and Testimony

As Kosuth and Greenberg both knew, artistic disciplines are defined by their conventions—or conditions. In premodern times, artists—say, painters—were practitioners of a given discipline who *knew* beforehand what technical and aesthetic constraints their productions had to meet in order to be conceptually identified as paintings. Their knowledge of painting was an inextricable mixture of intellectual familiarity, technical know-how and aesthetic discernment—all acquired through workshop apprenticeship or academic training and controlled by the painters' guilds or by the Academy. Which means they *knew* who they were and whom they addressed. The technical-aesthetic rules of their trade reigned inside the studio, but as conventions established with the outside world, for a convention is always a tacit, unreflected upon, semiunconscious social pact that ties artists to their public—something that Greenberg knew but rarely worked out explicitly. With the onset of modernism, painters began to challenge the technical-aesthetic conventions deemed necessary and sufficient to identify a given thing as a painting, by putting them through an aesthetic test. From then on, the appreciation of art, instead of bearing upon qualities contained within those conventions, began to bear upon those conventions themselves and upon whether or not the artist was allowed to transgress them. Thus, the test had to be read reflexively, as a testimony, witnessing to the necessity of renegotiating the social pact around a given technical-aesthetic rule. The Salon des Refusés brought the consequences into full daylight, involuntarily instituting the fact that henceforth the appreciation of modernist art, instead of expressing itself by formulas such as "this painting is beautiful," could not avoid taking the binary form of a yes or no specific to painting as such: "this is a painting" or "this is not a painting."[5] At this point (I'm summarizing horribly), "painting" has become a word void of a priori knowledge about the minimum rules and conventions its practice must obey; it is no longer a concept; instead it has become the proper name with which I baptize the things that I judge deserve

5. Something that Mallarmé's admonition to the 1874 Salon jury would take stock of: "Entrusted with the nebulous vote of the painters with the responsibility of choosing, from among the framed pictures offered, those that are really paintings in order to show them to us, the jury has nothing else to say but: this is a painting, or that is not a painting." See chapter 4.

to be so called. It remained for the history of modernist painting, as told by Greenberg, to empty actual paintings of even their most elementary rules and conventions so that the illusion is produced that one had arrived at stripping bare the one and only necessary and sufficient condition of all paintings: flatness.

Now, here is the crux of the matter. Duchamp read the binary choice between painting and not-painting as a "convention." He went straight to the tacit, semiunconscious pact that, since 1863, has bound artists to the Salon public. He perceived that, without really wanting to and without really knowing it, artists and public have since then played a game whose sole rule was that the former propose to the latter things designed to test its willingness to allow these things to enter the "category" of painting (or of sculpture), despite the occasionally crude way they manhandled the technical-aesthetic conventions of their craft. Whereas modernist painters took these conventions as the subject matter of their studio practice, tampering with them, deconstructing them and abandoning them one by one until there remained only the pure and simple flatness of the picture, Duchamp adopted this single rule of the game as the subject matter of his own practice, which was no longer a studio practice but, so to speak, a Salon practice. He made this rule explicit and treated it *as if* it were understood by convention that the *status* of the work of art were to be a thing to which the public had conceded the *quality* of painting or sculpture, and nothing else. The test, as we have seen, took place at the Independents' Show of 1917. Withdrawing from the thing he exhibited—*Fountain*—all trace of craft and every conventional alibi allowing one to identify it as painting or as sculpture, he insisted that it be appreciated for its quality as work of art, period. Art in general. In other words, he made the judgment (of quality) bear on the very fact of having to judge whether *status* equals *quality*.

With a gesture of exemplary economy, Duchamp went straight to the most primary convention, the most elementary (I don't say "essential") of all *modernist* artistic practice, namely that *works of art are shown in order to be judged as such*. It is as if, almost fifty years before Greenberg's "Modernist Painting" and Kosuth's conceptual art, he had seen through all the conventions that modernist painting had made opaque—including the flatness of the canvas, witness the *Large*

Glass—and had made opaque the one convention that all convinced modernists had seen through, because it had been their unconscious agreement: that works of art are shown in order to be judged as art, and nothing else (which means: for their quality as art; which also means: by way of a sentence such as "this is art").[6] He has thus made explicit the borderline between art and non-art; he has made visible the fact that each time the pact around a technical-aesthetic rule of the discipline is broken, another one needs to be negotiated about the legitimacy of breaking the first. Works of modernist art are shown to their public for no other purpose than begging approval and/or provoking disapproval.[7] Such is the convention he took as subject matter for *Fountain,* and which he submitted to a radical test. Behold a urinal. Either you judge that it's nothing, or that it's art. But once you judge it to be the latter, it carries, implicitly at least, a label saying: "this is art." *Fountain* passed the test and the label attached to it now remains as the testimony that it did pass. It is now a historical fact that *Fountain* was judged a work of art. Given this historical fact, it is tempting to say that *Fountain* has accomplished the reduction of art in general to its one necessary and sufficient condition; or that, in due modernist fashion, it has done for art at large what the blank canvas would have done for the art of painting. And this, with an advance of some fifty years.

In chapter 6, I spent some time with the aporias that would result from yielding to this temptation; in chapter 5, with the proper aesthetic understanding of the judgment that works of art are begging; in chapter 4, with a critical rereading of the parallel between the readymade and the blank canvas; in chapter 3, with Duchamp's regulative idea in comparison with that of the early modernist painters; in chapter 2, with a careful analysis of the particulars of the

6. See my reading of the articulation of Greenberg's formalism with his modernism in chapter 4.

7. Couched in the terms of the previous chapter, it may be said that Duchamp reinscribes the "Do whatever, in order to . . ." of the avant-garde into the "Do whatever provided . . ." of modernism.

Richard Mutt case; and in chapter 1, with a notion of art-historical facts as jurisprudence allowing both the initiated and the uninitiated to retain their freedom of judgment while accounting for the existence of an avant-garde tradition. And yet, a few puzzling things remain: the feeling that *Fountain* is perhaps the strongest instance of reductive *art about art* persists; the opposite feeling that *Fountain* is rich in meaning in no way reducible to a self-referential comment also insists; similarly, the feeling that it is not fair, even absurd, to cut off the readymades from the rest of Duchamp's oeuvre; and finally, the feeling that in spite of my conviction that a readymade is art only if you judge it as such,[8] the given fact that a label saying "this is art" is now attached to *Fountain* indicates a point of no return. "Given"—*étant donné*—is a very Duchampian word, and it prescribes a retrospective viewpoint that forbids the erasure of the label attached to *Fountain*. A break—perhaps a break with modernism—has happened, and it is worthwhile to ask wherein it consists. I said a little earlier that Duchamp has made *visible* the fact that each time the pact around a technical-aesthetic rule of the discipline is broken, another one needs to be negotiated about the legitimacy of breaking the first. But he certainly hasn't made this *visible* in the same way that a painter does, for whom the broken convention—in the sense of the broken pact—also materializes on the canvas in the visible form of broken conventions—in the sense of manhandled technique or violated aesthetic criteria. He has made the borderline between art and non-art visible, but then only to *gray matter,* not in a *retinal* sense. To all appearances, we are thus dealing with a boundary between a concept and its negation, a linguistic opposition and not a visible form, in Greenberg's sense.

8. This conviction is both a methodological and an ethical rule. Methodologically, it is always more fruitful to take sides with the nonbelievers, and ethically, with the adversaries of modern art, in order to arrive at a sound theory and at a strong defense of modernism. No serious, sophisticated plea in favor of a continuation of the avant-garde (whatever its new name might be) will succeed, unless it takes into account the vantage point of those who are left out of, or even who resist, the artworld and its conventions. The fact that more and more revisionists now dare to speak like philistines makes this ethical rule risky but all the more urgent to obey.

Of Critique: Linguistic and Enunciative Paradigm

Hence the strong impression that with this switch from the visual to the linguistic, the ultimate modernist reduction is no longer modernist; that by dint of having been exacerbated, the modernist mayonnaise turned into something else; that "the exacerbation of this self-critical tendency that began with the philosopher Kant," and whose "essence lies in the use of the characteristic methods of a discipline to criticize the discipline itself," has ended in the abandonment of all specific art disciplines and in the introduction of brand-new characteristic methods. Kosuth's "separation between aesthetics and art," his theory according to which "works of art are analytic propositions" that "express definitions of art," his conclusion that "art operates on a logic," are relatively coherent attempts to register the linguistic turn which the readymade had imprinted on the history of modernism as early as 1917. Why this linguistic turn had to wait until the sixties to prompt artists to act on it involves the particular conditions of reception in which the formalist/minimalist controversy thrived; it also has to do with the fact that not until the sixties had the humanities accomplished their own linguistic turn, when Saussurian linguistics provided the matrix for structuralism. It would soon be accommodated by art and art theory, at the cost, I should say, of a considerable misinterpretation of what art is about. I have been critical enough of Kosuth. Though he is a bit isolated in his usage of logical positivism, he is by no means alone among practitioners and commentators of conceptual art to have insisted on a complete break amounting to something of a paradigm shift from formalism to structuralism. The common view about conceptual art is to read in it the "awareness of the fact that art is a (visual) language system, determined . . . in a manner very analogous to the Saussurian model," or to see it as a way "to replace the object of spatial and perceptual experience by linguistic definition alone."[9] And its

9. Claude Gintz, "'L'art conceptuel, une perspective': Notes on an Exhibition Project," and Benjamin Buchloh, "From the Aesthetic of Administration to Institutional Critique (Some

common argumentation posits formalism—which is made a foil and caricatured in the process—as a theory for which meaning is a direct emanation of form, and structuralism as one for which meaning is born out of opposition. Allegedly, for the formalists certain meanings are attached to certain formal characteristics—the way, globally, "modernism" as a signified is attached to "flatness" as a signifier. For the structuralists, signification itself arises from sheer differences among opposed terms (cutting through signifiers and signifieds alike) rather than from those terms themselves.[10] In *Fountain,* the structuralist reading finds of course a privileged case, since its significance cannot be attached to its form but rather must arise from the very alternative—art or non art?—which it raises as a question. Answering the question by judging aesthetically doesn't interest the structuralist reading; whatever meaning it produces is a critical function of the opposition art/not art—critical, because the opposition needs to be maintained so that the whole enterprise does not fall back onto the "essentialist" position ascribed to formalism. There is nothing more passé for the structuralists than the choice between art and non-art. But there is nothing more relevant for the structuralists than the opposition of art and non-art *qua* opposition. It belongs to, indeed it constitutes, *Fountain*'s "art-meaning." Clearly, the structuralists take it for granted that *Fountain* has reached them with its label saying "this is art" attached to it. They read the point of no return that forbids an erasure of *Fountain*'s art status as if it meant that the most primary convention

Aspects of Conceptual Art 1962 1969)," both in *L'art conceptuel, une perspective* (Paris: Musée d'art moderne de la Ville de Paris, 1989), pp. 20, 41.

10. Exemplary of this structuralist view is an article by Rosalind Krauss on Peter Eisenman ("Death of a Hermeneutic Phantom: Materialization of the Sign in the Work of Peter Eisenman," *a + u,* January 1980), which takes as its explicit subject the cultural change involved in the passage from modernism to postmodernism, couched in terms of a paradigm shift from formalism to structuralism. It has exemplary value because it expresses the views of someone who openly acknowledges her ex-formalism and her ex-modernism at the very moment when she seeks her way out. (She had first expressed her initial struggle with her own formalist/modernist background in "A View of Modernism," *Artforum,* September 1972.)

of all modernist artistic practice, the one Duchamp precisely made explicit, namely that *works of art are shown in order to be judged as such,* were no more valid, whereas in fact it prescribes a retrospective viewpoint—something entirely different.

Of all the so-called conceptual artists, Marcel Broodthaers is the only one to have understood the real implications of that retrospective viewpoint, the only one to have seen that once the convention according to which works of art are shown in order to be judged as such has been made explicit and the work that tested this convention has successfully passed the test, then the new convention is that *works of art are shown already judged as such,* and that a new pact must be negotiated concerning the legitimacy of breaking that convention in turn. The 266 objects he gathered together and displayed in his role as curator for his exhibition at the Kunsthalle in Düsseldorf in 1972, titled *The Eagle from the Oligocene to the Present,* were all accompanied by a label stipulating "This is not a work of art."[11] Some of those objects were recognized works of art, some were mere cultural artefacts such as beer bottle labels or cigar bands. All depicted eagles, and all were borrowed from public or private collections. In the catalogue, Broodthaers specifies that these labels "illustrate an idea of Marcel Duchamp and of René Magritte," juxtaposes on two facing pages the photograph of Duchamp's *Fountain* and a reproduction of Magritte's *Treachery of Images,* and advises his reader in passing to read Michel Foucault's essay "This Is Not a Pipe," now famous but little known at the time.[12] How could we understand that "'This is not a work of art' is a formula obtained by the contraction of a concept by Duchamp and an antithetical concept by Magritte," as Broodthaers said in his interview with Irmeline Lebeer in 1974, if it were not by

11. *Museum,* catalogue in two volumes of the exhibition *Der Adler vom Oligozän bis heute,* subtitled *Marcel Broodthaers zeigt eine experimentelle Ausstellung seines Musée d'Art Moderne, Département des Aigles, Section des Figures,* Städtische Kunsthalle Düsseldorf, 1972.

12. Michel Foucault, *Ceci n'est pas une pipe* (Paris: Fata Morgana, 1973); trans. James Harkness, *This Is Not a Pipe* (Berkeley: University of California Press, 1983).

assuming that the "concept" inherited from Duchamp is to have transposed the given fact that a candidate for the status of art has successfully passed the test into words that say so ("this is a work of art"), and that the "concept" inherited from Magritte is to have translated the figurative or iconic function of painting (or of images) into words that speak of this translation.[13] Indeed, in *The Treachery of Images,* the drawing showing the pipe has to be translated by the ostensive statement, "this is a pipe," in order for us to understand that it is immediately contradicted by the explicit linguistic statement, "Ceci n'est pas une pipe," spelled out on the painting. It is obvious that without this translation from the ostensive to the discursive, which everyone spontaneously performs, the work wouldn't "function." And it is just as obvious that if Broodthaers hadn't understood that the contribution of this work was to make this translation explicit by playing on the convention according to which images show things ("this" designating at times the image, at times its referent), and that the contribution of *Fountain* had been to make the convention explicit according to which works of art are shown in order to be judged as such, the idea of contracting "This is not a pipe" and "this is a work of art" would never have occurred to him. Or better put, the idea that you would have to go through Magritte to negate "this is a work of art" would be absurd. Contrary to Kosuth, who claims to engineer the passage from restricted to general modernism when that had already been accomplished since the time of the very first unassisted readymade, Broodthaers registers its consequences, by contracting a convention that is restricted to iconic representation and a convention that is valid for art in general. Even though he sometimes seems to share the "conceptual" and structuralist view (as in the Düsseldorf catalogue, where he joins Kosuth by saying that "Since Duchamp the artist is the author of a definition"), his contraction of Duchamp and Magritte is the best plea I know in favor of the proper understanding of the

13. "Dix mille francs de récompense," interview by Irmeline Lebeer, in *Marcel Broodthaers, Catalogue* (Brussels: Palais des Beaux-Arts, 1974); trans. Paul Schmidt, "Ten Thousand Francs Reward," *October* 42 (Fall 1987): 47.

linguistic turn taken by art practice and theory alike in the days of conceptual art. His mention of Foucault's essay on Magritte is a clue.

For all the talk of paradigm shifts, the irony is that the structuralists and the conceptualists have acknowledged receipt of the given—of the *étant donné*—in Duchamp's readymade within the wrong paradigm. Structuralism is not the pertinent framework for the linguistic turn that *Fountain* imprinted on art. Neither the linguistic paradigm (signifier/signified, language/speech, synchrony/diachrony, etc.), nor the logical paradigm (analytical or synthetic propositions, etc.), nor even the pragmatic paradigm (which stresses the performativity of language), have replaced or dispaced the need for aesthetics, which remains as valid as ever when it comes to art, because the question is not one of paradigm shift but of translation (aesthetics is not a paradigm, in Thomas Kuhn's sense), and because the relevant framework is the *étant donné*. The shift matters, but it is not one of paradigms; it is simply the shift from before to after, and the retrospective view that it imposes. The paradigm matters too, but the choice of the right one requires no shift away from aesthetics. It puts aesthetics in abeyance, however, simply because retrospective does not mean retroactive. The paradigm we should be looking for is interpretive-after-the-fact and does not carry a judgment. It is not *critical*—neither in Greenberg's nor in Kant's sense—it is *archaeological,* in Michel Foucault's sense.[14] Broodthaers, who understood better than any so-called conceptual artist the consequences of the fact that we have inherited Duchamp's urinal with the label proclaiming its art status pinned to it, directs us to the right paradigm: it is the enunciative paradigm, such as it was theorized by Foucault in *The Archeology of Knowledge.*[15]

---

14. I have tried to lay out all the paradoxes of the archaeologist's position towards the end of chapter 1, speaking of "the tradition to which you must still belong—that is, from within which you judge without theory—in order to be able (but this time theoretically and without judging) to describe it as if you no longer took part in it."

15. Michel Foucault, *The Archeology of Knowledge,* trans. A. M. Sheridan Smith (New York: Pantheon Books, 1972).

A word of explanation about this enunciative paradigm, which has not had, at least in America, the critical success it deserves, which other aspects of Foucault's work, elaborated in *Discipline and Punish* or in *The History of Sexuality,* have had. Under the term *énoncé* (statement), Foucault postulates a discursive unit to be distinguished from the sign, from the sentence, and from the proposition. If by "unit" one would have to understand a basic, atomic element that some methodological reduction would reveal, Foucault does not find such a unit. The length of statements is variable; two linguistically different expressions sometimes form one and the same statement; conversely, two occurrences of one and the same linguistic expression sometimes form two separate statements; even a garbled sequence of letters is a statement in certain circumstances, and so on. Instead of an elementary unit, what Foucault brings to light is a mode of existence of linguistic signs insofar as they are stated (uttered, pronounced, registered . . .) and not insofar as they signify, of sentences insofar as they are stated and not insofar as they are grammatical, of propositions insofar as they are stated and not insofar as they are logical—a mode of existence that he calls the enunciative function. A statement is thus a linguistic "object" considered as the enactment of its enunciative function. Conversely, the enunciative function is this sheer function of existence of statements, recognized by the simple fact of having been stated. It operates in the discursive field.

Now, even if it is informed and crossed through and through by discursive practices, the field of the plastic arts, in which the readymades have attained their existence as works of art, is not discursive but ostensive, even for that art which calls itself conceptual. It is thus not legitimate to treat objects and images as *statements,* in Foucault's sense. However, the same reduction to which Foucault submitted signs, propositions, or discursive acts in general, anchoring them solely to the conditions of emergence that make them exist as statements, also allows us to relate images or objects to those conditions so long as we transpose them into the enunciative paradigm, that is, so long as we translate them into a statement that is always ostensive and thus always of the type "here is . . ." or "this is . . ." As Broodthaers well understood, it is exactly this transposition that Magritte's *Treachery of Images* effects, a transposition that is of course also valid for *Fountain:* a urinal that does nothing but show itself is translated by the ostensive statement, "here is a urinal." Since it shows itself further so as to test the convention according to which works of art are shown in order to be judged as such, and since it has successfully passed the test, it is also translated by the statement, "this urinal is a work of art," a statement that remains tagged onto it as the testimony that it indeed passed the test. Thus, the sentence "this is art," as it affixes itself to a readymade, is not the sign of the passage of artistic practice from a visual regime to a linguistic one, but the enactment and the manifestation of the enunciative function in which objects that show themselves as art and as art alone are caught up. It translates *the readymade,* as *statement.*

The readymade is not the concept that subsumes the fifty or so objects that Duchamp christened with that name.[16] We could designate them, one by one, but we could in no way collect them within a single category making up the concept of the readymade—in the singular—in that these fifty or so objects do not necessarily have characteristics in common at the level of medium, form, or style; in that all are not straight manufactured objects declared works of art; in that certain ones, called *aided* or *assisted,* imply a manipulation modifying the object, while still others have remained at the stage of an imaginary project, like the *Ice Tongs* or the *Woolworth Building;* and finally, in that in the *Green Box* the word "readymade" often has a textual existence semi-independent of its referents, above all when connected to a qualifier: *sick, unhappy, reciprocal* readymade, *semi-readymade,* etc. But one unassisted readymade—an ordinary object that nothing in its appearance distinguishes from its non-artistic counterpart, an object such as the bottle rack, the snow shovel, or of course, the famous urinal on which the test was performed—is enough to observe, in perfect concert with the Greenbergian description of modernism, and yet at the cost of a total dis-

16. I am here taking up the question of the singular in *the readymade,* raised in the previous chapter. As to the number of readymades, it is debatable. The most exhaustive list to date, which enumerates about fifty objects, is the one established by André Gervais in *La raie alitée d'effets,* pp. 81–83.

placement from *critique* to *archaeology,* that the convention or condition tested was indeed that works of art are shown in order to be judged as such. It is this self-referential folding over of the successfully passed test onto the tested condition that authorizes the reduction of the plurality of the readymades to the singular of *the readymade* and establishes its paradigmatic value for art in general: *the readymade* is simultaneously the operation that reduces the work of art to its enunciative function and the "result" of this operation, a work of art reduced to the statement "this is art," exemplified by Duchamp's readymades.

The Four Ingredients of Enunciative Mayonnaise

As *statement,* the sentence "this is art," pronounced over Duchamp's bottle rack, snow shovel, or urinal, raises the question of its enunciative conditions: given that the readymades' move has succeeded, to what conditions does it owe its success? More technically: to what conditions of enunciation does *the readymade* translate into the statement "this is art," given that the readymades are art? Let us generalize the question: since the test has shown that any ordinary object whatever could be a work of art, what are the conditions that made that possible? Or, more technically: what are the enunciative conditions that confirm the statement "this is art," whatever the thing designated, but given that the designated thing was indeed called art—art in general? For it is clearly the very Duchampian, retrospective point of view of the *given,* combined with the post-Duchampian opening of the "category" of art in general, or art at large, that allows us to say that these conditions validate the statement well beyond the handful of objects through which the demonstration was made. And consequently these conditions are—at least for a certain historical framework, for a certain cultural formation—the enunciative conditions of all works of art, of the Mona Lisa as well as the Mona Lisa with a mustache, or any one object chosen by Duchamp as well as any other candidate for the status of art, and *a fortiori* of the picture, of the piece of sculpture, of the traditional work, whatever its style. It is in this that *the readymade* is paradigmatic. What it says for itself in its particularity, it says for the work of art in general. The enunciative conditions it locates as its own are not the exception but the rule, the minimal formula, *stripped bare,* of the artistic enunciation, *even.*

Thus we need to extract the enunciative conditions of "this is art" as *statement.* (We should note that as a *sentence,* "this is art" has pragmatic conditions that are almost the same and grammatical conditions that are of an entirely different order; and that as a *proposition,* "this is art" has conditions of logical verification that are pertinent only within logic.) As with mayonnaise, they are four in number. The first might be called object-bound: "this" needs a referent. This object might be anything whatever provided that, designated a first time, it be an invariant from one occurrence of the statement to another (which is not required by the grammatical conditions of the sentence but indeed by its pragmatic conditions). The second and third are subject-bound: the statement requires an enunciator, who is free with regard to the object only for the first utterance, and who is thereby defined as enunciator or addressor by the fact that she or he was the first to take that liberty. And the statement needs a receiver who hears the sentence and repeats it. Whether he or she agrees with or contradicts it, this repetition is essential to the enunciative field (while it is not to the pragmatic one). It is the formal acknowledgement of receipt that assures the statement's function of existence and inscribes it on the surface of emergence where the regularities and the dispersals that compose a cultural formation, according to Foucault, are drawn. Finally, the fourth condition is precisely this surface of emergence and inscription, where the statement "this is art" is recorded and institutionalized, and reaches us at the level of the *given.*

These four conditions hold for *the readymade,* in other words, for the statement "this is art" when it directs us to any one of Duchamp's readymades. *The readymade* satisfies these conditions, and, indeed, its enunciative function is validated. Translation: Duchamp's readymades are the referents of these instances of "this" that are indeed considered and valorized as works of art; the utterance of the word "art" with regard to them has made Duchamp's reputation as an artist and has in fact consecrated him as their author; in judging that the readymades were art, the public has acknowledged receipt of the statement and has repeated it on its own behalf; finally, the statement has been recorded and institutionalized at the same time that the readymades have in fact been preserved, exhibited, fetishized as works of art by the museological institution. These conditions are the conditions of enunciation, they lay out the conditions that were necessary and sufficient for the statement "this is art" to be pronounced in relation to the objects Duchamp baptized readymades. They are in no way the conditions of production of these objects, since they were not even produced by Duchamp. Neither are they their conditions of reception, which only a historical or sociological inquiry could establish. Simply, as Foucault wanted for statements in general, enunciative conditions are conditions of existence (and not of essence; they have nothing to do with Greenberg's "essential conventions"): that a work of art *exists* as art in fact means that the statement "this is art" applies to it. That the statement in question be "this is art" (and not, for example "this is new" or "this is expensive") also means that the enunciative function is deployed in a particular field of the cultural formation—the artistic or aesthetic domain—where other enunciative regularities are noticeable, ones that specify this field by way of specific names. Thus, author and viewer (or public) are the conventional names of the first two enunciative conditions within the aesthetic field. In the economic field, it would be a matter of the couple producer/consumer; in the technical one, of the pair inventor/user; in communications, the pair sender/receiver; and finally, in the pragmatic field, the pair addressor/addressee. So, there are conditions for the existence of art in a given cultural formation. They are: given (1) an object, (2) an author, (3) a public, and (4) an institutional place ready to record this object, to attribute an author to it, and to communicate it to the public, the entity this formation calls work of art is possible, a priori. Such would be the thesis that must be demonstrated. How? One might do this externally, sociologically, but the survey threatens to be endless. Undoubtedly it would not be too difficult to show that these four conditions are necessary, but practically impossible to show that they are sufficient. It is perhaps more fruitful to stick to Duchamp and to consider the hypothesis that his work is modernist. If it is true that it is art about art and that it uses "the characteristic methods of a discipline [art in general] to criticize the discipline itself—not in order to subvert it, but to entrench it more firmly in its area of competence," if it is true moreover that it reduces art to its enunciative function, then it must declare the necessity and sufficiency of its own conditions of enunciation, four in number. And if we are able to show it, the thesis will at the same time be demonstrated by the existence, as art, of the readymades and the work of Duchamp in general (from which the readymades, as things, can't be cut away), by his life and his artistic success, all facts established until further notice. Does the statement "Duchamp's oeuvre is art" declare the concomitance of its enunciative conditions? and if it does, how?—those are the two questions to pose to the Duchampian corpus in order that it itself, methodically quoted, will thereby be sufficient to interpret the paradigm and validate the thesis.

The demonstration requires a method. So that the statement "this is art" may be validated, four concomitant conditions are thus required, which means that in their isolated state, outside their encounter, they cease being conditions of anything. There is no sense in speaking of an author if one does not suppose at the same time that he or she is the author of something. The artworld is full of things, but they are only objects in relation to subjects, one group of which could be called authors, and the other spectators. Even the institutions and the apparatuses of power have meaning only in relation to what they administer, and only for a given social group. It is thus logical that the analysis bear not on conditions in a state of isolation (as though in describing the eggs, oil, vinegar, and mustard, one hoped to deduce the nature of mayonnaise), but rather on those conditions at the "moment" when they join and, so to speak, when the mayonnaise "takes." Thus the combinatory of the four conditions of artistic enunciation authorizes six encounters two by two, four encounters three by three, and one encounter four by four which, ideally, should all be examined.[17] However, the essentials can be learned from the first three encounters two by two, and it is on those that our inquiry will focus.

17. That is, two by two: object/author, object/public, object/institution, author/public, author/institution, public/institution; three by three: object/author/public, object/author/institution, object/public/institution, author/public/institution; finally, four by four: object/author/public/institution.

The Encounter of an Object and an Author

Tracking the relation of object to author through Duchamp's work, we find in the *Green Box:*

> *Specifications for "Readymades". by planning for a moment to come (on such a day, such a date such a minute), "to inscribe a readymade"—The readymade can later be looked for.—(with all kinds of delays). The important thing then is just this matter of timing, this snapshot effect, like a speech delivered on no matter what occasion but at such and such an hour. It is a kind of rendezvous.—Naturally inscribe that date, hour, minute, on the readymade as information. Also the aspect of the readymade as exemplary instance.*[18]

As exemplary instance indeed: the readymade is a *kind of rendezvous.* It is born of the encounter of an object with an author. Object and author are nothing but the conditions of their encounter, nothing further being supposed about them. It is necessary and sufficient for them to exist to be able to meet. The object is a given, it exists somewhere, no matter where, available mentally. It doesn't even have to be in the artist's reach since, once decided on, *the readymade can later be looked for (with all kind of delays).* It could even be available only mentally and remain inaccessible to any appropriation: *find inscription for Woolworth Bldg as readymade.*[19] The author is likewise a given. The note from the *Green Box* doesn't grant him or her any talent, any interiority, any motivation. He or she has no truth to declare, only *a speech delivered on no matter what occasion but at such and such an hour.* He or she is without any intention other than that of *inscribing a readymade,* of being on time for the meeting. Given an object and an

18. *SS,* p. 32 (translation modified). From here on, with a few obvious exceptions, the use of italics in this chapter will be restricted to quotations from Duchamp.

19. *SS,* p. 75.

author, it is thus sufficient that they have a *rendezvous* for a readymade to be able to be *inscribed,* in other words, for an ordinary object to be able to be written into the register of those things onto which the statement "this is art" is affixed.

The *idea of fabrication* drops off with this encounter. It is a rule of modernism that a convention of art practice be tested by being tampered with, subverted, or even jettisoned. A readymade is an already-made object, and to admit it as an art object immediately leads one to eliminate the presupposition that the author has made the object with his or her own hands. Along with this presupposition of making goes the whole valorization of craft, everything that, legislating over the beautifully executed work, demands that the object be invested with technical know-how; all this disappears into *le refrain en durée,* the hackneyed formula, an ideological prejudice. A very peculiar administration regulates the artistic practice, one which, under the *Regime of Coincidence* and at the *Department of Weights and Measures,* drops, in the manner of the *Standard Stoppages* for which it serves as an epigram, *the idea of fabrication.*[20] However, it is another rule of modernism that a destroyed or jettisoned convention—which by that very fact becomes apparent as having been nothing but a mere convention—step aside to allow others hidden by the first to appear. If it is no longer required that the author be the fabricator, if henceforth it is enough to have a meeting between an artist and an object for the word "art," art at large, to be affixed to it, this *rendezvous* is, in its turn, not without conditions.

First condition: *to specify the readymades.* In other words, to choose. In an unpublished interview, Duchamp unequivocally puts forward the basis of a syllogism: *the work "art" means to make, and almost, to make manually,* he says, and a little further: *to make is to choose and always to choose.*[21] He leaves us nothing to do but conclude: the word "art" means to choose. What criterion, what *precision*

---

20. *SS,* p. 22 (translation slightly modified).

21. Marcel Duchamp, interview by Georges Charbonnier, radio interviews, RTF, 1961 (my translation).

optics will preside over this choice that has replaced fabrication? *You have to approach something with an indifference, as if you had no aesthetic emotion. The choice of readymades is always based on visual indifference and, at the same time, on the total absence of good or bad taste.*[22] The object's election is thus a first condition of the encounter, but the author should not be accountable for it, if by "author" one understands an intentionality, a taste, or a responsibility: *I object to responsibility.*[23] Without in any way renouncing the *painting of precision, and beauty of indifference.*[24] Skill enters into the choice, but with neither a goal in mind nor a preference, as in playing *the barrel game,* which *is a very beautiful "sculpture" of skill: "all the pieces in the frog's mouth" should not be preferred to "all the pieces outside"* or *(nor) above all to a good score.*[25] Such is the famous Duchampian impassiveness, which characterizes the author-condition. The formula of his free will is *Buridan's ass,* that donkey which the nominalist philosopher Buridan pictured between two buckets of oats, as tempted by the one as by the other, dying of starvation for not having known how to exercise its *freedom of indifference.*[26] It implies a subjective principle of choice that forces us to say, contrary to a going interpretation, that readymades do not belong to the category of found objects at all, but really

---

22. *PC,* p. 48.

23. Ibid. This is said in relation to the mechanical drawing adopted in the *Chocolate Grinder* to defend himself against taste and habit. See also what he says about the *Large Glass* returned broken from the exhibition in Brooklyn in 1927, in the cracks of which he sees *a curious intention that I am not responsible for, a ready made intention, in other words* (*SS,* p. 127). It was certainly in the face of the inflation of the author's ego that he wanted to position these objections to responsibility and intentionality: *I flatly refuse to write an autobiography. It has always been a hobby of mine to object to the written III's on the part of the artist.* (Letter of June 28, 1965, to Cleve Gray in reply to a request to tape his autobiography, cited by Marquis, *Marcel Duchamp,* p. 331.)

24. *SS,* p. 30.

25. *SS,* p. 23.

26. *Free will = Buridan's ass. Find a formula.* Marcel Duchamp, *Notes,* note 153. See chapter 6, n. 13.

to that of chosen objects. This principle of choice, however, is "unconscious" rather than intentional, it produces *canned chance* on its own and subverts authorship. To the question, "How do you choose a readymade?" Duchamp replied: *It chooses you, so to speak.*[27] One would not know how to put it better: outside his chance encounter with an already-made object, the author has no prerogative whatever. Epistemologically and psychologically, the subject in question is the Freudian or Lacanian subject, not the Cartesian or Kantian one.

Second condition of the encounter: *to inscribe a readymade.* And Duchamp adds: *Naturally inscribe that date, hour, minute, on the readymade as information.* Which in any case he never did, except on the *Comb,* inscribed with the sentence *3 or 4 drops of height* [*gouttes de hauteur* = goûts d'auteur?] *have nothing to do with savagery M.D. FEB. 17 1916 11 AM.* It was in 1914, he told Pierre Cabanne, in choosing *Hérisson* or the *Bottle Rack,* the first unassisted readymade, that *the idea of an inscription came as I was doing it,* replacing *the idea of fabrication.*[28] The sentence inscribed on the now-lost *Hérisson* would have to *enter into the choice a kind of flag or color that hadn't come out of a tube.*[29] And it was in 1915, at the time of doing *other objects with inscriptions, like the snow shovel,* that *the word "readymade" thrust itself on me.*[30] Thus, just as a readymade *chooses you so to speak,* so its generic name, readymade, *thrusts itself* on its author apart from his intention. Just as the *idea of an inscription* replaces *the idea of fabrication* in 1914, so a year later the title of the snow shovel, *In advance of the broken arm,* adds a proper name to the common noun designating the object. Just as its common noun, snow shovel (*pelle à neige*), whose anagram could be read "*elle a peigne,*" already contains the next-year's *Peigne (Comb)* through which Duchamp would register,

27. "I Propose to Strain the Laws of Physics," p. 62.

28. *PC,* p. 47.

29. Duchamp, interview by Charbonnier, RTF, 1961. For the relations of titles and names of works to the names of colors and to paintings, see the chapter "Color and Its Name," in my *Pictorial Nominalism,* pp. 119–142.

30. *PC,* p. 48.

in the subjunctive mode, his giving up of painting, so its proper name adds to it *a color that hadn't come out of a tube,* a color that's not ready-made, a painter's color, the medium of painters who *grind their own chocolate.*[31] The passage from the specific to the generic, from painting to art in general, from restricted to general modernism, is played out within Duchamp's enterprise through complex relations between works and their titles. About the *Nude Descending a Staircase No. 2,* Duchamp told Katharine Kuh that it *already predicted the usage of words as a way of adding a color* to the painting.[32] It is what brought the wrath of his cubist friends down on him, friends who, not judging it *proper to call a picture anything else but a landscape, a still-life, a portrait, or number so-and-so,* begged him at least to change the title in order that it not be a blot on the cubist installation at the 1912 Salon des Indépendants.[33] *Instead of changing anything, I withdrew it.*[34] Withdrawal of the picture, abandonment of painting, substitution of the choosing for the making, and passage to *pictorial nominalism.*[35]

Once the *idea of fabrication* has dropped off, the act of naming the object becomes a relevant condition for specifying its encounter with an author who chooses it as much as he is chosen by it, who, so to speak, trips over the happy find of a *three-dimensional pun,* as over the *Trébuchet.* And who, moreover, trips *in advance.* In relation to *Jeune homme triste dans un train* (*Sad Young Man in a Train*), contemporary with *Nude No. 2,* Duchamp explains: *The young man is sad* [triste] *because there is a later train. "Tr" is very* [très] *important.*[36] So important even that Buridan's ass must trip twice over the same stone, for example, over the nominalist delayed-action of *Trébuchet,* according to which the painting's title

31. See chapter 3.

32. Interview with Katherine Kuh, p. 83.

33. Cited by Arturo Schwarz, *Marcel Duchamp* (Paris: Georges Fall, 1974), p. 26.

34. Anne d'Harnoncourt and Kynaston McShine, eds., *Marcel Duchamp* (Philadelphia: Philadelphia Museum of Art, 1973), p. 258.

35. "A kind of *pictorial Nominalism,*" note from the *White Box,* dated on the back "1914," *SS,* p. 78.

36. *PC,* p. 47.

gets the delayed reading, *Je nomme tr . . . dans un tr . . .* ["I call tr . . . in a tr . . ."]. Duchamp tested all the variants of *pictorial nominalism,* experimenting with all the rhetorical relations of the object to its name. The hat rack is called *Hat Rack* but the urinal is called *Fountain;* the bicycle wheel mounted on a stool is called *Bicycle Wheel,* and the snow shovel answers to the inscription *In advance of the broken arm.* In this way are tested: tautology, metaphor, synechdoche, allegory. We could multiply the examples and see many other mechanisms at work: anagrams, acrostics, spoonerisms, paronymies, puns produced via *symétrie commanditée* or crossed through bilingualism, such as *Pulled at 4 Pins,* the limit having been reached by the *Verrou de sureté à la cuiller,* which refers to a spoonerism (*du dos de la cuillère au cul de la douairière*) at a three-dimensional level (it's an object), at an allegorical one (it relates to the chastity belt), and on the bilingual and self-referential mode, since in French *cuiller* means "spoon," alluding to "spoonerism."[37] The ultimate consequences of *pictorial nominalism* as authorial practice are rapidly drawn by Duchamp: in 1913 he had already asked himself: *Can one make works which are not works of "art"?*[38] In vain will the readymade's author object to his responsibility; in vain will the *objet-dard* oscillate ceaselessly from one aspect to the other of its double meaning; one can't take back a slip of the tongue.

Third condition of the encounter: to sign. One of the very last readymades, executed at the time of the first large retrospective celebrating the name and fame of the artist, that of Pasadena in 1963, has as its title *Signed Sign.*[39] It is a sign from the Hotel Green showing the image of a hand, index finger pointing, similar in every detail to the one Duchamp had indeed commissioned from a sign painter for the last painting executed by his own hand, *Tu m',* 1918. As with so many of the names of the readymades and like the word "readymade" itself, the title is in the past participle, thus acknowledging, at the time of the

37. There is an extraordinary and maddening exploitation of the inter-, intra-, and infratextuality of Duchampian wordplay in the book by André Gervais, *La raie alitée d'effets.*

38. *SS,* p. 74.

39. See Cleve Gray, "The Great Spectator," *Art in America* 57 (July–August 1969): 22.

retrospective, this perfectly self-referential *signed sign,* since the signature, a small, nearly invisible flourish in ball-point pen, is to be found just on the end of the pointing finger. But at the time the first readymade went public, in 1917 with *Fountain,* the signature had to be truly visible, manifestly drawn by a not-too-expert hand on the lower left of the urinal, as though it were a page of manuscript, or perhaps a painting. For lack of having been modeled by the artist's hand, the manufactured object flaunts, in place of "touch," a name. It is spelled *R. Mutt,* unknown to the boys. There where the relation of the object to its title is reduced to *a kind of pictorial nominalism* and that of the object to its author to *a kind of rendezvous,* the name of the author is as contingent as that of the object. Duchamp never contested the recognized value of the signature, he never dismissed this reassuring guarantee of causality, he never fled responsibility. Rather, he objected to responsibility, which is not the same. He unbalanced the relationship between the signature and the signatory and undid the *colles alitées* of authenticity by multiplying his name through pseudonyms. There were *Richard Mutt* and *Rrose Sélavy,* of course, but also *Marcel Douxami, Marsélavy,* and *Sélatz,* not to mention the ersatz names he was given by others: *Victor* and *Totor* by Henri-Pierre Roché, *Marchand du sel* by Robert Desnos, *Pierre Delaire* by Henri Waste, itself the pen-name of Henrietta Stettheimer.[40] In 1923, the list opened itself to infinity with the ready-made aliases chosen in *Wanted.* It is a handbill imitating police posters, on which, in the place reserved for the sought-after criminal, Duchamp set his own mug shot, frontface and in profile. The text goes as follows: *WANTED $2,000 REWARD For information leading to the arrest of George W. Welch, alias Bull, alias Pickens, etcetry, etcetry. Operated Bucket*

40. See André Gervais, *La raie alitée d'effets,* p. 29. According to Jacques Caumont and Jennifer Gough-Cooper (in *Rrosopopées* 16–17 [1987]: 344–345), *Marcel Douxami* really existed, which is almost too wonderful to be true. The name appeared as the signature on a letter of May 5, 1917, fairly insulting to Picabia, addressed to the editor of the little magazine *Rongwrong,* who was none other than Duchamp. (I thank Francis Naumann for having called my attention to this information.)

Shop in New York under name HOOKE, LYON and CINQUER. Height about 5 feet 9 inches. Weight about 180 pounds. Complexion medium, eyes same. Known also under name RROSE SELAVY.[41]

An author is sought, but to believe one will find him under his proper name is to swallow the bait, "hook, line, and sinker." No mention of Marcel Duchamp on the poster, and no manuscript trace offered to the sagacity of the graphologist art historian who would commit him- or herself to going back from Rrose Sélavy to the authentic signatory of *Wanted*. Indeed when it comes to authenticity, Rrose only looks for ready-made differences, preferring *infra-thin* ones: *Buy or take known or unknown paintings and sign them with the name of a known or unknown painter. The difference between the "style" and the unexpected name for the "experts," is the authentic work of Rrose Sélavy and defies forgeries.*[42] Everything that has been said about choice and about name as enunciative conditions at the point where an object and an author meet could be repeated for the signature. It is necessary to sign but it is sufficient to sign a list of aliases where the absent signatory, designated in the text he doesn't sign, remains nonetheless sought-after, *wanted*, outside the text, as the presumed author of his crime. One will look for him all the more in that his crime is to have only unauthorized, borrowed names. The author of *Wanted* is still in need of authorization and he had to wait for the moment of the retrospective—that of Pasadena, precisely, for which Duchamp executed *Signed Sign*—for *Wanted* to obtain an authorized signature. The work indeed reappeared as a quotation on the poster Duchamp designed for this retrospective, significantly called *A Poster within a Poster.* Appended to a space which is both that of the poster and that of the mat around *Wanted*, there finally appears, this time in cursive script and thus happily lending itself to the graphologist's test, the signature that removes all equivocation and grants authorship: *by or of Marcel Duchamp or Rrose Sélavy.*[43] This authorship is

---

41. *SS*, p. 181.

42. *Notes*, note 169.

43. The work this signature authenticates is, however, nothing but a printed poster and there the traces of the artist's hand are only mechanically reproduced. It answers as though by

not a natural right, it is an acquired right and it remains to be acquired *with all kinds of delays.* The name of the author, threaded through the string of pseudonyms, will only be validated by an authorization that will redound upon him through his fame: in the *mise-en-abyme* of *A Poster within a Poster,* once shouldn't underestimate the poster-ity that is implied.

The Encounter of an Object and a Public

Let us consider two important factors, the two poles of the creation of art: the artist on one hand, and on the other the spectator who later becomes the posterity.[44] It is with these words that Duchamp began one of the rare academic lectures, titled "The Creative Act," that he ever agreed to give. The creative process is thus not stopped at the chance relations that cause the word "art" to arise from the meeting of an object and an author. *After all, the public represents half of the matter; art is also made through the admiration one has for it; the masterpiece is declared in the final analysis by the spectator.*[45] In short, *it's the viewers who make the pictures.*[46] Duchamp is very clear in the evaluation of their responsibility: *art is a product of two poles; there's the pole of the one who makes the work and the pole of the one who looks at it. I give the latter as much importance as the one who makes it.*[47]

A modernist work is always, even if it denies this, an allegory of the practice to which it belongs. Contrary to an abstract painting, for example, which

symétrie commanditée to the very first work *by or of* Rose Sélavy, *Fresh Widow,* who signs it by means of the typeset notation: COPYRIGHT ROSE SELAVY. Dropping *the idea of fabrication,* the author is no longer someone his or her signature authorizes but someone who has the copyrights to his or her work. On this subject, see Molly Nesbit, "Ready-Made Originals: The Duchamp Model," *October* 37 (Summer 1986).

44. "The Creative Act," a lecture given at the meetings of the American Federation of Art, in Houston, April 1957, in *SS,* p. 138.

45. Duchamp, interview by Charbonnier, RTF, 1961, and *PC,* p. 39.

46. Michel Sanouillet, ed., *Duchamp du signe* (Paris: Flammarion, 1975), p. 247 (my translation).

47. *PC,* p. 70.

comments via painting on the conditions of painting, the *Large Glass* is not a *real allegory,* such as Courbet's *Studio of the Artist,* one of the first modernist paintings, had been. But it is clearly an allegory in the most traditional sense. And it is an allegory that comments via painting (since it is a painted object) on the fate of the painter once industrialization has transformed him into a *chocolate grinder,* and on the fate of the viewers once painting disappears into transparency (it is a glass object, contrary to the modernism of flatness) and moves into the fourth dimension, that of art in general. In the lower half of the *Large Glass* stand *the oculist witnesses,* who paradigmatically exemplify the viewers. They are simultaneously metaphors of the *bachelors* and their "gaze doctor." On the trajectory of their desire to look symbolized by the successive states, gaseous, frozen, spangled, then liquid, of the *illuminating gas* (in Lacanian terms we would say: on the circuit of their scopic drive), the *oculist witnesses* focus the gaze of the bachelors and dazzle it into a *sculpture of drops* that will be projected via *mirrorical return* in the region of the *nine shots* where it will rejoin, in a necessarily missed encounter, the *bride's* desire. Duchamp imagines the encounter of the object and the public in the manner of this missed encounter, missed at least for the bachelors chained in the three dimensions of space, but one which would succeed if the leap into the fourth dimension were possible. The manner in which the *oculist witnesses* are depicted thus illustrates the manner in which the real encounter of work and viewers is represented according to Duchamp. It is moreover what is clearly indicated by the *Kodak magnifying glass* whose image hangs over the *oculist witnesses* and which ends up being the only element in the lower half of the *Glass* not to have been represented in perspective, the only one, then, not to be in the space of the depicted witnesses but in that of the real witnesses.

Now this scenario of the object-public encounter is already to be found in the *Small Glass* of 1918, which is the sketch for the *oculist witnesses* and which itself includes, embedded in its glass surface, a real Kodak lens. Its title is at once its instruction sheet: *To Be Looked at (the Other Side of the Glass) with One Eye, Close-to, for about an Hour.* I did this (not for an hour; patience has its limits), and the experience is very instructive. My eye riveted to the magnifying glass,

I see—or rather I don't see—the work vanish from my visual field only for there to appear an inverted and reduced image of the gallery in the MoMA where the object is exhibited. A waiting period, uncomfortable and boring, begins. The revelation takes place when by chance another visitor passes who appears to me like a homonculus, upside down and in my former place, since I was initially on that side of the glass where the title/instruction was to be read. A missed encounter has just taken place—the glass serving as obstacle—between two spectators, he and I, two members of the public.[48] Between the two of us the work was nothing but the instrument of this encounter. But since he occupies the place where I was, it is also with myself that I had this missed rendezvous to which I arrived late, and it is with himself that he will have or that he already has a rendezvous, *with all kinds of delays.*

With a delay of more than fifty years from the *Small Glass* of 1918, Duchamp prepared himself to reveal to his posterity the "naturalist" and posthumous version of *The Bride Stripped Bare by Her Bachelors, Even.* Its title, *Etant donnés,* also serves as the *Preface* and the *Notice* for the first version, and it is no longer those things one must read (but perhaps one must have read them) for instruction on how to use the work. No more need either for a *Kodak magnifying glass* to symbolize the position of the *oculist witnesses.* This time the *illuminating gas* is furnished by the *bride,* who shamelessly displays herself. The most banal desire is enough to tell the most ordinary voyeur how to use the work and to attract him to the double peep holes drilled at eye level in the Spanish door that both gives and obstructs access to this peep-show. I also experienced it, at the Philadelphia Museum, led by my desire to see art, not pornography. However, it is as voyeur that I "ogle" and treat myself to the spectacle of this spread-eagled *bride* who offers herself to me and to me alone. Everything's there to see: in the gaping hole of the wall, the *bride,* the *cunt* of the *bride* (Duchamp writes:

48. Commenting on the same experience, Georges Roque makes similar remarks in a text called "Incompétence et performance," in *Performance, Textes & documents* (Montreal: Editions Parachute, 1980), pp. 149–156.

le con de la mariée[49]) focuses my whole visual field. And I am caught in the trap of denial that Freud showed to be the essence of fetishism: there is nothing to see, all the more so since the *bride* turns her head away and the wall masks her face from my view. She doesn't look at me, I don't see her looking at me. No view is taken: in vain am I *the one who plays the photographer,* she with her hairless vulva is not *celle qui a de l'haleine* [de la laine?] *en dessous*. The "*con*" is not the one you think, and the one seen is the one who thought he saw. Behind me in the museum's gallery someone has just entered, whom I do not see catching me in the act but whose gaze I feel prickling the nape of my neck, while, glued to the door and framed by its brick casing, I form a figure or a blot in the picture, rather pathetic at that.

It's the viewers who make the pictures, indeed. They are inside. If one folds onto the *Large Glass* the specifications of the instruction sheet formed by the work just preceding it, *To Be Looked at . . . ,* and its aftermath, *Etant donnés,* one realizes that the *oculist witnesses* do not stand in an outside space from which they look at the work but that they figure within it, in the transparent interworld of an encounter that is, moreover, necessarily missed. Of the salacious gaze of the bachelors, it is only the *image* that meets up with the *nine shots* by *mirrorical return*. It is thus useless to imagine the encounter from any point of view other than the encounter itself, in other words anywhere but from the *horizon,* which is also the *garment of the bride,* where the gaze loses itself but where the *stripping* occurs. Understood as enunciative conditions of art (of the *blossoming of the Mariée,* where "m'art y est," as Ulf Linde says),[50] the object and the public are given. But before or outside their meeting they are just any object and any public. A *chocolate grinder,* a urinal, would make no less good *objets-dard* than a fruit bowl. And the normally equipped man on the street is no less a voyeur

49. Anne d'Harnoncourt, ed., *Manual of Instructions for Marcel Duchamp, Etant Donnés: 1° La Chute d'Eau, 2° le Gaz d'Eclairage* (Philadelphia: Philadelphia Museum of Art, 1987), n.p.

50. Ulf Linde, "L'ésotérique," in *Abécédaire,* catalogue of the Duchamp retrospective (Paris: Centre Georges Pompidou, 1977), p. 74.

than the art lover. Nothing is prejudged about the nature of the object and the makeup of the public. On the other hand, the encounter itself conditions them. The title and the lens of the *Small Glass,* the peep holes in the door of *Etant donnés,* give the instructions that prescribe an individual encounter. Art does not address itself to the masses but rather to an individual, and the work of art, whatever it is, chooses its viewers one at a time. However, once the spectator falls into this viewing trap, it is another viewer that he sees looking at him or whom he sees looking. There the viewers are always double; following Lacan, we might say that the individual viewer gets split there. It is to an Other that his gaze is addressed and from an Other that it comes back to him. With that proviso does the *illuminating gas* flare up, does the *splash* dazzle, and does the poetic sparkle flash! Art takes place in the fourth dimension where the *voluntary, horizontal blossoming of the bride* goes to *meet the vertical blossoming of the stripping-bare* by her bachelors and produces the *blossoming through reconciliation.*[51]

However, in the lower part of the *Glass* where the illuminating gas manages to lower the *toboggan,* there are three *splashes* or three *crashes,* and in the upper part, where the *milky way* blooms, there are three *draft pistons* to convey the *bride's commandments.* In the Duchampian numerology, three is the number of the crowd. *When you've come to the word three, you have three million—it's the same thing as three.*[52] One might already wonder if a viewer who splits himself into two is able to understand himself. Of the two viewers who face each other on the two sides of the *Kodak lens* of the *Small Glass* or who succeed one another at the peep-holes of *Etant donnés,* we admit that they can *look at* (each other) *seeing,* but since they can't *hear hearing* it is out of the question that they hear one another.[53] *The blossoming by reconciliation* takes place, if it does at all, between

51. *Notes,* note 152.

52. *PC,* p. 47.

53. Note 252 of the *Notes* sets up an echo of the aphorism *One can look at seeing: one can't hear hearing,* published in the *Box of 1914,* which gives an idea of the resulting misunderstanding: *Thinking he heard me listening, he asked me to ask you if you knew that he knew that I had seen him looking at the one to whom I responded that I was responsible for nothing.*

the individual viewer and the work, but not between the viewers. In other words, consensus about art is not in the least a necessary condition in order to transform the crowd into a public. And since the work disappears into the transparency or behind the horizon, and since it basically shows nothing but the fetish where all gazes are trapped, the number of the crowd is raised to the power of the number that defines the encounter of the viewer with himself or with the Other: $3^2 = 9$.

The episode of the *nine shots* in the *Large Glass* produces the allegory of this. It is indeed a matter of an encounter, one that is certainly on the order of voyeurism since the story of the *Large Glass* is that of a stripping-bare. And it is truly a matter of intentionality, of aim, since the place of the *shots* on the *Glass* has been determined by means of a toy cannon, by shooting three salvos of three paint-dipped matches at the target from three different positions. In admitting that the *target* represents the object before or outside the encounter, and the three firing positions the public's expectations, the dispersal of the *nine shots*—each position multiplying itself into three experiences of voyeurism—then represents the impossibility of the members of the public's understanding each other about what they see and claim to call a work of art. The encounter took place; Duchamp even took the trouble to lay out its space-time: it is the sculptural space formed by the trajectories of the *nine shots,* also called *trajectory of observation out of the corner of the eye.*[54] As for the encounter itself, it is the *figure obtained,* that is, the *visible flattening of the demultiplied body.*[55] But the *target*—the goal of the scopic drive or the object of the desire—is lost. Nothing, either in the *Large Glass* or in the sketches and the notes, indicates where the target was placed when Duchamp fired the shots. If the *shots* still refer to it, it is through a *coefficient of displacement* which *is nothing but a souvenir.* The firing positions are not indicated either. The public has no collective strategy and its cohesion is only a *demultiplied body* whose unity is likewise nothing but a souvenir. The

54. *SS,* p. 84.

55. *SS,* p. 35.

only law that unifies it is nothing but a *regulation of regrets from one "deferee" to another.*[56]

The relations between object and public as Duchamp imagines them, produces and declares them, give rise neither to a community of viewers nor to a collection of objects. The work's only public status is a dispersal of privacies. At the point of the object-public encounter, the object vanishes and the public disperses, heterogeneous and divided. However, art is enunciated by such a failed meeting, far from the nuptials with the *retinal* joys of color, far even from the solitary pleasures of *olfactory masturbation.* No communication by means of *the smell of turpentine,* no transmission of the "little sensation" (Cézanne), no *taste.* Paul Klee's "visible" is not Duchamp's *viewable.* Thus there collapses the primary condition of the aesthetic experience, its phenomenological support, the gaze. Which goes pretty far—when we remember that nothing propels the bachelors' Odyssey but their desire to see the bride stripped bare at last. But the desire to see or the rage to look is not the gaze, even less so the gaze replete with aesthetic pleasure. Were it necessary, *Etant donnés* is there to convince us that in having fulfilled the viewer's expectations, the work has in no way satisfied his or her desire. In any case, it is not because of having been seen that *Etant donnés* is a work of art. Even the *Large Glass,* which is very beautiful, has garnered its artistic reputation from people who have never seen it and elicited from some of them, such as Jean Suquet, among the most sensitive of commentaries.[57] As for the readymade, it is *something one doesn't even look at, or something one looks at while turning one's head.*[58] Let's conclude with Duchamp: *this angle will express the necessary and sufficient corner of the eye.*

56. *Réglementation des regrets d'éloigné* [des lois niées?] *à éloigné. SS,* p. 23.

57. Jean Suquet, *Miroir de la mariée* (Paris: Flammarion, 1974); *Le guéridon et la virgule* (Paris: Christian Bourgois, 1976); *Le Grand verre rêvé* (Paris: Aubier, 1991). See also (in English) his contribution to the Duchamp conference held in Halifax in 1987, "Possible," in de Duve, *Definitely Unfinished Marcel Duchamp.*

58. "Conversations avec Marcel Duchamp," in Jouffroy, *Une révolution du regard,* p. 119; reprinted in *Opus International* 49 (March 1974), p. 89.

The idea of fabrication collapses with the three *Standard Stoppages,* a work apt to establish the thematic and methodological connection between the readymades and the *Large Glass.* With *Tu m'*—the last canvas the painter executed by hand, but also a commentary encoded by the *illuminatistic Scribism* on the relations between painting and the readymades—the gaze collapses. Too bad for the voyeur who confuses *Tu m's* instruction sheet with that of the almost contemporary *Small Glass.* The former work is to be read, it is not *to be looked at,* and above all not *close to.* Whoever would get too close would get his or her eye poked by the ready-made bottle brush which projects from it along the visual axis and would have his or her eye rinsed for good. *A plastic for plastic retaliation.* Over the act of gazing, over this gaze caught at the horizon of a fully rounded, aesthetic sensation, Duchamp prefers the *timid power* of the possible: *the possible is only a physical "caustic" (vitriol type) burning up all aesthetics or callistics.*[59] Vengeance has some potential, some "burning power" *in reserve.* If the viewer wants to avoid *feeling regret as soon as possession is consummated,* he must suspend his desire to see, slow down *the inevitable response to shop windows,* and defer his aesthetic pleasure: *the fruit still has to avoid being eaten.*[60] Which is to say that for the gaze [*regard*] Duchamp substitutes the *delay* [*retard*]. Thus, after the equation art = making = choosing, here is a second syllogism: *use "delay" instead of picture,* says a note from the *Green Box.*[61] Now, *the viewers make the picture.* Thus the viewers make the delay.

If the gaze is no longer a necessary condition of the encounter of the work with its public, delay is, to the contrary, one of them. *In the last analysis, the artist may shout from all the rooftops that he is a genius; he will have to wait for the verdict of the spectator in order that his declarations take a social value and that, finally, posterity includes him in the primers of Art History.*[62] The role of the author of a readymade

59. *SS,* p. 73.

60. *SS,* pp. 74 and 70.

61. *SS,* p. 26.

62. *SS,* p. 138.

was to trip over the object of a choice that chose him. *The role of the spectator is to determine the weight of the work on the aesthetic scale.*[63] *In planning for a moment to come to inscribe a readymade* and then to look for it *with all kinds of delays,* the author placed the object *in advance* on the *aesthetic scale* and the viewer, who arrives late, will have to determine its weight. The author has named the object *Hérisson, Peigne,* or *Trébuchet,* he has also given it the generic name *readymade,* but he has carefully abstained from calling it art. However, once the object is placed on the scale where it is a candidate for judgment, *can one make works which are not works of "art"?* Could one avoid the statement "this is art" being pinned on *Trébuchet* once it has given its viewers the same bump on the shin it gave its author? The word "trébuchet" has three meanings that the public of viewers, taken one by one, will refract according to the *Wilson-Lincoln system* in at least nine *trajectories from the corner of the eye:* it means a double-trayed scale for weighing gold, a bird trap, and a chessplayer's ruse consisting of sacrificing a pawn to the opponent in order for him to stumble over it. The birds caught in the trap are the *viewers who make the picture* in the manner of Pliny's birds from the fable: they take this coat rack nailed to the floor for a real object when it is merely, thanks to its title, something placed on the aesthetic scale—on the scale of the "art weigher"—for their attention. As for the chessgame of painting, in this case Duchamp is not so much Zeuxis as Parrhasios: the best ruse is the most transparent one, the one that catches the viewers in the trap of a *delay in glass.* There is hardly more to see behind the *bride's veil* than behind the curtain painted by Parrhasios, neither any *jacket,* nor any *vest,* nor any *uniform,* nor any *livery* to take down from this coatrack called *Trébuchet,* to realize that the *trajectories from the corner of the eye* are *strained and lose the nearly of the "always possible"—with moreover the irony to have chosen the body or original object which inevitably becomes according to this perspective*[64] . . . an *objet-dard.*

63. *SS,* p. 140.

64. *SS,* p. 36. The sentence remains unfinished.

The Encounter of an Object and an Institution

The sole encounter of object and author maintained the *objet-dard* in the metastable state of a slip of the tongue. Repeated, if only once but massively, by the public, re-viewed, if only *from the necessary and sufficient corner of the eye,* causing it to lose the *vitriol* and *the nearly of the "always possible,"* the slip congeals and becomes fixed there where metaphors, allegories, and other figures of speech all freeze into catechreses: in art as an institution. Again we must first know what "art as an institution" means, or more concretely, if all artistic institutions (that is, places where the statement "this is art" is recorded and receives social sanction) institutionalize the same thing under the name "art." Even this last question is too vast. No more than for the question of author and public should we unglue ourselves from Duchamp's work to find out what it has to say of the relation between an ordinary object—not made but chosen, named and signed by its author, not viewed but evaluated by its delayed public—to the institution through which the recording of its claim to art is achieved. Or yet again: given that the readymades have received social sanction, what do they have to say of the institutions where that social sanction took effect?

The public life of the readymade begins at the same time as its institutional life. Two readymades (we don't know which) were exhibited in April 1916 at the Bourgeois Galleries in New York, and at the same time, *Pharmacy* was shown at the Montross Gallery. But as we might have expected they went unnoticed: the readymade is *something one doesn't even look at.* Exactly a year later, the Richard Mutt affair blew up. "Affair" is after all a big word for an event that had no public impact at the time but only found its reverberations much later, in the art of artists who would get their own authority from the readymade's move and would give Duchamp his posterity. In December 1916, the Society of Independent Artists, Inc. was founded, modeled on the Société des Artistes Indépendants of Paris, and programmed to hold an annual Salon after the fashion of its French model. The same slogan, "No jury, no prizes," was adopted and the first Salon scheduled for April 1917. That's when the hanging committee received from a certain R. Mutt from Philadelphia a more-than-embarrassing package: a urinal posed flat on its back, flagrantly signed and dated, and baptized *Fountain*. The urinal was conjured away; it didn't figure in the catalogue; there was no public scandal. The show was a big success and it wasn't until May, at the time of the closing, that an unsigned editorial, called "The Richard Mutt Case," appeared in the second issue of *The Blind Man,* that took up the cause for Mr. Mutt's selection. The editorial was accompanied by a photographic reproduction of the urinal entitled *Fountain by R. Mutt,* captioned THE EXHIBIT REFUSED BY THE INDEPENDENTS, and duly credited to its author: *Photograph by Alfred Stieglitz*.

The Richard Mutt Case is exemplary in showing how the conditions of artistic enunciation gather together and go into effect at the meeting point of an object and an institution. The object is given, made available to the artist by its manufacturer, *The J. L. Mott Iron Works*. It is unforeseen by the institution, to say the very least, but it has been chosen, named *Fountain,* and signed R. Mutt, in a transparent parody of the name of its manufacturer; it was therefore authorized, even if it was by a perfect unknown. And it will be rechosen, and renamed art, and resigned *by or of Marcel Duchamp* by the viewers who, even if they have never seen it, will "have made the pictures" *with all kinds of delays*. As for the institution, Society of Independent Artists, Inc., it too is given, and its access is open to everyone. Even though it is willing to recognize anyone as an artist, it can't swallow the urinal and doesn't agree that Mr. Mutt is the author of anything artistic whatever. It is only as an epilogue, and thus too late for the exhibition, that *The Richard Mutt Case* will credit, in the most paradoxical way, an institution that wanted nothing to do with the existence of the famous and infamous urinal. Duchamp's most celebrated readymade—perhaps his most celebrated work—is an object that has disappeared, that practically no one has seen, that never stirred up a public scandal, about which the press at the time never spoke, which never figured in the catalogue of the Independents' Show but made it into a discreet Salon des Refusés, and whose very existence could be doubted were it not for Stieglitz's photograph. This readymade is only known through its reproduction.

The double-page spread of *The Blind Man* where the Richard Mutt case was presented has been reproduced again and again in monographs on

Duchamp and elsewhere.[65] *In the last analysis, the artist may shout from all the rooftops that he is a genius; he will have to wait for the verdict of the spectator in order that his declarations take a social value and that, finally, posterity includes him in the primers of Art History.* This is what happened, and widely. *Given* that it has happened, it is possible for me to say here and now that with the Richard Mutt case, the modernist reduction of art at large to its necessary and sufficient conditions is accomplished. No reduction to essence, however. These conditions involve neither a kind of Greenbergian flatness, which has lept from painting to art at large, from the specific to the generic, nor a kind of Kosuthian "nature of art," which has been discovered at the end of an inquiry carried out by means of "analytic propositions." The conditions in question are those of enunciation, no more and no less. And they only concern the *statement* "this is art," as it affixes itself to whatever object, as it also leads art back to its most elementary function of existence, the one Foucault calls the enunciative function, which is that of statements validated by the sole fact of having been uttered. Let's return to the Richard Mutt case, then. (1) To validate the statement there must be a case, a referential "this" whose existence is designated by an ostensive act. The urinal as such disappeared, yet here it is, in the position of referent in the photograph, which plays, as does every photograph (contrary to painting or drawing), the role of reality's index and proof. *Ecce* the object; it's a urinal. It no longer exists; it existed. (2) To validate the statement there must be an enunciator, an "I" who chooses, names, and signs the object. This is *Fountain by R. Mutt.* On the facing page, the editorial's argument emphasizes that "by" has to read "chosen by" and not "made by." (3) To validate the statement there must be a viewer who doesn't look, or who looks *while turning one's head,* like a photographer for example, who lets his camera look in his stead, but who repeats the statement as if it were his, a "you" who says "I" in turn: *Photograph by Alfred Stieglitz.* (4) To validate the statement there must be an institution which, if need be, refuses

65. Thanks to Arturo Schwarz, the two issues of the journal are available today in facsimile (Archivi d'arte del XX secolo, Rome–Milan, Gabriele Mazzotta Editore, 1970).

to validate the object but nonetheless effectuates, *with all kinds of delays,* the concomitance of the first three conditions, and registers it. This is *The exhibit refused by the Independents.* QED. The four enunciative conditions of *the readymade* are spelled out in the presentation of *this* readymade, which is nowhere present.

Modernism "Without Walls"

The readymade, I said before, is a work of art reduced to the statement "this is art." After *the idea of fabrication,* after the gaze, what drops away at the point where an object and an institution meet is the work itself, that which tradition, including the entire tradition of restricted modernism, calls the work: the work as material object, the work as an author's *opus,* the work as visual phenomenon offered to a viewer, the work as institutionalized value. Tradition made that quadruple implication of the word "work" into a causal theory: something is a work because it is made by human hands, because the hand that made it is unique and left its traces on it, because it shows itself and is beautiful, sublime, meaningful, or simply good, because its value is recognized. Then came conceptual art, and this set out programmatically to deconstruct and to negate this quadruple understanding. (1) To negate the work as material object: this is the theme of the *dematerialization of the art object,* a theme that was promoted by Lucy Lippard beginning in 1968 and later served as a title for her well-known book on the first six years of conceptual art.[66] (2) To negate the work as being the *opus* of an author: this is the theme of *the death of the author,* the title of Roland Barthes's famous essay, whose first appearance was in English in *Aspen Magazine,* for an issue edited by the conceptual artist Brian O'Doherty.[67] (3) To negate the work as visual phenomenon offered to a viewer: this is the theme of

66. Lucy Lippard and John Chandler, "The Dematerialization of Art," *Art International,* February 1968; Lucy Lippard, *Six Years: The Dematerialization of the Art Object from 1966 to 1972.*
67. Roland Barthes, "The Death of the Author," *Aspen Magazine* 5–6 (1966).

the end of aesthetics, of the refusal of the judgment of taste, of the rejection of formalism, of the exclusion from art of every practice grounded in a "morphological basis," a theme of which Kosuth was the main defender. (4) To negate the work as institutionalized value: this is the theme of the denunciation of the museum, of the contesting of the art market, of the invention of alternative spaces, of the critique of institutions, a theme which sustained purely "conceptual" pieces (these are no longer called "works"), like Robert Barry's *Closed Gallery Piece* of 1969, as well as "contextual" interventions, like those of Michael Asher on the walls of the Toselli Gallery in Milan in 1973.

There is no doubt that the strong period of conceptual art, American especially (Lippard's "six years"—1966–1972—are a good indication), represented a moment of great creative élan, of intense reflective activity, of active debate and awareness. Everyone began to taste the modernist mayonnaise concocted by Duchamp, not for the pleasure of exercising his or her judgment of taste, but for the sharpening of intellectual discernment. Tastebuds aroused (which, it seems, are individually sensitive to sweetness, saltiness, acidity, and bitterness), each tucked in to the analytic, deconstructive, or—why not?—critical (in the Greenbergo-Kantian sense) task of extracting the individual ingredients that made up the ready-made emulsion spooned out onto his or her plate. In good modernist form, each took it into his or her head to pursue the critique of mayonnaise via the means of mayonnaise and to experiment with the recipe by varying the proportions and seasoning, some overdoing the pepper, others the salt. The results have various flavors, but since it is with mayonnaises just as with works of art, you have to taste each one individually, something it is not my intention to undertake here. Happily, art has no need of correct theory to be appreciated. All the same—irony of ironies—it is at the conceptual level that conceptual art gets it wrong. I used "recipe" metaphorically, but I could have said "program" just as well and that wouldn't have been a metaphor. Conceptual art (at the very point at least where it laid claims to concepts) conducted its program of deconstructing or critiquing the four ingredients of the mayonnaise as if they were causes when they were nothing but conditions. It rightly laid the blame on the tradition that made the quadruple understanding of the word "work" a causal theory, but in attacking what it believed the four causes of traditional art to be, it left causality itself entirely intact. John Cage, by contrast, was a lot more on target. Conceptual art thus committed two cardinal errors. It wanted to fight *for a good cause,* yet it didn't recognize the degree to which Duchamp had already undone the causalities—*colles alitées,* as he put it—of authorship, of spectatorship, and of institutionality. In other words, conceptual art identified enunciation with production at the same time that it projected into the future what already belonged to the past. The most flagrant aspect of this misunderstanding was to have interpreted the linguistic turn that Duchamp gave to art in general within the structuralist-semiological paradigm and not to have seen that the relevant paradigm was the enunciative one.

For the enunciative paradigm these four senses of the word "work"—handmade object, trace of its author, visual phenomenon, institutionalized value—are superfluous conditions ("expendable" is Greenberg's word). Not necessary, contingent. It might be that they remain indispensable or inevitable within the field of production, as the obvious failure of conceptual art to have gotten rid of them would seem to confirm. But the enunciative paradigm has nothing to say about the field of production, it only addresses the field of enunciation. And in this field, it is necessary and sufficient that a "this" designated by an "I" be shown to a "you" by means of an ostensive statement, and that this statement be repeated and registered under the rubric "art," for an *archaeologist* like Foucault, or Broodthaers, or myself for that matter, to gather it, to attest to its regularity and dispersal, and to relate it to its enunciative conditions. These conditions are those of art, and even, if we please, of the work, of the work of art in general, and thus of no matter which work, but only insofar as it states itself or is stated, only insofar as it is the referent of the statement "this is a work of art." Everything that is named art, even and above all what tradition—modernist or not—is capable of accounting for, implicitly bears this statement. The readymades bear it explicitly, which is why they are modernist. Given that a readymade is art, it carries a label that says this. It is a truism, but it is not a tautology, as Kosuth thinks. *The readymade* is certainly art about art, but the power of the statement "this is art" to lead back to its own conditions of enunciation and to strip them of everything that would allow a confusion of conditions and causes, is not *sui generis.* It passes through *this* readymade, it requires the designation of a referent which has nothing self-referential about it. Which is why it was essential, in order for the enunciative paradigm to be validated, that *this* readymade, *Fountain* in this case, disappear in its condition as work so that it is no longer manifested except in the guise of the referent. This is indeed the way things transpired: as object, *opus,* spectacle, and value, and even as support of the statement "this is art," *Fountain* has disappeared.

This statement has another support, then, namely the photograph that testifies to the existence, in the sole guise of referent, of this urinal. It tacitly declares, "this (the urinal) is art," and even more tacitly, "this (the photo) is its proof." Nothing is proved, however, because the "proof" must still be submitted to the test of the delay that takes charge of it as a new object giving rise to new statements, around which the enunciative conditions permute. In the place of "this is *Fountain by R. Mutt*" we find "this is *Photograph by Alfred Stieglitz.*" In the position of the object we thus encounter a photograph, that is, a readymade painting. In place of the author we find a photographer, that is, strictly speaking, someone who replaces making with choosing and the hand with the eye, and to whom the acknowledgement that *it's the viewers who make the pictures* applies better than to anyone. Finally, instead of viewers—of the photo and of its referent, in place of this *spectator who later becomes the posterity,* there is *The Blind Man* and his progeny: the crowd of visitors who hurried to the Independents' Show in 1917 without even a hint of *Fountain's* existence, and the mass of readers of Duchamp monographs who will harvest, *with all kinds of delays,* the statement, "this (the work reproduced by means of its reproduction by Stieglitz) is art." Today the waiting period is over, the delay is achieved, and it is as though the photographic print reproduced in 1917 in a little avant-garde journal with a tiny circulation had been sufficient to propel its referent into the museum, so that at the present time that is where it is to be found, exemplary, paradigmatic of its own enunciative conditions.

That should now be clear: the museum to which the readymade has been propelled is what Malraux called *le musée imaginaire,* the museum-without-walls.

Indeed, *Fountain* is nowhere else: the Moderna Museet in Stockholm, the National Gallery in Ottawa, the Musée national d'art moderne in Paris, and a few others possess replicas of it, but replicas are reproductions. Other replicas of *Fountain* exist, moreover, miniature replicas, in as many copies as there are *Boîtes-en-valise*. But the *Boîte-en-valise,* little portable museum of images, does nothing but instantiate the museum-without-walls as a gathering together of the enunciative conditions of everything it contains. Basically it is a monograph on Duchamp's oeuvre in its totality, presented *as if* it were a museum object or a collector's item.[68] *Fountain* only exists as the lost referent of a series of ostensive statements (photograph in the Stieglitz case, miniatures in that of the *Boîte en valise,* full-size replicas in that of museums) that swear to the fact that it existed but that it no longer exists at the moment one learns of its existence, and that's why its whole public belongs to the progeny of *The Blind Man.* This is the ever-expanding public whose artistic culture is almost entirely formed by the museum-without-walls and who, rather than visually checking with original works, submits to reproductions in books and art magazines for what they are in fact: nothing more than an institutional statement that presents all sorts of things in the position of referent as if their artistic quality were merely a matter of status, or, to use Walter Benjamin's terms, as if their aura, their cult value, had been entirely reabsorbed into their exhibition value. And the enunciative paradigm that *the readymade* translates, up to now formal, begins to reveal its historical purport and its ethical content. It states the enunciative conditions of art "in the age of mechanical reproduction," once the copy precedes the original, once the museum-without-walls is first and the real museum second. Indeed, a reproduction of art is an object the artist hasn't made, from which its viewer does not draw a full aesthetic experience, and which the museological

68. Obviously one could neglect the "as if" and treat the *Boîte-en-valise* as a work in the traditional sense. In this case, singularity will assert itself sooner or later, and one will be led to remark the differences between one *Boîte* and another. This is what Ecke Bonk has done in his excellent *Marcel Duchamp, The Box in a Valise* (New York: Rizzoli, 1989).

institution neither valorizes nor legitimates as a work. A reproduction of art does nothing beyond declaring the existence, as art, of the work that is its referent.

There was a historical necessity for the enunciative paradigm, then; it didn't fall from the sky. Duchamp didn't reduce the work of art to its enunciative function on a whim, and I haven't interpreted his action in these terms out of methodological artifice. The readymade's enunciative conditions, as I said before, are valid for the work of art in general, for the Mona Lisa as well as for the Mona Lisa with a mustache. But I added: at least for a particular historical framework, a particular cultural formation. Malraux called this cultural formation the museum-without-walls and Benjamin called it art's "age of mechanical reproduction," an age for which *the* condition is precisely to see *all* the conditions of reception, of circulation, and of enjoyment of art reduced to enunciative conditions. Everything the regime of the museum-without-walls considers to be "art," whether this be a Rembrandt, an African fetish, a palm print on the cave walls of Pech Merle, or a readymade, everything that it calls art, carries at least implicitly a label on which "this is a work of art" is written. A readymade is nothing but a work of art reduced to this label. If it makes us acknowledge that insofar as they are "art," the Rembrandt and the African fetish allow themselves to be equally reduced, it must make us reflect on the converse as well: it is insofar as the Rembrandt and the fetish support this reduction that they authorize a readymade to be found in their company. It would not be there—or its presence would be inexplicable and illegitimate—if the enunciative conditions it reveals as its own were not valid for every work of art. It would not be there moreover if it had not transferred to the plane of production the conditions that regulate its reception, its circulation, and its enjoyment. To produce a readymade is to show it, to transmit a readymade is to make it change context, to enjoy a readymade is to wonder what it is doing in the museum. But the real museum no longer comes first. If Manet inaugurates modernism by the fact that he paints for the museum, then Duchamp ends it because he understands that the real museum comes second in relation to the museum-without-walls, for which it is nothing any longer but the referent, the way the gold lying in the vaults of central banks is nothing but the symbolic guarantee for the money in circulation. The artistic patrimony of the world has nothing in common but the statement, "this is a work of art." It is shown in museums of objects, which is where one can see it with one's own eyes and take pleasure in it. But it is only in the museum of images that the patrimony is a patrimony, that it is worldwide and that it circulates in the "sequence [of reproductions]—which brings a style to life, much as an accelerated film makes a plant live before our eyes," as Malraux said. And Malraux, again: "For all alike—miniatures, frescoes, stained glass, tapestries, Scythian plaques, pictures, Greek vase paintings, 'details' and even statuary—have become 'colorplates.' In the process they have lost their properties as *objects;* but, by the same token they have gained something: the utmost significance as to *style* that they can possibly acquire."[69] It is only in reproduction that Scythian plaques and Greek vase paintings, that a Rembrandt and an African fetish assemble without resembling each other; elsewhere the fetish returns to its sacred function or its ethnological meaning, and Rembrandt becomes once again a Dutch seventeenth-century painter, the one who made the author an introspective psychologist rather than a technician of paint-application, who allowed viewers to make the pictures by projecting themselves into a foggy chiaroscuro, and who had trouble with his institutional patrons, whether Captain Cock's Company or the Drapers' Guild.

We still have to wonder whether an elsewhere besides the museum-without-walls still exists; if Malraux hasn't written the first and last of the great aesthetic tracts on *style* founded on the precedence of the reproduction over the original; if the history of art, become fiction about itself through Malraux, isn't in the process of becoming, as it is more and more widely perceived, a simulacrum of itself; and if the antidote for the museum-without-walls that Georges Duthuit had called, in a violent attack on Malraux, *The Off-the-Wall Museum* (*Le musée inimaginable*), hasn't become, indeed, unimaginable. It has if, as for

69. André Malraux, *The Voices of Silence,* trans. Stuart Gilbert (Princeton: Princeton University Press, 1978), pp. 46, 44.

Duthuit, what one means by "art" must recede back beyond modernism, and if one dreamt that the work as object, *opus,* visual phenomenon, and institutionalized value should seek refuge in "the neutral warehouse of the heteroclite," as way back then, before the museum, in the *Wunderkammer.*[70] It hasn't at all if, as with Duchamp, one makes the practice of art—its meaning, its ambition, its quality—depend on the most explicit recognition of its actual conditions of operation. Once something, no matter what, has been cited by the museum-without-walls, it is art. To Duchamp's question, "*Can one make works which are not works of 'art'?*" the enunciative regime of the museum-without-walls replies: no, art is inevitable. There's no need for a King Midas to explain this transsubstantiation. Malraux called it *metamorphosis,* and he wasn't mistaken in giving the photograph as its author and time—the delay of the viewers—as its agent.[71] But understood this way, the name "art" is only a status, and has nothing honorific about it. And that of "artist" will only sanction the success of an opportunistic strategy with nothing honorable about it. These days it is enough to be reproduced in *Flash Art* to be an artist, but the test isn't there. Every object that is a candidate for art status—and God knows there have been enough of them on the heels of Duchamp—should be submitted to the test of the *Reciprocal Readymade = Use a Rembrandt as an ironing board.*[72]

A rebours

Before hastening to say that in 1972, in Düsseldorf, Marcel Broodthaers submitted 266 objects depicting eagles to the test of the *reciprocal readymade,* we should wonder why, in order to contract Duchamp and Magritte, he preferred the

70. Georges Duthuit, *Le musée inimaginable* (Paris: José Corti, 1956), 2: 258.

71. In an earlier text, I tried to show that we should agree with Malraux on Duchamp's grounds rather than disagree with him on his own grounds. We would then see that the readymade is synchronic with the museum-without-walls ("Le temps du readymade," in *Abécédaire,* pp. 166–184).

72. *SS,* p. 32.

imagery of the eagle to that of the pipe or the male-gendered fountain, and remember that in the second volume of the catalogue (published when the exhibition was well under way), he revealed that "the concept of the exhibition is based on the identity of the eagle as idea and of art as idea."[73] Each of the 266 objects on display is too obviously accompanied by a placard specifying "This is not a work of art" for there not to be something more there than meets the eye. The warning does not affix itself in the same manner to the exhibited objects that are recognized works of art as it does to those which are not. And the placards are not discreet in the way those in museums are: they are black, too large, and their material and graphic quality are out of place. They give neither the title, nor the artist's name, nor the provenance, but instead a number that refers to the catalogue where this information can be found. They have two holes so that they can be screwed onto something, but they are not mounted onto the objects they accompany, looking rather as if they had been dismounted in order to be displayed for their own sake. Finally, their obsessional repetitiveness, in three languages in alternation, succeeds in making it clear that something's up. So many signs that one should read them self-referentially, and that they are the objects submitted to the test of the "Rembrandt as ironing board," rather than those to which they affix themselves. Broodthaers's reciprocal readymade is *the readymade*—that is, the work of art reduced to the *statement* "this is art." It is *the eagle from the Oligocene to the present*—that is, art as idea from Pech Merle to conceptual art. It is the whole content of Malraux's *Voices of Silence,* in other words. It uses the museum-without-walls as a museum, and the museum as a work of art.

As the only one among the conceptual artists, who generally confuse Duchamp's lesson with the dematerialization of the work of art or with the substitution of language for visuality, to have seen that the enunciative paradigm was the apposite one, Broodthaers acknowledges reception of the enunciative paradigm and draws the consequences, taking it up in his own turn as the subject

73. *Museum, Der Adler vom Oligozän bis heute,* 2: 19.

matter of his work. In the subtitle of his Düsseldorf exhibition—"Marcel Broodthaers Shows an Experimental Exhibition of His Musée d'Art Moderne, Départment des Aigles, Section des Figures"—each word counts. *Marcel Broodthaers shows:* if Duchamp tests the convention according to which works of art are shown in order to be judged as such, Broodthaers tests the convention according to which works of art are shown, already judged as such. In order to test this convention, he had to undo this previous judgment, this prejudice—whence its implacably repeated negation—and to make the ostensive gesture explicit: the artist is no longer the one who makes, and if he is still, like Duchamp, the one who chooses, he is above all, like Magritte, the one who shows. And what does he choose to show? The test itself: *an experimental exhibition.* And what does this exhibition show? 266 objects coming from a good 60 museums or public collections and 15 private ones. And what do these objects, all of which belong to the imagery of the eagle, show? Always the same image blinding the public who wants to see nothing there but a theme and its variations: "the eagle in art, in history, in ethnology, in folklore . . ." "Publikum, wie bist du blind!" Broodthaers writes in the catalogue.[74] But also, for those for whom "information on so-called modern art had an effective role": 266 images exemplifying 266 times "art as idea," art as concept. And further: 266 times the same statement, "This is not a work of art," for which the objects are nothing but the referents. And finally, 266 numbers which, conforming to the *théorie des figures*—"image of theory" and perfect contraction of the Duchampian object and the Magrittian image—each manifest a "theory of the image."[75] So that *Section des figures* can be translated as "section of ostensive statements," and *Départment des Aigles* as "department of conceptual art." All that in understanding, of course, that in place of the artist as author we find the artist as director of *his*

74. Ibid., 1:16: "Public, how blind you are!"

75. "A theory of the figures would serve only to give the image of a theory. But the Fig. as a theory of the image?" writes Broodthaers on the reverse side of a work consisting of two cut-out numbers, the 0 and the 1 of the binary code, which he had so often parodied. See Dirk Snauwaert, "The Figures," *October* 42 (Fall 1987): 134.

Musée d'Art Moderne, that in place of the traditional, which is to say modern, museological institution, we find the museum-without-walls, that is, the actual enunciative regime of all that modernity calls art; and finally, that in place of the viewers we find, as always, those who arrive late.

It is rather indifferent to me to decide if Broodthaers is still modernist in the Greenbergian sense. Does Broodthaers really use "the characteristic methods" of art—of art in general, of art after Duchamp—"to criticize the discipline itself," and does he do that "not in order to subvert it, but to entrench it more firmly in its area of competence"? One is at first tempted to day no, and then yes. In support of the no is the fact that Broodthaers's "characteristic methods" are deliberately literary, even if they often have painting as their *subject,* and thus they are not drawn from the criticized discipline itself. In support of the yes is the fact that art at large acknowledges no boundaries between the disciplines of literature and painting: every method is fair game. Broodthaers's mayonnaise is impure and its self-reference—this typically modernist way of taking its own conditions of possibility for subject matter—systematically calls for a mysterious *praise of the subject.* In support of the no, is the fact that the *method* that he clearly proclaims in the Düsseldorf catalogue—to contract Duchamp and Magritte—announces unambiguously that if the institution of contemporary art, "supported by collectors and dealers," is critiqued, this is certainly not to entrench it more firmly in its area of competence.[76] In playing museum director, Broodthaers seeks to delegitimize the museum's institutional authority. But in support of the yes, there is the fact that it is unfair to confuse "area of competence" and "institution." It is unfair to ascribe this confusion to Broodthaers, once we want to apply the word "art" to his own work, and it is unfair to ascribe it to Greenberg, once we have read him closely.

We should never forget that Greenberg was not content to identify modernism with "the intensification, almost the exacerbation, of this self-critical tendency that began with the philosopher Kant," but that he was convinced as

76. *Museum, Der Adler vom Oligozän bis heute,* 1: 13.

well that "Modernism defines itself in the long run, not as a 'movement,' much less a program, but rather as a kind of bias or tropism: towards aesthetic value, aesthetic value as such and as an ultimate."[77] All mayonnaises are not modernist, of course, but the best ones are. Now, it seems to me that if I say (and I do say it) that Broodthaers is an infinitely better artist than Joseph Kosuth, better by far than Douglas Huebler, much better than Robert Barry, and even better than Lawrence Weiner, I say that what places him in my personal hierarchy is just this "tropism towards aesthetic value as such." The sentence by which I judge that Broodthaers is a great artist doesn't invest the word "artist" with the same meaning as when I state that it suffices nowadays to be reproduced in *Flash Art* to be an artist. In the former case I am speaking of a quality, in the latter of a status. It is this issue of difference between quality and status that the very particular modernism of Broodthaers's work—a modernism clothed in nineteenth-century garb, a modernism made of a reflexiveness that rubs history against the grain (*à rebours,* the reference to Huysmans is deliberate)—opens or reopens all the better to go forward. So, let me recapitulate. *The Eagle from the Oligocene to the Present* tests the convention according to which works of art are shown, already judged as such. How is that a "convention"? Like all conventions, this one is a tacit, unreflected upon, semi-unconscious social pact. But contrary to the conventions that painters have tested over the course of modernist painting, as Greenberg describes it, this one is not a convention of artistic practice. It is proper to the enunciative regime of the museum-without-walls; it is the pact linking the editors of Skira—or of *Flash Art,* for that matter—to their readers, and not that which links artists to their public. Broodthaers takes it as given that every object from a museum or private collection comes to him—via the museum-without-walls—already awarded the status of work of art. But, in submitting this status to the test of its negation—"this is not a work of art"—he acts as if this pact linked artists and their public. He's right.

He's right because it is not only from the cultural formation that Malraux called the museum-without-walls and Benjamin called art's "age of mechanical

77. Clement Greenberg, "Necessity of Formalism," p. 207.

reproduction" that he has inherited his own *fictional museum,* but from Duchamp and Magritte "contracted." From Duchamp he has inherited *the readymade,* that is, the work of art reduced to the statement "this is art," and from Magritte he has inherited *The Treachery of Images,* that is, the understanding of ostensive statements (Foucault may have provided assistance here). This is how he could translate the Duchampian making (= to choose) by the Magrittian showing (= to state). Thus one must go back up the trail and repeat that if Broodthaers tests the convention according to which works of art are shown, already judged as such, Duchamp tested the convention according to which works of art are shown in order to be judged as such. Again, how is that a "convention"? Like all conventions this one is also a tacit, unreflected upon, semi-unconscious social pact, and this time it is a pact that ties artists to their public. I said at the outset that this was the most elementary convention of all *modernist* artistic practice, and a little further on, that it sufficed for a single, unassisted readymade to have passed the test successfully for it to be revealed that such was indeed the tested convention. Thus, I read the test reflexively, as a testimony attesting to the necessity of renegotiating the social pact around the four ingredients of the Duchampian mayonnaise. The fact that the readymades have passed the test successfully does not absolve us from having to judge them again. Their presence on the jurisprudential record has not made them immune to further revisionist erasure. They are not in Malraux's *Voices of Silence,* by the way, which is a sure sign that even though "they have lost their properties as *objects,*" by the same token they have not gained "the utmost significance as to *style* that they can possibly acquire." To call them art is not to lend them style—or *quality,* in Greenberg's sense, but neither is it to refuse them access to quality—one of those words that formalism has mortgaged and which it is therefore urgent to reclaim. It is to make our judgment as to their quality bear on the very fact of deciding whether, in their case, status equals quality. Whether, in other words, we simply read the label pinned on them, or whether we write it.

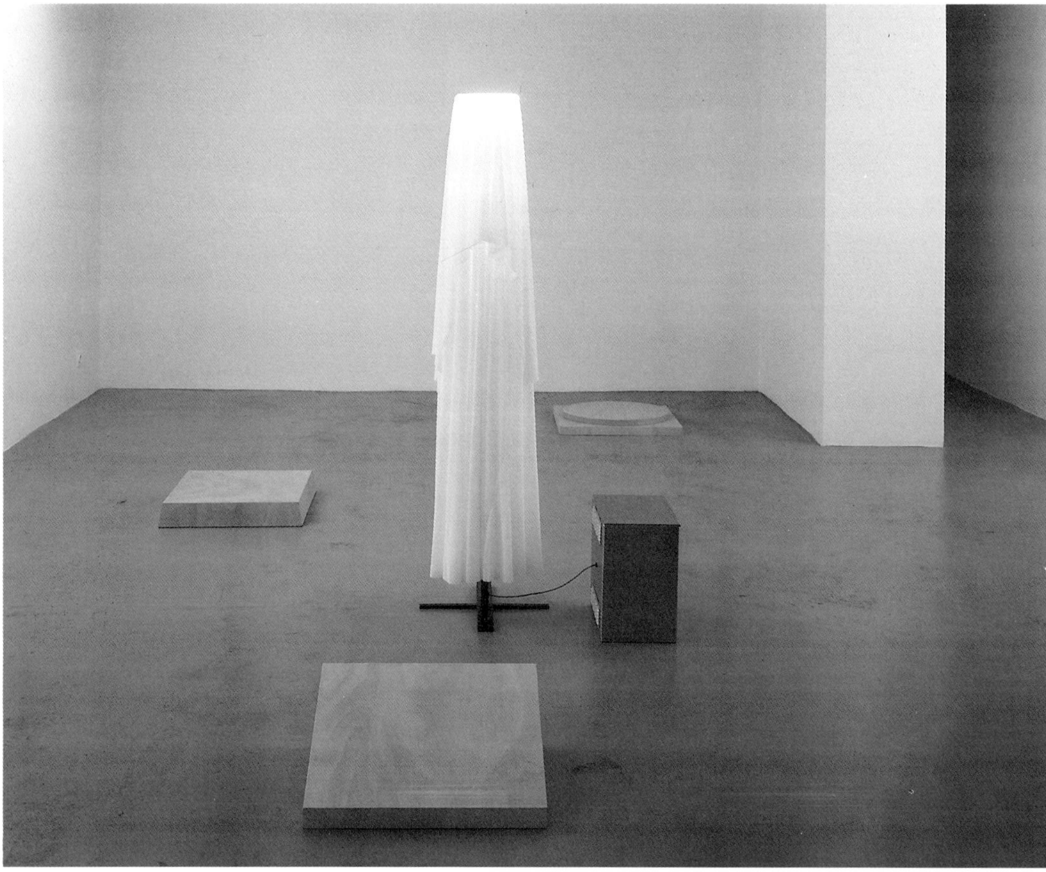

Sylvie Blocher, *Déçue la mariée se rhabilla,* 1991. "La D.M.R.," steel, neon light, synthetic fabric, height 166 cm, diameter 22 cm; "Le fil à la patte," stainless steel box, 34.5 × 23 × 35.5 cm; "Le socle vide," plywood, 57 × 57 × 9 cm; "Le niveau zéro de l'architecture," plywood, 65 × 65 × 7.5 cm; "Le trou du souffleur," plywood, 54.5 × 45 × 16 (tapering to 3) cm. Courtesy Galerie Roger Pailhas, Marseille-Paris.

8

Archaeology of Practical Modernism

> The world experiences the consequences not of the death of God, but of the death of Project. This project has sometimes been called Progress, sometimes Revolution. Their name is worn out.
>
> —*Octavio Paz*

With a Grain of Salt

What about an avant-garde mayonnaise, indigestible as hell for the average mortal, quasi-aphrodisiac for the aficionado? It brings off the feat of dispensing with the art of cuisine, with appetizers, entrees, desserts, with simmering soups, hearty main courses, side dishes. Nothing is left but the trimmings, the dressing, the superfluous having become the essential. And indeed, it has the sublime taste of the essential. It has freed the converted from the drudgery of the kitchen, the rules of table manners, the bourgeois taste for juicy meat, and rewarded their critical tongue with a devilish tang; it has the flavor of the future. It has set out to conquer the world and is about to become the universal diet, the only regimen, the basic nutrition of all people, of all peoples. With an egg yolk, some oil, vinegar, and a dash of mustard, humanity will be emancipated from its egoistic dependency on the fruits of the earth. It's coming soon.

The grain of salt is a must, since even laced with all the humor in the world, the bill is spicy. For this ideological sustenance has had its day; it is still on our plate, even though it has been discreetly taken off the menu. It promised progress, at once religion and politics, utopia served for dinner. It has become, over the five or six generations of cooks dedicated to it, the very height of refinement. It still pleases, there are still sensitive palates that will accept nothing else. But its aftertaste is bitter; the dinner is cold, and next door people are having simmering soups, hearty main courses, side dishes, appetizers, and desserts. The temptation is strong to indulge, to forget mayonnaise and avant-garde, to abandon all critical sense, to lose sight of the project of humanity freed from its selfish taste for the fruits of the earth.

Art's Critical Function and the Project of Emancipation

But enough of glib allegory. It's been a while now since the demise of the avant-garde has appeared on the menu and the table set to celebrate—but can it be a celebration?—the end of the ideology of progress. When this ideology was still in active use, in other words, as long as it was both carried by history and carrying it into the future, it never meant that art was improving with the passage of time. Or that its quality was following an ascending curve similar to the one followed by scientific discovery or technological invention. Rather, it meant simply that ambitious art could not be conceived as anything but progressive—socially, politically, or ideologically; it meant that art had to accompany or even anticipate the project of emancipation that, in various guises, underwrote the advent of modernity; finally, it meant that art achieved its utopian ambition through a critical function organically linking the aesthetic domain with the ethical, or, in concrete "infrastructural" terms, the artistic with the political. So, for art and culture, the discussion on the end of the ideology of progress boils down to one single question—is artistic activity able to maintain a critical function if it is cut off from an emancipation project? Such a question requires a "yes" or "no" answer, accompanied by a hopefully justificative commentary. I would like to try to answer directly, but I can't, because implicit in the very way the question is posed, there are two assumptions and one prejudice which I am not sure to share. The two assumptions are: (1) when artistic activity is not cut off from an emancipation project, it has a critical function; and (2) artistic activity might well be cut off from it. The prejudice is: artistic activity should have a critical function. This would set the true value of art and/or define quality in art. It seems to me, then, that first I have to decide whether the two assumptions underlying the question are well-founded, and if the prejudice implicit in the question is indeed right.

First of all, let's ask about the meaning, in this context, of "emancipation project" and "critical function." "Emancipation" connotes a liberation, but it is more precise than that. The word is used to indicate the premature granting of legal, civic, or political (let's say ethical in general) majority to a minor. This granting means: you have not yet reached adulthood, but I consider you to be mature enough nonetheless to be able to morally anticipate your majority, and as a consequence I grant you autonomy, in other words, the right to free self-determination. The expression "critical function" in this context refers to a vigilance that also operates in the ethical domain. Artistic or aesthetic activity would function as judge, guardian, guarantor of the achievement of an ethical or political project of emancipation. Such is roughly the meaning of the first assumption, whose content now needs to be further analyzed.

Given that one has as a project the premature granting of ethical majority to minors, who is this "one," and who are these minors? This "one" cannot be anyone except someone who is already in his majority, otherwise how could he decide who deserves emancipation? And he could not be anyone but someone who is already in power, otherwise how could he grant autonomy? Let's say that this "one" is an enlightened despot, or the duo of a despot and a philosopher: Voltaire and Frederick the Great, for example, or Diderot and Catherine the Great of Russia. Or, if he is not in power, this "one" will be an instance in which a scientific project of mastery is combined with a political project of the conquest of power, in the alliance of a correct theory and a just practice: the Communist Party guided by the writings of Marx, for example. An enlightened despot promising autonomy, a republic of men of science and philosophers, or a political party carried along by class struggle—here are three possible versions for an avant-garde.[1] It is, we might say by somewhat playing with words, a major minority acting on behalf of and for the benefit of a minor majority. As the term itself indicates, the avant-garde is in advance. Its advance lies in the adult status it enjoys sooner than the "minors" who are to be emancipated. Who are they? Ethics—whether based on the representativity of the people's elected officials, or rooted in Rousseau's notion of the general will, or articulated in Hegelian or Marxist dialectics, or justified by the democratic centralism within the proletarian party—requires the emancipation of all humanity: all men and women, universally, with no restrictions of class, race, or sex. Consequently, it appears (I'm oversimplifying terribly) that emancipation rhymes with revolution, peace with progress, power struggles with the direction of history, and the motto that summarizes the project—Liberté, Egalité, Fraternité—with universality.

Alongside politicians and men of science, artists linked their activity with such an emancipation project or were invited to do so by the philosophers, and even sometimes were given the leading role.[2] This is a historical fact, starting

1. Just one example, from Victor Hugo's *Les misérables* (1862): "The encyclopedists, led by Diderot, the physiocrats, led by Turgot, the philosophers, led by Voltaire, and the utopists, led by Rousseau—these are the four sacred legions. The great advance of humanity toward light is due to them. They are the four avant-gardes of mankind as it marches toward the four cardinal points of progress—Diderot toward the beautiful, Turgot toward the useful, Voltaire toward truth, Rousseau toward justice." Quoted (in part) by Matei Calinescu, *Faces of Modernity* (Bloomington and London: Indiana University Press, 1977), p. 108.

2. Thus, Saint-Simon: "in this great undertaking the artists, the men of imagination will lead the march" (*De l'organisation sociale,* 1825). Or, another Saint-Simonian, Olinde Rodrigues: "It is we, artists, that will serve as your avant-garde; the power of the arts is indeed the most immediate and the fastest. . . . We address ourselves to the imagination and feelings of people: we are therefore supposed to achieve the most vivid and decisive kind of action; and if today we seem to play no role or at best a very secondary one, that has been the result of the arts'

with the Enlightenment, and from this perspective, my chosen question doesn't come out of the blue—it is a question that is familiar to us all. It is based on the indisputable fact that a good deal of modern art has considered its critical function to be the guarantor of an ethical emancipation project aligned with history, anchored in the political field, and in ideological solidarity with a revolution. Examples abound: David and the French Revolution, Géricault and the one of 1830, Courbet and the one of 1848, Tatlin and the one of 1917, and so on. To those directly political alliances should be added the innumerable idealistic or materialistic, utopian or pragmatic variations of artistic practices whose fate was linked to the aspirations of a material, cultural, or spiritual revolution. I need not go any further. This phenomenon defines the very notion of an artistic avant-garde. Its essential ideological purport is the transitive link it establishes between ethics and aesthetics. Accordingly, aesthetic liberation or revolution might be seen as announcing, preparing, provoking, or accompanying ethical liberation or revolution, or the other way around. In any case the implication is transitive: if aesthetic freedom, then moral freedom; or vice-versa, if political freedom, then artistic freedom.

The first assumption I mentioned—when artistic activity is not severed from an emancipation project, it has a critical function—is consequently based on these historical sequences, or on similar ones. At issue is whether it is also rooted in the supporting ideology, in other words, in the prejudice also mentioned earlier—that it is good for artistic activity to have a critical function and that this defines quality in art. If the answer is "yes," then the presence of that

lacking a common drive and a general idea, which are essential to their energy and success" (*L'artiste, le savant et l'industriel,* 1825). Or again, this time from Gabriel Désiré Laverdant, a disciple of Fourier: "Art, the expression of Society, communicates, in its highest soaring, the most advanced social tendencies; it is the precursor and the revealer. So that in order to know whether art fulfills with dignity its role as initiator, whether the artist is actually of the avant-garde, one must know where Humanity is going, and what the destiny of our species is" (*De la mission de l'art et du rôle des artistes,* 1845). All three are quoted in Calinescu, *Faces of Modernity,* pp. 102, 103, and 106–107.

critical function—or its absence—would work simultaneously as a criterion of periodization and of value. Obviously this critical function had to be absent from artistic production prior to the historical emergence of the project of humanity's emancipation, a project that dates from the Enlightenment and marks the beginning of modernity. Before the Enlightenment, the function of art was to honor the dead, serve the Church, ornate bourgeois interiors, placate taste, and so on, but its function was never—at least, never programmatically—to exert critical vigilance over the ethical realm. Once it appears in the artworks, this very function of critical vigilance—precisely because it is new—radically severs them from their pasts; it further forbids anyone to valorize art forms that failed to make the same break on their own. The only modern art of significance and quality is avant-garde art, and any art that is satisfied with exerting functions that predate modernity (placating taste, for instance) loses its value as well as its critical function simply by being retarded, retrograde. When push comes to shove, Rodchenko is an artist and Bonnard is not.

The Rodchenko/Bonnard Alternative

We easily see the problem that is our legacy, and we are all aware of it. It is twofold, and it is the product of disenchantment. On the one hand, the political has betrayed the ethical; on the other, the ideological has hijacked the aesthetic. In the political sphere, revolutions have bred the Terror and the Gulag, and their emancipation project can no longer be trusted. In the artistic sphere, the very idea of the avant-garde no longer has much currency; revisionism rules the day. Bonnard is rehabilitated, and the prejudice—it is good for artistic activity to have a critical function—is judged as wrong.[3] In this vein, the revisionists revalue the late Derain at the expense of the cubist Derain, the Picasso of the

3. Hilton Kramer's piece on Bonnard in his *The Revenge of the Philistines* (New York: The Free Press, 1985) is a good case of sensitive, intelligent, and revisionist rehabilitation. Sensitive because it is based on unprejudiced dealing with the profundity which, apparently to his

"rappel à l'ordre" at the expense of Picasso the collagist, the metaphysical Carrà at the expense of the futurist Carrà, the Picabia of the forties at the expense of the dadaist Picabia, and so on—or, to intrude briefly into the other arts, place Richard Strauss above Schönberg or Thomas Mann above James Joyce.[4] All of which brings me to the second assumption underlying the question: it might be true that artistic activity, from now on, is severed from the emancipation project. It is probably not true for everyone (for instance, it is not true for Habermas, but let's not go into that). The chances are that the emancipation project is no longer tenable, for having generated disillusionment and degenerated into totalitarianism. Without this assumption, the question I am asking (and which was already Adorno's dilemma) would make no sense. I repeat,

---

own surprise, Kramer has discovered in Bonnard's painting when he visited the retrospective organized by Gérard Régnier (alias Jean Clair, more about him in n. 6) at the Pompidou Center in Paris in 1984. Intelligent and revisionist, because it was not lost on the author that rehabilitating Bonnard involved looking at the School of Paris not in terms of "an avant-garde renaissance" but in terms of "the glorious twilight of an epoch drawing to a close" (something that avant-gardists would certainly agree to), and that this in turn was "going to entail some drastic revisions in the way the history of modern painting will be written." Now, what I find amusing is that there is no flirtation with revisionism that avoids the perhaps silly game of pitting names against each other. (I leave it to the reader to estimate whether I myself will wiggle out of the Rodchenko/Bonnard alternative satisfactorily.) In any case, Kramer's alternative is not the Rodchenko/Bonnard one, and I hope that what I have written until now will suffice to distance myself from his position: "The priority given to ideas in Duchamp guarantees him a high position in any scenario that favors ideas at the expense of artistic realization. By contrast, Bonnard is an artist who seems to have had no 'ideas' at all—except, of course, those that could be articulated by his paint-brush. Yet can anyone really doubt that Bonnard is the superior artist?" (p. 85).

4. For a thorough critique of revisionism in the visual arts, issued from a position that I shall shortly refer to as that of the last partisans of the avant-garde, see Benjamin Buchloh, "Figures of Authority, Ciphers of Regression: Notes on the Return of Representation in European Painting," *October* 16 (Spring 1981).

pushing the question: is artistic activity capable of maintaining a critical function, granted that it is now indeed severed from an emancipation project?

The revisionists say "no," and the consequence follows immediately: by the same token, modernity is over. The terms "postmodernity" and "postmodern" would at least carry the meaning of that break; their substance would be "to abandon the emancipation project." They would also imply the reinstatement of premodernist values. If critical function and quality in art do not run together any longer, then placating taste, ornating bourgeois interiors, or even (replacing the Church) exalting multinational companies again become permissible. This is precisely the reproach expressed by the last partisans of the avant-garde who reply: "Yes, even cut off from a project of emancipation, art can and must keep its critical function." But they do periodize as well, proclaiming the advent of postmodernity, since, inevitably and fatally, they give to the term "critical function" a meaning that is no longer modern, or is so only negatively.

Let's recall once again what this critical function essentially was as long as modernity lasted, or (which amounts to about the same thing) as long as the avant-garde was carried by history. It implied a transitivity from aesthetics to ethics, or vice versa. Thus, it saw it as its duty to deny, incessantly, any kind of autonomy to the aesthetic or artistic field with regard to the ethical or political one. On the artist's side, the freedom to make forms—or anti-forms—could never be simply formal and autonomous (as in art-for-art's-sake), but it had at least to stand for an incitement to take similar steps toward freedom in the social and historical realms. Art would be revolutionary and emancipatory only to the degree that it acted on "life"—that is, on civic life. On the art lover's side, the delight in the forms created by the artist had to avoid reabsorption into the private space of merely subjective personal pleasure; at the very least, it had to work as a stimulus for desires for change which, in some future time, would subvert the social order. As long as artistic activity is not cut off from an emancipation project, critical function and utopian function are one and the same. Or better, utopia resorts to the ends, critique to the means: utopia is a promise, a projection into the future, an anticipation, a daydream; and critique is the vigilance watching over the conditions that make the dream possible, translating itself into the rejection of the past and the negation of the present, and implementing a strategy for change.

How do the last partisans of the avant-garde conceive of a critique that might survive the loss of the project of emancipation and the collapse of utopias? By turning utopian critique into the critique of utopias.[5] By accusing, for instance, the "historical avant-gardes" of having been recuperated, autonomized, and subsequently betrayed by the neo-avant-gardes that followed. By applying critical vigilance not so much to the conditions of the dream but rather to the conditions of its failure. By showing this through art works that manage to negate both the existing social reality and the flight into utopia, works that no longer anticipate but rather state the fact that anticipation was premature. Thus, artistic activity maintains its critical function. The freedom enjoyed by the artist within a free-market society should only be used to show how it is alienated or illusory, to reveal that such freedom is only an alibi for oppression or a privilege acquired at the expense of the others' freedom. The art lover's pleasure must be denied him or her because it is only a private one, or, for the same reason, be made to be perceived as something morbid, usurped, incompatible with the pleasure of others. Critical function is maintained. From aesthetics to ethics, from the artistic to the political, the implication remains transitive, and this is what matters: if aesthetic reification, then moral alienation. Or the other way around: if absence of political freedom, then false autonomy in artistic freedom. This may be called the postmodern condition, and the art that is lucid about it gives to "postmodernism" at least the meaning of a negatively signified memory of hope: even scratched out, utopia is not forgotten.

5. "One of the crucial antinomies of art today is that it wants to be and must be squarely Utopian, as social reality increasingly impeded Utopia, while at the same time it should not be Utopian so as not to be found guilty of administering comfort and illusion. If the utopia of art were actualized, art would come to an end." Theodor W. Adorno, *Aesthetic Theory*, trans. C. Lenhardt (London: Routledge & Kegan Paul, 1984), p. 47.

The question—is artistic activity able to maintain a critical function if cut off from an emancipation project?—demanded a "yes" or "no" answer. Two opposing camps have answered: the revisionists said "no"; the last partisans of the avant-garde said "yes." The former pay by relinquishing all ethical ambition for art, the latter with a sense of despair. As for me, at the very outset I stated that I was unable to answer, for I was not sure to share the assumptions and the prejudice implicit in the question's formulation. I now realize that I do in fact share them, but not without having to redefine them from top to bottom. Let's start with the second assumption, since it is shared by both camps: artistic activity might very well be cut off from an emancipation project. Agreed. I would even say: I hope so. How do I dare say so? Have I joined the revisionist camp? Did I yell, "Down with that notion of the avant-garde! Down with nihilism disguised as 'glorious singing tomorrows,' with these black squares and urinals pretending to be art when they only testify to the impotence of their authors! Down with the so-called quintessential reduction—to primary colors, to elementary forms, indeed, to blank canvases—which is only the unending impoverishment of painting!"? Did I say that it was time to return to technique, to the bronze, to pastels, to muddy colors? Did I scream that an inflatable rabbit cast in stainless steel could only be art for a handful of decadent snobs? Did I pontificate about Bonnard being worth all of the Mondrians combined? Not at all.[6] If you want my opinion, Mondrian is by far a greater painter than Bonnard,

6. Whether in politics or in art, the revisionist literature is growing every day, and the fact that its intellectual level is dwindling (say, from Daniel Bell to Fukuyama) is either the reassuring sign of its growing ridiculousness or the alarming sign of its growing appeal—I can't decide. In any case (to stay with art), when revisionism is dumb it certainly is a revenge against the "revenge of the philistines" that is equally philistinic (I allude to Hilton Kramer because he is an intelligent revisionist), as one recent book by Jean-Philippe Domecq (*Artistes sans art?* [Paris: Editions Esprit, 1994]) demonstrates. Only when revisionism is intelligent is it worth being taken seriously, and I know no revisionist more intelligent than Jean Clair, who was the editor of *L'art vivant* before he became curator at the Pompidou Center, and who is now director of the Picasso Museum in Paris. It is he who organized the Bonnard retrospective

but Bonnard is infinitely better than Mondrian's epigones, Fritz Glarner or Jean Gorin. I rather like Jeff Koons's rabbit and I love the one watertank with two basketballs floating midwater, though I hate the rest of his work. I am more excited by some of Barry Flanagan's bronze sculptures than by Carl Andre's plates these days, but I would not dare compare Sandro Chia's bronzes to Richard Serra's steel sculptures. As for pastels, I would praise them only by saying that Degas excelled in them whereas he was not too good in oils. This doesn't seem particularly revisionist to me nor, for that matter, particularly avant-gardist. And yet I did say that I wanted artistic activity to be cut off from an emancipation project.

PROJECT VERSUS MAXIM

The problematic term is not "emancipation" but rather "project." Let's go back to the definition of emancipation. This word is used to indicate the premature granting of a legal, civic or political (let's say ethical in general) majority status to a minor. The Enlightenment thinkers—I named Diderot, Rousseau, and Voltaire, but here I am primarily thinking of Kant—chose the word well. Emancipated humanity is not an adult humanity; it is a humanity that is allowed to anticipate its adulthood, in spite of the fact that it has not reached it, but *as if* it had reached it. Today, we know that humanity will never reach adulthood—understood as the entirely rational and autonomous state of the enlightened

---

that drew Kramer's comments cited in n. 3, but he also presented a Balthus retrospective, the *Réalismes* show at Pompidou in 1981, and . . . the Duchamp retrospective with which the Pompidou Center was inaugurated in 1977! His revisionist enterprise began, very pointedly, with three articles on the return to perspective in the work of three paragons of avant-garde art: Duchamp, Malevich, and Magritte. It is Jean Clair I have in mind when I speak of returning to technique, to the bronze, to pastels, to muddy colors, for these are some of the pleas he makes in his *Considérations sur l'état des beaux-arts, Critique de la modernité* (Paris: Gallimard, 1989), as well as in his *Paradoxe sur le conservateur* (Paris: L'échoppe, 1988), and they are the signs of his true conservatism.

subject. This we know not as a consequence of our historical disillusionment but as a consequence of the biological fact distinguishing humans from other animals: humans are born prematurely. Let me stop here very briefly, for it is, if you remember, on this very same biological fact that I ended chapter 5 and the same one again that I alluded to at the end of chapter 6. Neoteny, the fact—long recognized by embryologists—that the human brain is not completed, and not completely "wired," at the time of birth is what has given the cortex and the neocortex their phylogenetic prevalence over older (both in embryological and evolutionary terms) cerebral structures and has allowed the formidable development of the human intellectual capacities. It is this fact that makes the growth of young humans vulnerable and dependent on stimuli from the outer world, on the presence of language in their environment, on parental care and affection, on social relations in general, and thus on culture, in a way that is not true for any other species, not even the primates. It is also this fact that accounts for the human species having developed this intricate set of mechanisms—repression, censorship, resistance, denial, disavowal, sublimation, but also the return of the repressed, symptoms, dreams, slips of the tongue, compromise-formations, in one word, the whole neurotic (sometimes psychotic) machinery regulating the "psychopathology of everyday life"—with which humans negotiate the discrepancies between the rational capacities of their brain and the instinctual remnants of earlier stages of natural evolution which their physiology also contains. It is this fact and its consequences that explain why the subject can never hope to reach the transparent rationality dreamt of by the Enlightenment, but constitutes its identity *imaginarily,* through a "drama whose internal thrust is precipitated from insufficiency to anticipation" (Lacan, on the "mirror stage").[7] The incompleteness at birth of the human central nervous system is an

7. Lacan's epistemological oscillation between Hegel and cybernetics makes the passage from "The Mirror Stage," from which I extracted a sentence worth quoting in full. If interpreted "phylogenetically," it almost reads like a disenchanted summary of the Marxo-Hegelian view of history, and especially, of the history of the visual arts (given the function of the *imago,* or image):

ontogenetic handicap that has proved to be a selective advantage in the process of natural evolution, otherwise we wouldn't be here. But it forever remains a

---

> I am led, therefore, to regard the function of the mirror-stage as a particular case of the function of the *imago,* which is to establish a relation between the organism and its reality—or, as they say, between the *Innenwelt* and the *Umwelt.* In man, however, this relation to nature is altered by a certain dehiscence at the heart of the organism, a primordial Discord betrayed by the signs of uneasiness and motor unco-ordination of the neo-natal months. The objective notion of the anatomical incompleteness of the pyramidal system and likewise the presence of certain humoral residues of the maternal organism confirm the view I have formulated as the fact of a real *specific prematurity of birth* in man. It is worth noting, incidentally, that this is a fact recognized as such by embryologists, by the term *foetalization,* which determines the prevalence of the so-called superior apparatus of the neurax, and especially of the cortex, which psycho-surgical operations lead us to regard as the intra-organic mirror. This development is experienced as a temporal dialectic that decisively projects the formation of the individual into history. The *mirror stage* is a drama whose internal thrust is precipitated from insufficiency to anticipation—and which manufactures for the subject, caught up in the lure of spatial identification, the succession of phantasies that extends from a fragmented body-image to a form of its totality that I shall call orthopaedic—and, lastly, to the assumption of the armour of an alienating identity, which will mark with its rigid structure the subject's entire mental development. Thus, to break out of the circle of the *Innenwelt* into the *Umwelt* generates the inexhaustible quadrature of the ego's verifications." (Jacques Lacan, *Ecrits: A Selection,* trans. Alan Sheridan [New York and London: W. W. Norton & Co., 1977], p. 4)

See also, in *Ecrits,* in connection with what I called earlier "the dialectic of anticipated retrospection and retrospective anticipation in avant-garde art" (chapter 4, n. 74), "Le temps logique et l'assertion de certitude anticipée" (*Ecrits* [Paris: Seuil, 1966], pp. 197–213). As to Lacan's epistemology oscillating between Hegel and cybernetics, see *Le Séminaire, Livre II, Le moi dans la théorie de Freud et dans la technique de la psychanalyse* (Paris: Seuil, 1978), in particular "Freud, Hegel et la machine," pp. 83–97.

handicap: as acquired characters are not genetically transmissible, there remains only the "exo-cortex" called culture or civilization in charge of ethical and political progress. Biologically speaking, every generation starts from scratch as far as its constitutive immaturity is concerned.[8] Humanity is bound to be perpetually emancipated because humans are in a sense emancipated from the start: their birth hurls them into the world with such an advance on their real capacities for autonomy (a six-month-old chimpanzee has a more developed instrumental intelligence than a six-month-old human), that anticipation is the matrix of most survival strategies the species has developed. In that sense, and with a bit of humor, every man and woman on earth is his or her own avant-garde. The knowledge of this cluster of facts—to which Darwin's evolution theory, genetics, embryology, ethology, animal and human psychology, sociobiology, all have contributed—should be the basis on which to rest the problem of ethics, after the collapse of those many ideologies—not the least of which is Marxism—that have dreamt of changing man's nature in the name of a project of emancipation.[9] Although I obviously take some shortcuts (the problem being

8. I don't deny the possibility that Darwinian selection has acted, and still acts, on our cultural "exo-cortex" in the same way it has acted on our biological features—which is the premise of, among others, Edward O. Wilson's *Sociobiology* (Cambridge, Mass.: Harvard University Press, 1975). But positing neoteny (itself of course the result of a long evolutionary process) at the root of culture and civilization in general rather than this or that selection (for example, the paradoxical selection of "altruistic" behaviors) at the root of the particulars of culture and morals is, it seems to me, the only way of not taking ethics out of "ethics," in other words, of not erasing the radical heterogeneity between moral duty and the biological substrate which might explain its presence in human conscience and consciousness. Moreover, it seems to me the only way, compatible with present-day scientific knowledge, to account for our existence as *natural* beings without falling prey to the more than dubious biological determinism pervading the conclusions of Wilson's book and other researches in sociobiology.

9. Again: that is what *the problem of ethics* should rest upon, not ethics itself, a catastrophic confusion that has led some scientists and philosophers—starting with Herbert Spencer—to accept social Darwinism as something inevitable, or worse, to promote it. For a recent survey

so broad and so complex), my conviction is that it is the handicap of being born prematurely that forces humans to an ethical behavior instead of an instinctual one, and that should drive them towards progress in civilization, democratic freedom, a legal State, and an international political order; and that thereby, they would accomplish their "nature." There is still a long way to go, as the present state of the world demonstrates. It will always be too soon to grant autonomy to human beings, and this is why humanity cannot be freed but only emancipated. It is bound to anticipate an adult stage that its very nature precludes—"bound," in both the sense of a natural determination and of a moral obligation.[10]

In the question I am trying to answer, the emancipation project at issue was only a project. Inasmuch as it declared itself ready to emancipate humankind, it was supposed to grant humanity an advance on its future capacity for self-determination, to anticipate on its not yet attained adulthood, and thus to wager on time, that is, on history, in the hope that progress will, in the end, align reality with the ideal. But inasmuch as it remained a project, emancipation itself was withheld and necessarily postponed. Actually granted (or conquered) emancipation, by contrast, would still wager on time, but only symbolically or analogically. It would still anticipate a majority yet to come, but it would not expect a supply of future time to fill in the gap between the childhood and the adulthood of humankind. Its premise would be to recognize the irredeemably premature nature of autonomy, and its first act would be to grant autonomy nonetheless, *as if* humanity were ready to spontaneously order its conduct according to maxims like Liberté, Egalité, Fraternité. Saying that the motto of the

of the state of the debate around the issues raised by both the scientific facts and their polemical interpretation, see Jean-Pierre Changeux, ed., *Fondements naturels de l'éthique* (Paris: Odile Jacob, 1993). See also Arthur L. Caplan, ed., *The Sociobiology Debate* (New York: Harper & Row, 1978), and Matthew H. Nitecki, ed., *Evolutionary Progress* (Chicago: The University of Chicago Press, 1988).

10. This is perhaps why, as I said in chapter 6, the categorical imperative is received from no one knows whom or what.

French Revolution is a maxim precisely implies the "as if." Indeed, it is obviously not a reality: men are neither free nor equals nor brothers. To make a project of it is to believe—and then to will—that some day men will be able to be free, equals, and brothers. Such is the goal, the end, generous and noble; now the means remain to be fixed, vile and ignoble though they be. Revolutions begin to go wrong when maxim and project are confounded. Then an avant-garde takes possession of the emancipation maxim and claims to direct history in the name of the end of history, to educate people in the name of the people, to postpone the advent of liberation because humanity is not ready yet. Thus, Robespierre: "No freedom for the enemies of freedom!" Terror begins, and we have not yet seen the last of the despot/philosopher duo: for example, there is Hegel believing that he sees the Spirit of the World passing under his window in the guise of Napoleon; there is Lenin appropriating Marx; there is Mao deifying himself into "the Mao-Zedong-thought." Terror has begun, and soon will come the dictatorship of the proletariat, spearhead of emancipated humanity. But the proletariat is not ready yet; it will have to be educated first. Enter the Party, avant-garde of the avant-garde. But the Party itself needs to be kept under the iron fist of the Central Committee, until . . . I don't have to draw you the whole picture. Terror is the ineluctible consequence of an ideology of the avant-garde that confounds emancipation as a maxim and emancipation as a project. (This is what Ian Hamilton Finlay decided to shoulder, symbolically, as an artist.)

Now let's get on to the first assumption: when not severed from a project of emancipation, artistic activity does have a critical function. I probably share this assumption with just about everyone. It is even almost a tautology, since it is the emancipation project that defines the character of the critical function. And reviewing the "historical" avant-gardes, I observe that artistic activity has had a critical function, indeed. But I also observe that the "historical" avant-gardes never fulfilled their promise nor achieved their project, and that they were betrayed by being autonomized or reified. I, too, would share the last partisans of the avant-garde's state of despair were I to hold onto critical function in the way they understand it. Luckily, I don't see it in the same way, since

I don't confuse maxim and project. Thus, I reformulate the assumption as follows: when not severed from a *maxim* of emancipation, artistic activity does have a critical function. And suddenly, the term "critical" takes on quite another meaning. The gist of the emancipation *project* was that the critical function had to guarantee that a transitive linkage be established between aesthetics and ethics. For instance, if artistic liberty (absence of norms and constraints), then political liberation. If aesthetic equality (creativity shared by all rather than individual talent for a few), then social egalitarianism. If cultural fraternity (sharing of the means of production rather than capitalist division of labor), then moral community. Or vice versa (I am summarizing horribly): when true communism actually rules the planet and the State disappears, everyone will be an artist. For the emancipation project, the purpose—the end, which is also the end of the road—is always universal. Whether political or artistic, action is the means. The avant-garde is the guide that leads from means to ends, and the critical function is the judge watching over the appropriateness of means to ends.

Now, what is the meaning of the term "critical" for the *maxim* of emancipation? One must act, in art as well as in politics, in aesthetics as well as in ethics, *as if* men were free, equals, and brothers, that is, *as if* they were adult, rational, and reasonable beings. One ought to regulate one's conduct on the Idea of humanity. Its universality does not rest, as with Rousseau, on a general will; nor, as with Marx, on a productive capacity; it does rest, as with Kant, on a simple feeling of belonging to the human species—let's say, a sense of solidarity. Kant called it *sensus communis,* common feeling.[11] Facts—oppression, inequality, war—deny daily that this feeling is actually shared. But without assuming that it does indeed exist within each person, it is impossible to even imagine the end of oppression, inequalities, and wars. The chances are slim that an end will ever be put to them in historical reality, but the Idea of humanity—whose political name is universal peace—requires that our behavior be regulated according to that end. An end which is therefore an end without end (in

11. See chapter 5.

Kant's vocabulary: *purposiveness without a purpose*), a goal with no historical ending, no prescribed term, and no other purpose but respecting the maxim, with no criterion justifying the means.

That is obviously idealistic. What's the use of deconstructing the emancipation project, in order to find a way out of the disillusionment generated by its historical failure, if the result is to smuggle in another utopia through the back door, and a very stale one at that, smacking of Christianity on the one hand and reeking of bourgeois self-righteousness on the other? Too many oppressions have been conducted in the name of precisely such a universal Idea of humanity. And every concrete struggle for emancipation, that of the working class being neither the first nor the last, has been conducted in the name of one specific group rising against the one who claimed to have universality on its side. Agreed. The point is precisely that no one can claim to have universality on his or her side. To define ethical behavior as "acting *as if all* humans were rational and reasonable beings" does not entail presenting the left cheek when the right one has been slapped. But on the other hand, to implement ethical behavior in political institutions does not mean setting up apparatuses of power serving only the interests of those who act *as if they* were rational and reasonable. Although things are far from being perfect, modern democracies have created their political, judicial, and repressive institutions knowing full well that they are necessary because humans are not and will never be entirely rational and reasonable, and they operate those institutions according to the Idea that humans ought to behave as if they were. The "as if" indicates a regulative idea, not a mystique, and not an appropriation of universality either. Though every concrete struggle is local and specific and has to be fought as such, its compatibility with the common good is its only legitimacy. There is a growing tendency among socially committed intellectuals to accuse universality of being in essence a falsely idealistic alibi justifying oppression, or inhibiting concrete struggles, or erasing differences with bland, generalized humanism. Many of today's specific struggles supporting civil rights, gay and lesbian rights, the homeless, and multiculturalism, or against racism and sexism, are conducted in view of particular claims and deliberately underscored by an antiuniversalist discourse. Though I agree that in order to be efficient these struggles must be focused, their relinquishment of the Idea of universality is dangerous. The results are already appearing here and there, for example when the laws of a democratic State, on the pretext of "respect for cultural differences," are no longer equally applied. (That there is even any debate at all about whether Africans living in the West should be allowed to practice excision on their daughters with impunity is distressing.)

The fashionable attacks on universality have not even spared Marx, whose "Workers of all countries, unite!" is sometimes mocked as idealistic because of its underlying anthropology, endowing all human beings with potentially unalienated labor power. Certainly the Marxian utopia is gross in many respects, and it was indirectly responsible for half of the political tragedies this century has seen; but if Marx's redeeming quality was not to have justified class struggle and the revolution as a step towards the liberation of the whole of humankind, then what would it be? His idealism is not in his universalism, but rather in the transformation of a merely regulative idea into a determining one. He has made Kant's "as if . . . so that" into "if . . . then." The irony is that the transitive implication he thought he could establish between "infrastructure" and "superstructure," and vice versa, which he called dialectical materialism, is the very mark of the idealism of his system. The power of explanation of his system is largely intact: there are certainly material causes—social, historical, even natural—that propel history. They are indeed to be found in the ubiquity of struggle. They are indeed not mechanistic (in a Newtonian sense) but dialectical, in a cybernetic sense. But when Marx decided that ideology should redirect the course of history and dialectically act on its material causes, even on the natural ones, then dialectics meant magic. Not because spirit doesn't act on matter (it does in the technical realm, for example: I design a house, I avail myself of the knowledge of how to build a house, then of the necessary materials and tools, and then I build it), but because in the practical realm (practical in the Kantian sense of ethical), spirit doesn't rule over matter by way of logical implication: from a correct theory, it does not follow that the practice is just. That's simply not how reality works. Which is why, to come back to the meaning of the term "critical" for the *maxim* of emancipation, it is a mere feeling, a subjective signal, which is in charge of inciting us, humans, to behave as if all humans were mature, even though the correct theory tells us that they—that we—being constitutively premature, are forever in our infancy.

The aesthetic is somewhere in between the theoretical and the ethical, the material and the ideological, the somatic and the spiritual. Its realm is feeling, and feeling is by necessity subjective, personal. Kant's *sensus communis*—the feeling of belonging to the "Family of Man"—is therefore not a common demonstrable reality. If it were, the maxim of emancipation would not be in need of a critical function. Love would draw us together all by itself. But since this Christian dream is a dream, what is it that the critical function of aesthetic or artistic activity watches over? It watches over the requirement of universality which in its own sphere—the aesthetic—reminds us that the same requirement should regulate ethical action in its sphere. And it warrants a passage from the aesthetic to the ethical, a passage, however, which is not transitive and ideological but rather reflexive and analogical. No causal link, no logical implication binds art to politics on the material terrain of social history, nor aesthetics to ethics on the spiritual terrain of ideology. It is not true that artistic freedom derives from political freedom, nor conversely that artistic liberation or revolution necessarily announces, prepares, provokes, or accompanies political liberation or revolution. At most, it may be said that aesthetic freedom, or the lack thereof, is to art what ethical freedom, or the lack thereof, is to politics: *Arrhe est à art ce que merdre est à merde.* Duchamp's words for this equation are "algebraic comparison" and "allegorical appearance," and Kant's words for it are "analogy" and "symbol": "Now I maintain that the beautiful is the symbol of the morally good."[12]

I am finished with the two assumptions underlying the question raised by the collapse of the ideology of progress. I declared that I agreed with them,

---

12. Immanuel Kant, *Critique of Judgment,* trans. Werner S. Pluhar (Indianapolis: Hackett, 1987), p. 228. And later:

but not without a sweeping conceptual reformulation. Here it is, in a nutshell: "emancipation project" has to be replaced by "emancipation maxim," and the critical function of art has to be considered as reflexive and analogical rather than transitive and ideological. Well, this done, I can now say that I even subscribe to the prejudice underlying the question: it is good for artistic activity to

---

> Hence all intuitions supplied for a priori concepts are either *schemata* or *symbols*. Schemata contain direct, symbols indirect, exhibitions of the concept. Schematic exhibition is demonstrative. Symbolic exhibition uses an analogy (for which we use empirical intuitions as well), in which judgment performs a double function: it applies the concept to the object of a sensible intuition; and then it applies the mere rule by which it reflects on that intuition to an entirely different object, of which the former object is only the symbol. Thus a monarchy ruled according to its own constitutional laws would be presented as an animated body, but a monarchy ruled by an individual absolute will would be presented as a mere machine (such as a hand mill); but in either case the presentation is only *symbolic*. For though there is no similarity between a despotic state and a hand mill, there certainly is one between the rules by which we reflect on the two and how they operate. This function [of judgment] has not been analyzed much so far, even though it very much deserves fuller investigation; but this is not the place to pursue it. (*Ibid.*, p. 277)

The fact that Kant's remarkable choice of examples for his analogy—which in modern terms we might translate: a dictatorship is to a democracy what a mechanical machine is to a cybernetic "organism"—draws both from the political realm and from what Engels would have called "the Dialectics of Nature" almost reads like an advance rebuttal of the "if . . . then" transitive implication of Marxism. For we might rewrite it as such: it is *as if* a dictatorship were ruled by the causal one-way laws governing mechanical devices, *so that,* by comparison a democracy would then seem to be ruled by the self-regulating, dialectical laws of "control and communication in the animal and in the machine" (to use Norbert Wiener's phrase). Needless to say, if dialectical materialism forgets the "as if," so does ultra-liberalism. Pushed to its extremes, it would leave all social regulations to the "cybernetics" of the market and do away with all references to Ideas of reason.

have a critical function; this would indeed define both the value of art and quality in art. But here again, there is a nuance that is significant. As I insisted in the first chapter, an expression like "the value of art" (meaning the general value of art, or the value of art in general) is meaningless as long as you have not mentioned which works of art you are talking about. And quality *in* art cannot be defined either, except by pointing at particular works, by judging them to have quality—first of all, the quality of being art at all—and by offering their unique qualities as examples (not as models) of the kind of quality to be expected from all art, if it is to be on the level. In other words, value and quality are themselves the outcome of a reflexive judgment based on a feeling—Kant's definition of an aesthetic judgment. And so too with art's critical function: when I sense that a critical function is active in the work of art I am beholding, it prompts me to activate in myself a similar critical function. The prompting itself (the incitement and the excitement—Kant's paraphrase for it would be "the quickening of imagination and understanding in their free play")[13] is reflexive and does not guarantee the artistic quality of the work. Art's critical function provides no criterion. All it does is present "something that prompts the imagination to spread over a multitude of kindred presentations that arouse more thought than can be expressed in a concept determined by words."[14]

So, it is good for artistic activity to have a critical function; this would define the general value of art as being "food for thought" and the particular qualities of works of art as depending on my sensing the presence of such a critical function in a given work. I am thus asked to produce a case. Why not go back to that of Joseph Beuys touched on in chapter 5? It is most exemplary because it is most problematic. The motto "Everyone an artist" was for him both a belief and a project. Which is why he belonged—and how!—to this very modernity motivated by the project of emancipation. He believed in universal creativity as *the* faculty defining Man/Woman—understanding, imagina-

13. I myself am condensing Kant's paraphrase. See *Critique of Judgment*, §9.

14. Kant, *Critique of Judgment* (trans. Pluhar), p. 183.

tion, and practical reason rolled into one. He was convinced that everyone was a potential artist, an artist in his or her childhood, not emancipated yet. But he knew very well that not everyone was an artist; rather, he wanted everyone to become one. He had even imagined the political utopia that would allow his project to become reality. Therefore, he committed the mistake—I should say, the fault—of introducing a transitive link from art to politics, or from politics to art. If I had to evaluate his work by the yardstick of his own ideology, I would have to measure it against the lack of realism of his political utopia, and I would be forced to consider the work as dreadful. But that is not how I judge. Although Beuys's ideology is more than problematic to me, what matters is whether it hijacks the works, or whether the works stand on their own, formally; whether, in order to appreciate his work, I ought to believe the myth he constructed around himself, or whether its aesthetic qualities resist even the cruelest political and psychoanalytic deconstructions of the myth;[15] whether I am supposed to buy into the symbolic meanings he gave to fat and felt, or to Eurasia, or to his economic fantasy, or whether I can look at the works the way an atheist looks at a Memling madonna; whether I even need to know those meanings, or whether their possibly hidden truth cannot be inferred from the reading of the works, in good old modernist fashion; whether the judgment with which I severely condemn his assumption—clearly our assumption number one: that art retains its critical function only when it is not cut off from an emancipation *project*—entails an equally severe judgment on his prejudice clearly the same as ours too: that it is good for art to retain a critical function. So, the judgment through which I declare Beuys's assumption erroneous and the one through which I declare his prejudice just are heterogenous, and I evaluate his work as an artist with neither of them. My judgment on his assumption is of the order of knowledge (science, theory, understanding), my judgment on his prejudice is of the order of will (ethics, practice, reason), and my

15. See Benjamin Buchloh, "Beuys: The Twilight of the Idol, Preliminary Notes for a Critique," *Artforum*, January 1980.

judgment on his work is on the order of feeling. Though some works are better than others and many do not seem to be much more than relics to me, I don't feel that his best works have in any way been taken as hostages to his "theories." I don't feel that the meaning he ascribes to his use of materials, to his desire to unite East and West in Eurasia, or to creativity as the true capital, have mortgaged other interpretations.[16] I don't even feel his explanations are the best entry into the work. But I do feel the aesthetic power of his ideological convictions; I do feel that it is they which give the works their unique form; and I do feel their failure in the forms, which is precisely what, to my eyes, gives those forms their artistic relevance and authenticity. What moves me, in the end, is the tragic sense of impossibility that exudes from Beuys's works. Nothing like Duchamp's *impossibilité du fer,* however—Beuys never suffered from that kind of "impotence." But he never enjoyed that kind of lucidity either. What exudes from his work is the impossibility of *soziale Plastik* (social sculpture) actually to change the world, whether architecturally (see *Tallow,* 1977), politically (see *Dürer, ich führe persönlich Baader + Meinhof durch die Dokumenta V,* 1972), or economically (see *Wirtschaftswerte,* 1980). To me, such is the truth of Beuys's work (and truth has to do with knowledge and understanding); such is also its ethical significance (and ethics have to do with will and practical reason). But this I can say only because the works and their forms succeeded in "quickening" imagination and understanding in me, in activating my critical vigilance reflexively, and in prompting me to surrender to the works' quality. What would you call this involuntary "free play of my cognitive powers" if not an aesthetic judgment? The critical function of artistic activity is exerted via this aesthetic

---

16. Although I would add that these interpretations would have to be of an "archaeological" kind. Beuys's position at the very end of modernity commands this. I have attempted precisely such an interpretation elsewhere, when I read Beuys's "creativity" as synonymous with Marx's "labor power" so as to make retrospective sense out of the most important, and the most tragic mistakes (and faults) of modernity, namely, the mapping of the aesthetic field onto that of political economy. See Thierry de Duve, "Joseph Beuys, or the Last of the Proletarians," *October* 45 (Summer 1988): 47–62.

judgment, although of course it doesn't stop there—rather, that's more where it starts. It offers an analogical and reflexive bridge linking knowledge to will, theoretical or ideological activity to practical or ethical action, but it doesn't confound them; it doesn't mix them; it doesn't make one derivative of the other; it doesn't mortgage the one or hijack the other. It abandons the work of art not to its autonomy, but, as stated in Kant, to its *heautonomy*.[17]

---

17. Kant, *Critique of Judgment* (trans. Pluhar), p. 25.

> Hence judgment also possesses an a priori principle for the possibility of nature, but one that holds only for the subject, a principle by which judgment prescribes, not to nature (which would be autonomy) but to itself (which is heautonomy), a law for its reflection on nature. This law could be called the *law of the specification of nature* in terms of its empirical laws. . . . So if we say that nature makes its universal laws specific in accordance with the principle of purposiveness for our cognitive power . . . then we are neither prescribing a law to nature, nor learning one from it by observation (although observation can confirm the mentioned principle). For it is a principle not of determinate but merely of reflective judgment.

The word "heautonomy" appears only in this passage, extracted from §V of the introduction, entitled "The Principle of the Formal Purposiveness of Nature Is a Transcendental Principle of Judgment." The judgment in question is of course the teleological judgment. This is the place to remind the reader who is not familiar with Kant that the *Critique of Judgment* has two parts, the first being the *Critique of Aesthetic Judgment* and the second the *Critique of Teleological Judgment*. It is the second part that really mattered to Kant, for that is where he sought to understand how nature seems to orient itself spontaneously according to purposes (even though nature knows of no purpose and obeys causality alone), and thereby to explain why man, who is definitely also a product of nature, is entitled to claim that he has moral freedom. It is amazing how Kant succeeded in avoiding the traps of both determinism and finalism which usually set the terms of any debate on man's free will. Of course, Kant could not have known of cybernetics, which solves the riddle of the apparent teleonomy of nature through the concept of feedback and makes the *Critique of Teleological Judgment* scientifically obsolete.

Kant was the first to point out, once and for all, the contradictory—antinomic, he said—character of an aesthetic judgment. He was talking about the judgment of taste, in other words, about the evaluation of beauty, mostly in nature. When you say, for instance, looking at the sunset, "it's beautiful," you express a personal feeling. You are free to have such a feeling, therefore your neighbor should be just as free to experience this sunset as in no way beautiful at all. Yet, you didn't say "I like this sunset"; you said that it was beautiful, *as if* its beauty were objective. Saying so implies that it should be, and that it ought to be, beautiful for everyone, *as if* the sunset's beauty were both a natural fact that should be recognized and a moral quality that ought to be approved, although it is neither, being merely the result of your feeling. (Hence beauty as a symbol of morality, and the faculty of aesthetic judgment as a cognitive power, even though it "cognizes" nothing.) You therefore are asking for universal acceptance of your judgment of taste. (Perhaps, being a convinced pluralist, you

---

However, I believe that its ethical importance is intact and remains, with the distinction between empirical and transcendental, the best line of resistance, on the one hand, against a totally cybernetic view of the world (in economics, in ecology, in sociobiology, for instance), a view which, though scientifically (i.e., empirically) true, eliminates the need for transcendental Ideas, and on the other hand, against a dialectical view of the world, whether idealist (as in Hegel) or materialist (as in Marx and Engels), which conflates the empirical and the transcendental. In the Kantian system, the teleogical judgment bridges (but does not fill) the gap between the first and the second *Critiques,* the first having to do with how pure understanding conforms to the laws of nature (causality) and the second with how pure practical reason conforms to the law of liberty (purposiveness or "free causality"). The interesting thing is that Kant had to go through the detour of his inquiry into aesthetics to find the solution he was looking for, the reflexive aesthetic judgment providing him with a model for the teleological judgment, according to which we are indeed entitled to ascribe purposiveness to nature, but only reflexively. Now that cybernetics has done away with the reflexive teleological judgment, there remains only the aesthetic judgment to bridge (but not fill) the gap between science and ethics, a responsibility which I tend to see as one of art's main cultural functions.

don't believe that this is what you are doing, but you can't avoid it; it is a property of the sentence you are using.) How to reconcile your claim to a universal consensus with your neighbors' freedom to disagree? You assume necessarily that your neighbors are as capable of experiencing the beauty of the sunset as you are, and that in following their personal feeling, they will make the same judgment that you made (but not necessarily this time). And so on for all human beings. You therefore attribute to all of humanity a *sensus communis* which is nothing other than the capacity to make aesthetic judgments.

In the aesthetic realm of taste, Kant was seeing a sign—a symptom—testifying to the existence of a feeling of belonging to the species, itself merely indicative—symbolic—of the possibility of reaching universal agreement in matters of ethical conduct. This possibility itself he saw as no more than an Idea of reason, yet a necessary one, one that is mandatorily required so as to regulate emancipated ethical action. And he saw in art—man-made beauty—an exemplary terrain in which this claim to universality finds its social and material expression. Although having a social existence, it is only through an analogy that the beautiful in art is political (the beautiful is to art what ethics is to politics). As I have been arguing throughout this book, the phrase through which we express an aesthetic judgment concerning some man-made works—precisely those which comprised the avant-garde—switched in the course of modernity from "this is beautiful" to "this is art." Duchamp's readymades brought that switch out into the open. What remained to be understood in Duchamp's aftermath was that "this is art" continues to be an aesthetic judgment in the Kantian sense, not in the sense where it would remain a judgment of taste, however—this is no longer necessarily the case, and certainly not when a readymade is at issue—but in the sense that it requires one to suppose that everybody is endowed with the faculty of aesthetic judgment, defined, after Duchamp, as the capacity of judging, that is, of choosing, that is, of *making* what deserves to be called art. "Everyone an artist," indeed—Joseph Beuys was vindicated in advance. Only in theory, though, and this perhaps justifies Beuys's anger against Duchamp. For something else besides theoretical understanding remained to be done in order to appreciate the practical (i.e., the ethical) consequences of

Duchamp's move properly. Not, as Beuys himself believed, to act transitively on Duchamp's theory,[18] but rather, to insist, after and perhaps against Duchamp, that the Kantian-after-Duchamp formula, "this is art," being the paradigmatic formula for the *modern* aesthetic judgment, be regulated by the *modern* maxim of emancipation for which the political paradigm remains Liberté, Egalité, Fraternité, and of which the subjective signal remains *sensus communis.*

Contra Duchamp

Common sentiment? Pfuii! Art can be made out of every possible human feeling, and every possible human feeling can enter the love of art, including disgust, ridiculousness, and the particularly socially relevant feeling of dissent that in the first chapter I called the sentiment of dis-sentiment—the opposite of common sentiment. Among the feelings that sustained both the making and the appreciating of avant-garde art, anger was on top of the list. It is in anger that I want to finish this book. Against Duchamp, first. Who is this aloof prodigy who manages to trap the viewers into making his pictures, sacralizing his *objets-dard,* and overrating his silence? Who is this cool disciple of Pyrrho who fosters beauty of indifference, this grinning ironist incapable of enthusiasm and commitment? Who is this misogynous young man who paints his sisters Yvonne and Magdeleine "torn in tatters"? Who is this charming bachelor who pictures an idealized bride in the fourth dimension of his *Glass* and neglects his perhaps boring but rich bride-in-life, Lydie Sarazin-Levassor, to go and play chess all night during their honeymoon on the Riviera? Who is this tactician who embarks on the *Rochambeau* in 1915 having invented melancholic stratagems against compulsory military service and who leaves his friend Apollinaire behind to be wounded at Verdun? Who is this strategist of his own fame who manages to wriggle his way through the second World War smuggling *Boîtes en valise* across the demarcation line, and then to embark for America once again,

18. See chapter 5.

this time on the *SS Serpa Pinto*? Who is this Narcissus who poses as a woman after having considered taking on a Jewish name, and who doesn't seem to notice, later on, that six million Jews are wiped from the surface of the earth? Who is this dandy who plays chess sovereignly but eschews every concrete historical battle fought by the foot soldiers of the avant-garde? Who is this salon revolutionary, who is he? *Un anarchiste de droite*? Are we all pawns in his game? How can we have sympathy for the man? Yet, how can we avoid being under his spell? Love affairs are not simple, and the question about Duchamp is the same as that about Beuys: does the work resist the man? Do aesthetics transcend morals? "Transcend" is the wrong word: aesthetics and morals have nothing to do with each other.

But then, what are we to do with the next set of questions? If aesthetics and morals have nothing to do with each other, how come the kind of art history that is written by the last partisans of the avant-garde—who believe in a transitive link between aesthetics and morals, or between art and politics—has given Duchamp a choice place in the lineage that starts with Courbet? Should we think, then, that they are talking about the elderly, alcoholic Courbet who brags about toppling the Colonne Vendôme but paints lousy stags in the forest? Of course not. They are thinking about the Courbet of 1848, the socialist Courbet, Proudhon's friend. And rightly so. But I am angry at them as well. Whom do they think they are helping when they put Duchamp in the same avant-garde category as Rodchenko, Tatlin, John Heartfield, or Raoul Hausmann? They know very well that Hausmann is not quite on Duchamp's level, as an artist, and if they were really honest, they would also admit that Rodchenko, as a photographer, is not on the level of Sander, and that as a painter he is neither on the level of Mondrian—that goes without saying—nor on that of Bonnard—and that is a lot more embarrassing. Whom do they think they are helping? Hans Haacke? Haacke has his own anger against Duchamp; the trouble is, when he lets it ooze into his work, he's not too good. *Baudrichard's Ecstasy,* it's called. Beware! The discourse of the last partisans of the avant-garde is in danger of helping not Hans Haacke but rather the young wolves of radical opportunism for whom Duchamp's apolitical aloofness *and* status as a super-avant-gardist are the best alibi for their career moves. They have read all of Baudrillard and digested Jeff Koons, and they serve him wrapped in political correctness at the Whitney Biennial.

My anger is not directed at them as much as at the art schools that have produced them. That is where they have been fed on a critical discourse that stopped midway in its deconstruction of modernism and forgot to reconnect the utopias of modernity, along with their failure, to their historical roots. A well-intentioned discourse, most of the time, but academic, and whose perverse effect is to backfire. Teaching "critical theory"—and not much else—to art students today is like teaching Barthes's *Mythologies* to advertising students. When they leave the school with their portfolios tucked under their arms, they have already understood that political art is no longer really the issue and that the transitive link between art and progressive politics is almost as passé as the link between art and religion. They know that art is a slot in the leisure industry, with avant-garde art as a submarket catering to a clientèle with a nostalgic taste for avant-garde mayonnaise. As they have been educated, so they educate the public, providing assistance in the critical decoding of our culture. This was McLuhan's use of art, and it is now being fed back into the products of art—something inevitable, I guess: we have all become anthropologists of our own culture.[19] The problem is that culture does that very well on its own, without the help of art. Popular culture is very sophisticated, and it is perhaps a safe assumption that there are more Oprah-watchers than we intellectuals might think who see the show through a perfectly integrated "Lenny Bruce filter" of sorts.

Why art, then? My anger against the educational system that has taught the young wolves of radical opportunism to erase "critically" the boundary between art and popular culture in no way entails a kind of "Avant-garde and Kitsch" argument. In fact, I am angry at Greenberg too. I am angry at him for having taken the pungent taste of negativity out of the *avant-garde* mayonnaise and for

19. See the starting point of the first chapter, as well as the whole of chapter 7.

serving it back with the edulcorated flavor of a *modernist* mayonnaise.[20] He and Adorno are perhaps the two thinkers who understood best that what art had meant for millennia was threatened with disappearance pure and simple by the sudden development of industrial capitalism in the nineteenth century, and that the avant-garde was the only serious survival strategy for tradition. Their understanding of the phenomenon of the avant-garde explains more facts and gives more meaning to them than all the apologies of liberation and the antitraditionalist manifestos with which the artists of the "historical avant-gardes" authorized themselves. But Greenberg (not Adorno) wronged those artists when he cut their works off from their words, as if their revolt against the status quo was irrelevant and only their anxiety about the fate of art—or the plight of culture—mattered. He once said about the artists (he had Clyfford Still in mind): "I like them better without the soundtrack"—and I cannot pardon him this insult. I guess the words of a painter do not belong to "the characteristic methods of a discipline" that a modernist painter is supposed to use "to criticize the discipline itself—not in order to subvert it, but to entrench it more firmly in its area of competence." I guess a good art critic maps out this area of competence only with his eye, not with his ear. Fine. I wish there were more art critics of this breed these days, who look at the work rather than interviewing the artist in order to build up an opinion. I even admire Greenberg the critic for his inalterable empiricism, for his positivism. But there are times when I like him better without the soundtrack, too. As a critic—and one of the best, no doubt—he should perhaps have kept to his personal ethics of "pointing, pointing, pointing," of attracting the reader's attention to the works he valued, and have kept some of his comments to himself. Once he began to feel seriously threatened by the most advanced art of his time, he spoke carelessly, and he

20. In other words, for having neglected *practical* modernism and paid attention only to "pure" or *theoretical* modernism; or still, for having conceived of modernism solely as an involuntary tropism towards aesthetic value as such, and having silenced the voluntary call for emancipation that was the ideological content of many modern art movements.

unwittingly encouraged the prevailing oversimplified reading of his own doctrine, with the unfortunate result of offering a totally self-enclosed view of modernism, as art about art that is of interest to the artworld only. At that point, the maxim of emancipation is forsaken, art's universal address is forgotten, and with it, art's critical function. We might as well accept that works of art, including those of avant-garde art, are luxury goods and nothing else.

As to the conservatives and the revisionists, is it worth being angry at them? The conservatives no longer have much power in the artworld, even though they control a huge market of luxury goods, flattering a clientèle that is unlikely to disappear as if by magic. Sometimes I tend to pity them, for they are the true philistines whose taste "froze" somewhere along the way, depending on what generation they belong to. Sometimes I am even thankful to them—as I am thankful that there are specialists who still understand Latin—for keeping areas of connoisseurship alive which would otherwise have eroded. But most of the time I am very angry at them, especially now that they have been joined by the revisionists, for having put a mortgage on some of the key words that should regulate our dealings with works of art. Among them are tradition, aesthetics, and universality. While claiming to be traditionalists, the conservatives and the revisionists are in fact the true anti-traditionalists of our time, because they stubbornly refuse to see that the avant-garde *is* tradition, that it is the only art which, in its betrayal of academic standards, was faithful to tradition while acknowledging the real conditions of modernity. Their usurped claim on the word "tradition" makes it difficult, but all the more urgent, to reclaim it from them. The same holds true for "aesthetics." They take advantage of the anti-aesthetic discourse which—this is true—has nurtured the provocative self-legitimation of the avant-gardes, in order to dismiss them and to throw out the baby (i.e., the works) with the bathwater (i.e., the discourse). Finally, they claim to have universality on their side, which is the sin against universality *par excellence.* At that point, the maxim of emancipation is forsaken once again; a particular class appropriates art's universal address, and its critical function collapses into good taste and erudite culture. We might as well accept that all works of art except those of the avant-garde, which the revisionists love to hate for their "esoteric intellectualism," are their private property.

We are really living through interesting times: the ideology of progress has collapsed; postmodernity has been proclaimed through wishful thinking; the best young artists have learned to split their practice and their discourse as if in conscious schizophrenia; and the world of art critics and historians is funnily divided by a battle of words. The revisionists claim tradition, aesthetics, universality, and, as if their claim had any credibility, those words become immediately taboo for the last partisans of the avant-garde. Fully aware of the intricacies of dialectics, these then reply with anti-tradition, anti-aesthetics, and anti-universality, to which they add anti-formalism and postmodernism—anti-art and non-art being a bit out of fashion. A little slow on the uptake but determined to outwit the avant-gardists, the revisionists now buy the concepts of anti-art and non-art wholesale and then announce very proudly that they have seen the emperor's new clothes. How long is this ping-pong game going to last? As long as either side believes that the use of certain words automatically puts you in one camp or in the other, as if they had fixed referents. As long as on either side of the ping-pong table Rodchenko means anti-tradition and Bonnard tradition, with tradition meaning "quality" for the revisionists, and "institution" for the avant-gardists. As long as Duchamp's "this is art" is read on both sides of the table as an anti-aesthetic move: "anything goes" versus "critique of the art institution." Funny, but tiresome. Isn't it a lot more fruitful, and a lot more economical, to suppose that during modernity "this is art" has had the same critical function as "this is beautiful" had in Kant's time?

Perhaps the switch of formulation from "beautiful" to "art" was not correctly understood, because if the beautiful is just a subjective feeling, art on the contrary is a social practice with its own existence in public life. Even with a built-in claim to universality, aesthetic preferences are a matter of taste; because of its implementation in social institutions, a claim on art seems more directly political. The consensus on the beautiful is only a community of feeling assumed to be shared by everyone; consensus on art apparently requires actual agreement on its rules and conventions. But, as the ping-pong players had better recognize, when anything goes, then the critique of the art institution is accomplished. When all rules are gone, then all conventions are dissolved. You can interpret this by saying that within the artworld it is understood that artists can do what they want, use any material to say whatever they want, respect or manhandle their technique, cultivate or transgress any available style, and that they are accountable only to themselves (which infuriates the revisionists), or (and this would be the avant-gardist justification) that they are dialectically accountable to the artworld for relentlessly criticizing it from within. This is the current view, worse, the current convention, and if it continues to prevail, then the ping-pong players have a long game ahead of them, with an ever-dwindling audience: the artworld speaks to the artworld, and it gets smaller every day. Or you can interpret the same phenomenon—that when all rules are gone, then all conventions are dissolved—by saying that the social pact that binds together the artists and their public extends to include anyone and everyone.

Is this a reality? Yes and no. It is a historical reality that the demise of the *ancien régime* and the advent of modern democracies have broken the traditional boundaries between the professional artists and the class of their patrons; that the Church has lost its position of purveyor of public art obeying strict aesthetic, technical and ideological constraints; that the universal spread of capitalism has thrown artists into the marketplace where the encounter between producers and consumers is more or less haphazard; that industrialization has eroded the technical definition of all crafts, including those crafts called fine arts; that the Salons have brought artists in direct contact with an anonymous crowd and rendered their art vulnerable to its verdict; that the Academy has lost its quasi-monopoly on the schooling of artists; that since then, no one really knows beforehand whom art addresses and who is legitimately an artist. In order for two parties to sign a convention, they need to know who they are, and then each other. If they doubt their identity, if they don't know who their interlocutor is, then where is the social pact? Avant-garde artists are those who understood this and translated the dissolution of the social conventions that in the past assigned them a place in society into an active dissolution of the technical and aesthetic conventions of their trade. They are the ones who faced their identity crisis and its anxieties, who did not expect to circumscribe their audience in advance, who addressed the void. As it broke the aesthetic bond, the artistic avant-garde imaginarily and symbolically affiliated itself with the marginal, the oppressed, the revolted, with that part of society that was excluded from the social bond but stood for the political avant-garde of emancipated humanity. It did that while eating out of the hand of "an elite among the ruling class of that society from which it assumed itself to be cut off, but to which it has always remained attached by an umbilical cord of gold."[21]

With Greenberg's famous disabused remark from "Avant-garde and Kitsch," we are cruelly reminded that it is not a reality that the social pact that binds together the artists and their public extends to include anyone and everyone. You may say that it *was* a dream, a utopia, or a project, but no longer that it *is* any of those things. Remember? It may very well be that artistic activity is now definitively severed from an emancipation project—hence the despair of the last partisans of the avant-garde. But there is no need for despair if you replace dream with Idea and project with maxim. And if you say: the pact that binds together the artists and their public *ought to* extend to include anyone and everyone. And if you understand that this pact is therefore not a "real" pact but a symbolic one; that it is not directly a social, a political, an ideological pact; that it is rather the outcome of the aesthetic negotiation between the artwork's form and the individual viewer's feelings, expressed in such a way ("this is art") that it claims universal assent. There is no need for despair if you hold on to art's critical function, which is to watch over the requirement of universality, which, in today's thoroughly institutionalized artworld, ought to remind its members that whatever it produces, shows, appreciates, sells, and consumes, does have meaning beyond being mere luxury goods only insofar as it negates this artworld's actual boundaries. And if you understand Duchamp's readymade—this anything whatever that could have been made by anyone—to be the symbolic embodiment of art's address to everyone. And if you interpret the

21. Clement Greenberg, "Avant-Garde and Kitsch," p. 8.

historical fact—revealed by the readymade—that all specific artistic conventions have been dissolved, as testifying to the political imperative of modernity, which, as far as I can see, our postmodernity has not made obsolete: to dissolve every social pact that would rest on bases other than transcendental Ideas—be those bases sexual, religious, racial, tribal, or national. Better not trust *sensus communis;* it rarely extends the limits of the ethnic group. Ideas are safer. However, the idea of humanity, or, to evoke Kant's even broader Idea, that of a *community of reasonable beings,* has perhaps proved its obsolescence, inasmuch as humanism, human rights, humanitarian action, are obviously not the most adequate responses to the political needs of the day. There are signs that the Idea of an *ecosystem of self-regulated organisms* might in the near future replace that of a *community of reasonable beings,* an ecosystem of which in any case those prematurely emancipated animals called humans, fortunately capable of regulative Ideas, are in charge. Again, better not trust *sensus communis,* however, and not forget the abyss between empirical reality and transcendental Ideas. Environmentalists who do so believe that the social contract extends to include nature, and they end up speaking of the "rights of trees." But *community* is the issue, and I am not dreaming. I guess I am mourning the *Idea* of communism and gathering strength for the next century. Vis-à-vis communism as an ecosystem, I have not one single regret. I guess I am waking the corpse of Project, whose other names are Progress and Revolution (as Octavio Paz said in the epigraph of this chapter). I guess I am trying to make sense of a century of political disasters and artistic breakthroughs. To drill a hole in the wall and let the sun in. I guess I am trying to understand why Marcel Duchamp was such a great artist.

Index

Page numbers in italics indicate illustrations.

Names

Works by Duchamp

General Concepts

DUCHAMPIAN CONCEPTS

Kantian Concepts